Big Data, Little Data, No Data

Big Data, Little Data, No Data

Scholarship in the Networked World

Christine L. Borgman

The MIT Press
Cambridge, Massachusetts
London, England

MIT Press books may be purchased at special quantity discounts for business or sales promotional use. For information, please email special_sales@mitpress.mit.edu.

This book was set in Stone Sans and Stone Serif by the MIT Press. Printed and bound in the United States of America.

Library of Congress Cataloging-in-Publication Data

Borgman, Christine L., 1951–
  Big data, little data, no data : scholarship in the networked world / Christine L. Borgman.
       pages cm
  Includes bibliographical references and index.
  ISBN 978-0-262-02856-1 (hardcover : alk. paper)
1. Communication in learning and scholarship—Technological innovations.
2. Research—Methodology. 3. Research—Data processing. 4. Information technology. 5. Information storage and retrieval systems. 6. Cyberinfrastructure.
I. Title.
  AZ195.B66 2015
  004—dc23

                                                          2014017233

10 9 8 7 6 5 4 3 2 1

For Betty Champoux Borgman, 1926–2012,
and Ann O'Brien, 1951–2014

Contents

Detailed Table of Contents

Preface

Big data begets big attention these days, but little data are equally essential to scholarly inquiry. As the absolute volume of data increases, the ability to inspect individual observations decreases. The observer must step ever further away from the phenomena of interest. New tools and new perspectives are required. However, big data is not necessarily better data. The farther the observer is from the point of origin, the more difficult it can be to determine what those observations mean—how they were collected; how they were handled, reduced, and transformed; and with what assumptions and what purposes in mind. Scholars often prefer smaller amounts of data that they can inspect closely. When data are undiscovered or undiscoverable, scholars may have no data.

Research data are much more—and less—than commodities to be exploited. Data management plans, data release requirements, and other well-intentioned policies of funding agencies, journals, and research institutions rarely accommodate the diversity of data or practices across domains. Few policies attempt to define *data* other than by listing examples of what they might be. Even fewer policies reflect the competing incentives and motivations of the many stakeholders involved in scholarship. Data can be many things to many people, all at the same time. They can be assets to be controlled, accumulated, bartered, combined, mined, and perhaps to be released. They can be liabilities to be managed, protected, or destroyed. They can be sensitive or confidential, carrying high risks if released. Their value may be immediately apparent or not realized until a time much later. Some are worth the investment to curate indefinitely, but many have only transient value. Within hours or months, advances in technology and research fronts have erased the value in some kinds of observations.

A starting point to understand the roles of data in scholarship is to acknowledge that data rarely are *things* at all. They are not natural objects with an essence of their own. Rather, data are representations of

observations, objects, or other entities used as evidence of phenomena for the purposes of research or scholarship. Those representations vary by scholar, circumstance, and over time. Across the sciences, social sciences, and the humanities, scholars create, use, analyze, and interpret data, often without agreeing on what those data are. Conceptualizing something as data is itself a scholarly act. Scholarship is about evidence, interpretation, and argument. Data are a means to an end, which is usually the journal article, book, conference paper, or other product worthy of scholarly recognition. Rarely is research done with data reuse in mind.

Galileo sketched in his notebook. Nineteenth-century astronomers took images on glass plates. Today's astronomers use digital devices to capture photons. Images of the night sky taken with consumer-grade cameras can be reconciled to those taken by space missions because astronomers have agreed on representations for data description and mapping. Astronomy has invested heavily in standards, tools, and archives so that observations collected over the course of several centuries can be aggregated. However, the knowledge infrastructure of astronomy is far from complete and far from fully automated. Information professionals play key roles in organizing and coordinating access to data, astronomical and otherwise.

Relationships between publications and data are manifold, which is why research data is fruitfully examined within the framework of scholarly communication. The making of data may be deliberate and long term, accumulating a trove of resources whose value increases over time. It may be ad hoc and serendipitous, grabbing whatever indicators of phenomena are available at the time of occurrence. No matter how well defined the research protocol, whether for astronomy, sociology, or ethnography, the collection of data may be stochastic, with findings in each stage influencing choices of data for the next. Part of becoming a scholar in any field is learning how to evaluate data, make decisions about reliability and validity, and adapt to conditions of the laboratory, field site, or archive. Publications that report findings set them in the context of the domain, grounding them in the expertise of the audience. Information necessary to understand the argument, methods, and conclusions are presented. Details necessary to replicate the study are often omitted because the audience is assumed to be familiar with the methods of the field. Replication and reproducibility, although a common argument for releasing data, are relevant only in selected fields and difficult to accomplish even in those. Determining which scholarly products are worth preserving is the harder problem.

Policies for data management, release, and sharing obscure the complex roles of data in scholarship and largely ignore the diversity of practices

within and between domains. Concepts of data vary widely across the sciences, social sciences, and humanities, and within each area. In most fields, data management is learned rather than taught, leading to ad hoc solutions. Researchers often have great difficulty reusing their own data. Making those data useful to unknown others, for unanticipated purposes, is even harder. Data sharing is the norm in only a few fields because it is very hard to do, incentives are minimal, and extensive investments in knowledge infrastructures are required.

This book is intended for the broad audience of stakeholders in research data, including scholars, researchers, university leaders, funding agencies, publishers, libraries, data archives, and policy makers. The first section frames data and scholarship in four chapters, provoking a discussion about concepts of data, scholarship, knowledge infrastructures, and the diversity of research practices. The second section consists of three chapters exploring data scholarship in the sciences, social sciences, and humanities. These case studies are parallel in structure, providing comparisons across domains. The concluding section spans data policy and practice in three chapters, exploring why data scholarship presents so many difficult problems. These include releasing, sharing, and reusing data; credit, attribution, and discovery; and what to keep and why.

Scholarship and data have long and deeply intertwined histories. Neither are new concepts. What is new are efforts to extract data from scholarly processes and to exploit them for other purposes. Costs, benefits, risks, and rewards associated with the use of research data are being redistributed among competing stakeholders. The goal of this book is to provoke a much fuller, and more fully informed, discussion among those parties. At stake is the future of scholarship.

Christine L. Borgman
Los Angeles, California
May 2014

Acknowledgments

It takes a village to write a sole-authored book, especially one that spans as many topics and disciplines as does this one. My writing draws upon the work of a large and widely distributed village of colleagues—an "invisible college" in the language of scholarly communication. Scholars care passionately about their data and have given generously of their time in countless discussions, participation in seminars and workshops, and reading many drafts of chapters.

The genesis of this book project goes back too many years to list all who have influenced my thinking, thus these acknowledgments can thank, at best, those who have touched the words in this volume in some way. Many more are identified in the extensive bibliography. No doubt I have failed to mention more than a few of you with whom I have had memorable conversations about the topics therein.

My research on scholarly data practices dates to the latter 1990s, building on prior work on digital libraries, information-seeking behavior, human-computer interaction, information retrieval, bibliometrics, and scholarly communication. The data practices research has been conducted with a fabulous array of partners whose generative contributions to my thinking incorporate too much tacit knowledge to be made explicit here. Our joint work is cited throughout. Many of the faculty collaborators, students, and postdoctoral fellows participated in multiple projects; thus, they are combined into one alphabetical list. Research projects on scholarly data practices include the Alexandria Digital Earth Prototype Project (ADEPT); Center for Embedded Networked Sensing (CENS); Cyberlearning Task Force; Monitoring, Modeling, and Memory; Data Conservancy; Knowledge Infrastructures; and Long-Tail Research.

Faculty collaborators on these projects include Daniel Atkins, Geoffrey Bowker, Sayeed Choudhury, Paul Davis, Tim DiLauro, George Djorgovski, Paul Edwards, Noel Enyedy, Deborah Estrin, Thomas Finholt, Ian Foster,

James Frew, Jonathan Furner, Anne Gilliland, Michael Goodchild, Alyssa Goodman, Mark Hansen, Thomas Harmon, Bryan Heidorn, William Howe, Steven Jackson, Carl Kesselman, Carl Lagoze, Gregory Leazer, Mary Marlino, Richard Mayer, Carole Palmer, Roy Pea, Gregory Pottie, Allen Renear, David Ribes, William Sandoval, Terence Smith, Susan Leigh Star, Alex Szalay, Charles Taylor, and Sharon Traweek. Students, postdoctoral fellows, and research staff collaborators on these projects include Rebekah Cummings, Peter Darch, David Fearon, Rich Gazan, Milena Golshan, Eric Graham, David Gwynn, Greg Janee, Elaine Levia, Rachel Mandell, Matthew Mayernik, Stasa Milojevic, Alberto Pepe, Elizabeth Rolando, Ashley Sands, Katie Shilton, Jillian Wallis, and Laura Wynholds.

Most of this book was developed and written during my 2012–2013 sabbatical year at the University of Oxford. My Oxford colleagues were fountains of knowledge and new ideas, gamely responding to my queries of "what are your data?" Balliol College generously hosted me as the Oliver Smithies Visiting Fellow and Lecturer, and I concurrently held visiting scholar posts at the Oxford Internet Institute and the Oxford eResearch Centre. Conversations at high table and low led to insights that pervade my thinking about all things data—Buddhism, cosmology, Dante, genomics, chirality, nanotechnology, education, economics, classics, philosophy, mathematics, medicine, languages and literature, computation, and much more. The Oxford college system gathers people together around a table who otherwise might never meet, much less engage in boundary-spanning inquiry. I am forever grateful to my hosts, Sir Drummond Bone, Master of Balliol, and Nicola Trott, Senior Tutor; William Dutton of the Oxford Internet Institute; David de Roure, Oxford eResearch Centre; and Sarah Thomas, Bodley's Librarian. My inspiring constant companions at Oxford included Kofi Agawu, Martin Burton, George and Carmella Edwards, Panagis Filippakopoulos, Marina Jirotka, Will Jones, Elena Lombardi, Eric Meyer, Concepcion Naval, Peter and Shirley Northover, Ralph Schroeder, Anne Trefethen, and Stefano Zacchetti.

Others at Oxford who enlightened my thinking, perhaps more than they know, include William Barford, Grant Blank, Dame Lynne Brindley, Roger Cashmore, Sir Iain Chalmers, Carol Clark, Douglas Dupree, Timothy Endicott, David Erdos, Bertrand Faucheux, James Forder, Brian Foster, John-Paul Ghobrial, Sir Anthony Graham, Leslie Green, Daniel Grimley, Keith Hannabus, Christopher Hinchcliffe, Wolfram Horstmann, Sunghee Kim, Donna Kurtz, Will Lanier, Chris Lintott, Paul Luff, Bryan Magee, Helen Margetts, Philip Marshall, Ashley Nord, Dominic O'Brien, Dermot O'Hare, Richard Ovenden, Denis Noble, Seamus Perry, Andrew Pontzen, Rachel

Quarrell, David Robey, Anna Sander, Brooke Simmons, Rob Simpson, Jin-Chong Tan, Linnet Taylor, Rosalind Thomas, Nick Trefethen, David Vines, Lisa Walker, David Wallace, Jamie Warner, Frederick Wilmot-Smith, and Timothy Wilson.

Very special acknowledgments are due to my colleagues who contributed substantially to the case studies in chapters 5, 6, and 7. The astronomy case in chapter 5 relies heavily on the contributions of Alyssa Goodman of the Harvard-Smithsonian Center for Astrophysics and her collaborators, including Alberto Accomazzi, Merce Crosas, Chris Erdmann, Michael Kurtz, Gus Muench, and Alberto Pepe. It also draws on the research of the Knowledge Infrastructures research team at UCLA. The case benefited from multiple readings of drafts by professor Goodman and reviews by other astronomers or historians of astronomy, including Alberto Accomazzi, Chris Lintott, Michael Kurtz, Patrick McCray, and Brooke Simmons. Astronomers George Djorgovski, Phil Marshall, Andrew Pontzen, and Alex Szalay also helped clarify scientific issues. The sensor-networked science and technology case in chapter 5 draws on prior published work about CENS. Drafts were reviewed by collaborators and by CENS science and technology researchers, including David Caron, Eric Graham, Thomas Harmon, Matthew Mayernik, and Jillian Wallis. The first social sciences case in chapter 6, on Internet research, is based on interviews with Oxford Internet Institute researchers Grant Blank, Corinna di Gennaro, William Dutton, Eric Meyer, and Ralph Schroeder, all of whom kindly reviewed drafts of the chapter. The second case, on sociotechnical studies, is based on prior published work with collaborators, as cited, and was reviewed by collaborators Matthew Mayernik and Jillian Wallis. The humanities case studies in chapter 7 were developed for this book. The CLAROS case is based on interviews and materials from Donna Kurtz of the University of Oxford, with further contributions from David Robey and David Shotton. The analysis of the Pisa Griffin draws on interviews and materials from Peter Northover, also of Oxford, and additional sources from Anna Contadini of SOAS, London. The closing case, on Buddhist scholarship, owes everything to the patient tutorial of Stefano Zacchetti, Yehan Numata Professor of Buddhist Studies at Oxford, who brought me into his sanctum of enlightenment. Humanities scholars were generous in reviewing chapter 7, including Anna Contadini, Johanna Drucker, Donna Kurtz, Peter Northover, Todd Presner, Joyce Ray, and David Robey.

Many others shared their deep expertise on specialized topics. On biomedical matters, these included Jonathan Bard, Martin Burton, Iain Chalmers, Panagis Filippakopoulos, and Arthur Thomas. Dr. Filippakopoulos

read drafts of several chapters. On Internet technologies and citation mechanisms, these included Geoffrey Bilder, Blaise Cronin, David de Roure, Peter Fox, Carole Goble, Peter Ingwersen, John Klensin, Carl Lagoze, Salvatore Mele, Ed Pentz, Herbert van de Sompel, and Yorick Wilks. Chapter 9 was improved by the comments of Blaise Cronin, Kathleen Fitzpatrick, and John Klensin. Paul Edwards and Marilyn Raphael were my consultants on climate modeling. Sections on intellectual property and open access benefited from discussions with David Erdos, Leslie Green, Peter Hirtle, Peter Murray-Rust, Pamela Samuelson, Victoria Stodden, and John Wilbanks. Christopher Kelty helped to clarify my understanding of common-pool resources, building on other discussions of economics with Paul David, James Forder, and David Vines. Ideas about knowledge infrastructures were shaped by long-running discussions with my collaborators Geoffrey Bowker, Paul Edwards, Thomas Finholt, Steven Jackson, Cory Knobel, and David Ribes. Similarly, ideas about data policy were shaped by membership on the Board on Research Data and Information, on CODATA, on the Electronic Privacy Information Center, and by the insights of Francine Berman, Clifford Lynch, Paul Uhlir, and Marc Rotenberg. On issues of libraries and archives, I consulted Lynne Brindley, Johanna Drucker, Anne Gilliland, Margaret Hedstrom, Ann O'Brien, Susan Parker, Gary Strong, and Sarah Thomas. Jonathan Furner clarified philosophical concepts, building upon what I learned from many Oxford conversations. Will Jones introduced me to the ethical complexities of research on refugees. Abdelmonem Afifi, Mark Hansen, and Xiao-li Meng improved my understanding of the statistical risks in data analysis. Clifford Lynch, Lynne Markus, Matthew Mayernik, Ann O'Brien, Katie Shilton, and Jillian Wallis read and commented upon large portions of the manuscript, as did several helpful anonymous reviewers commissioned by Margy Avery of the MIT Press.

I would be remiss not to acknowledge the invisible work of those who rarely receive credit in the form of authorship. These include the funding agencies and program officers who made this work possible. At the National Science Foundation, Daniel Atkins, Stephen Griffin, and Mimi McClure have especially nurtured research on data, scholarship, and infrastructure. Tony Hey and his team at Microsoft Research collaborated, consulted, and gave monetary gifts at critical junctures. Thanks to Lee Dirks, Susan Dumais, Catherine Marshall, Catherine van Ingen, Alex Wade, and Curtis Wong of MSR. Josh Greenberg at the Sloan Foundation has given us funds, freedom, and guidance in studying knowledge infrastructures. Also invisible are the many people who invited me to give talks from the book-in-progress and those who attended. I am grateful for those rich opportunities

for discussion. Rebekah Cummings, Elaine Levia, and Camille Mathieu curated the massive bibliography, which will be made public as a Zotero group (Borgman Big Data, Little Data, No Data) when this book is published, in the spirit of open access.

Last, but by no means least, credit is due to my husband, George Mood, who has copyedited this manuscript and everything else I have published since 1977. He usually edits his name out of acknowledgments sections, however. Let the invisible work be made visible this time.

I Data and Scholarship

1 Provocations

The value of data lies in their use.
—National Research Council, *Bits of Power*

Introduction

In 1963, Derek de Solla Price famously contrasted "little science" and "big science." Weinberg (1961) recently had coined the term *big science* to refer to the grand endeavors a society undertakes to reflect its aspirations. The monuments of twentieth-century science to which Weinberg referred included huge rockets, high-energy accelerators, and high-flux research reactors. They were "symbols of our time" comparable to the pyramids of Egypt, Versailles, or Notre Dame. This was the age of Sputnik and a time in which vast sums of money were being poured into the scientific enterprise. Price and Weinberg questioned the trajectory of big science, asking about the relative value of big and little science (Price), whether big science was worth the monetary investment, and even whether big science was ruining science generally (Weinberg).

"Big data" has acquired the hyperbole that "big science" did fifty years ago. Big data is on the covers of *Science*, *Nature*, the *Economist*, and *Wired* magazine and the front pages of the *Wall Street Journal*, *New York Times*, and many other publications, both mainstream and minor. Just as big science was to reveal the secrets of the universe, big data is expected to reveal the buried treasures in the bit stream of life. Big data is the oil of modern business (Mayer-Schonberger and Cukier 2013), the glue of collaborations (Borgman 2007), and a source of friction between scholars (Edwards et al. 2011; Edwards 2010).

Data do not flow like oil, stick like glue, or start fires by friction like matches. Their value lies in their use, motivating the *Bits of Power* (National

Research Council 1997) report. The unstated question to ask is, "what are data?" The only agreement on definitions is that no single definition will suffice. Data have many kinds of value, and that value may not be apparent until long after those data are collected, curated, or lost. The value of data varies widely over place, time, and context. Having the right data is usually better than having more data. Big data are receiving the attention, whereas little trickles of data can be just as valuable. Having no data is all too often the case, whether because no relevant data exist; they exist but cannot be found; exist but are not available due to proprietary control, embargoes, technical barriers, degradation due to lack of curation; or simply because those who have the data cannot or will not share them.

Data are proliferating in digital and in material forms. At scale, big data make new questions possible and thinkable. For the first time, scholars can ask questions of datasets where n = all (Edwards et al. 2013; Mayer-Schonberger and Cukier 2013; Schroeder 2014). Yet digital data also are far more fragile than physical sources of evidence that have survived for centuries. Unlike paper, papyri, and paintings, digital data cannot be interpreted without the technical apparatus used to create them. Hardware and software evolve quickly, leaving digital records unreadable unless they are migrated to new versions as they appear. Digital records require documentation, not only for the rows and columns of a spreadsheet but also for the procedures by which they were obtained. Similarly, specimens, slides, and samples may be interpretable only via their documentation. Unless deliberate investments are made to curate data for future use, most will quickly fade away.

It is the power of data, combined with their fragility, that make them such a fascinating topic of study in scholarly communication. Data have no value or meaning in isolation. They can be assets or liabilities or both. They exist within a knowledge infrastructure—an ecology of people, practices, technologies, institutions, material objects, and relationships. All parts of the infrastructure are in flux with shifts in stakeholders, technologies, policies, and power. Much is at stake, not only for the scholars of today and tomorrow but also for those who would use the knowledge they create.

Big Data, Little Data

This book's title—*Big Data, Little Data, No Data*—invokes Price's legacy and the concerns of all fields of scholarship for conserving and controlling their intellectual resources. Data are inputs, outputs, and assets of scholarship. Data are ubiquitous, yet often ephemeral. Questions of "what are data?"

often become "when are data?" because recognizing that some phenomena could be treated as data is itself a scholarly act (Borgman 2007, 2012a; Bowker et al. 2010; Star and Bowker 2002).

A nominal definition of data can be found in the *Oxford English Dictionary:* (1) "an item of information; a datum; a set of data"; (2) "related items of (chiefly numerical) information considered collectively, typically obtained by scientific work and used for reference, analysis, or calculation"; also (3) "quantities, characters, or symbols on which operations are performed by a computer, considered collectively. Also (in non-technical contexts): information in digital form." These definitions are narrow and circular, failing to capture the richness and variety of data in scholarship or to reveal the epistemological and ontological premises on which they are based. Chapter 2 is devoted to explicating the concept of data.

Features of data, combined with larger social and technical trends, are contributing to the growing recognition that data are becoming more useful, more valuable, and more problematic for scholarly communication.

Bigness

Derek de Solla Price (1963) recognized that the important distinctions between little and big science are qualitative. Big science, in his view, was dominated by invisible colleges that constituted community relationships, exchanged information privately, and managed professional activities of the field (Crane 1970; Furner 2003b; Lievrouw 2010). Little science is conducted on a smaller scale, with smaller communities, less agreement on research questions and methods, and less infrastructure. The conduct of science, and of all forms of scholarship, has changed considerably since Price's observations. He was among the first modern historians of science and his perspective was influenced considerably by the post–World War II growth of the research enterprise (Furner 2003a, 2003b). The distributed, data-intensive, and computation-intensive practices that dominate much of today's research activity were barely visible at the time of Price's death in 1981. However, his insight that little and big science are qualitative distinctions holds true in an era of big data.

Big data and little data are only awkwardly analogous to big science and little science. Price distinguished them not by size of projects but by the maturity of science as an enterprise. Modern science, or *big science* in his terms, is characterized by international, collaborative efforts and by invisible colleges of researchers who know each other and who exchange information on a formal and informal basis. Little science is the three hundred years of independent, smaller-scale work to develop theory and method

for understanding research problems. Little science, often called *small science,* is typified by heterogeneous methods, heterogeneous data, and by local control and analysis (Borgman, Wallis, and Enyedy 2007; Cragin et al. 2010; Taper and Lele 2004). As Price noted, little science fields can become big science, although most will remain small in character.

Distinguishing between big and little data is problematic due to the many ways in which something might be big. Only in 2013 did the *Oxford English Dictionary* accept *big data* as a term: "data of a very large size, typically to the extent that its manipulation and management present significant logistical challenges; [also] the branch of computing involving such data." Other definitions of big data are concerned with relative scale rather than absolute size. Mayer-Schonberger and Cukier (2013), when considering business and government applications, think of big data in terms of insights that can be extracted at large scale that could not be done at smaller scales. In the scholarly realm, big data is the research made possible by the use of data at unprecedented scale or scope about a phenomenon (Meyer and Schroeder 2014; Schroeder 2014).

Data are big or little in terms of what can be done with them, what insights they can reveal, and the scale of analysis required relative to the phenomenon of interest—whether consumer-buying behavior or drug discovery. An early definition that distinguishes the ways in which data can be big remains useful: volume, variety, velocity, or a combination of these (Laney 2001). A substantial increase in any of these dimensions of data can lead to shifts in the scale of research and scholarship.

The ubiquity of data also contributes to its bigness. As more of daily life is instrumented with information technologies, traces of human behavior are easily captured. Barely two decades ago, telecommunications access was measured in terms of the proportion of households that had a telephone line. Now each individual may have multiple communication devices, each with its own unique identifier. Even in developing countries, digital delivery of information is feasible because of the exponential growth of mobile communication technologies. These ubiquitous devices are much more than telephones, however. They can sense, communicate, and compute. They can capture and distribute text, images, audio, and video. Traces can be marked with coordinates of time and place, creating continuous records of activity. Buildings, vehicles, and public places are instrumented with similar technologies. These traces can be combined to create rich models of social activity. Data, and the uses to which they can be put, are proliferating far faster than privacy law or information policy can catch up.

The rise of the concept of *data* in the media hype cycle and in scholarly discourse reflects the ubiquity of data sources and the sheer volume of data now available in digital form. Long predicted, critical mass has been achieved in the sciences, medicine, business, and beyond. In business parlance, big data has reached the "tipping point" when an idea crosses a threshold of popularity and then spreads rapidly (Gladwell 2002). In all sectors, digital data have become easier to generate, mine, and distribute.

The ability to ask new questions, map new trends, and capture phenomena never before capturable has created a new industry—one that is sometimes compatible with scholarly concerns and sometimes not.

Openness

Trends toward open models of software, government, standards, publications, data, services, and collaborative production of knowledge have changed relationships among stakeholders in all sectors (Benkler 2007; Hess and Ostrom 2007a; Kelty 2008; Raymond 2001). Openness is claimed to promote the flow of information, the modularity of systems and services, and interoperability. However, openness has economic and social costs, as is evident from the "free software" movement. Open is more akin to free speech than to free beer, to invoke Richard Stallman's (2002) distinction.

Open access publishing is usually dated to the Budapest Declaration in 2002, which has roots in electronic publishing experiments that began in the 1970s (Budapest Open Access Initiative 2002; Naylor and Geller 1995). Open access to data has even older roots. The World Data Center system was established in the 1950s to archive and distribute data collected from the observational programs of the 1957–1958 International Geophysical Year (Korsmo 2010; Shapley and Hart 1982). CODATA was founded in 1966 by the International Council for Science to promote cooperation in data management and use (Lide and Wood 2012). In 2007, principles for access to research data from public funding were codified by the Organization for Economic Co-operation and Development (Organisation for Economic Co-operation and Development 2007). Policy reports on access to research data continue to proliferate (Arzberger et al. 2004; National Research Council 1997; Esanu and Uhlir 2004; Mathae and Uhlir 2012; Pienta, Alter, and Lyle 2010; Wood et al. 2010). Open access publishing and open data are examined more fully in chapter 3.

Open access is partly a response to trends toward the commodification of information resources. Although this trend has roots in policy changes in intellectual property and economics of information, critical mass has led to new markets. Medical records, consumer-buying behavior, social media,

information searching, scholarly publishing, and genomics are among the areas in which sufficient concentrations of data exist to create and move markets. Some of these data are exchanged wholly within the business sector, but many span research and business interests. Data from academic research can have commercial value and commercial data can serve academic inquiry, leading to new partnerships and new tensions (Lessig 2004; Mayer-Schonberger and Cukier 2013; Schiller 2007; Weinberger 2012).

Open access, in combination with the commodification of data, is contributing to shifts in research policy. Governments, funding agencies, and journals are now encouraging or requiring scholars to release their data (Finch 2012; National Science Foundation 2010b; "National Institutes of Health 2003; Research Councils UK 2012a). Open access to publications and data is accelerating the flow of scholarly content in many areas, while contributing to tensions between stakeholders.

The flow of information depends ever more heavily on technological infrastructure. Telecommunications networks are increasing in capacity and penetration, both wired and wireless. Technology investments to support the supply and demand for information, tools, and services continue unabated. However, technology investments do not lead directly to improvements in information exchange. Technical infrastructures also are targets for espionage—whether corporate, political, or academic. Privacy, confidentiality, anonymity, and control of intellectual assets are at stake. Moving data, scholarly and otherwise, over networks involves a delicate balance of security, rights, protections, interoperability, and policy.

The Long Tail

"The long tail" is a popular way of characterizing the availability and use of data in research areas or in economic sectors. The term was coined by Chris Anderson (2004) in a *Wired* magazine article describing the market for goods in physical stores versus online stores. The statistical distribution—a power law—is well known (figure 1.1). In Anderson's model, about 15 percent of the distribution is in the head of the curve; the remaining 85 percent of cases are distributed along the tail. When applied to scholarly research, a small number of research teams work with very large volumes of data, some teams work with very little data, and most fall somewhere in between. At the far right of the curve, a large number of scholars are conducting their research with minimal amounts of data (Foster et al. 2013).

The long tail is a useful shorthand for showing the range of volumes of data in use by any given field or team of researchers. It is also effective in emphasizing the fact that only a few fields, such as astronomy, physics,

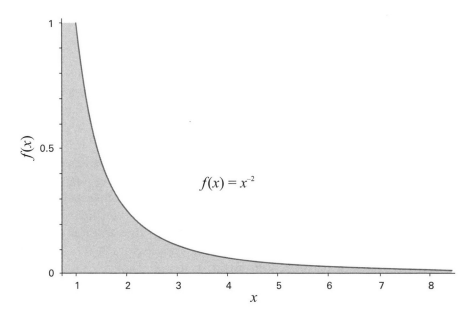

Figure 1.1

The power law distribution commonly known as the long tail. *Credit:* Jillian C. Wallis.

and genomics in the sciences; macroeconomics in the social sciences; and some areas of digital humanities; work with very large volumes of data in an absolute sense. In sum, volumes of data are unevenly distributed across fields.

The weakness of the long tail metaphor lies in the suggestion that the data practices of any field or any individual can be positioned on a two-dimensional scale. Scholarly activities are influenced by countless factors other than the volume of data handled. Research questions usually drive the choice of methods and data, but the inverse also can be true. The availability of data may drive research questions that can be asked and the methods that might be applied. Choices of data also depend on other resources at the disposal of individual researchers, including theory, expertise, laboratories, equipment, technical and social networks, research sites, staff, and other forms of capital investment.

One generality can be claimed about the long tail of data distribution in scholarship, however: the data used by the small number of scholars working at the head of the curve tend to be big in volume but small in variety. Big science fields that generate large masses of data must agree on

common instruments (e.g., telescopes, DNA sequencers) and formats (e.g., metadata, database structures). These data tend to be homogeneous in content and structure. The ability to standardize data structures facilitates the development of shared infrastructure, tools, and services. Conversely, the further down the tail of the distribution that a research specialty falls, and the more its practices are small science or small scholarship in character, the greater is the variety of content, structure, and representations. Those in small scholarship areas, working alone or in small teams, can adapt their research methods, data collection, instrumentation, and analysis to the problem at hand much more readily than can those big scholarship researchers who must depend on space telescopes, linear colliders, or mass digitization projects for their data. The downside to such flexibility is the lack of standards on which to base shared infrastructure and the lack of critical mass to develop and sustain shared data resources.

The majority of scientific work today, and the majority of scholarly work overall, is conducted by individuals or small teams of researchers, usually with minimal levels of research funding (Heidorn 2008). Some of these teams are partners in very large, distributed, international big science collaborations. They may produce or analyze big data and may exchange those data through community repositories (National Science Board 2005; Olson, Zimmerman, and Bos 2008). However, many of these individuals and teams are conducting scholarship that is exploratory, local, diverse, and lacks shared community resources.

No Data

As researchers, students, governments, businesses, and the public at large come to assume the existence and availability of data on almost any topic, the absence of data becomes more apparent. Fields vary greatly in the volumes, velocity, and variety of data available to address their research questions. Data-rich fields often pool their data resources, which promotes common methods, tools, and infrastructure. With a greater abundance of data than any individual or team can analyze, shared data enables mining and combining, and more eyes on the data than would otherwise be possible. In data-poor fields, data are "prized possessions" (Sawyer 2008, 361) that may drive the choice of methods and theory. As with the long tail metaphor, the data-rich and data-poor dichotomy oversimplifies the complexity of data resources used in any research endeavor. The following are but a few of the reasons that no data or minimal data may be available for a particular research question or project.

Data Are Not Available

In most fields, scholars are rewarded for creating new data. It is much easier to get a grant to study something new via observations, experiments, surveys, models, ethnographies, or other means than to get a grant to reanalyze existing data. Scholars gain competitive advantage by pursuing topics for which no data exist. Examples of areas in which scholars do search for reusable data include astronomy, social media, modeling cities and climates, and "dry lab" research in the biosciences.

Relevant data may exist but are held by entities that are under no obligation to release them or that may be prohibited by law from releasing them. Such data include business records, patented processes, museum curatorial records, educational records, and countless other forms of information potentially useful for research. Some of these data may be available under license or under conditions such as the anonymization of individual identities. The trend toward open data in research, government, and business has resulted in the availability of data that previously were considered proprietary.

Data on clinical trials of drugs or other medical interventions are particularly contentious. These data can have high monetary and competitive value. They also serve essential roles in clinical care. Patients want more access to these data and findings, because they serve the public interest. Selective release and reporting of clinical trial data has become a public policy concern. Although not explored in depth in this book, biomedical data such as clinical trials are on the front lines of shifting policies toward open access and changes in relationships among stakeholders (De Angelis et al. 2005; Edwards et al. 2009; Fisher 2006; Goldacre 2012; Hrynaszkiewicz and Altman 2009; Kaiser 2008; Laine et al. 2007; Lehman and Loder 2012; Marshall 2011; Prayle, Hurley, and Smyth 2012; Ross et al. 2012; Wieseler et al. 2012).

Human subjects data in the social sciences and humanities, as explored in chapter 5, also can be very sensitive and not subject to release. Data that can be anonymized to a reasonable degree, such as general social surveys, are the most likely to become available for reuse. Ethnographic and other forms of qualitative data rarely are available for use beyond the investigators and teams that collected them.

Data Are Not Released

Open access to data has a long history in some areas of scholarship, but positive attitudes toward data release are far from universal. In some areas, the failure to release data is considered scientific malpractice; in others, the inverse is malpractice, as explored in chapter 8. In chemistry, for example,

the practice of collecting and storing data for reuse has been trivialized as "stamp collecting" (Lagoze and Velden 2009a, 2009b). Data can be valuable assets to be exchanged, bartered, and used as leverage in negotiations with collaborators or funders. Once released to the public, researchers lose control of who, how, when, and why those data may be used. Often investigators are concerned that their data might be used selectively, misused, or misinterpreted, all of which would reflect badly on their research (Hilgartner and Brandt-Rauf 1994).

Recent policy changes to require data management plans as part of grant proposals are steps toward data release. However, few of these policies mandate open access to data. Rather, investigators must specify what data they will collect, how they will manage those data, and the conditions under which they will make them available to others. Similarly, a small but growing number of journals require the data reported in their articles to be released. Data release can occur by many mechanisms such as contributing them to community archives or institutional repositories, including them as supplementary materials to journal articles, posting on local websites, or releasing upon request (Alsheikh-Ali et al. 2011; Wallis, Rolando, and Borgman 2013).

In some fields, investigators are given embargo periods—also called proprietary periods—to control their data before releasing them. The length of time investigators can control their data typically ranges from a few months to a few years. The period is intended to be long enough to analyze the data and to publish their findings, but short enough to encourage the release of data to the community. When funding agencies or journals require scholars to release their data, they generally do so at the time findings are published, or later upon request. Rarely are scholars expected to release their data prior to publication, unless they have exceeded their embargo or proprietary periods, or other rules apply such as the release of clinical trials data.

In the data-poor fields described by Steve Sawyer (2008), withholding data is commonly accepted practice. Scholars in the humanities, for example, may protect their access to rare manuscripts, letters, or other sources as long as possible. In the social sciences, they may protect access to materials, research sites, and associated data. In the physical and life sciences, researchers may protect access to research sites, species, observations, and experiments. Countries may hoard archeological sites, cultural heritage materials, and other data resources, allowing access only to indigenous scholars and their research partners. Scholars from poor countries, in any field, may protect the trove of resources they bring back from a rare and precious trip abroad.

Scholars in many fields may continue to mine datasets or other resources over the course of a career, never being "done" with the data. Some datasets become more valuable over time, such as cumulative observations on a species or phenomenon. The notes, records, and materials of a scholar can be valuable data to others but might become available only at the end of a career, if and when offered to archives.

Data Are Not Usable

Documenting data for one's own use is difficult enough. Documenting data in ways to make them useful for others to discover, retrieve, interpret, and reuse is much more difficult. Motivations to invest effort in making data useful to others vary by countless social, technical, political, economic, and contextual factors, as discussed in chapters 8 and 9.

Releasing data and making them usable are quite different matters. The information necessary to interpret the data is specific to the problem, the research domain, and the expertise and resources of those who would reuse the data, as explained further in chapter 4 and the case studies. Codebooks, models, and detailed descriptions of the methods by which the data were collected, cleaned, and analyzed usually are necessary for interpretation. In addition, digital datasets can be opened only with certain software, whether statistical tools, instrument-specific code, or software suited to applications in the domain, ranging from art to zoology. Many such software tools are proprietary. Information about the origins and transformations on data can be essential for reuse. The farther afield that the reuse is from the point of origin, whether in terms of time, theory, discipline, or other measure of distance, the more difficult it may be to interpret a dataset or assess its value for reuse.

Unless data are documented quickly, while those with the expertise are available to describe them, they may soon cease to be useful. Similarly, datasets quickly fall out of synchronization with versions of hardware and software used to create and analyze them.

At the core of the data curation problem are questions of what data are worthy of preserving, why, for whom, by whom, and for how long? What responsibilities for data curation should fall to investigators, communities, universities, funding agencies, or other stakeholders? These questions are explored in chapter 10.

Provocations

As should be apparent by now, *data* is a far more complex subject than suggested by the popular press or by policy pronouncements. It remains

large and unwieldy, even when constrained to research and scholarship. Although the literature on research data is growing rapidly, each journal article, conference paper, white paper, report, and manifesto addresses but one part of the elephantine problem. This book is the first monograph to assess the whole elephant of data from social, technical, and policy perspectives, drawing on examples from across the academic disciplines. It picks up where the more general exploration of scholarship in the digital age left off (Borgman 2007), addressing the radical expansion of interest in data in the interim, as exemplified by the trends outlined above.

Ambitious as the goals of this book may be, yet more questions about the nature, roles, and uses of data in scholarship remain. Theory, evidence, and practice are deeply entangled. Points of intersection are identified and disentangled when possible. The arguments presented herein explore the issues of the day, based on deep concerns about what is at stake for scholarly research and the academic enterprise in the foreseeable future. The narrative is framed by six provocations intended to provoke a deeper conversation among the many stakeholders in the scholarly enterprise:

1. Reproducibility, sharing, and reuse of data are issues that have been discussed for decades, and in some cases for centuries. Addressing matters such as who owns, controls, has access to, and sustains research data will determine how their value can be exploited and by whom.

2. Transferring knowledge across contexts and over time is difficult. Some forms and representations of data can be shared readily across disciplines, contexts, and over time but many cannot. Understanding what features matter and which do not is necessary to inform scholarly practice and policy and to guide investments in knowledge infrastructures.

3. The functions of scholarly publication remain stable despite the proliferation of forms and genres. Data serve different purposes in scholarly communication than do journal articles, books, or conference papers. Treating data as publications risks strengthening the roles of vested interests at the expense of exploring new models of scholarly communication. The functions of data in scholarship must be examined from the perspectives of diverse stakeholders.

4. Scholarly work is being disseminated more widely through movements such as open access publishing, open data, and open source software. The different purposes of data and publications in scholarship influence the incentives, means, and practices for dissemination. Providing open access to data has implications for scholars, libraries, universities, funding agencies, publishers, and other stakeholders that are poorly understood.

5. Knowledge infrastructures are evolving to accommodate open access, data-intensive research, new technologies, social media, and changes in practice and policy. Some stakeholders gain advantage and others lose. Costs, benefits, risks, and responsibilities are being redistributed. New kinds of expertise are needed but their application will vary across contexts and research domains.

6. Knowledge infrastructures develop and adapt over generations of scholars. A long view of design and policy is needed, but research funding operates on short cycles. Substantial investments in infrastructure are necessary to acquire, sustain, and exploit research data today, tomorrow, and beyond. Those investments will be contentious, because choices that are made today will determine what data and other information resources will be available tomorrow and well beyond.

These provocations are explored in ten chapters, arranged into three parts. The first four chapters provide an overview of data and scholarship, laying out the premises for all six provocations. The second part consists of three case study chapters. Multiple cases in the sciences, social sciences, and humanities are explored, each providing evidence for the provocations. Data policy and practice comprise the third part, providing a comparative analysis for the availability and use of data across disciplines and contexts (chapter 8); exploring issues of credit, attribution, and discovery of data (chapter 9); and concluding with questions of what to keep and why (chapter 10). The last part draws out the implications of these provocations for scholarly practice and research policy, proposing further questions to be addressed.

Conclusion

A healthy intellectual community depends on the vigorous pursuit of knowledge by scholars in high-energy physics and high Tibetan culture alike. The challenge is to develop knowledge infrastructures that serve the diversity of ideas, questions, methods, and resources that each contributes to scholarship. Across the spectrum, scholars agree that the enthusiasm for big data puts smaller scale scholarship at risk (Alberts 2012; Berlekamp 2012; Gamazon 2012; Meyer 2009; Sawyer 2008; Siminovitch 2012).

This book opens up the black box of "data," peering inside to examine conceptions, theories, practices, policy, values, incentives, and motivations. Data, per se, is not a terribly exciting topic. It is, however, an extremely useful environment in which to view radical shifts in scholarly practice

and how they intersect with technology, education, and policy. The six provocations are intended to broaden and deepen the conversation about research data, with all stakeholders at the table. None of these provocations has a simple or clear answer. Many of the questions will be negotiated individually, often on a daily basis. All of them will influence how scholarship is conducted, now and in the future. Therein lies the heart of this book.

2   What Are Data?

Introduction

Although a newly popular concept, *data* is not a new term. The *Oxford English Dictionary* dates the use of *data* to 1646 in theology, already in plural form. Daniel Rosenberg's (2013) analysis of the use of *data* in the Eighteenth Century Collections Online (ECCO) (Gale Cengage Learning 2013) showed a steady growth in mentions from the seventeenth century onward. The earliest usage was in Latin, with *data* entering English through mathematics and theology. Singular and plural usage was debated throughout the eighteenth century. Data was invoked either as (1) the set of principles accepted as the basis of an argument or (2) as facts, particularly those taken from scripture. Rosenberg found that only in the latter eighteenth century did data come to imply facts in the form of scientific evidence gathered by experiments, observations, and other investigations. His searches of the Google Books online corpus showed the steady growth of the term in twentieth-century literature, but these analyses were less conclusive than those in ECCO.

Rosenberg's historical analysis, albeit constrained to English language usage, concludes that *data* remains a rhetorical term without an essence of its own. Data are neither truth nor reality. They may be facts, sources of evidence, or principles of argument that are used to assert truth or reality. The tripartite division of data, information, and knowledge (Machlup and Mansfield 1983) oversimplifies the relationships among these complex constructs. Meadows (2001, 3) comments that "what we take to be the basic data always has an element of arbitrariness in it." Michael Buckland's comment that data are "alleged evidence" comes closest to capturing the ambiguity of the term (Buckland 1991, personal communication, 2006; Edwards et al. 2007).

The question of "what are data?" is better addressed as "when are data?" as noted in chapter 1. The interesting and important questions about

the role of data in scholarship address the processes by which something becomes data. How do individuals, teams, and communities create, select, or use data? What factors in these decisions are associated with the data per se? Which are associated with the research questions or methods? Which are functions of how data are represented? How do these considerations vary by field, discipline, and research problem? How do they vary by relationships to the data, from creator to curator? How do notions of data evolve throughout a research project or over the lifetime of the data? How are all of these questions changing as more data—or more signals that could be treated as data—become available in digital form?

Data are not pure or natural objects with an essence of their own. They exist in a context, taking on meaning from that context and from the perspective of the beholder. The degree to which those contexts and meanings can be represented influences the transferability of data, as framed in the second provocation. This chapter explores efforts to define data in theoretical and operational terms, concluding with a working definition for use throughout the book.

Definitions and Terminology

Scholarly literature, policy pronouncements, and the popular press are rife with discussions of data that make little attempt to define their terms. Even histories of science and epistemology, as Rosenberg (2013) comments, mention data only in passing (Blair 2010; Daston 1988; Poovey 1998; Porter 1995). Other foundational works on the making of meaning in science discuss facts, representations, inscriptions, and publications, with little attention to data per se (Bowker 2005; Latour and Woolgar 1986; Latour 1987, 1988, 1993). In the humanities, the term is rarely mentioned, despite scholars' use of facts, numbers, letters, symbols, and other entities that would be categorized as data in the sciences and social sciences. As the humanities come to rely more on digital collections, borrow more tools from other fields, and develop more of their own analytic methods for digital objects, their notions of data are becoming more explicit (Borgman 2009).

Data are forms of information, a larger concept that is even more difficult to define. Epistemological and ontological problems abound, resulting in many books devoted to explicating information and knowledge (Blair 2010; Brown and Duguid 2000; Burke 2000, 2012; Day 2001; Ingwersen and Jarvelin 2005; Liu 2004; Meadows 2001; Svenonius 2000). Buckland (1991) distinguished between information as process, as knowledge, or as thing. Donald Case (2002, 2012) collected dozens of definitions of information,

grouping them by how they dealt with uncertainty, physicality, structure and process, intentionality, and truth. Jonathan Furner (2004a) applied three criteria to selecting definitions of information: coherence, parsimony, and utility. Later, he identified three families of conceptions of information that are broadly useful: semiotic, sociocognitive, and epistemic (Furner 2010).

The concept of data is itself worthy of book-length explication. For the purposes of analyzing data in the context of scholarly communication, a narrower approach will suffice. This overview is constrained to useful definitions, theories, and concepts for exploring commonalities and differences in how data are created, used, and understood in scholarly communities.

Definitions by Example

Data are most often defined by example, such as facts, numbers, letters, and symbols (National Research Council 1999). Lists of examples are not truly definitions because they do not establish clear boundaries between what is and is not included in a concept. The definition offered by Peter Fox and Ray Harris (2013, 10) is typical: "'Data' includes, at a minimum, digital observation, scientific monitoring, data from sensors, metadata, model output and scenarios, qualitative or observed behavioral data, visualizations, and statistical data collected for administrative or commercial purposes. Data are generally viewed as input to the research process."

Paul Uhlir and Daniel Cohen (2011), in the context of data policy, encompass a wide array of attributes in their examples of data:

The term "data" as used in this document is meant to be broadly inclusive. In addition to digital manifestations of literature (including text, sound, still images, moving images, models, games, or simulations), it refers as well to forms of data and databases that generally require the assistance of computational machinery and software in order to be useful, such as various types of laboratory data including spectrographic, genomic sequencing, and electron microscopy data; observational data, such as remote sensing, geospatial, and socioeconomic data; and other forms of data either generated or compiled, by humans or machines.

The Uhlir and Cohen definition recognizes that data can be created by people or by machines and acknowledges relationships between data, computers, models, and software. However, any such list is at best a starting point for what could be data to someone, for some purpose, at some point in time.

Jorge Luis Borges (1999) provided the most charming commentary on why defining things by lists is unsatisfactory. In his 1942 essay, he presented a classification of animals in a putative Chinese encyclopedia

entitled *Celestial Empire of Benevolent Knowledge*: "(a) belonging to the emperor, (b) embalmed, (c) tame, (d) sucking pigs, (e) sirens, (f) fabulous, (g) stray dogs, (h) included in the present classification, (i) frenzied, (j) innumerable, (k) drawn with a very fine camelhair brush, (l) et cetera, (m) having just broken the water pitcher, (n) that from a long way off look like flies." The thinking of Foucault (1994), Lakoff (1987), and many other philosophers and scholars has been influenced by Borges's subtle skewering of classification mechanisms.

Operational Definitions

The most concrete definitions of *data* are found in operational contexts. Institutions responsible for managing large data collections should be explicit about what entities they handle and how, but few of these definitions draw clear boundaries between what are and are not data.

Among the best-known principles for data archiving are those in the *Reference Model for an Open Archival Information System* (OAIS) (Consultative Committee for Space Data Systems 2012). This consensus document on recommended practice originated in the space sciences community and is widely adopted in the sciences and social sciences as guidelines for data archiving. The OAIS Reference Model uses *data* as a modifier: dataset, data unit, data format, database, data object, data entity, and so on, while defining *data* in general terms with examples:

Data: A reinterpretable representation of information in a formalized manner suitable for communication, interpretation, or processing. Examples of data include a sequence of bits, a table of numbers, the characters on a page, the recording of sounds made by a person speaking, or a moon rock specimen. (Consultative Committee for Space Data Systems 2012, 1–10)

The OAIS model distinguishes data from information as follows:

Information: Any type of knowledge that can be exchanged. In an exchange, it is represented by data. An example is a string of bits (the data) accompanied by a description of how to interpret the string of bits as numbers representing temperature observations measured in degrees Celsius (the Representation Information). (Consultative Committee for Space Data Systems 2012, 1–12)

The Data Documentation Initiative (DDI) is a set of metadata standards for managing data throughout their life cycle (Data Documentation Initiative 2012). The DDI is widely used in the social sciences and elsewhere for data description but does not define data per se. The DDI metadata specifications, which are expressed in XML, can be applied to whatever digital objects the DDI user considers to be data.

Among the partners in developing the DDI is the Inter-University Consortium for Political and Social Research (ICPSR). ICPSR is a leading international center that has been archiving social science research data since the early 1960s. ICPSR allows contributors to determine what they consider to be their data. Their instructions to prospective depositors offer the following guidance:

In addition to quantitative data, ICPSR accepts qualitative research data (including transcripts and audiovisual media) for preservation and dissemination. ICPSR is committed to digital preservation and encourages researchers to consider depositing their data in emerging formats, such as Web sites, geospatial data, biomedical data, and digital video. (Inter-University Consortium for Political and Social Research 2012, 4)

Thus, even institutions that collect and curate large volumes of data may not impose precise definitions of what they do and do not accept. Data remains an ambiguous concept, allowing archives to adapt to new forms of data as they appear.

Categorical Definitions

In operational and general research contexts, types of data may be distinguished by grouping them in useful ways. Data archives may group data by degree of processing, for example. Science policy analysts may group data by their origin, value, or other factors.

Degrees of Processing   Among the most discrete categories of data are the processing levels defined by NASA's Earth Observing System Data Information System (EOS DIS). Data with a common origin are distinguished by how they are treated, as shown in figure 2.1. (NASA's Earth Observing System Data and Information System 2013).

These fine distinctions are necessary for operational purposes. EOS DIS data products originate at level 0, which is "raw data at full instrument resolution." Level 0 data products already have been cleaned to remove communications artifacts; thus, they are not signals directly from the instrument. The next level of data product, 1A, is at full resolution and has added metadata for time references, instrument parameters, and other information. At level 1B, data products are further divided into sensor units for instruments with that capability. Levels 2, 3, and 4 are processed further to add more metadata, to reconcile data products with standard space-time grids, and to aggregate data into models. As indicated in figure 2.1, all instruments have at least level 1 data products, most have data products at level 2 or 3, and some instruments have data products processed to level 4.

DATA PROCESSING LEVELS

EOSDIS data products are processed at various levels ranging from Level 0 to Level 4. Level 0 products are raw data at full instrument resolution. At higher levels, the data are converted into more useful parameters and formats. All EOS instruments must have Level 1 products. Most have products at Levels 2 and 3, and many have products at Level 4.

Data Level	Description
Level 0	Reconstructed, unprocessed instrument and payload data at full resolution, with any and all communications artifacts (e.g., synchronization frames, communications headers, duplicate data) removed. (In most cases, the EOS Data and Operations System (EDOS) provides these data to the data centers as production data sets for processing by the Science Data Processing Segment (SDPS) or by a SIPS to produce higher-level products.)
Level 1A	Reconstructed, unprocessed instrument data at full resolution, time-referenced, and annotated with ancillary information, including radiometric and geometric calibration coefficients and georeferencing parameters (e.g., platform ephemeris) computed and appended but not applied to Level 0 data.
Level 1B	Level 1A data that have been processed to sensor units (not all instruments have Level 1B source data).
Level 2	Derived geophysical variables at the same resolution and location as Level 1 source data.
Level 3	Variables mapped on uniform space-time grid scales, usually with some completeness and consistency.
Level 4	Model output or results from analyses of lower-level data (e.g., variables derived from multiple measurements).

Figure 2.1

NASA EOS DIS Processing Levels. *Credit:* Figure redrawn by Jillian C. Wallis.

The degree of processing of data such as those from NASA instruments depends on many factors, such as the capability of the instrument and the uses to which the data may be put. Most scientists want level 4 data so they can compare them to other models of phenomena. Those data products will be the most comparable between instruments and missions. Some scientists want level 0 data or possibly even more native data without the communication artifacts removed so they can do their own data cleaning. If they are testing theories, they may wish to make their own decisions about outliers, calibration, imputing missing values, ways to account for weather and technology anomalies, and so on. If they are searching for patterns that are wholly unknown, such as the search for extraterrestrial intelligence (SETI), they want the most raw and comprehensive set of signals possible (Anderson et al. 2002; Sullivan et al. 1997).

These levels of processing have significant implications for how data are curated and maintained for future use. Data may need to be managed at each level, especially for observational data that cannot be replicated, as is the case with NASA missions. If data are maintained at the lowest levels only, then processing algorithms and documentation to transform data to higher levels may be required. In many areas of physics, chemistry, and biology, the most raw instrument data are too voluminous to maintain, so curation effort is directed toward the most processed products that represent the findings of a project. The pipeline software used to clean, calibrate, and reduce observational data is constantly under revision as instruments, computing technologies, and research questions evolve, as errors are discovered, and as analytic methods improve. Data streams from an instrument may be processed multiple times, leading to multiple data releases. Version control is an essential part of managing large observational data archives.

Origin and Preservation Value   While developed for a specific system and purpose, NASA's processing levels also are used to categorize data in other operational environments. In science policy contexts, much more general groupings are needed. The categorization promulgated by the US National Science Board (NSB) is intended to reflect data used in the sciences, social sciences, and technology. Although the humanities, arts, medicine, and health are outside the remit of the NSB, these data categories are intended for use in those domains. The origins of data may influence operational decisions on what data are worthy of preservation and for how long they should be curated (National Science Board 2005).

Observational data, the first of the three NSB categories, are those that result from recognizing, noting, or recording facts or occurrences of phenomena, usually with instruments. In the sciences, examples include observations of weather, plants, and animals, whether by satellite, sensor network, or pen in notebook. In the social sciences they include economic indicators and interviews, whether from self-report by businesses, online interviews, or ethnographies. Any of these observations may be associated with specific places and times or may involve multiple places and times (e.g., cross-sectional, longitudinal studies). Observational data are considered the most important to preserve, because these data are the least replicable.

Computational data are the products of executing computer models, simulations, or workflows. While most common in the physical and life sciences, they also are found in the social sciences and humanities. Physicists

model the universe, economists model the interactions of people and markets, and classicists model ancient cities and sites. To reuse a computational model in the future, extensive documentation of the hardware, software, input data, and interim steps may be required. Sometimes the model inputs are preserved; sometimes the model outputs are preserved. Sometimes only the algorithms are retained on the grounds that the model can be run again if needed.

Experimental data, the third category, are the results of procedures in controlled conditions to test or establish hypotheses or to discover or test new laws. Examples include outputs of chemistry research in a wet laboratory, physical experiments in a linear collider, and psychology experiments controlled in a laboratory or in field sites. If an experiment is designed to be replicable, those data may be easier to replicate than to preserve. If the conditions of the experiment cannot be replicated, the data also may need to be preserved.

The *Long-Lived Data* report emphasizes the policy implications of these three categories of data, each of which has different requirements for curation. They also distinguish between levels of data within each of the three origin types. Data may be gathered in "raw form" and refined through successive versions. In many circumstances, preserving data in multiple forms may be warranted (National Science Board 2005, 19–20). The report acknowledges that the boundaries between these categories are porous. For example, observational data may be used in experiments and computational models, and findings from experiments and models are used to refine methods of gathering observations. Edwards (2010) examines the interplay between observational data and models, documenting the century-long process in climate research by which data became mobile.

Various types of records are associated with observational, experimental, and computational data, such as historical records, field records, and handwritten notes. *Record* is another fundamental term that is rarely defined, despite broad usage in law, archives, data handling, and daily language. Relying on the *Oxford English Dictionary,* a *record* (noun form) is the attestation or testimony of a fact and implies witness, evidence, or proof. When used in the sense of "on record" or "of record," the gist is the fact or condition of being preserved as knowledge or information. *Record,* in this sense, is a very old term, dating to the fourteenth century.

Records is useful as a fourth category of data origin, encompassing forms of data that do not fit easily into categories of observation, experiment, or computation or that result from any of these categories. Records of almost any phenomenon or human activity can be treated as data for research.

They can include documentation of government, business, public, and private activities; books and other texts; archival materials; documentation in the form of audio and video recordings, glass plates, papyri, cuneiforms, bamboo, and so on. Authoritative records are similar to observations in that they cannot be replicated and thus have high value for preservation.

Collections Efforts to categorize digital data collections also shed light on the origins and value of data to communities. The three functional categories of collections established by the same National Science Board report are applied widely (Cragin and Shankar 2006; National Science Board 2005). In order from least to most formal, these are research data collections, resource or community data collections, and reference data collections. The same data may be incorporated into multiple collections but represented differently in each. Many finer distinctions about collections can be made, such as physical versus digital collections, digital versus digitized records, surrogates versus full content, static images versus searchable representations, and searchable strings versus enhanced content. The latter distinctions are deferred to chapter 7, where they are discussed in the context of humanities data.

Research data collections, the first of the three NSB categories, are those that result from one or more research projects. These data have had minimal processing or curation and may not conform to community standards for format and structure—if such standards exist at all. These collections usually are developed by and for a research group and may not be preserved beyond the end of a project. Many thousands of these collections exist. Examples include "fluxes over snow surfaces," genomes for a particular yeast, and other specific but important collections for small communities (National Science Board 2005, appendix D).

Research data collections that serve a continuing need may become *resource* or *community data collections.* These collections may establish standards for their community, whether by adoption or by developing new standards. Resource data collections may receive some direct funding, but without a commitment to sustain them beyond the immediate priorities of the community or the funding agency. Examples in this category range from the PlasmoDB, for the genomics of a specific malaria parasite, to the Ocean Drilling Program, which is supported by the US National Science Foundation and twenty-two international partners.

Reference data collections, the third category, are those that serve large communities, conform to robust standards, and are sustained indefinitely. These collections have large budgets, diverse and distributed communities,

and established governance structures. Examples in this category include large international collections that are essential community resources, such as the Protein Data Bank, the SIMBAD astronomical database, and reference datasets included in the ICPSR collections (Protein Data Bank 2011; Genova 2013; National Science Board 2005; Inter-University Consortium for Political and Social Research 2013).

These three categories of data collections are useful for assessing the degree of investment that communities make in their data and in the amount of sharing that occurs. Community data systems are one of the seven types of collaboratories identified by Nathan Bos and colleagues (Bos et al. 2007; Olson, Zimmerman, and Bos 2008).

Conceptual Distinctions
No matter how sharp these distinctions between categories may appear, all are arbitrary to some degree. Every category, and name of category, is the result of decisions about criteria and naming. Even the most concrete metrics, such as temperature, height, and geo-spatial location, are human inventions. Similarly, the measurement systems of feet and inches, meters and grams, and centigrade and Fahrenheit reflect centuries of negotiation. The fundamental constants of weights and measures are under continual revision by the authority of an international standards body (Busch 2013; Lampland and Star 2009; Lide and Wood 2012; Meadows 2001).

Weights and measures, in turn, are applied in many ways. Scales for measuring atomic weights are far more accurate than those found in grocery stores. Water-quality standards differ greatly between those that governments apply to drinking water and those that surfers apply to the ocean water in which they swim. A person's height is measured with different degrees of accuracy at a physician's office or at a sporting competition. A yet wider array of circumstances governs how categories of data are distinguished in research and scholarship.

Sciences and Social Sciences   Although NASA makes explicit distinctions between raw and processed data for operational purposes, *raw* is a relative term, as others have noted (Bowker 2005, 2013; Gitelman 2013). What is "raw" depends on where the inquiry begins. To scientists combining level 4 data products from multiple NASA missions, those may be the raw data with which they start. At the other extreme is tracing the origins of data backward from the state when an instrument first detected a signal. Instruments are designed and engineered to detect certain phenomena, under certain conditions. Those design and engineering decisions, in turn, shape

what can be detected. Identifying the most raw form of data may be an infinite regress to epistemological choices about what knowledge might be sought.

To social scientists who collect observations in the form of surveys and interviews, raw data may be the forms filled in by interviewees or by the interviewers. These forms typically are riddled with incomplete or unintelligible answers. They also contain errors, as when a respondent appears to have mistaken the ordering of a scale or has entered an improbable year of birth. Such errors are detected by comparing answers that should elicit similar responses and by constraining variables to numerical ranges. In other cases, respondents may have answered randomly, whether out of confusion or mischief.

Cleaning these kinds of data is as much art as science, requiring considerable methodological and statistical expertise (Babbie 2013; Shadish, Cook, and Campbell 2002). The cleaned data become the basis for the analyses from which research conclusions are drawn. Decisions about how to handle missing data, impute missing values, remove outliers, transform variables, and perform other common data cleaning and analysis steps may be minimally documented. These decisions have a profound impact on findings, interpretation, reuse, and replication (Blocker and Meng 2013; Meng 2011).

Humanities   The meaning of *data* is particularly ambiguous in the humanities (Borgman 2009; Unsworth et al. 2006). Distinctions between primary and secondary sources are the closest analog to raw and processed groupings in the sciences and social sciences. In common parlance, a *primary source* is an original document or object, such as a historical manuscript or a sculpture, whereas a *secondary source* is any analysis or later work about that entity. *Tertiary sources,* a term less often used, are compilations such as catalogs and indexes. Usage of these three terms varies widely within the humanities and within library and archival practices (University of Maryland University Libraries 2013). As explored in chapter 7, primary sources also can be representations of originals that no longer exist or might be edited compilations that improve on the readability of originals.

Much historical scholarship in the humanities is devoted to identifying relationships among centuries-old books, treatises, and other important documents as they were copied, interpreted, translated, and transferred between cultures and contexts over time. Primary sources may be long since lost, destroyed, or deteriorated. Secondary sources branched off into an unknown array of variants, and may have been split and combined in many ways for many purposes. The choice of what is primary depends on

context and on one's starting point. One scholar's secondary source may be another's primary source.

An important distinction about data in the humanities is how uncertainty is treated in knowledge representations (Kouw, Van den Heuvel, and Scharnhorst 2013). Uncertainty takes many forms, whether epistemic, statistical, methodological, or sociocultural (Petersen 2012). Ambiguity and heterogeneity are sources of uncertainty in historical records, for example. As scholars in the humanities apply technologies developed for other forms of inquiry, such as statistical tools and geographical information systems, they are caught in the quandary of adapting their methods to the tools versus adapting the tools to their methods. New tools lead to new representations and interpretations. Each field, collectively, and each scholar, individually, assesses how much uncertainty can be tolerated and what constitutes "truth" in any inquiry. Implicit in research methods and in representations of data are choices of how to reduce uncertainty.

Conclusion

Now in its fifth century of use, the term *data* has yet to acquire a consensus definition. It is not a pure concept nor are data natural objects with an essence of their own. The most inclusive summary is to say that data are representations of observations, objects, or other entities used as evidence of phenomena for the purposes of research or scholarship. An entity is "something that has a real existence," per the *Oxford English Dictionary*, "as distinguished from a mere function, attribute, relation, etc." Those entities may have a material existence, such as texts on paper or papyri, or they may be digital, such as signals from sensors or completed forms from an online survey. Entities become data only when someone uses them as evidence of a phenomenon, and the same entities can be evidence of multiple phenomena. Photographs in an old family album or high school yearbook may become data when a researcher uses them as evidence for hair and clothing styles of a period. Another researcher may use them as evidence of family groupings or social identity. Weather records in old ship logs, gathered for business and navigation purposes, now are used as data to study climate change. Patent records may be a source of evidence for when and where some found object may have been manufactured.

Lists of entities that could be considered data are unsatisfactory as definitions, yet such "definitions" abound in the scholarly literature and in policy documents. The inability to anchor the concept in ways that clarify what are and are not data in a given situation contributes mightily to the

confusion about matters such as data management plans, open data policies, and data curation. Concrete, bounded definitions are most often found in operational contexts, such as the OAIS definition quoted earlier: "A reinterpretable representation of information in a formalized manner suitable for communication, interpretation, or processing." Categorical definitions, such as those for origins of data or types of collections, also are useful in the contexts for which they were developed. Agreement on a general definition is necessary to gain traction on the local and global issues associated with research data, however.

The term *data* is used as consistently as possible throughout this book. When referring to data as entities, the word is used in the plural form, following the standard editorial usage (Bryson 2008) common in the literature of scholarly communication. This acknowledges that data is a plural noun, and that plural and collective nouns acquire different grammatical forms throughout the English-speaking world. Data is used in the singular form when referring to the concept; for example, "*data* is not a new term" or "big data is the oil of modern business." However, use of the term *data* varies by context and by user, often in subtle and significant ways. Particularly in the case studies, usage follows the conventions of the field being discussed. Unless used as a concept or when conventions are noted, *data* refers to *entities used as evidence of phenomena for the purposes of research or scholarship.*

3 Data Scholarship

Introduction

Data scholarship is a term coined here to frame the complex set of relationships between data and scholarship. Data have taken on a life of their own, or so it would seem from the popular press, independent of the scholarly context in which they are used as evidence of some phenomena. Scholars, students, and business analysts alike now recognize that having enough data and the right techniques to exploit them enables new questions to be asked and new forms of evidence to be obtained. Some of the things that can be done with data are extremely valuable. However, it can be very difficult to determine just how valuable any set of data may be, or the ways in which they may be valuable, until much later.

The notion of data scholarship was first framed as "data-intensive research" in policy initiatives that began early in the 2000s, including *eScience, eSocial Science, eHumanities, eInfrastructure*, and *cyberinfrastructure* (Atkins et al. 2003; Edwards et al. 2007; Hey and Trefethen 2005; Unsworth et al. 2006). The first three terms eventually coalesced into the collective *eResearch*. The UK program on Digital Social Research consolidated earlier investments in eSocial Science, which encompassed data-intensive research in the social sciences and the study of eResearch (Digital Social Research 2013). *eScience* often refers collectively to data scholarship in all fields, as exemplified by "eScience for the humanities" (Crane, Babeu, and Bamman 2007). *Cyberinfrastructure* remains a distinctly American concept that spans data scholarship and the technical framework that supports these activities.

Historically, scholarship has meant the attainments of a scholar in learning and erudition. Scholarship is an interior activity that encompasses how one learns, thinks about intellectual problems, and interprets evidence. Research—"systematic investigation or inquiry aimed at contributing to knowledge of a theory, topic, etc." per the *Oxford English Dictionary*—is a

form or act of scholarship. In the sciences and social sciences, research and scholarship often are used interchangeably, whereas the term *scholarship* is often preferred in the humanities. *Scholarship* is the broader concept and more aligned with *scholarly communication*. The latter term encompasses formal communication among scholars such as research, publishing, and associated activities such as peer review; and informal communication, including collaboration, personal exchanges, talks and presentations, and so on.

Individuals and individual scholarly communities may know how to exploit their data for their own purposes but know little about what data or methods from adjacent communities might be of value to them, or vice versa. Scaling up to much larger volumes of data leads to qualitative differences in methods and questions. Old approaches are no longer viable, and yet old data often must be combined with the new. Expertise may not transfer easily across domains or methods. The reactions to these challenges are many. Some would release data widely, in whatever forms they exist, to let others exploit at will. Some would hoard data indefinitely, rather than let others extract value that they had failed to anticipate. Many are paralyzed by risks such as misuse, misinterpretation, liability, lack of expertise, lack of tools and resources, lack of credit, loss of control, pollution of common pools of data, and the daunting challenges of sustainability. Only now is the range of problems in dealing with data becoming apparent. Some of these problems are beginning to be understood sufficiently to make progress toward solutions. Others appear intractable.

While scholars may view dealing with data as one more individual responsibility in a time of declining resources for the research and education enterprise, data scholarship is embedded deeply in knowledge infrastructures. As framed in chapter 1, tensions around data arise from concerns for ownership, control, and access to data; the difficulty of transferring data across contexts and over time; differences among forms and genres of scholarly communication; larger shifts in technology, practice, and policy; and needs for long-term sustainability of data and other scholarly content. Much is at stake for scholars, students, and the larger societies in which scholarship is conducted. Knowledge infrastructures provide a framework to assess social and technical interactions, the implications of open scholarship, and converging forms of scholarly communication.

Knowledge Infrastructures

The term *knowledge infrastructure* builds on earlier developments in information, infrastructure, and the Internet. Scholarship on infrastructure per

se has blossomed, the Internet has become wholly embedded in academic life, and information remains a constant flow. The phrase *information infrastructure* has narrowed in use from suggesting a comprehensive view of the information world to connoting technical communication architectures. Similarly, *national information infrastructure* and *global information infrastructure* now refer to policy frameworks of the 1990s (Borgman 2000, 2007; Busch 2013; Kahin and Foray 2006; Wouters et al. 2012).

Infrastructures are not engineered or fully coherent processes. Rather, they are best understood as ecologies or complex adaptive systems. They consist of many parts that interact through social and technical processes, with varying degrees of success. Paul Edwards (2010, 17) defined *knowledge infrastructures* as "robust networks of people, artifacts, and institutions that generate, share, and maintain specific knowledge about the human and natural worlds." These networks include technology, intellectual activities, learning, collaboration, and distributed access to human expertise and to documented information. A later community exploration of these ideas addressed three themes: how are knowledge infrastructures changing? How do knowledge infrastructures reinforce or redistribute authority, influence, and power? How can we best study, know, and imagine today's (and tomorrow's) knowledge infrastructures? (Edwards et al. 2013).

Data is a form of information that seems always to be in motion, difficult to fix in a static form. Borders between tacit knowledge and common ground also are shifting, as multiple parties negotiate how data are understood across disciplines, domains, and over time. The norms for knowledge, while never stable, are even more difficult to establish in an age of big data. What does it mean to "know" something if the computational result cannot be fully explained? How much can or should be known about the origins of data to transfer them across contexts? The "trust fabric" implicit in the exchange of information between collaborators is difficult to replicate in exchanges with unknown others, especially across communities and over long periods of time. Some transfers can be mediated by technology, but many will depend upon the expertise of human mediators, whether they are data scientists, librarians, archivists, or other emerging players in the research workforce. Commercial interests also are entering this space.

Knowledge infrastructures overlap with the "knowledge commons" framework, as developed further in chapter 4. A commons is also a complex ecosystem, defined simply as a "resource shared by a group of people that is subject to social dilemmas" (Hess and Ostrom 2007a, 3). Examples of how these complex ecologies reinforce or redistribute authority, influence, and power are threaded throughout this book. Individuals with skills in big

data analytics are more valued. Scholars with the resources to exploit new forms of data also benefit. New forms of knowledge such as data mining and crowdsourcing help to remap and to reshape the intellectual territory.

Massive investments in infrastructure are good for everyone to the extent that a rising tide lifts all boats. The rising tide metaphor is countered by other social and economic trends, such as the knowledge gap theory (Ettema and Kline 1977; Tichenor, Donohue, and Olien 1970), media literacies (Jenkins et al. 2009), and the Matthew effect (Merton 1968, 1988, 1995). Generally speaking, the rich get richer. Those with greater abilities to take advantage of new technologies and new information gain differential benefits. The Matthew effect applies to scholarship and was originally formulated in studies of Nobel Prize winners. Those individuals and academic centers held in highest prestige tend to acquire recognition and resources disproportionately. New discoveries by established centers of excellence will receive more attention than those from less-known centers. Conversely, scholars in lower-tier institutions and in less-developed countries typically have fewer skills and fewer local resources to use technological innovations effectively.

Invisibility is a concern in the design and maintenance of infrastructures in at least two respects. One is the defining characteristic of infrastructures that they may be visible only upon breakdown (Star and Ruhleder 1996). People often are unaware how much they depend on an infrastructure, whether the electrical grid or the interoperability between two instruments, until that infrastructure ceases to function. Second is the amount of invisible work necessary to sustain infrastructures, whether electrical grids, networks of scientific instruments, or distributed repositories of research data. Those who benefit from using these infrastructures are often unaware of the background effort involved in keeping all the parts working smoothly together. Invisible work is a salient characteristic of knowledge infrastructures, because labor to document, organize, and manage scholarly information is essential for others to discover and exploit it. Invisible work is both glue and friction in collaborations, in the development of tools, in the sharing and reuse of data, and many other infrastructure components (Bietz and Lee 2009, 2012; Birnholtz and Bietz 2003; Borgman 2003; Edwards et al. 2011; Ehrlich and Cash 1999; Lee, Dourish, and Mark 2006; Paisley 1980; Ribes and Jackson 2013; Star and Strauss 1999).

Knowledge infrastructure may be a new term, but the idea is not. Since the earliest days of intellectual inquiry, scholars have learned how to swim—or how to design better boats—to avoid drowning in the deluge, flood, or tsunami of data headed their way. Scholars have complained about being overwhelmed with information since at least the first century CE, as Ann

Blair (2010) reports in *Too Much to Know.* Concerns for the abundance of books arose well before the early modern period. By the mid-thirteenth century, solutions to the information problem were being formulated. These included title pages, concordances, and florilegia. Florilegia, literally "selected flowers," were compilations of the best sections of books on a topic. Indexes were popular by the sixteenth century. Blair explores how early scholars coped individually with their reading and interpretation through sophisticated note taking and organization mechanisms. As Price (1975) reports in *Science since Babylon,* the growth of indexing and abstracting services paralleled the growth of journals from the mid-nineteenth century onward. Relationships among authors, publishers, indexers, libraries, booksellers, and other stakeholders have been in flux ever since.

The Social and the Technical

Data scholarship is rife with tensions between the social and the technical. Rarely can these factors be separated, because they are reflexive and mutually influencing. The tool makes data creation possible, but the ability to imagine what data might be gathered makes the tool possible. Rather than attempt to resolve those long-standing debates, the premise of the provocations is that the social and the technical aspects of scholarship are inseparable. Neither the data nor the tool can be understood without the other; their meaning lies in the relationship between them (Bijker, Hughes, and Pinch 1987; Bijker 1995; Hughes 1989, 2004; Latour and Woolgar 1979; Latour 1987, 1988, 1993; Meyer and Schroeder 2014; Schroeder 2007).

Bruno Latour (1987) coined the term *technoscience* to explain how scientific practice is coupled with technologies. As a philosopher, Latour tends to use *science* in ways that encompass most forms of scholarly inquiry. In North American parlance, the sciences frequently are distinguished from the social sciences and the humanities. Further distinctions can be made, such as separating disciplinary topics from professional pursuits in engineering, medicine, law, and education. Although useful to identify institutional boundaries such as academic departments, such distinctions are arbitrary with respect to knowledge and scholarship. Science is sometimes used herein in the general sense of scholarly knowledge and practice. When distinctions by discipline are useful, as in case studies, the sciences, social sciences, and humanities are invoked.

Larger questions of the history and philosophy of science are at play in the rising attention to data. Science is an expensive public investment. Since World War II, and particularly since the end of the Cold War, the

public has demanded more accountability, more voice in research directions, and more access to the results of research (Kwa 2011; Latour 2004). As relationships between the scientific enterprise and the public shifted, social scientists became more eager to study scholarly work. Scientists and other scholars also became more willing to be studied, both to have their voices heard and to benefit from external observations of their work (Salk 1986). Since the early 1950s, a growing body of scholarship has addressed the history, philosophy, and social studies of science and technology (Hackett et al. 2007; Latour and Woolgar 1986; Lievrouw and Livingstone 2002; van Raan 1988; Woolgar 1988). That body of work, in turn, spawned studies of scholarly practices in the social sciences and humanities (Borgman 2009; Case 2006; De La Flor et al. 2010; Friedlander 2009; Jirotka et al. 2006; Wouters et al. 2012).

Communities and Collaboration

Policies, practices, standards, and infrastructure for data usually refer to the communities associated with those data. Data management plans are a prime example: "What constitutes such data will be determined by the community of interest through the process of peer review and program management" (National Science Foundation 2010a). Similarly, policies for digital archiving are framed in terms of the "designated community" (Consultative Committee for Space Data Systems 2012). Data often are "boundary objects" that exist tenuously on the borders between the domain areas (Star and Griesemer 1989). By examining the roles that data play in collaborations, the boundaries, scope, agreements, and disagreements of communities come into view.

Collecting, creating, analyzing, interpreting, and managing data requires expertise in the research domain. Many kinds of expertise are required, some theoretical and practical, some social and technical. Parts of this expertise can be readily taught, or learned from books, journals, or documentation, but much of it is deeply embedded knowledge that is difficult to articulate. Best known as "tacit knowledge"—which is itself a complex construct—the expertise most critical to exploiting data is often the least transferrable between communities and contexts (Agre 1994; Collins and Evans 2007; Darch et al. 2010; Duguid 2005; Polanyi 1966; Schmidt 2012).

Community is a theoretical construct well known in the social sciences. In social studies of science and of scholarship, communities of practice and epistemic cultures are core ideas. *Communities of practice* is a concept originated by Lave and Wenger to describe how knowledge is learned and shared in groups (Lave and Wenger 1991; Wenger 1998), a concept subsequently

much studied and extended (Osterlund and Carlile 2005). *Epistemic cultures,* by contrast, are neither disciplines nor communities (Knorr-Cetina 1999). They are more a set of "arrangements and mechanisms" associated with the processes of constructing knowledge and include individuals, groups, artifacts, and technologies (Van House 2004). Common to communities of practice and epistemic cultures is the idea that knowledge is situated and local. Nancy Van House (2004, 40) summarizes this perspective succinctly: "There is no 'view from nowhere'—knowledge is always situated in a place, time, conditions, practices, and understandings. There is no single knowledge, but multiple knowledges."

Knowledge and Representation

Despite efforts to commodify them, data are "bright shiny objects" only in the sense of being a popular topic that attracts and distracts attention (Schrier 2011; Starke 2013). Signals, recordings, notes, observations, specimens, and other entities came to be viewed as data through a long cultural process within research fields, disciplines, and specialties. Documentations of scientific practices are known as "inscriptions" (Latour and Woolgar 1979, 1986; Latour 1988; Lynch and Woolgar 1988a, 1988b). Each field develops its own inscriptions to document, describe, and represent what it considers to be data. Common methods of representing data—metadata, markup languages, formats, labeling, namespaces, thesauri, ontologies, and so on—facilitate the exchange of data within a field. A common form of representation can define the boundaries of a community. Similarly, those boundaries can become barriers for those who wish to move data between fields that employ competing forms of representation. Various diseases, drugs, flora, fauna, and phenomena go by many different names. The ability to combine data from multiple sources depends on these inscriptions.

Data, standards of evidence, forms of representation, and research practices are deeply intertwined. Differences between communities often become apparent only when attempts are made to use or combine external data sources, to collaborate, or to impose practices from one community onto another. Transferring knowledge across contexts and over time is difficult, as framed in the second provocation. Data are no easier to move than are other forms of knowledge. Often they are among the most difficult because their meaning depends on the apparatus that surrounds them—the software, hardware, methods, documentation, publications, and so on.

Journal articles, conference papers, books, and other genres of publication are packages of information that are intended to be interpretable, at least by the sophisticated reader, as an independent unit. They are representations

of scholarly knowledge and often include representations of data in forms suitable for dissemination, discovery, and exchange. Forms in which scholarly publications are represented evolved over the course of centuries. Title pages, statements of authorship, tables of contents, indexes, and other features that are now accepted components of scholarly books developed incrementally. Some of these features, such as statements of responsibility, were transferred from books to articles with the first publication of scholarly journals in 1665, the *Journal des Scavans* in Paris and *Transactions of the Royal Society* in London. In the time since, expansive knowledge infrastructures have arisen around scholarly publishing. Publishers, peer reviewing, bibliographic citation, indexing and abstracting services, information-retrieval systems, and evaluation metrics such as journal impact factors are all part of this knowledge infrastructure, as explored in chapter 9.

Theory, Practice, and Policy

Data scholarship is a concept that transcends theory, practice, and policy. Data policy writ small is the set of choices made by researchers about matters such as what they consider data, what they save, what they curate; what they share, when, with whom; and what they deposit, when, and for how long. Data policy writ large is the set of choices made by governments and funding agencies about matters such as what they consider to be data; what they require researchers to save; what they require researchers to release, when, how, and to whom; what data they require to be curated, by whom, and for how long; and how these requirements are implemented in grant proposals, in awards, and in the provision of data repositories. Data policy in the middle range is the choices made by research institutions, universities, publishers, libraries, repositories, and other stakeholders about what they consider to be data and their role in curating and disseminating those data. In turn, these rest on larger policies about research funding, intellectual property, innovation, economics, governance, and privacy.

Policies of governments, funding agencies, journals, and institutions that are intended to improve the flow of scholarly communication often make simplifying assumptions about the ability to commodify and exchange information. While usually intended to promote equity across communities and disciplines, policies that fail to respect the substantial differences in theory, practice, and culture between fields are likely to be implemented poorly, be counterproductive, or be ignored by their constituents. Individual communities may have their own moral economies that govern how data are collected, managed, and shared, for example (Kelty 2012; McCray 2000). As explored in the case studies and in chapter 8, current policies for

data management plans and data sharing tend to focus on releasing data rather than on the means to reuse them or to sustain access, which are complex and expensive aspects of knowledge infrastructures.

Open Scholarship

Open access, open source, open data, open standards, open repositories, open networks, open bibliography, open annotations ... the list continues indefinitely. The open access movement has been under way since the 1970s, as introduced in chapter 1. Today's knowledge infrastructures were shaped by, and continue to shape, developments in open access to research; mechanisms to improve interoperability among systems, tools, and services; advances in distributed computing networks and technologies; and nearly ubiquitous access to the Internet.

Open scholarship is no more easily defined than is data scholarship. It is most closely equated to open science. For the purposes of discussion here, open scholarship encompasses the policies and practices associated with open access publishing, open data, data release, and data sharing. Among the expectations for open scholarship are to speed the pace of research, to encourage new questions and forms of investigation, to minimize fraud and misconduct, to facilitate the growth of a technically and scientifically literate workforce, and to leverage public investments in research and education (David, den Besten, and Schroeder 2010; Esanu and Uhlir 2004; Nielsen 2011; Boulton et al. 2012; Uhlir and Schröder 2007).

The use of a single term such as *open scholarship*, however, risks masking substantial differences in these many forms of open access. Publications and data each play distinct roles in scholarship, as framed by the third provocation and explicated below. What open access to publications and open data have in common are the intent to improve the flow of information, minimize restrictions on the use of intellectual resources, and increase the transparency of research practice. Where they differ are in their kinds of value for scholarship, the array of stakeholders involved, and their mobility across contexts and over time.

Open Access to Research Findings

Scholarship moved from the realm of private letters and meetings to open dissemination with the advent of the first journals in 1665. Readers had access to books, journals, and other publications through libraries, booksellers, and personal subscriptions. Private exchange of letters, drafts, manuscripts, and preprints continued in parallel.

Open access to research findings made a giant leap forward in 1991 with the launch of arXiv, originally known by its address xxx.lanl.gov, as it predated the World Wide Web (Ginsparg 1994, 2001). In the twenty-plus years since, arXiv has expanded to other scientific fields, moved from Los Alamos National Laboratories to Cornell University, and gained a broad base of support from member institutions. Its usage continues to rise exponentially. More than eight thousand papers per month are contributed to arXiv, and more than sixty million papers were downloaded in 2012 alone (ArXiv.org 2013).

Several lessons from the launch of arXiv are important for today's considerations of open access to data. One is that the system was an outgrowth of the active preprint exchange culture in high energy physics. It built on an existing knowledge infrastructure that supported the flow of information within networks of close colleagues, known as invisible colleges (Crane 1972).

The second lesson is that arXiv disrupted that knowledge infrastructure by changing relationships among authors, publishers, libraries, and readers as stakeholders in the scholarly communication of physics. Researchers and students alike, in countries rich and poor, gained access to papers much sooner than the official date of publication. Journal editors and publishers in physics had little choice but to accept the existence of arXiv, given its rapid adoption. Previously, many journals refused to consider papers posted online on the grounds that such posting constituted "prior publication." Similar policies remain in place in many fields today.

A third lesson is that the success of arXiv did not transfer quickly or well to other fields. Whereas preprint servers in other disciplines are gaining in size and popularity, none became as deeply embedded in scholarly practice as has arXiv. However, even arXiv is not embedded in all of physics, mathematics, astronomy, or the other fields it covers. In some research specialties, usage is ubiquitous. In other specialties it is only lightly used.

Open access to publications built on those early lessons. Open access is a simple concept that is commonly misunderstood, in no small part due to the competing interests of many stakeholders. Peter Suber's (2012a, 4) definition is the most succinct: "Open access (OA) literature is digital, online, free of charge, and free of most copyright and licensing restrictions." As Suber hastens to point out, open access to the literature of research and scholarship operates in a much different realm than does open access to other forms of content. One principle on which OA literature rests is that authors are the copyright holders of their work, unless and until they transfer the ownership to another party such as a publisher. The second is that

scholars rarely are paid for writing research articles. They can distribute their work widely without losing revenue, which is not the case for most other authors, artists, or creators. Scholarly authors write research articles for impact or influence, rather than for revenue. It is in a scholar's best interests to reach as wide an audience as possible. The primary sources of funding for scholarly research are academic salaries and research grants. It is also in the best interests of the institutions that employ and fund scholars that their publications achieve the highest possible impact.

Open access to literature can be accomplished by many means, under multiple governance models, and goes by many names (e.g., *green, gold, gratis, libre,* etc.). What these models have in common is that they rest on the two principles described above. Authors generally retain copyright or license their work for open access distribution. Authors also retain the rights to be attributed as the creators of the work. Different considerations apply for open access to scholarly books, textbooks, and other works for which authors generally do receive direct revenue (Budapest Open Access Initiative 2002; Directory of Open Access Journals 2013; Howard 2013a; Jacobs 2006; Laakso and Björk 2013; Leptin 2012; Pinter 2012; Research Councils UK 2013; Suber 2012a; Van Noorden 2013b; Wickham and Vincent 2013; Wilbanks 2006; Willinsky 2006).

Since the mid-2000s, a growing number of research universities around the world have adopted open access policies for the journal publications of their faculty. In the United States these include Harvard, Massachusetts Institute of Technology, California Institute of Technology, and the University of California (Harvard University 2010; MIT Libraries 2009; Caltech 2013a; Office of Scholarly Communication 2013). Generally, these policies grant the universities a nonexclusive license to disseminate the work, usually through a public repository. Seismic shifts toward open access to publications occurred in 2012 and 2013. In 2012, the Research Councils of the United Kingdom (RCUK) announced that all peer-reviewed journal articles and conference papers resulting in whole or in part from their funding are to be submitted to open access journals, effective April 2013. The definition of "open access journal" in the policy has been modified and interpreted several times since, being particularly contentious. It involves embargo periods, an array of business models, and some interim subsidies (Research Councils UK 2012a, 2012b). In 2013, the executive branch of the US government announced a similar policy for open access to publications resulting from federal funding, generally following the embargo periods and policies established by the National Institutes of Health and PubMed Central (Office of Science and Technology Policy 2013; Holdren

2013b). The European Union, Australia, and other countries are debating similar policies.

These various policies, business models, and new genres of publishing have resulted in broader public access to the scholarly journal literature. Accounting for embargo periods, about half of journal articles are freely available online within a year of publication, and that proportion is expected to grow (Laakso et al. 2011; Van Noorden 2013a). While the devil is in the details, open access to scholarly journal articles is becoming the norm. Tensions between stakeholders have not disappeared, however. Authors continue to post articles, papers, and other works online for which these open access policies do not apply, and some publishers are becoming more aggressive about policing access to works for which they are the exclusive copyright holder (Howard 2013b; SHERPA/RoMEO 2014).

Open Access to Data

Many funding agency policies for open access to data are linked to policies for open access to publications. The UK policy is most explicit about the relationship (Research Councils UK 2012b, 1): "The Government, in line with its overarching commitment to transparency and open data, is committed to ensuring that published research findings should be freely accessible." The RCUK policy on publishing in open access journals requires authors to specify how data associated with the publication can be accessed, but acknowledges the complexities of doing so (Research Councils UK 2012b, 4): "to ensure that researchers think about data access issues … However, the policy does not require that the data must be made open. If there are considered to be compelling reasons to protect access to the data, for example commercial confidentiality or legitimate sensitivities around data derived from potentially identifiable human participants, these should be included in the statement."

The National Institutes of Health in the United States requires that publications resulting from their grant funds be deposited into PubMedCentral. They also require data management plans with grant proposals (Basken 2012; National Institutes of Health 2013; PubMed Central 2009; Zerhouni 2006). The National Science Foundation has requirements for data management plans but not for open access publishing. However, the subsequent US federal policy on open access publishing will apply to NSF, NIH, and other federal agencies that spend more than $100 million annually in research and development. The policy directs each agency to develop an open access plan for scientific publications and digital scientific data (Holdren 2013b; Burwell et al. 2013).

Open access to journal articles and open data differ with respect to both of Suber's (2012a) principles, however. Whereas authors are the copyright holders on journal articles, at least initially, the same is rarely true for data. As explored further in chapter 9, determining who qualifies for authorship is a much-debated topic within and between fields. Once settled, certain rights and responsibilities accrue to the authors of a work. Determining who qualifies as an "author" of data is a barely explored topic within most collaborations (Wallis 2012). Even when individuals and groups assign authority for data, the rights and responsibilities may remain unclear. Many forms of data are created and controlled by scholars, but ownership is a different matter. Some forms of data are deemed to be facts that cannot be copyrighted. Researchers use data that are owned by other parties or acquired from common pools of resources. Some types of data, such as confidential records on human subjects, are controlled by scholars but cannot be released. Rights policies may vary by institution, funding agency, contract, jurisdiction, and other factors.

Suber's second principle is that scholarly authors write journal articles and many other forms of publication for impact, not for revenue. Scholars, their employers, and their funders are motivated to disseminate their publications as widely as possible. Neither situation is true for most data. Journal articles are packaged for dissemination to an audience, whereas data are difficult to extricate from the processes of scholarly work. Releasing data often requires substantial investment over and above the conduct of the research and the writing of publications. Data can be valuable assets that are accumulated over the course of a career, to be released carefully, if at all.

Governance models for open access to data are nascent at best, as discussed more fully in chapters 4 and 10. "Freely accessible," as in the RCUK policy quoted, appears to be in the sense of free speech rather than free beer, following Stallman's aphorism quoted in chapter 1. The essential questions to address about any commons concern equity, efficiency, and sustainability (Hess and Ostrom 2007a). Only a few fields have found ways to address equity and efficiency through the use of repositories to ingest, curate, and provide access to data. Private exchange suffices in some fields. Others are turning to research libraries for assistance. In all cases, sustainability is a problem. Some repositories have long-term funding, others only short term. Some provide data to anyone without a fee, others serve data only to members of the consortia that fund them. Data shared by private exchange or by posting on a research team's website may be available only in the short term, as discussed in chapter 8.

Open data is thus substantially distinct from open access to scholarly literature. Little consensus exists on what it means for data to be "open." The earliest framing of open data, by Peter Murray-Rust and Henry Rzepa (2004), encompasses most of the later ideas. Both chemists, they are concerned with free access and with the ability to mine structured data. When entities such as molecules are represented in ways that an algorithm can identify their structure, they become useful as data for mining, extraction, and manipulation. When those same molecules are represented only as images in a text file, human eyes are necessary to identify their structure. Open data, in their formulation as a "datument," are data that are structured for machine readability and that are freely accessible.

Murray-Rust and others, under the aegis of the Open Knowledge Foundation, later developed a succinct legal definition of open data: "A piece of data or content is open if anyone is free to use, reuse, and redistribute it — subject only, at most, to the requirement to attribute and/or share-alike" (Open Data Commons 2013). In business contexts, definitions are more ambiguous: "Open data—machine-readable information, particularly government data, that's made available to others" (Manyika et al. 2013). The *OECD Principles and Guidelines for Access to Research Data from Public Funding* (Organisation for Economic Co-operation and Development 2007) frames open access to data in terms of thirteen principles, as explained in chapter 8. The UK Royal Society report called *Science as an Open Enterprise* (Boulton et al. 2012, 14) defines open data as "data that meets the criteria of intelligent openness. Data must be accessible, useable, assessable and intelligible." Implications for biomedical data include cost-benefit trade-offs, triggering and timing of data release, means to ensure data quality, scope of data to include, confidentiality, privacy, security, intellectual property, and jurisdiction (Boulton et al. 2011).

Openness can facilitate the creation of data. Open access to texts, for example, enables the entities in those texts to be treated as data. Using text-mining techniques, it becomes possible to locate all the articles or books describing a particular molecule, celestial object, person, place, event, or other entity. Publication databases, data archives, and collections of digitized books begin to look alike from a data-mining perspective (Bourne et al. 2011; Bourne 2005; Crane 2006; Murray-Rust et al. 2004). However, they look much different from an intellectual property perspective, as examined in chapter 4.

Open data also can include the ability to treat representations of research objects as data, whether or not the objects being described are open. An example is the creation of open tags or annotations for publications,

datasets, and other content. Annotations and bibliographies add value to the items described, making them more discoverable. Interest in sharing annotations arose early in digital library research, leading to competing methods and to standards efforts for the interoperability of annotation systems (Foster and Moreau 2006; Hunter 2009; Phelps and Wilensky 1997, 2000). Early tools to manage personal bibliographies, such as ProCite, BiblioLink, RefWorks, and EndNote were predicated on sole-author writing and on files held locally. By the early 2000s, individuals began to tag and annotate websites, images, publications, and data and to share those tags on social networks such as Delicious and Flickr. By the latter 2000s, personal bibliographies and open annotation were converging. Zotero, Mendeley, LibraryThing, and other tools enable bibliographies, tags, and notes to be shared. The open bibliography movement got a large boost when national libraries began to release cataloging records for open use (Open Bibliography and Open Bibliographic Data 2013). As more bibliographic records become openly available, they can be treated as data to be mined. Annotation tools support a growing array of data types (Agosti and Ferro 2007; Das et al. 2009; Kurtz and Bollen 2010; Renear and Palmer 2009; Rodriguez, Bollen, and Van de Sompel 2007).

Open Technologies

Open scholarship is part of a forty-plus-year transition from closed to open networks and technologies. Stories of the origin and trajectory of the Internet are tales of this transition (Abbate 1999; Goldsmith and Wu 2006; Kraut et al. 2002; Levien et al. 2005; MacLean 2004; O'Brien 2004; Odlyzko 2000; National Research Council 2001; Zittrain 2005). It is generally agreed that computer networks were developed with government funding to serve research and military purposes. From the first international interconnections of networks in the late 1960s until the policy changes of the early 1990s, the Internet was available only to the research, academic, and military communities via government contracts. These became known as National Research and Education Networks (NRENs). Developed initially to share expensive computer cycles over the network, Internet capabilities expanded to include e-mail, file transfer, and similar features. Parallel commercial packet-switched networks, such as Telenet and Tymnet, provided commodity communications to private enterprise in support of business activities and new information services such as bibliographic databases (Borgman, Moghdam, and Corbett 1984; Borgman 2000).

Policy changes in 1993–1994, under the rubrics of *national information infrastructure* and *global information infrastructure,* allowed government

and commercial interconnections. This was the launch of the commodity Internet and the conversion of communication networks from government-owned or protected systems to commercial operations. The Internet was declared "open" to interconnection and to the provision of services by public and private entities alike. Opening the network coincided with the first demonstration of the World Wide Web and with the first browser interfaces. In the two decades since, Internet technologies, capacity, and user communities have scaled beyond even the wildest imaginations of the original designers. However, new business models, shifts in the balance of stakeholders, and unforeseen challenges of security and privacy are contributing to redesign of the infrastructure (Borgman 2000; Estrin et al. 2010).

Moving data over open networks is a different matter from being able to use those data once acquired. Data in digital form and representations in digital form are readable only with appropriate technologies. To interpret a digital dataset, much must be known about the hardware used to generate the data, whether sensor networks or laboratory machines; the software used to encode or analyze them, whether image processing or statistical tools; and the protocols and expertise necessary to bring them together. Technologies evolve very quickly, especially in research environments. Many instruments produce data that can be read only with proprietary software. To use or reuse those data requires access to the right version of the software and perhaps to the instrument. Many analytical tools are proprietary, thus analysis of data may yield datasets in proprietary formats, independent of how open the data were at the time of ingest. Scholars often build their own tools and write their own code to solve problems at hand. Although an efficient practice in the short term, local code and devices can be very hard to maintain in the long term. Rarely are they constructed to industrial standards for software engineering. Local tools are flexible and adaptable, often at the expense of portability across sites and situations (Easterbrook and Johns 2009; Edwards et al. 2013; Segal 2005, 2009).

The degree of openness of data, standards, and technologies influences the ability to exchange data between tools, labs, partners, and over time. Standards can improve the flow of information within communities but also can create boundaries between them. They may be premature or inappropriate, creating barriers and preventing innovation. Technical interoperability of systems and services has long been the holy grail of digital libraries and software engineering. Interoperability allows some data and

stakeholders in and keeps others out. Policy, practice, standards, business models, and vested interests often are greater determinants of interoperability than is technology, per se (Brown and Marsden 2013; Busch 2013; DeNardis 2011; Lampland and Star 2009; Libicki 1995; Palfrey and Gasser 2012).

Converging Communication

Formal and informal communications are converging in business, government, and scholarship alike. To stay in business, it is no longer sufficient for a company to be visible on Main Street and in the daily newspapers. Now businesses also need a presence on the World Wide Web, social networks, blogs and microblogs, and video channels. Governments must be available to citizens in capital cities and in individual neighborhoods. With the growth of digital government, they also must be available online, providing public services 24/7. Similarly, scholars are exerting their influence not only through the literature of their fields but also via web pages, preprint servers, data archives, institutional repositories, archives of slides and figures, blogs and microblogs, social networks, and other media as they are invented. New technologies facilitate new means of communication, but they also destabilize existing models. As old models are mapped onto the new, metaphors may be stretched to their breaking points.

Data Metaphors

The roles that publications and data play in scholarly communication are conflated in metaphors such as "data publication" and "publishing data." The simplifying assumptions in these metaphors pose risks to new models of scholarly communication, as stated in the third provocation.

Strictly speaking, publishing means "to make public," thus many acts could be construed as publishing. In the context of scholarship, however, publishing serves three general purposes: (1) legitimization, (2) dissemination, and (3) access, preservation, and curation (Borgman 2007). The first function is usually accomplished by peer review. The fixed point of publication, which typically is the document of record, manifests the legitimization process, conferring a stamp of quality and trust awarded by the community. Citations accrue to published units as the legitimized records of research. The dissemination function is essential because research exists only if it is communicated to others (Meadows 1974, 1998). Publishers disseminate research as journals, books, conference proceedings, and other

genres. Authors disseminate their own work by distributing publications to colleagues, posting them, and by mentioning them in talks, blogs, social networks, and beyond. The third function is to make the work available and discoverable, to ensure that copies are preserved, and usually also to ensure that a copy is curated for long-term use. The latter function tends to be a joint responsibility of authors, publishers, and libraries. Scholars are motivated to publish their work, since publishing is the primary form of recognition for hiring, promotion, and other rewards.

The data publishing metaphor is apt only in the narrow use of the term, analogous to journal and book publishing. For example, the Organisation for Economic Co-operation and Development (OECD) publishes a wide array of national and international statistics on gross domestic product, employment, income, population, labor, education, trade, finance, prices, and such. Various governmental bodies publish census data and similar statistics. Outside the scholarly arena, data publishing may refer to distribution of documents consisting of lists, facts, or advertisements rather than narrative. A company by that name has been producing directories of local telephone numbers and similar information since 1986 (Data Publishing 2013).

Beyond that narrow usage, the data publishing metaphor breaks down. Most often, it refers to the release of datasets associated with an individual journal article. Data may be attached to articles but they rarely receive independent peer review because they are difficult to assess. In this sense of data publication, the data often are deposited in an archive and linked to the article, rather than published as a unit. The dataset may become discoverable and be curated, but it is not distributed as an entity that stands alone, nor is it self-describing in the way that journal articles are. Data publication also can refer to posting data on the author's website, in which case none of the three functions of publishing is well served. In a few cases, the term refers to an archive that collects data and makes them accessible to others (PANGAEA: Data Publisher for Earth & Environmental Science 2013). Discovery and curation may be accomplished, but peer review and dissemination are not core activities of most data archives.

The argument in favor of the metaphor is familiarity—scholars understand how to publish and cite articles. Implicit in this argument is that familiarity will encourage data release (Crosas et al. 2013; Klump et al. 2006; Lawrence et al. 2011; Murphy 2013; Parsons and Fox 2013). Although often stated as fact, little evidence exists that data citation is an incentive to release data. The data publication metaphor also promotes the interests of publishers who would package data as units to disseminate, extending current business models.

The arguments against the data publication metaphor are many, but it persists. Calls to "publish your data" with each journal article are risky because they reify a binary link between articles and datasets. In fields where a binary relationship exists and where papers are expected to be reproducible based on those datasets, the mapping may serve the interests of the community. Those fields are few and far between, however, as discussed in chapter 9. For such a one-to-one mapping to be effective, it must be supported by a larger knowledge infrastructure that includes peer review of datasets, the availability of repositories, journal policies and technologies to facilitate linking, and access to the necessary hardware, software, and other apparatus for reproducibility.

A one-to-one mapping between a journal article and a dataset is but one of many possible relationships between publications and data. Relationships frequently are many-to-many. The full scope of data and information resources associated with a given publication can be impossible to specify. Direct links are useful to the extent that they support discovery and reproducibility, but an architecture that requires one-to-one links constrains the ability to discover or reuse datasets for other purposes. The open data movement is predicated on the ability to assemble and compare data from many sources, which requires open technologies.

Data publication is but one of the five metaphors for data stewardship identified by Parsons and Fox (2013), all of which they find to be problematic and incomplete. Their second metaphor is "big data" or "big iron," referring to the industrial production and engineering culture associated with data in astronomy, climate science, high energy physics, and similar areas. Big iron is concerned with quality assurance, data reduction, versioning, data and metadata standards, and high throughput. "Science support" is their third metaphor, referring to areas such as field ecology in which it can be difficult to separate the science from the data or the data collectors from the curators. "Map making," their fourth metaphor, refers to the geospatial data essential for climate models, land use, surveys, and many other purposes. These data are integrated in layers, published as a map rather than as an article or paper.

"Linked data" is their last metaphor. While a means of linking datasets and publications, it is part of a larger movement to aggregate related units of data, publications, and documentation. Notions of linked data are fundamental to the semantic web. To be effective, they rely on graph models of organization and require agreements on ontologies and standards. Open data is central to this worldview, but preservation, curation, and quality assurance are not high priorities.

Units of Data

The metaphors associated with data make simplifying assumptions about the appropriate unit to disseminate, cite, use, or curate. Data can be represented in units of any size, whether pixels, photons, characters, strokes, letters, words, cells in a spreadsheet, datasets, or data archives. Even the term *dataset* is problematic, referring to at least four common themes—grouping, content, relatedness, and purpose—each of which has multiple categories (Renear, Sacchi, and Wickett 2010). Datasets ranging in size from a few bits to many terabytes can be treated as independent objects. The appropriate unit depends on the intended use. Sometimes it is useful to aggregate many units of data for comparison and mining; at other times it is useful to extract portions of larger resources.

Books and journal articles, once existing only on paper as convenient units of communication, now can be broken down into much smaller units. Search engines retrieve articles as independent entities, not part of a journal issue carefully assembled by editorial staff. Within those articles, each table, figure, and dataset may have its own identifier so that it can be retrieved independently—separated from the context of the research method, theory, and conclusions. Books, journal articles, and other forms of text can be treated as units or aggregates of data, searchable by words, phrases, and character strings.

The boundary between formal communication such as publications and informal communication such as presentations and conversations continues to blur as scholarly content becomes more atomized and treated as data. Journal articles, preprints, drafts, blog posts, slides, tables, figures, video presentations of talks, tweets, Facebook and LinkedIn posts, and countless other entities can be distributed independently. Public, albeit commercial, repositories for slides and figures are popular for their ease of deposit and access and because they accept useful entities not readily published elsewhere. The flexibility of unitizing and linking digital objects promotes new forms of communication. For example, when journals require substantial page charges to publish color figures—even in digital form—authors may publish only the grayscale version with the journal article, depositing or posting the full-color figures elsewhere. Because the color image is necessary to interpret the findings, these authors have chosen an affordable means to reach their audience, at least in the short term. Some of this content will be sustained, but much will not. Links break early and often.

The usual response to the problem of disaggregation is to reaggregate content both to reconstruct original relationships among parts and to

create new aggregations. Linked data approaches can be used to reconstruct the value chain of scholarship, connecting articles, data, documentation, protocols, preprints, presentations, and other units. This approach is suitable for units that are readily networked but is not a generic solution for linking resources across systems and services (Bechhofer et al. 2013; Goble, De Roure, and Bechhofer 2013; Pepe et al. 2010; Van de Sompel et al. 2012). Similarly, data mining of the open literature may identify data in texts, tables, and figures, but not in supplemental materials or archives. Multiple approaches are needed to the problems of disaggregation, reaggregation, citing, and units of publication (Bourne et al. 2011; Parsons and Fox 2013; Uhlir 2012).

Documents of Record

As scholarly communications are fragmented, dispersed, and reaggregated in new ways, maintaining the evidentiary record becomes more difficult. Cited objects disappear, links break, and search algorithms evolve as proprietary secrets. Data are even less stable than publications because they can serve multiple purposes in multiple contexts. Publications are units fixed in a place and time after long periods of development. At the moment of publication, works are assigned unique and persistent identifiers, whether digital object identifiers (DOIs); volume, issue, and page numbers; or other registrations. To be assigned persistent identifiers, units of data must be frozen in time, version, and form. Questions of what units constitute the evidentiary trail loom large.

The problem of proliferating versions of documents is hardly new. Major newspapers such as the *New York Times* publish multiple editions throughout the day. In the print world, "the late city edition" was considered the document of record. In a digital world, the *New York Times* exists in multiple print and digital versions tailored to local, national, and international audiences. Individual articles may change continuously.

In a print world, the document of record is usually unambiguous: the journal issue, the conference proceedings, the published book. Once documents were published in print, they stayed published. Bibliographic citations accrue to the published version of the work. Readers can trace the flow of ideas and evidence by following these bibliographic references, knowing they can obtain a stable copy of the work from a library, a colleague, or a bookstore, even years later. Journal articles now appear online weeks or months prior to print publication, if indeed printed at all. Until recently, the online version was considered a preview and the print version

was the document of record to be referenced. Online versions have become the document of record and the DOI is rapidly replacing volume, issue, and page number referencing.

Data can be disseminated in ways that capture their dynamic character better than can journal articles in static formats. The *Journal of Visualized Experiments,* for example, publishes peer-reviewed reports of experiments accompanied by videos that demonstrate how the experiment is performed (*JoVE: Peer Reviewed Scientific Video Journal* 2013). Authors are enhancing publications with interactive visualizations such as 3D PDFs that enable readers to rotate astronomy data models within the article (Goodman et al. 2009). Many other such experiments are under way (De La Flor et al. 2010; Dutton and Jeffreys 2010; Wouters et al. 2012).

Research methods and findings also can be disseminated by means other than formal publications in journals and books. Short videos, for example, are a popular way to demonstrate laboratory techniques. Other concepts can be illustrated with drawings and voiceovers. Searching a video site for *proteomics, differential equations, econometrics,* or *intertextuality* yields dozens of free recordings, some of which have been viewed a half-million times. Authors are using social media to promote their work and readers are using them to learn new ideas, findings, and skills. Tweets and blog posts have become important alerting services for scholarly content. *Science* runs a popular annual competition, *Dance Your PhD,* for which doctoral candidates submit short music videos that illustrate their theses (Bohannon 2013a). These resources may be on the current fringes of scholarly publishing, but they are increasingly important parts of the knowledge infrastructure that scholars inhabit.

Conclusion

Data and scholarship are inextricable from each other. They exist together in a complex ecology best understood as a knowledge infrastructure. Knowledge infrastructures are in a continuous state of flux as research and technologies advance, policies shift, and stakeholder interests are rebalanced. They adapt and evolve over long periods of time. Social and technical influences on knowledge infrastructures are similarly inextricable. Scholars are members of multiple and overlapping communities, each with their own methods, cultures, practices, and means of representing their knowledge. Shared representations facilitate the sharing of data and other resources, but they also create boundaries between communities.

Scholarship is becoming more open in many respects, but each form of openness reveals new barriers to communication and to exchanging resources such as data. The lack of consensus on what it means for something to be open is due to the many ways some entities, policies, technologies, or services might be considered open and the extenuating circumstances for each. Formal and informal scholarly communications are converging in some respects and diverging in others. Metaphors of scholarly publishing break down when mapped onto data. The atomization of units of communication offers opportunities to aggregate and disaggregate knowledge in new ways, but undermines traditional understandings of what to value, trust, and curate as the evidentiary record of scholarship and what to discard.

4 Data Diversity

Introduction

Given the diversity of theories, methods, cultures, and questions in scholarly inquiry, it is unsurprising that data are equally diverse. Effective knowledge infrastructures are those that lay common ground, support distinctive methods and requirements to the extent possible, and facilitate the transfer of data, methods, tools, technologies, and theories across communities, contexts, and over time, when appropriate. In the best of all possible worlds, scholars can draw on knowledge infrastructures from a broad spectrum of domains.

What is good for physics may not be good for philology, and vice versa. Domains differ in many ways, including their volume, variety, velocity (Laney 2001), and types of data; their cultures of sharing and reuse; and their criteria for assigning authorship and responsibility, whether for publications or for data. A close analysis of data practices—what and how data are collected, managed, used, interpreted, released, reused, deposited, curated, and so on—can identify the range of variance, approaches that are common across fields, approaches that require extensive local adaptation, and opportunities for transfer. Often the most transformative research is that which borrows practices from other domains. Some individuals look inward to their communities and others look outward for expertise and ideas. Approaches may remain relatively static over the course of a career or may adapt continually to new sources of data, tools, questions, opportunities, and constraints. Pockets of innovation arise in unexpected corners of the scholarly universe, but so do pockets of stagnation. The provocations in chapter 1 vary by domain and by other factors. This chapter develops a model that is applied to cases in the sciences, social sciences, and humanities in the three chapters following, laying the foundation for comparative analyses of data policy and practice in part III.

Disciplines and Data

Data practices differ as widely as does any other aspect of scholarly work. The conduct of research is learned over the course of a career, resting on deep expertise and experience. Theory, questions, methods, and resources influence the choices of data to address a problem. Conversely, recognizing that something could be used as data influences the ways in which questions are pursued and methods are applied. These choices often rest on tacit knowledge and on suppositions that are difficult to articulate.

Disciplines are a convenient, if far from perfect, way of categorizing the differences in data practices. The boundaries between the sciences, social sciences, and humanities are porous and artificial. Any broad categorization of human activity is fraught with difficulty, yet some grouping is necessary to frame an argument. Many categorizations of disciplinary distinctions exist, none of which have broad consensus. Common dichotomies of research approaches include basic versus applied, hypothesis-driven versus discovery-driven, deductive versus inductive, and theoretical versus empirical. Despite the widespread use of these terms in science policy, they have been contentious since Francis Bacon's time in the sixteenth and seventeenth centuries.

Donald Stokes (1997) explored the Western origins of research practices, revealing the many ways in which such categories are treated and how distinctions such as basic versus applied research vary with their roles in the research, over time, and by other circumstances. He asks whether research is a quest for fundamental understanding and whether investigators consider applications of findings. When the answer to both questions is yes, the work can be categorized as "use-inspired basic research," which Stokes labels as "Pasteur's quadrant." Louis Pasteur was concerned with fundamental understanding of the fermentation process and also with how that understanding could be applied to preventing spoilage of milk. Pure basic research, epitomized by Niels Bohr, is the quest for fundamental understanding without consideration of how that knowledge might be used. Thomas Edison exemplifies pure applied research, deeply concerned with use and little concerned with fundamental understanding. As Stokes comments (74–75), the fourth quadrant, where the answer to both questions is no, is not empty. Scholars may simply be curious and not motivated either by application or fundamental theory. That fourth quadrant is particularly interesting when considering the temporal characteristics of data. For example, field guides to birds and butterflies, devoid of use or theory at the time when created, later became valuable records for climate change.

Kwa (2011) traces the history of scientific reasoning back to Greek and Latin primary sources, going well beyond Western traditions. Building on the work of Alistair Crombie (1994), Kwa explores six distinct styles: deductive, experimental, hypothetical-analogical, taxonomic, statistical, and evolutionary. Meyer and Schroeder (2014) compare eResearch approaches to Kwa's (and Crombie's) styles of knowing. They also apply Whitley's (2000) model of social organization in the sciences to eResearch across the disciplines. Whitley's dimensions are mutual dependence and task uncertainty. Some fields have high mutual dependency, requiring aggregation of resources and formalization of governance structures, whereas fields with low mutual dependency have less need for these structures. Mutual dependency interacts with degree of task uncertainty, whereby fields low on that dimension (i.e., having higher certainty), such as high energy physics, develop integrated bureaucracies to govern their fields.

Thomas Kuhn (1962, 1970) made similar arguments about the degree of agreement within communities as to what questions are worthy of pursuit. Tony Becher (1989, 1994) is among those who distinguish between "hard" and "soft" approaches to science and to scholarship in general. He draws on the work of Biglan (1973) and Kolb (1981) to make a further dichotomy between pure and applied, resulting in a two-by-two model analogous to those of Stokes and Whitley. The hard-pure quadrant constitutes the abstract-reflective approaches found in the natural sciences; the soft-pure are the concrete-reflective modes of the humanities and social sciences; hard-applied are the abstract-active characteristics of the science-based professions; and the soft-applied are the concrete-active modes found in the social professions. Although all of these models are based on extensive empirical study of the domains, each attempts to reduce the work of complex and diverse communities to a few simple elements (Furner 2010).

Styles of research in the social sciences and humanities have received less attention of this sort than have those of the sciences. Those quadrants that correspond to scientific approaches are applicable to the social sciences, especially in quantitative areas that border the sciences. Theory and interpretation are terms more commonly found in the humanities and in areas of the social sciences that border the humanities. Task uncertainty is higher in these areas and shared resources are fewer. Scholars in the humanities are the most likely to work alone, exhibiting less mutual dependence. All of these practices are changing with advances in distributed technologies. Teams are getting larger, more shared resources are being developed, and

tasks are becoming more systematized (Beaulieu, de Rijcke, and van Heur 2012; Burdick et al. 2012; Friedlander 2009; Meyer and Schroeder 2014; Unsworth et al. 2006; Wouters et al. 2012).

Size Matters

Big data is a matter of scale, not absolute size, as explained in chapter 1. Differences in the scale of data, in turn, influence what entities become data, the methods applied, the forms of inquiry, and the goals and purposes of the research. Big science, in Price's (1963) terms, are mature sciences typified by large, distributed teams, international collaborations, large data collections, and large instrumentation facilities. The little sciences, small sciences, or small scholarship refer to everyone else.

The middle ground can be the most interesting, however. As is evident from the case studies, no field functions solely within rigid boundaries of big science or little science. Fields with massive data collections, shared instrumentation, international partners, and elaborate governance structures also have pockets of activity in which individual investigators collect and maintain local data collections that never become part of shared resources. Similarly, sole investigators may rely on massive data collections assembled by others.

The dimensions by which data vary in size, scale, or scope are influenced by what entities become data, the practices associated with them, how those data are represented, and how they could be released or reused. Institutional factors also can be important, such as norms and symbols, intermediaries, routines, standards, and material objects (Mayernik, in press). Size dimensions are independent of field or discipline and interact with many other considerations, such as the goals of the project, the means by which data are collected, and how they are analyzed. They can be indicators of where transference is appropriate and not, and where investments in knowledge infrastructure are needed.

Project Goals

The goals of a research project influence the scope of evidence required. For exploratory research, for example, a scholar may wish to collect small sets of data that describe particular events or phenomena, often in a flexible manner. If the goal is to model entire systems, consistent collection of large volumes of data is necessary. When first framing a problem, researchers are open to many possible sources of data. As they narrow a problem, they often narrow the scope of their data collection.

Weather and climate data are examples of how much the scope of data collection may differ depending on the goal of research. Weather data are local measurements collected for the purposes of short-term prediction of temperature, rain, snow, clouds, wind, storms, and other events. Rarely are weather predictions reliable more than ten days in advance. Local meteorological measurements for weather data may be consistent over time, if taken at the same site, with the same instruments, at regular intervals, and following established protocols. However, local data taken at one site are not necessarily consistent with local data taken at other sites, because sites may use different instruments and different protocols for data collection.

Climate science, in contrast to weather prediction, requires observations taken at widely distributed locations over long periods of time. Climate data might be collected systematically through satellite observations or derived from multiple sets of weather data. Such climate data are used as inputs to models of physical processes for studying the earth's climate. The same observations may be input to multiple models, each developed by different research teams, and each with its own set of parameters and theories. Paul Edwards (2010) provides a comprehensive account of the scientific, technical, social, and political efforts that were required—over the course of a century—to implement the international agreements that resulted in the consistent data collection necessary for climate science. Today, these data are used to predict storms, floods, droughts, and other climate patterns that transcend international boundaries.

Climate models, although far from perfect, represent a success story to the extent that local and global interests eventually converged (Edwards 2013). Convergence appears not to be the norm, since failures are less well documented than are successes. David Ribes and Thomas Finholt (2009), for example, identified tensions in long-term development of four large scientific infrastructures. In the beginning, and especially from the outside, each of these infrastructures appeared to have common goals. As the collaborations progressed, differences in end goals, motivations, user communities, technologies, and other factors became increasingly apparent. Reconciling data about water—an essential topic in an era of climate change—is particularly problematic, given fundamental differences in the approaches taken by fields such as environmental engineering, hydrology, public policy, architecture, and urban planning. Differences in goals can be attributed to Stokes's dimensions of application versus fundamental understanding, temporal factors, standards and interoperability, and the local context (Jackson and Buyuktur 2014; Jackson et al. 2011; Jackson 2006; Lampland and Star 2009; Ribes and Finholt 2009; Ribes and Jackson 2013).

Data Collection

Whether observations, records, or other entities become data is partly a function of who collects them and how. Big data are usually those collected by machine, such as the massive volumes of photons captured by telescopic instruments or the discrete sampling of water-quality indicators by sensor networks. Many years of labor may be invested in developing the technology, but once developed it yields data of high volume and velocity. These are the data of Parsons and Fox's (2013) "big iron" metaphor, characterized by industrial production and an engineering culture. Individuals and small teams also can collect big data, whether from social networks or sensor networks. At the other extreme is artisanal data collection, which requires considerable craft knowledge. These include samples of water and soil that are collected by hand, processed by dilution and centrifuge, cultured, and counted (Wallis, Rolando, and Borgman 2013). Local artisanal data tend to be maintained locally by the teams that collect them. Collecting, using, and interpreting data—big or little—usually depends heavily on expertise in the domain (Beaulieu, de Rijcke, and van Heur 2012; Collins and Evans 2007).

Methods of data collection can be significant determinants of the motivation and ability to exchange data. Hilgartner and Brandt-Rauf (1994) distinguish between the availability of a technique and the competitive edge it provides. Their continuum ranges from "magic hands," in which new techniques can be applied only by those with specialized skills, to "kits," in which the techniques are sufficiently routinized to be sold as standardized kits. "Standard protocols" lie in the middle range of the continuum. A single technique within a single laboratory may evolve from magic hands to kits. Pritchard, Carver, and Anand (2004) found that groups cluster around data collection practices rather than fields. Data produced by industrial, standardized, or kit methods are more readily documented than are data resulting from artisanal methods and magic hands.

Units of data, as discussed in chapter 3, and their relationship to publication practices also influence what become data and the amount of data collected. A one-day field trip may yield enough data for several papers. In other cases, one journal article may represent many years of data collection. One large dataset may be analyzed for multiple research questions, whether alone or in combination with other sources of evidence. Notes taken in an archive may yield a few data points or many years of evidence to be explored. Researchers may cumulate data on one site, species, community, or rare manuscript over the course of their careers. Rarely does one research trip—whether to a field station or to an archive—yield exactly one publication. When data are precious, they are most likely to be carved

into multiple papers, known variously as "least publishable units," "smallest publishable units," or "minimum publishable units." This practice is sometimes referred to as "salami slicing" (Owen 2004).

The degree of control a scholar or team has over the collection of data also influences practices, motivations, and constraints on transfer and reuse. When taking data from a repository or other resource, investigators must rely on available documentation to know how data were collected. Data collection can be outsourced, whether by hiring survey interviewers or by crowdsourcing. In the latter case, scholars have found ways to train volunteers to spot birds, invasive species, or other phenomena. Tools are provided, such as websites and mobile applications, and data collection is supervised and verified by experts (eBird 2013; "What's Invasive!" 2010). While not a generalizable approach to data collection, crowdsourcing can capture large amounts of data by engaging an interested public.

Data Analysis

Investments made in data at the analytical stages, and in iterations among collection, analysis, and interpretation, also are determinants of how readily data are used, reused, exchanged, and curated. Some data become useful with minimal intervention; others require substantial cleaning, calibration, and other handling. Early decisions about what to collect, how, and why cascade through later processes. Measurements may be direct, such as taking the dimensions of leaves and assigning geo-spatial and temporal parameters to them (e.g., precise location and time gathered). Others are indirect, requiring models for interpretation, such as a sensor voltage that represents a type of nitrate. Information on the type of machine; its calibration; the time, date, and place of data collection; and the method by which the sample was captured may be necessary to interpret any given data point. Data might be analyzed and documented immediately, creating a permanent record. Others may cumulate to be analyzed later. Some samples are fragile, such as water samples containing protozoa that die within hours. Others, such as text on parchment, can remain relatively stable for centuries.

Practices for data analysis are a function of project goals; concerns for application or theory; availability of tools, expertise, and infrastructure; and many other factors. Just as some people maintain meticulously organized households and others live happily in chaos, scholars vary widely in their personal habits for data collection and analysis. Some organize their data quickly, discretely, and fully as early as possible. Others let data accumulate for days, months, or years before tackling the pile. Some write analytical memos at each step of collection and analysis, others make their

assessments post hoc. Some establish clear protocols and procedures for their labs or teams, promoting consistent practices that facilitate comparative and longitudinal analyses. Others prefer more flexibility, exploiting the array of expertise that each team member brings to the collaboration. Whereas data practices may cluster by community, the specifics of data handling are as diverse as the array of data themselves (Bowker 2005; Edwards et al. 2011; Jackson et al. 2011; Mayernik 2011, in press; Wallis 2012).

While not generalizable, some kinds of data analysis can be crowdsourced, as exemplified by Zooniverse. This organization supports projects in which the classification or interpretation of data is not amenable to computational methods, minimal training and domain expertise are required, and objects can be classified by a few parameters. In current projects, participants classify weather on Mars, transcribe weather data from old ship logs, hear whales communicate, and analyze cancer data. The gamelike interface encourages people to contribute their time to these research projects. More than one million people are members of Zooniverse as of early 2014. Data are presented to multiple volunteers for classification. The accuracy of each classification is assessed, as is the speed and accuracy of each volunteer (Zooniverse 2014).

When Are Data?

Rarely can a magic moment be established when things become data. Typically it involves a process in which a scholar recognizes that an observation, object, record, or other entity could be used as evidence of phenomena and then collects, acquires, represents, analyzes, and interprets those entities as data. A simple example will help to illustrate the many points at which things might become data. A researcher has determined that public parks are an appropriate location to study children's behavior. The researcher visits a park and observes a child running across the playground. Depending on the research question, the phenomena under study, the theoretical framework, the research method, and the goals of the study, many different aspects of that observation might become data. The researcher might be observing the child's gait to assess age, health, and type of activity. The starting and ending point of the run may be of interest: does the child appear to be running aimlessly, between two parents or caregivers, or with other children? Is the child playing in isolation or interacting with others? The researcher might be collecting observations on the individual child as the unit of analysis, on a parent-child dyad, or on a group of children.

The park might also be the unit of analysis, if the researcher is comparing activity at many different parks, each with different demographics. Alternatively, the researcher may be conducting a long-term ethnographic study at one site. Contextual information may be gathered such as date and time of day, socioeconomic data on the neighborhood, transportation options to reach the park, weather data, or levels of air pollution or pollen.

Observations about the child's activities could be recorded in many different ways, depending upon what is known about the research subjects and the degree of consent that has been obtained to observe them. The researcher might sit alone on a bench in an unobtrusive spot, quietly taking notes on paper. If the researcher has the informed consent of the participants, more extensive information may be gathered. Multiple observers might be present. Cameras, microphones, and other sensors might be installed in the playground. Participants might even be fitted with sensors to gather records of their activity, patterns of movement, heart rates, and so on. The researcher might interview the children and their caregivers before or after the playground activity.

What aspects of the researcher's observations of the child in the park are data? Observations must be represented in some way to be treated as data, as introduced in chapter 3. The human observer captures the child's activities in her mind's eye, then documents them as entities on paper or in a computer. They might be narrative notes, sketches, a table of entries, or some other form of representation. They might be entered directly into an analytical tool or might be transcribed for later entry. If participants were interviewed, those responses could be combined with the notes. Contextual information about the park and conditions at the time of observation may be input to a spreadsheet or statistical package. Audio and video recordings of the child's activity may be captured as digital representation with some automated tagging of place, date, time, light levels, and other parameters. Additional representation could include manual segmentation of the recordings to match them to other records on individual participants. These representations can be analyzed in many ways, depending on the goal of the research. Detailed models of the activities of each child, each dyad, or each park might be compiled. Alternatively, the analysis may address aggregate groups of activity and larger patterns. In all cases, the observations are selective, recording details of interest for the given research study and ignoring others.

Thus, many aspects of the research context influence what become data and how those data are recorded and represented. Relationships between knowledge and data can be partitioned in many ways (Furner 2010). Factors

influencing when and how things become data are grouped into two general categories for describing the case studies in the following chapters. First are considerations of the distance of the scholar from the origins of the data. This category includes sources and resources, metadata, and provenance. Second is the set of external influences on what becomes data, grouped into economics and value, property rights, and ethics.

Distance Matters

Distances from the origins of data to their use can be measured in many ways. Time, context, method, theory, language, and expertise can be important. Geographic distance between collaborators also can contribute significantly to the ability to share, interpret, and use data (Cummings et al. 2008; Hollan and Stornetta 1992; Olson and Olson 2000). *Origins* is a similarly problematic term, used here to mean the first time that someone treats something as data. Origins and distance become significant factors in representation and reuse.

The closer that a scholar's work is to the origins of the data, along any of these dimensions, the less that interpretation may depend on formal knowledge representations. At one extreme are the scholars who have personal and intimate relationships with their data, such as the ethnographer who spends a career studying a community or a phenomenon. A lone scholar studying the child's behavior in the park may be able to write a journal article from her handwritten notes alone, never representing those notes in ways that others could interpret them for other purposes.

At the other extreme are scholars who work only with datasets collected by others, often very large datasets compiled from many sources over long periods of time. The demographer mapping the activity in the parks of a city, county, or country must rely on representations of data that were recorded by many people and institutions, perhaps for many purposes. Rarely does the demographer or other big data analyst have intimate knowledge of how, when, or why those data were collected. Later users of these data must rely on representations or inscriptions of those data, on the availability of software to read those digital formats, and on other documentation. The opportunities are great, both for new interpretations and for misinterpretations.

Sources and Resources   Scholars sometimes collect their own data, sometimes acquire existing data about a phenomenon, and oftentimes combine new and old data. The distance between new and extant data—framed here as sources and resources—is useful when considering how to manage data,

how to transfer data across contexts and time, and how to assess which data are worthy of preservation. *Sources* are data that originate with the investigators on a given project. *Resources* are existing data reused for a given project. The source-resource distinction follows usage in the *Oxford English Dictionary* and is developed more fully elsewhere (Borgman 2007).

Researchers have more control over sources they generate themselves than data they obtain from other resources. Sources usually are managed by the individuals or research teams that created them, at least until the data are deposited, destroyed, or left to decay. When researchers use resources they do not control, whether personal datasets of others, data archives, manuscripts, social network feeds, or government records, they depend on other parties for access to those resources and for rights to release, publish, or reuse their resulting data.

Whether something is a source or resource for a particular research endeavor depends upon how those data are used. When astronomers study the sky, they are using telescopes to capture observations of a particular region, during a particular range of time, with a particular instrument. Each set of observations is a unique and original source of data. When others reuse data from an astronomy archive, they are treating those data as resources.

Records not created for research purposes also can be viewed as resources. For example, demographic information about the neighborhood of a park, weather records, and daily pollution and pollen records are resources for those studying activities in the park. Similarly, a scholar studying changes in language over time could rely on historical manuscripts as resources. Those manuscripts were written to communicate ideas to contemporaries. It is today's scholar who is treating them as resources for textual research. However, today's scholar also can create new data sources by capturing information that previously could not be captured, such as by encoding handwriting patterns or extracting text from historical materials with new optical character recognition algorithms.

Metadata "To classify is human," as Geoffrey Bowker and Susan Leigh Star (1999, 1) framed the problem of "classification and its consequences." People classify their worlds with file names, folders, colored stickers, book shelves, kitchen cupboards, stacks of paper and other media, and by countless other means. The first step in classification is usually to name things. Once named, those categories can be organized as hierarchies, networks, graphs, or other relationships with varying degrees of formality. Those choices of names for data and for relationships among them can have profound effects on the ability to discover, exchange, and curate data.

Metadata, most simply defined as "data about data," are a means to name things, to represent data, and to represent relationships.

Definitions and Discovery   The multiplicity of definitions for metadata is a manifestation of the many uses to which it can be put. A general definition from the standards community is that "metadata is structured information that describes, explains, locates, or otherwise makes it easier to retrieve, use, or manage an information resource" (National Information Standards Organization 2004, 1). NISO distinguishes three main types of metadata: descriptive, structural, and administrative. The latter type has two sub-types: rights management and preservation metadata. A similar typology is used in the archives community: administrative, descriptive, preservation, technical, and use metadata. Technical metadata includes hardware and software documentation, authentication data, and other system-specific information. Use metadata includes use and user tracking, content reuse, and versioning information (Gilliland 2008; Gilliland-Swetland 1998). Library organization methods such as cataloging rules, indexes, and the-sauri are descriptive metadata in the above sense, although library practice further distinguishes descriptive and subject cataloging (Svenonius 2000). Among the many ways to evaluate scientific metadata are these require-ments: scheme abstraction; scheme extensibility, flexibility, and modu-larity; comprehensiveness and sufficiency; simplicity; data interchange or exchange; data retrieval; data archiving; and data publication (Willis, Greenberg, and White 2012).

Whether particular units of information are data or metadata often depends on what is being described and for what purposes. Bibliographic records are metadata about the books, journal articles, conference papers, and other documents they describe. In turn, bibliographic records can be treated as data for social network studies to show who cites whom, and as data for scholarly communication studies of the transfer of ideas across disciplines over time (Borgman and Furner 2002; Borgman 1990). One per-son's data is another's metadata, and vice versa.

Distinctions between data and metadata were among the most revela-tory news in the 2013 leak of classified files from the US National Security Agency (NSA) ("The NSA Files" 2013). Whereas the NSA cannot legally col-lect information on the contents of phone calls or obtain names or addresses of customers without a warrant, they can—and do—collect data on what they refer to as metadata: "the phone number of every caller and recipient; the unique serial number of the phones involved; the time and duration of each phone call; and potentially the location of each of the participants

when the call happened" (Ball 2013). US government lawyers have equated these items to information on the envelope of a letter. Although they may be metadata in this legal opinion, these units of information can serve as data to model who calls whom, when, from where, to where, and for how long. Public opinion views these as personal data; the legal distinction between data and metadata is less persuasive to those under surveillance (Gallagher 2013).

Forms of metadata and the means to create them are aligned with methods of data collection to varying degrees. When data are collected or generated by computational technologies, automated metadata may result. Examples include telephone calling records, credit card transactions, and the output of scientific instruments. Automated metadata are embedded in audio, video, text, and image files to facilitate retrieval, processing, and tracking of licenses ("Embedded Metadata Initiative" 2013). For example, photo- and video-sharing sites use these metadata to tag and geo-locate uploaded files. Media management software such as iPhoto uses these metadata to tag objects with time stamps, dates, location, faces, camera exposure, and other information. Analytical tools for research data have yet to exploit automated metadata as widely as have tools for consumer products and social media.

When data are collected manually, metadata creation is usually a manual process, as when researchers record dates, times, procedures, and results of gathering and testing physical samples of water or soil in the field. However, even when data are collected through automated means, whether telescopes or online surveys, some amount of manual metadata production may be necessary. Research staff members on duty may be responsible for recording the contextual information necessary to interpret data, such as weather conditions, instrument artifacts, and software errors. Researchers assign variable names to survey items and assign labels to rows and columns in spreadsheets. To make effective use of digitized texts, human readers often must tag chapters, sections, paragraphs, names, places, and other units. Important information about research objects, whether material or digital, may not be part of the item itself. Depending upon its age and condition, a printed book may lack author, date, and publisher information. The identity of the book's owners, printers, binders, and writers of marginal annotations also may be necessary to determine its origins. Rare book catalogers search far and wide to create authoritative metadata for objects such as these.

Whether created automatically or manually, metadata are the means by which others can discover the existence of the objects they represent. They

also may be the means by which data are matched, compared, and distinguished. Metadata can be cumulative, with representations added as data are used and reused in new contexts, migrated to new technologies and formats, and curated over long periods of time. Metadata can become more voluminous than the data they represent.

Communities and Standards   Metadata can bridge distances from sources to resources by formalizing and standardizing how data are named and described. When communities develop a thesaurus, taxonomy, ontology, or similar structure for organizing their knowledge, they are making agreements on what categories of things exist and the relationships among those categories. For local use within a research team, a simple ontology of a few dozen terms and relationships might suffice to analyze a dataset and report findings. For general use among large communities that exchange data, far more elaborate ontologies are required. In the biosciences, for example, taxonomies of organisms are essential forms of metadata. The taxonomy database of the National Center for Biotechnology Information of the US National Library of Medicine contains descriptions of more than 230,000 species that have been formally named—yet the contents of the database are estimated to represent only about 10 percent of the described species of life on the planet (Bard 2013; "Taxonomy Database" 2013). Individual areas of the biosciences have developed their own classifications, a growing number of which are available as open and interoperable resources ("Open Biological and Biomedical Ontologies" 2013). They are not necessarily compatible, however. The existence of so many competing ontologies is an indication of deep divisions within and between research domains (Bowker 2005; Hine 2008).

Classification mechanisms such as ontologies, taxonomies, and thesauri, and metadata structures such as FITS files in astronomy, the DDI in social sciences, and TEI in the humanities (all discussed in the case studies), facilitate interoperability within communities. By agreeing on what to name things and on relationships between categories, researchers can discover, mine, and combine data from multiple sources. For the same reasons, these mechanisms create friction between domains that have incompatible metadata schema. The fruit fly Drosophila melanogaster is studied for so many different purposes that multiple, incompatible classifications were developed by individual communities of researchers. The roots of some of these mechanisms date back to early twentieth century exchanges of Drosophila data through community newsletters (Kelty 2012). Other metadata layers arose to bridge these metadata schemes. OpenFlyData, for example, is a

proof-of-concept proposal to integrate gene expression data for this organism across multiple systems (Miles et al. 2010).

Despite the maturity of metadata schema in many areas of the sciences, other areas lack metadata schemes or lack wide implementation of the schemes that do exist (Bowker 2005; Mayernik 2011; Wallis, Rolando, and Borgman 2013). The degree to which collections deploy metadata standards is among the characteristics that distinguish research, resource, and reference collections of data (National Science Board 2005). The Digital Curation Centre (DCC) maintains an extensive catalog of metadata specifications developed by individual fields in the sciences, social sciences, and humanities. The DCC resource also is organized by metadata specifications, profiles, uses, and associated software tools (Digital Curation Centre 2013).

Investments that individual scholars and communities make in metadata are indicators of what they consider to be valuable as data. However, the inverse does not necessarily follow: many valuable data do not receive much metadata, which limits their dissemination and use (Mayernik 2011). Metadata can be expensive to create, whether investments of individuals in describing their own datasets or investments of communities in developing and maintaining classification schema. These are not static resources. They must be revised and adapted continuously as language changes and as research fronts advance. Sustaining metadata schema often is invisible work that is essential to the success of scholarship but receives little extrinsic recognition (Borgman 2003; Star and Strauss 1999).

Stories abound of how standards generally, and information standards in particular, can create as many problems as they solve. Bowker and Star's (1999) *Sorting Things Out* is rife with examples of the politics of classifications. Taxonomies of diseases are less about medical knowledge than they are about power relationships between physicians and nurses and about fees that can be charged for procedures. The cause of death in the public record may reflect the physician's choice of a socially acceptable form of death, given the multiple causes often involved. Suicides and syphilis can easily be attributed to stroke, heart failure, or perhaps pneumonia. In some countries it is more acceptable to die of stomach than heart problems (Bowker and Star 1999). Birth certificates are equally problematic, created on demand for the immediate "doable" job (Pine, Wolf, and Mazmanian 2014). Behind every mechanism for organizing knowledge are unstated and undocumented assumptions about the reasons for which data and metadata are created and will be used. When data and metadata are used for other purposes, in other contexts, and at later times, documentation of those assumptions may not exist or cannot be found. Statistics on birth,

death, marriage, and the number of fish in the sea all rest on shaky ground, yet public policy and research fronts depend on them. The same is true of all forms of data and metadata. Metadata are necessary to discover, interpret, and use data, but must be handled with care. "Data bite man," as David Ribes and Steven Jackson (2013) put it so well.

Provenance   Metadata can represent many aspects of data. One aspect of particular importance for knowledge infrastructures is the ability to represent where data originated and how they made the journey from there to wherever they are now. *Provenance,* in the sense the term is used commonly in museums and archives, is the continuous chain of history of an object. One method by which museums assess authenticity is through records of ownership or control. If a continuous record exists back to the object's origins, it is more likely to be what it purports to be. Multiple chains of provenance may be important: the chain of custody, of where an object was made and later altered, or of the cultural context in which it was used (Contadini 2010).

Provenance has meanings both narrower and broader than *metadata.* The term was borrowed from French in the eighteenth century to indicate the origin or source of something. It can mean simply the fact of the origin or the history of something and the documentation of that record, per the *Oxford English Dictionary.* In the narrower sense, provenance can be a type of metadata that describes the origin of the data. As digital objects become legal and scientific records, the notion of provenance has expanded in theory and practice. Provenance on the World Wide Web includes aspects such as the attribution of an object, who takes responsibility for it, its origin, processes applied to the object over time, and version control (Moreau 2010; "Provenance XG Final Report" 2010). The ability to establish the provenance of a dataset, for example, may influence whether a result is deemed trustworthy, reproducible, admissible as evidence, or to whom credit is assigned (Buneman, Khanna, and Wang-Chiew 2001; Moreau et al. 2008). Among the arguments for data citation is better recording of provenance (Uhlir 2012). Similarly, arguments for the preservation of research workflows are based on the need for better provenance records (Gamble and Goble 2011).

Just as museums use provenance information to assess the authenticity of a sculpture, researchers may use provenance information to assess the authenticity, trustworthiness, and usefulness of a dataset. Provenance records may document the protocols by which the data were collected, whether observing a child in a park or gene expression in Drosophila

melanogaster; transformations made on a dataset; criteria for cleaning and reducing a dataset; software routines applied at each stage; and documentation of other information necessary to replicate or interpret the findings. The more distant the researcher is from the original source of data, the more that reuse depends upon the availability of provenance information. Provenance also can be critical when combining data from multiple sources: the provenance of each component dataset will influence decisions about use, analysis, and trust. Licensing and other rights information may be needed to determine what can be used, when, how, and with what attribution.

External Influences

Scholars make choices about what to use as data within the opportunities and constraints of the knowledge infrastructures in which they work. Like Dr. Pangloss, scholars may wish to exist in the best of all possible worlds. Like Candide, they must cope with the external influences of the real world (Voltaire 1759). These influences can have powerful effects on what can become data and on what data can be transferred across contexts and over time. As technologies, policies, and players interact, the power of individual stakeholders also shifts. Social norms, markets, law, technical architectures, and software code are rebalanced continuously (Lessig 2004).

Economics and Values Data have many kinds of value, only one of which is monetary. While a comprehensive analysis of the economics of research data is much needed, it is well beyond the scope of this book. For the purposes of discussion here, research data are best understood as a commons resource, as introduced in chapter 2. Data clearly fall within the commons definition of a "resource shared by a group of people that is subject to social dilemmas" (Hess and Ostrom 2007b, 3). A commons is a shared resource to be governed, not a space free of costs or ownership. Commons and market models of production coexist; the question is usually one of balance. Similarly, the outcomes of commons approaches can be good or bad (Bollier 2007; Disco and Kranakis 2013; Hess and Ostrom 2007b). Following Hess and Ostrom's usage of *commons* as an inclusive term, this discussion combines commons as a shared resource system and a property rights regime. Competition and free riding are social dilemmas that often arise because not all interests are shared. Threats to knowledge commons include commodification, degradation, and lack of sustainability. Knowledge, in the context of knowledge commons, is defined as "all intelligible ideas, information, and data in whatever form in which it is expressed or obtained" (Hess and Ostrom 2007b, 7).

The commodification of scholarly literature and the rapid rise in prices charged to libraries were among the drivers of the open access movement. Commons analyses were spurred in the mid-1990s as digital resources began to be distributed widely and as intellectual property regimes became more restrictive. Shared scholarly resources were becoming very expensive by the latter 1980s and potentially underused due to lack of access. Similar concerns appear to be influencing the open data movement. Digital data are fragile and vulnerable to loss; sustainability is difficult to achieve. Concerns arise about whether data are too valuable as shared resources to be controlled as commodities, from the human genome to maps of public spaces.

Garrett Hardin's (1968) metaphor of "the tragedy of the commons" is far better known than are the many studies that challenged his assumptions and conclusions. The commons can be governed by multiple and competing stakeholders if basic principles are followed. However, these principles do not translate into any formulaic set of rules. Governance is a continual process of negotiation among stakeholders (Hess and Ostrom 2007b; Ostrom and Hess 2007). These are the early days of scoping the knowledge commons for data. The World Data Centers began as a way to formalize exchanges of data that previously were bartered. These governance models continue to mature (Hugo 2013; Shapley and Hart 1982). Communities in the biosciences and elsewhere are learning to govern commons resources such as large reference collections of data.

Some basic principles of the economics of information are important to the discussion of the value of research data. Goods can be classified along two dimensions into a simple two-by-two matrix. The first dimension is the degree to which individuals can be excluded from use. This is the classic distinction between pure public goods such as sunsets, when exclusion is difficult, and pure private goods such as physical objects that can be owned, when exclusion is easy. The second dimension is subtractability, also known as rivalry. If subtractability is high (rivalrous), then one person's use takes away from use by others, as in owning a computer or a car. If subtractability is low (nonrivalrous), then one's person's use does not hamper another's, as in journal subscriptions (Hess and Ostrom 2007b, 8–9). The economic characteristics of information goods may depend as much on their packaging as on their content. For example, the same software can be distributed as open source or sold as a commercial product. The same information can be distributed as a digital file or as a printed book. The file may be nonrivalrous, but only one person can own or read the physical book at a time (Disco and Kranakis 2013; Kelty 2008).

Research data can fall into any of the four categories in this two-by-two matrix, as illustrated in table 4.1. Public goods, those for which exclusion is difficult and subtractability is low, have received the most attention in discussions of the value of data. When data are released with minimal restrictions on their use, they can be treated as public goods (Berman et al. 2010; David, den Besten, and Schroeder 2010; David 2004a; Guibault 2013; Murray-Rust et al. 2010; Pearson 2012; Wilbanks 2009, 2011).

Ostrom and others place libraries in the category of common-pool resources, those with high subtractability and for which exclusion is difficult (Hess and Ostrom 2007b; Ostrom and Ostrom 1977). Most data repositories fall into this category. They are common-pool resources because communities invest in them as shared content and because governance is necessary. As the cost of books and journals rose, the knowledge commons became threatened with enclosure, which turns public goods into private goods. Libraries could acquire fewer resources and their ability to provide access to those resources became more restrictive. The success of the knowledge commons depends on the ability to limit enclosure, to make exclusion difficult, and to sustain effective governance models. Libraries, archives, data repositories, and other shared-information resources are under continual threat of free riders, enclosure, and sustainability (David 2003, 2004b; Disco and Kranakis 2013; Kranich 2004, 2007; Lessig 2001, 2004).

Hess and Ostrom place journal subscriptions in the toll or club goods category, which is those for which exclusion is easy and subtractability is low. Data that are available only as supplements to toll-paid journals fall into this category, as do services that offer access to data on a subscription basis. Data repositories that are accessible only to paying members of the consortium can be considered club goods. Also included are commercial

Table 4.1

Types of data in a knowledge commons

| | | Subtractability | |
		Low	High
Exclusion	Difficult	Public goods Open data	Common-pool resources Data repositories
	Easy	Toll or club goods Data by subscription	Private goods Competitive data, "raw" data

Source: Adapted from matrix of types of goods (Hess and Ostrom 2007b, 9).

data such as social media feeds. The last quadrant, private goods, where exclusion is easy and subtractability is high, consists of physical or consumable goods in most economic analyses (Hess and Ostrom 2007b; Ostrom and Ostrom 1977). Many forms of data can be considered private goods because they are not "plug and play" like software. Expertise, instruments, software, and hardware can create rivalries for data.

In the best of all possible worlds, digital data may appear to be public goods. Paul David (2003, 4), in explaining data, information, and knowledge as economic goods, equates ideas to fire rather than to coal, and quotes Thomas Jefferson in 1813, "He who receives an idea from me, receives instruction himself without lessening mine; as he who lights his taper at mine receives light without darkening me." Although data are not ideas, multiple perfect copies of digital objects can be made without degrading the original. However, data can become private goods in cases when exclusion is easy and subtractability is high. Exclusive control of data can gain competitive advantage for researchers, scholars, institutions, governments, or private companies. For example, controlling access to data about drug discovery and clinical trials can determine which company is first to market. Data such as these, which have scientific and commercial value, are on the front lines of governance for the knowledge commons. As universities, public funding agencies, and pharmaceutical companies partner in drug discovery, they are negotiating ways to release data in the public interest while protecting private commerce (Boulton 2012; Edwards et al. 2009; Edwards 2008a; Goldacre 2012; Thomas 2013).

Research data tend to have high subtractability because of the expertise and apparatus associated with them. Even within communities that have expertise and access to the apparatus, data may be treated as commodities in a gift-exchange culture. They can be traded and bartered for other data, for research funding, or for social capital (Hilgartner and Brandt-Rauf 1994; Lyman 1996; Wallis, Rolando, and Borgman 2013). In other cases, data are best viewed as raw material rather than as goods that can be traded in a market. Extracting data from the expertise and apparatus associated with them may require considerable investment in representations, metadata, and provenance. Software, code, scripts, and other tools may need to be released along with the data. Here the distinction between data and representations is essential. It is the representations that are being exchanged, and new representations may be necessary to make those data useful to other parties.

Thus, these four categories of data depend on their use, not on inherent characteristics of the data. A protein structure, for example, may be a

private good when controlled by a pharmaceutical company, a toll good when appended to a journal article available only by paid subscription, part of a common-pool resource when contributed to a data repository such as the Protein Data Bank, and a public good if released as open data with minimal license restrictions.

Property Rights   Are data property? The lawyerly response would be, "It depends." Laws, policies, and practices applying to the ownership, control, and release of data vary by funding agency, government, and jurisdiction. Property law, intellectual property law, database law, contracts, and regulations intertwine in ways that confuse scholars, lawyers, librarians, students, legislators, and the general public. Property rights and the economics of data are deeply intertwined in research policy (Dalrymple 2003; David and Spence 2003; David 2003; Esanu and Uhlir 2004; Scotchmer 2003; Uhlir 2007). Any of these factors may influence when and how a scholar can treat something as data.

Whether or not data are intellectual property, they often are treated as such. Even data declared "open" are being licensed by researchers, universities, and other parties (Ball 2012; Hirtle 2011; Korn and Oppenheim 2011; Wilbanks 2013). Confusion over ownership, rights to release data, responsibility to release data, and the conditions under which to release data are significant constraints on their availability (David and Spence 2003; Erdos 2013a, 2013b). A few examples will help to illustrate the property issues that may arise in collecting or creating data. Researchers may wish to acquire information from publisher databases or social networks (e.g., Twitter, Facebook). This may be possible under conditions specified by contracts with the companies that operate them. If the researcher acquires data through an application programming interface (API), by "scraping" websites, or by other automated means, the content is still subject to property laws, although property rights may be more difficult to determine or to enforce. Similar conditions may apply to data from public agencies, such as student performance data gathered by school districts. Researchers gain access to these data under contracts that govern uses of the data, by whom, over what period of time, how results may be published, and the conditions under which data might be deposited or otherwise shared.

To reproduce material in a publication usually requires written permission from the owners, which can be a nontrivial process. If the owner can be identified, contacted, and grants permission, then the author can follow the guidelines of the publisher and laws of the jurisdiction. Rules may differ among texts, photographs, images, audio and video recordings, and other

genres. Guidelines for the use of specific types of materials are helpful, but definitive rules are unlikely since technology evolves more rapidly than does law (Hirtle, Hudson, and Kenyon 2009; Visual Resources Association 2012).

Scholars are not freed of property constraints by working only with materials old enough to be out of copyright. Representations of objects are copyrightable independent of the copyright status of the object. Archives and museums may sell or license digital versions of manuscripts or other special collection materials they own. An artist may sell a painting to a museum but retain the rights to make reproductions of that painting. To publish a photograph of an object, an author may need to acquire permission from the owner of the object, the photographer, and yet other parties. Museums have restricted the access to images of works in their collections but are starting to release more content on an open access basis (Getty Research Institute 2013; Whalen 2009).

The most difficult set of property issues for scholars involves "orphan works," which are works for which the copyright status cannot be determined, or if it can be determined, then the owner cannot be identified or reached or does not respond (Hirtle 2012; Society of American Archivists 2009; US Copyright Office 2006). As many as 75 percent of all known books may be orphan works (Grafton 2007) and as much as two-thirds of the Google Books corpus is estimated to be orphan works (Courant 2009; Lewis et al. 2010; Samuelson 2009a; 2010).

Orphan works are an example of the anti-commons, which is the case of scarce information resources being underused due to excessive intellectual property rights or patents (Hess and Ostrom 2007a). Scholars may be forced to choose materials less appropriate to their line of inquiry or to abandon inquiries altogether when they cannot reproduce, reuse, or quote from materials of interest (J. E. Cohen 2012; Lessig 2001, 2004; "Library Copyright Alliance" 2005). Data that are governed as common-pool resources, such as weather data and Drosophila genomes, can be underused when members attempt to restrict access or to violate governance rules (Edwards 2013; Kelty 2012).

A partial solution to the orphan works problem is to embed computer-readable license information as metadata in digital documents. To the extent that property rights and license information can be specified, searchers—whether human or machine—can retrieve digital objects that meet their usability requirements. In principle, scholars could determine what objects are usable without restriction, those that are not, and those that can be used under certain license conditions. Such technical solutions

are problematic, however. Encoding license information is more difficult than was initially apparent. Creative Commons licenses—the most widely used form of open access licenses—are designed to be machine readable, human readable, and lawyer readable (Creative Commons 2013). General categories of use are identifiable, but reuse of objects may be subject to additional conditions. Open access to journal articles is difficult to specify because they can be open in multiple and competing respects. Some are available without fee, some as structured and searchable content. Some articles, books, and other works may be licensed for use in their entirety, others may allow reuse of subsets, and each may have different requirements for attribution. The atomization of intellectual property licenses, also known as "license stacking," has created legal and technical barriers to data reuse (Houweling and Shaffer 2009). Complicating matters further is the legal distinction between reading texts for their content and "nonconsumptive use," such as indexing or statistical analyses that do not "trade on the underlying creative and expressive purpose of the work" (Australian Law Reform Commission 2014). Exceptions to intellectual property law for the purposes of nonconsumptive use were a salient feature of the proposed Google Books settlement (Samuelson 2009b).

Scholars encounter these property rights issues in the control and release of their own data and in gaining access to materials they wish to use as data. They should not need to be intellectual property lawyers to determine what data they can or should release, when, and how. Scholars may be reluctant to use data for which rights cannot be determined, are difficult to obtain, or for which they risk undue liabilities. Rights and responsibilities associated with data are on the forefront of information policy.

Ethics Questions of what is right and wrong in any situation vary in untold ways over time, across cultures, and by circumstance. Choices of research data are as subject to ethical considerations as any other part of life. Data collection that was considered innovative in decades past, such as the Tuskegee study of syphilis (Jones 1981) or the Milgram (1974) experiments in social psychology, was later considered abhorrent. Although these are extreme examples that appear clear-cut by today's standards, many areas remain gray and others are subject to legal and policy regulation.

The ethics of what can be treated as data, how, when, and why are evolving rapidly as digital records become the norm and as data mining becomes more sophisticated. Data about people are among the most contentious. Conceptions of confidentiality, anonymity, and privacy are shifting in unforeseen ways. Data on human subjects that once were considered

securely anonymized now can be reidentified by combining them with data from other sources, allowing data miners to assemble rich profiles on individuals. In some arenas, data will be released only under more severe restrictions. In others, research subjects are being named and identified, whether to give credit for their contributions or to facilitate the combining of records. Some researchers are analyzing social network data collected by private companies, whereas others are questioning the ethics of companies being allowed to collect such data on individuals (Bruckman, Luther, and Fiesler, forthcoming; Ohm 2010; Wilbanks 2009; Zimmer 2010).

Research on living persons—known as human subjects—is governed by regulations to ensure that people are treated ethically and that records about people are treated confidentially. Researchers are to respect privacy in collecting, reporting, and releasing data. Informed consent of the subjects is usually mandatory. Local human subjects review committees often are the final arbiters of whether data are to be released or destroyed at the end of a research project, which leads to uneven application of ethics rules ("Ethics Guide: Association of Internet Researchers" 2012; National Research Council 2013; US Department of Health and Human Services 1979).

Whether a study involves human subjects depends on how *research* and *human subjects* are defined. These terms are established clearly in the regulations of each funding agency, policy body, and local review committees. Social scientists learn these rules and procedures as part of their graduate training. They learn the applicable rules of their fields, agencies, and universities. If they move to another university or another country, or partner with people elsewhere, they often learn new rules or variants.

Researchers in the humanities, sciences, and technology tend to be less familiar with these regulations because they are not as ingrained in their graduate training or their research practices. Data that are considered ethical to collect in one field may not be considered so in another. Researchers may not be aware that their research activities are subject to a particular set of regulations. If an engineering team mounts cameras in a campus hallway to perfect face recognition algorithms, is that human subjects research? Does it matter whether the hallway is in the engineering building or in a dormitory? Does it matter whether the data are destroyed at the end of the project? Or who has access to the data? If a philosophy graduate student observes children playing sports in a public park to study how they handle conflict, is that human subjects research? Does it matter if the student obtained permission from the park, the team, or the parents? Is a signed consent form from each child and parent necessary? The answer to most of these questions is a lawyerly, "it depends."

Data associated with research on animals, endangered species, hazardous waste, infectious diseases, and other sensitive topics are subject to regulations and to ethical concerns about data release (J. Cohen 2012; Enserink and Cohen 2012; Enserink 2006, 2012b; Fouchier, Herfst, and Osterhaus 2012). Climate data have become sensitive in recent years due to the politics of climate change. Cases in which data are taken out of context or deliberately misrepresented have led to caution in the release of these data (Kintisch 2010).

Common-pool resources, in the economic sense, can be highly contentious. Valuable sources of scholarly data such as archeological sites, rare manuscripts, and rare species can be viewed as world heritage materials, as cultural property of individual countries or communities, or as private goods. Opinions differ strongly on whether controlling such sources to gain competitive advantage is ethical. In some fields and in some countries, protecting materials for indefinite exploitation is accepted practice, and in others it is considered unethical. Practices change over time and geography, colliding in international and interdisciplinary collaborations. As data exchange becomes more common, technologies become more sophisticated and more widely available, and national and domain boundaries continue to fade, these ethical tensions are likely to accelerate.

Conclusion

The diversity of data is due not only to the breadth of research approaches across domains of inquiry but also to the many ways in which individual observations, objects, records, texts, specimens, persons, animals, or other entities can be represented as data. Fields of study differ by these and many other factors, such as the goals of their research projects, the ways in which they collect and analyze data, and their choices of new sources or existing resources for data. Scholars may work very close to the origin of ideas or phenomena or at great distance, whether that distance is in time, space, theory, method, language, or other metric. The same entity may be represented in many ways, by many means, and for many purposes, over long periods of time. In the process of representation, those entities may acquire many names and those names may be arranged in many ways. Metadata, the structured information that is used to manage data and other information resources, includes the names, labels, and relationships used to represent data. Classification mechanisms such as taxonomies, thesauri, and ontologies are used to organize metadata. Since the same entities can be represented in many ways to serve as evidence of different phenomena, context determines when something is data and when it is metadata.

Metadata, provenance, and classification mechanisms facilitate the exchange of data within communities. They also can be sources of friction within collaborations and markers of the boundaries between communities. External factors may determine how, why, and whether data are treated as economic goods. The same data could be pure public goods, pure private goods, common-pool resources, or club goods at different stages, or even concurrently. Property rights and ethics associated with data similarly depend heavily on context. Recognizing the diversity of data, their representations, and the competing perspectives of stakeholders on the matters of value, rights, and ethics is essential to the design of effective knowledge infrastructures. The sources of tension are many, as developed in the case studies that follow.

II Case Studies in Data Scholarship

Part II lays the groundwork for the analyses in part III, "Data Policy and Practice." Although the literature is rife with studies of research activity within individual fields, especially in the sciences, the differing methods and purposes of each study make them difficult to compare. Research practices in the social sciences and in the humanities are less well studied, especially in regard to their uses of data. Part II compares data scholarship in the sciences, social sciences, and humanities by the factors identified in chapter 4.

Each of the three chapters that follow has a pair of case studies. The first case in each chapter is an example of data scholarship that requires larger volumes of data, while the second case explores data scholarship that uses smaller and more localized types of data. About half the cases draw on the author's empirical work with an array of collaborators. The publications in which those findings are reported are cited throughout. The other half were developed specifically for this book. The science cases in chapter 5 contrast astronomy with sensor-networked science and technology. In chapter 6, surveys and social media are contrasted with sociotechnical studies of sensor-networked science and technology. Chapter 7, on data scholarship in the humanities, develops cases in classical art and archeology in contrast with a close analysis of Chinese Buddhist philology. Some of the cases include multiple exemplars. Support for these cases is explained further in the acknowledgments section in the front matter of this book.

Case studies, by their nature, are more concerned with depth of analysis than with generalization. By presenting each case in a parallel structure, comparisons and larger generalizations are possible. However, several caveats are necessary. Each case represents the work of one or a few teams of researchers through the lens of their data scholarship. No example should be read as prototypical of how research is conducted in all parts of a field. The six cases are drawn narrowly enough to characterize the practices of an

individual researcher or team but broadly enough to suggest the range of issues faced by researchers in the larger domain.

Each case is presented through the lens of data scholarship, taking an information studies–theoretic perspective. The scholars are unlikely to describe themselves in such a way; rather, these are reflections on their work. The cases are used to explicate the provocations presented in chapter 1, providing evidence for the knowledge infrastructure requirements of these domains, the tensions among stakeholders, and the range of motivations and practices for collecting, sharing, and reusing data.

5   Data Scholarship in the Sciences

Introduction

The sciences encompass research on the natural world, studying flora and fauna, biological and physical phenomena, and interactions among them. For discussion here, the umbrella of the sciences includes those known collectively as the STEM fields (science, technology, engineering, and mathematics). Whether big or little, the sciences today employ software, computational methods, and statistics in their research. Digital collections, tools, and technologies are the norm—as are specimens, slides, chemicals, and all manner of material objects. The provocations arise from the diversity of data and scholarship within and between domains. In some domains, knowledge infrastructures are functioning adequately, at least for now. In others, fundamental matters of data ownership, control, sharing, exchange, sustainability, risk, and responsibility are hotly contested. In a few, tensions are just beginning to surface.

Research Methods and Data Practices
The sciences are as cosmopolitan as other areas of inquiry. References to "the scientific method" or "scientific norms" are misleading because there exists not one method, but many. The classic set of scientific norms set forward by Robert Merton several generations ago (Merton 1963a, 1970, 1973; Storer 1973) have yielded the stage to a much more nuanced understanding of the emergent and varied character of scientific practices. Notions such as communities of practice (Lave and Wenger 1991) and epistemic communities (Knorr-Cetina 1999) are more useful frameworks to study data practices today.

The big science–little science dichotomy set forth by Derek de Solla Price is another way of thinking about the range of research methods applied in the sciences. Some fields, such as astronomy and physics, work in large

and distributed collaborations, often sharing massive instrumentation infrastructures that take years to build. Others, such as field ecology or the biology of bird behavior, work in small groups and use locally adapted technologies. Dimensions such as the quest for theory or for use, as developed in chapter 4, also profoundly influence data practices and the requisite knowledge infrastructures.

Digital collections of data are essential community resources in some fields and nonexistent in others. Methods developed in one field may remain local or be adapted to other domains. For example, the "basic local alignment search tool," known as BLAST, was developed for matching sequences of DNA (Altschul et al. 1990). A fast algorithm for identifying strings, BLAST since has been applied as a similarity identification method for text, audio, and images. Spreadsheets, which were developed for business applications, are widely used in the sciences. In some cases they are a primary means to manage data. In others, spreadsheets are a lowest common denominator solution to sharing data among groups that use incompatible tools. How, when, and why methods and tools are transferred between domains is poorly understood.

Science Cases

As one of the oldest areas of human inquiry, and one that is familiar to scholars and the public alike, astronomy is an ideal case study to begin the exploration of data practices within individual fields. Astronomical records were essential for agricultural, navigational, and religious purposes, and these uses continue today. Galileo was the first scientist to recognize the value of telescopes for observing the sky, improving current technology for his own purposes. Galileo's notes on his observations in 1610 of the movements of Jupiter's satellites are canonical records of modern science. Astronomy research offers insights into big data, physical sciences, and knowledge infrastructures. It is a science with a very long time frame, and one that relies heavily on information technologies to collect, analyze, and visualize data.

Sensor-networked science and technology, the second case study in this chapter, offers an array of contrasts to astronomy. Remote sensing with cameras on satellites revolutionized the environmental sciences by providing expansive views of the Earth from above. Embedded sensor networks reverse the role of these technologies, providing microscopic views of the environment at ground level. They can be deployed for continuous data collection over long periods of time or for short explorations of specific phenomena.

Research on the use of sensor networks offers insights into little science, life sciences, technology research, and cross-disciplinary collaborations.

These two case studies, drawing examples from individual projects within these fields, provide comparisons of how data in the sciences are selected, created, used, shared, reused, managed, and curated, and how scholarship is evolving in the networked world. No two cases can represent the diverse array of data scholarship, however. These cases, and those in the following two chapters, were selected for their contrasts, for the availability of evidence, and their resonance with the provocations.

The science cases illustrate the complexity and messiness of the research process, the difficulty of separating observational data from the instruments used to collect them and the methods used to analyze them, and the many stages of data handling before they become interpretable as evidence of some phenomena. Each case begins with an examination of data sources and ends with an explanation of how research is conducted using those data.

Astronomy

Astronomy has a long, illustrious, and well-documented history. In modern usage, per the *Oxford English Dictionary,* astronomy "deals with the universe beyond the Earth's atmosphere, comprising the study of celestial objects and extraterrestrial phenomena, and of the nature and history of the universe." As with any research area, the boundaries are porous. Astronomers commonly collaborate with physicists, engineers, and computer scientists. Some have partners in statistics, medicine, biology, art and design, and elsewhere.

Astronomy has many characteristics that help to elucidate larger themes of this book. It is a big data field that has several decades of experience with digital data and computation. In that time period, astronomers have encountered radical changes in data practices, shifting from sole-investigator work to large team collaborations and from local control over instruments to shared international resources. Astronomy has become a field as diverse as any other, consisting of pockets of big data, little data, and occasionally no data. Some astronomers are pioneers in data sharing and reuse; others are known to hoard their data resources. They have constructed a sophisticated knowledge infrastructure to coordinate information resources on a global scale, yet rely on human expertise to identify relationships between individual objects. Substantial gaps in their ability to discover and exploit information resources remain.

The case study focuses on astronomy as an observational science, recognizing that these examples do not encompass the entire field. The scope is sufficiently broad to explore the sources, uses, and disposition of data, yet narrow enough to offer coherent explanations about the choices of data in a research area and to lay the foundations for discussions of sharing, reuse, and responsibility in later chapters. Material is drawn from published literature and from current research on data practices in the field. The example of conducting research in astronomy is developed through interviews, observations, and other analyses of the work of a team based at the Harvard-Smithsonian Center for Astrophysics (CfA) (Borgman 2013; Borgman et al. 2014; Sands et al. 2014; Wynholds et al. 2011, 2012).

Size Matters

Astronomy varies widely in the size of collaborations and the volumes of data handled. Until the latter part of the twentieth century, astronomy remained a sole-investigator science. Galileo owned his own telescopes and had complete control over his own data. Modern telescopes, including the 200-inch Hale telescope at Palomar Mountain that remained the world's largest for many years, were privately owned with access by only a select few astronomers. Between the time the Hale telescope was dedicated in 1948 and the first of the Gemini eight-meter telescopes was dedicated in 1999, the telescope became a very different research tool. At the same time, more public funding was invested in astronomy, resulting in cultural changes in the field. Telescope time was available to many more astronomers, as was access to the data (McCray 2004). The community of professional astronomers in positions at universities and other research centers around the world has grown at least four-fold since the 1970s. Current estimates range from ten thousand to fifteen thousand active researchers (International Astronomical Union 2013; DeVorkin and Routly 1999; Forbes 2008). The astronomy enthusiast community is immense, swelling the ranks of those with astronomy expertise.

Big Science, Little Science Astronomy is a big science, in the terms of Weinberg (1961) and Price (1963)—large, ambitious, long term, and requiring substantial social and economic investment. It is now an international field with high levels of coordination in the design of instruments and missions. Teams both large and small conduct astronomy research. Modern telescopes require one to two decades to design, build, and deploy; thus, very long-term planning is required. Time constraints are partly social and political—the work to form and coordinate teams and to secure multiple

cycles of funding; partly technical—instruments and software must be designed to anticipate the state of technology at the time of deployment; and partly physical—the construction of instruments, including casting, cooling, and polishing of the glass in telescope mirrors, is a multiyear process (University of Arizona Science Mirror Lab 2013; McCray, in press). The design of instruments and missions, in turn, influences decisions about the resulting data, how those data will be captured and curated, and the conditions under which astronomers have access to the instruments and the data. As each new telescope is launched into space or the ones on the ground see "first light," the design of the next generation of instruments is well under way.

As astronomy came to depend more on public funding and on community collaboration, they began to build consensus on research priorities (McCray 2004; Munns 2012). Since the 1960s, the US astronomy community has conducted a "decadal survey" to identify the highest priority projects. The scientific categories of projects change from decade to decade, reflecting shifts in the field. Among the nine panels in 2010 were Cosmology and Fundamental Physics, Planetary Systems and Star Formation, Electromagnetic Observations from Space, and Optical and Infrared Astronomy from the Ground (The National Academies 2010). The decadal survey is a set of recommendations to the national and international funding agencies for areas the community requests support. It is not a guarantee of funding or of priorities of allocation, however. Actual funding is subject to negotiation with the agencies, with parent entities such as the US Congress, and with international partners.

Big Data, Long Tail   Astronomy also has become a big data field in terms of observational data available, putting astronomers at the head of the long tail curve. The absolute volume of astronomy data continues to grow by orders of magnitude with each new generation of telescope. Astronomy data are big in terms of volume and velocity, to use Laney's (2001) terms introduced in chapter 2. Their scaling problem is continual as new instruments capture more data at faster rates. Nearly all astronomy data are measurements of the intensity of electromagnetic radiation (e.g., X-rays, visible light) as a function of position on the sky, wavelength, and time.

Astronomy's shift to digital technologies occurred over a period of several decades, resulting in qualitative changes in the forms of data captured. For generations of astronomers, data capture was analog, consisting of long and continuous exposures on glass plates, charge-coupled devices (the basis of digital photography), or spectrographs. Astronomers spent entire nights at

a telescope, carefully moving the instrument to obtain a continuous exposure of a celestial object or region over periods of minutes or hours. Only a few records might result from each night on the mountain. In contrast, digital capture results in discrete, rather than continuous, images. Digital records are much more readily copied intact and transferred to other storage devices. They are more manipulable and more easily disseminated than analog data. The transition from analog to digital astronomy began in the 1960s, accelerated in the 1970s, and was almost complete by the late 1990s (McCray 2004, in press).

By the late twentieth century, telescopes were producing data at rates well beyond human consumption. Many parts of the process can be automated. To the extent that data collection can be specified precisely, robots can operate instruments during the night, sending datasets to be read the morning after. Frequently, however, instruments are under the direct control of the astronomer. Taking one's own data may still require staying up all night, even if the conditions are more comfortable than in times past. Computer-based data analysis and visualization are the norm for the current generation of astronomers. However, many working astronomers learned their trade in analog days, bringing that analytic expertise to today's data analysis. Some manual data collection continues, such as the observation of sunspots (Curwen 2013). Analog data collected over the last several centuries remains valuable as permanent records of the skies in earlier eras. Some of those data have been converted to digital form and made available in public repositories. Others remain private, in the control of the astronomers and institutions that collected them.

Sky surveys are research projects to capture large amounts of data about a region of the sky over a long period of time. The Sloan Digital Sky Survey (SDSS), named for its primary funder, the Alfred P. Sloan Foundation, was the first sky survey designed for immediate public use. Data collection began in 2000, mapping about one-quarter of the night sky with an optical telescope at Apache Point, New Mexico. In a series of nine data releases from 2000 to 2008, the SDSS captured data at higher rates and better resolution because of new instruments added to the telescope, advances in charge-coupled devices (CCDs) for the cameras, and improvements in computer speed and capacity (Ahn et al. 2012; Bell, Hey, and Szalay 2009; Finkbeiner 2010; Gray et al. 2005; Sloan Digital Sky Survey 2013a; Szalay 2011).

Pan-STARRS, the next generation sky survey, is mapping a larger area of the sky at greater levels of detail and has the additional capability of identifying moving objects. The telescope, based in Hawaii, is being deployed in stages. Pan-STARRS' gigapixel cameras are the largest and most sensitive

cameras built to date. The Large Synoptic Survey Telescope (LSST), a ground-based telescope in Chile planned as the next major sky survey after Pan-STARRS, claims to be the "fastest, widest, and deepest eye of the new digital age." It will obtain thirty terabytes of data nightly. The Square Kilometre Array (SKA), planned to be the world's largest radio telescope, is expected to capture fourteen exabytes of data per day. Data from sky surveys and from the main missions of public telescopes tend to be curated in archives, available for public use after periods of embargoes and processing. Data management is among the principal challenges facing missions such as Pan-STARRS, LSST, and SKA (Pan-STARRS 2013a; Large Synoptic Survey Telescope Corporation 2010; Square Kilometre Array 2013; Shankland 2013).

Not every astronomer is a big data scientist, however, nor are all astronomy data released for public use. Some astronomers still spend nights on the mountain, collecting small amounts of highly specialized observations. Others obtain "parasitic" data from secondary instruments on telescopes in space. Yet others build their own instruments to capture precise kinds of data needed to address their own research questions. Data from smaller projects such as these may be stored indefinitely on the local servers of the investigators. Such data may be large in volume, highly specialized, and difficult to interpret. Astronomers of the analog era tended to trust only data they had collected themselves. Those who collect data know them best, whether analog or digital. Artifacts such as computer malfunctions or changes in weather that occlude an image are difficult to document in automated pipelines, but can be essential knowledge for interpreting results.

Theorists may have big data or no data—depending upon what they consider to be data. Analytic theories in astronomy consist of equations that are solvable with pencil and paper or nowadays with supercomputers. Analytic theories are used to model observed phenomena or to make predictions about phenomena. Computational or numerical theories are those in which astrophysical phenomena and objects are simulated to model, predict, and explain phenomena. Computational simulations are a middle ground between theory and observation because they employ principles of pure analytic theory to information that looks much like observational data. Modelers may synthesize what a particular telescope would see if a source, event, or region with the properties they have simulated were to be observed. Most models depend upon real observations gathered by other astronomers as inputs. Those who build computational models of astronomical phenomena sometimes consider the output of their models to be their data. Others will say they use no data.

Simulations typically produce a time series showing the evolution of a phenomenon. Models are run with multiple combinations of input parameters to simulate a range of potentially realistic conditions. Each parameter combination can be run for many time steps (each of which is called a "snapshot"). As a result, each run (and even just one snapshot) may produce several terabytes of output—far more than can be kept indefinitely. Modelers may say their data consist of the few kilobytes of empirical observations they need to initiate a model run. Some make fine distinctions between simulations, the code associated with the output of simulations, parameters, and data. Synthetic data can be created in the same format as observational data, enabling statistical comparisons with the same sets of analytical tools.

When Are Data?

Astronomy data are more difficult to characterize than might be imagined by the nonspecialist. Many people, with many different talents, are involved in the design, development, and deployment of astronomy missions. Some astronomers are involved in these earlier stages, but observational research with public telescopes may rely on data for which the instruments were conceived decades earlier. Astronomers may devote large parts of their careers to a long-term collaboration, move between projects, draw data from multiple missions, or focus on specialized topics with their own instrumentation. Some write observing proposals to collect their own data; some use extant data from archives; some build their own instruments; and some use combinations of all of these sources and resources. The point at which some entity becomes useful astronomical data depends upon choices such as these.

People involved at each stage may know only enough about the prior stages to do their own job. By the time an instrument sees first light, no single person has a comprehensive view of all the decisions that led to the resulting stream of observations. To the physicist who led the instrument design, the voltage on the CCDs may be data. To the theorist studying the origins of the universe, data may be the output of simulations that model how stars, galaxies, and other celestial objects form, evolve, and die. To the empirical astronomer, data may be "image cubes" consisting of coordinates on the sky and spectra. To the software engineer, data may be the output of the pipeline from the CCDs to the cleaned, calibrated, and structured files that are ingested by repositories.

"Constructing an astronomy paper is like building a house," to quote one of the astronomers interviewed. Rarely is the beginning point clear. Families

renovate and extend a house over periods of years and decades. Even if one family starts with an empty plot, a structure may have stood before. Yet earlier, someone decided how the land was to be divided, which determines the possibilities for the size and orientation of the house, and so on.

Sources and Resources The COMPLETE Survey (COordinated Molecular Probe Line Extinction Thermal Emission Survey of Star Forming Regions [COMPLETE] 2011) discussed in the case study can be understood only in the larger context of how data are collected, selected, used, and managed in observational astronomy. The sources and resources for data in astronomy are many and varied. They are difficult to extricate from the instruments, domain expertise, scientific principles, and forms of representation specific to the field. While their data are "observations of the sky," these observations rely on instruments with specialized sensing capabilities. Signals captured by these instruments are cleaned and calibrated to community standards. Metadata are used to represent these signals in ways that they can be reconciled with data from other instruments. Structures for data standards enable astronomers to apply a common set of tools for analysis, visualization, and reporting. Overlaid on these technologies, tools, and standards are institutions and professional practices to link data and publications from the international community of astronomers.

Telescopes Telescopes are the most basic, and yet the most complex, technologies in astronomy. Optical technologies are much improved since Galileo's day, resulting in telescopes that capture digital images. Modern telescopes have multiple instruments, each with its own capabilities. These can be swapped out over time, extending the life of the telescope.

Telescopes are of several physical types and may be located on land, above part of the atmosphere on planes and balloons, or in space, high above the Earth's atmosphere. Ground-based telescopes are typically located at higher altitudes or at remote locations away from city lights. Optical telescopes are those with mirrors or lenses to focus light, such as those at Palomar in California or the La Silla Observatory in the Atacama Desert of Chile. Radio telescopes use dish antennas, rather than mirrors or lenses, to focus signals. The Square Kilometre Array, which is being constructed as an array of many dishes in Australia and South Africa, is so named because it will have an effective collecting area of one square kilometer. An international project, it is located in the Southern hemisphere to get the best view of the Milky Way Galaxy; the region also has less radio interference than other suitable sites (Square Kilometre Array 2013).

Telescopes launched into orbit around the Earth can peer much deeper into space, with views well beyond the Earth's atmosphere. These instruments can be decades in planning, and can generate data for decades. Hubble is among the best-known space telescopes, currently orbiting 353 miles above the Earth. Conceived in 1946 by Lyman Spitzer Jr., Hubble launched in 1990. In between were a series of development and design projects with international collaboration and funding. The Hubble Space Telescope (HST) is in its third decade of delivering scientific data from space. With five sets of instruments, each capable of gathering light in different ways at different wavelengths, the HST is an orbiting laboratory for astronomy. Additional instruments power the satellite, monitor its health, and are used to make adjustments. Although most space instruments are launched into orbit or into deep space without further physical intervention, Hubble has been visited several times to add, repair, and swap instruments. More than ten thousand publications have resulted from Hubble data (HubbleSite 2013b).

The actual collection of data from telescopic instruments is often an industrial process managed by the project mission, such as Hubble or Chandra. The HST, for example, sends its signals to a tracking and relay satellite, which sends them to a ground station in New Mexico, which sends them to the Goddard Space Flight Center in Greenbelt, Maryland, which sends them to the Space Telescope Science Institute (STScI) in nearby Baltimore. Validation and error checks are made at each stage in the process. Astronomers may use the observational data from STScI, once fully calibrated and released. They also can submit observing proposals to use particular instruments, for particular periods of time, to study their own research questions. About two hundred proposals are approved each year, which represents about a 20 percent success rate for the applicants (HubbleSite 2013b).

Electromagnetic Spectrum   Each instrument, whether in space or on the ground, is designed to obtain signals over a particular range (or ranges) of wavelengths. Radio telescopes take signals at the low-frequency end of the spectrum, which is also known as low energy or long wavelength. Gamma ray telescopes take signals at the highest frequency end of the spectrum, also known as high energy or short wavelength. Gamma rays and X-rays are largely blocked by the Earth's atmosphere, so gamma- and X-ray telescopes operate outside the Earth's atmosphere, and thus are located on rockets or satellites. The electromagnetic spectrum is continuous. Divisions commonly made in astronomy include, in order of increasing energy, radio, microwave, infrared, optical, ultraviolet, X-ray, and gamma ray. Finer divisions may include far-infrared, medium-infrared, near-infrared, soft X-ray,

hard X-ray, and so on. Wavelengths sometimes are named after their size in metric distances, such as millimeter or submillimeter. Visible light (colors seen by the human eye) available to Galileo is only a very narrow band of the spectrum.

Celestial Objects   Celestial objects, also known as astronomical objects, are observable entities in the universe that occur naturally. These include stars, planets, galaxies, and comets, as well as other less familiar objects like nebulae, supernova remnants, and black holes. Most astronomy research involves the study of celestial objects, whether individually or in combination with other phenomena. Objects may occur in certain regions of the sky and be visible at certain wavelengths. To study a given celestial object, an astronomer needs observations of that region, taken with instruments capable of capturing the phenomena of interest. In some cases, an astronomer would apply for observing time on a specific telescopic instrument, on some number of days at the right time of year, to be pointed at the region. In many other cases, the astronomer would search for data from instruments that already have gathered observations of the region at the desired wavelengths. Stars, planets, and asteroids move around in the sky, so astronomers need 3D models of trajectories to derive the (2D-projected) sky coordinates of these kinds of celestial objects at any given time.

Astronomy Data Products   Observations from telescopic instruments go through many steps of cleaning, calibration, and data reduction before becoming available in astronomy data repositories. The processing steps are known as *pipelines* (European Southern Observatory 2013; National Optical Astronomy Observatory 2013b). Pipeline processing may require some months; thus, observations often are made available as a "data release," accompanied by the "data paper" that documents them. The ninth data release of the SDSS, for example, includes all of the data from a new instrument added to the telescope after the eighth data release, plus corrected astrometry (sky positions) for the eighth release (Ahn et al. 2012; Sloan Digital Sky Survey 2013b). Thus, the same observations of the sky may be released more than once, as improvements are made to the pipeline. Astronomers are careful to identify which data release was used for any study. Interpretation of findings varies accordingly.

When astronomers gather their own data via observing proposals, they may do their own pipeline processing. A manual of recommended tools and steps may be provided for guidance. Those using well-calibrated instruments can compare their data to those of prior data products from the same

instrument. Those using a new instrument or their own instrument have advantages for new discoveries but also limitations in the lack of comparative data products for validating their results. They may turn to other data resources to calibrate some of their measurements, whether or not acknowledged in their publications (Wynholds et al. 2012). Those who prefer less-processed observations may be seeking new phenomena or other patterns that are obscured by standard data reduction methods.

Many other kinds of data products result from astronomical observations. These include star catalogs and surveys of regions or celestial objects. Star catalogs date to ancient observations of the sky, when positions and brightness were charted over the course of the year. They also provided essential information for navigation at sea and on land. Modern catalogs draw upon data repositories for precise descriptions of what is known about each star (National Aeronautics and Space Administration, Goddard Space Flight Center 2014). Known stars can be referenced by catalog number. Catalogs and other data products can be searched to determine whether an object is known or unknown. Real-time sky surveys rely on these types of data products for almost instant identification of new celestial objects. Transient event-detection methods can send "skyalerts" to telescopes, smartphones, and other devices (Caltech 2013b). Data release may be instantaneous or be delayed for years, as discussed further in chapter 8.

Knowledge Infrastructures   Astronomy has the most extensive knowledge infrastructure of all the fields covered in the case studies. Agreements on standards for data structures, metadata, and ontologies, combined with international coordination and large community investments in repositories, tools, and human resources, have resulted in a complex network of information resources. Despite the highly automated data collection in astronomy, substantial portions of the infrastructure require human expertise to assign metadata and to identify links between related objects.

The manual labor required to interpret observations and to document relationships between digital objects is an example of the "invisible work" that often is required to make infrastructures function effectively. The work is visible to those who do it, of course, but those who rely on the infrastructure may not be aware of those investments unless the system breaks down.

Metadata   Astronomy observations typically are acquired either as *spectra* (intensity as a function of wavelength), *images* (the distribution of intensity on the sky at a particular wavelength), or *cubes* (a 3D dataset giving intensity as a function of position and wavelength, from which images and

spectra can be extracted). In some cases, an instrument known as a *bolometer* is used to measure intensity at a single position over a very narrow range of wavelengths. Increasingly, astronomy observations are acquired as time series, meaning a series of samples, over time, of any of the types of data listed above. Telescopic instruments can generate metadata automatically for sky coordinates, wavelength, and time of observation. Object names are entered by hand at the time of observation, since human judgment is required. Other information useful to interpret observations, such as weather conditions and instrument errors, also may be recorded manually in observing logs.

To present images taken at wavelengths far beyond the visible part of the spectrum, astronomers assign colors to parts of the wavelength; for example, red = radio; green = optical; blue = X-ray. However, few metadata standards exist for false color in images. Techniques for assigning colors vary widely, resulting in published images that are largely irreproducible. Although colorful "pretty-picture" composites are popular with the public, many astronomers are reluctant to present these images in their research publications. Artistry must be carefully balanced with scientific validity (Kessler 2012).

Essential information about the instrument, conditions of observation, wavelength, time, and sky coordinates are represented in a standard data format known as Flexible Image Transport System (FITS). FITS was developed in the 1970s and widely adopted by the latter 1980s as part of the transition from analog to digital astronomy. Analog observations could be calibrated to the positions and conditions of each telescope. Digital capture offered the opportunity to combine observations from multiple instruments, but to do so, agreements on data structures and coordinate systems were necessary (National Aeronautics and Space Administration, Goddard Space Flight Center 2013a; Hanisch et al. 2001; McCray, in press; Wells, Greisen, and Harten 1981).

Most astronomy data repositories now provide data resources in FITS formats; thus, astronomers can use the metadata in FITS files to locate observational data by sky coordinates, spectra, time of observation, and other characteristics associated with the instruments. A few astronomers prefer the more raw "pre-FITS" forms of data at the lower levels of processing described in chapter 2 (NASA's Earth Observing System Data and Information System 2013).

Coordinate Systems   Astronomy is based on the simple organizing principle that there exists only one sky. However, establishing a coordinate system

that could reconcile the positions of objects in the sky required several centuries of scientific and engineering innovation. Latitude (north-south) could be computed on land or sea via the stars. Longitude (east-west) required exact calculations of time as the Earth moves in its orbit. A precise clock that functioned aboard a ship at sea, accomplished in the latter eighteenth century, transformed both navigation and astronomy (Sobel 2007). Coordinate systems in astronomy depend upon precise temporal measurements because the motion of the Earth in its orbit causes the position and wavelength of an object's emission to change subtly with time.

Astronomers agreed on a standard mapping system, known as the World Coordinate System (WCS), as part of the FITS standards for describing observations of the sky (National Aeronautics and Space Administration, Goddard Space Flight Center 2013b). Each pixel in an image of the sky is assigned X and Y coordinates for its location. These coordinates, usually expressed as *right ascension* and *declination,* are the equivalent of longitude and latitude for the positions on the Earth. The electromagnetic spectrum is the third dimension used in astronomical observations. This dimension may be expressed as frequency or wavelength, and it can be translated to a velocity in many cases due to the Doppler effect. For objects far outside the Milky Way, Hubble's law is incorporated into the calculation of an object's distance.

Observations taken by different instruments, at different times, can be reconciled via these coordinate systems. Sky images that were captured on glass plates more than a century ago can be matched to images taken with today's telescopes (Harvard-Smithsonian Astrophysical Observatory 2013b; Johnson 2007). Similarly, photographs of the sky taken today may be matched to their sky locations using the WCS, star catalogs, and other astronomical data products. The process is imperfect, as reconciliation sometimes requires knowledge of why an image was taken (Hogg and Lang 2008; Lang et al. 2009).

Celestial Objects   Celestial objects and other astronomical phenomena have their own sets of metadata. These are cataloged manually, after papers are published, through coordinated multinational efforts. Celestial objects in our galaxy are cataloged in SIMBAD (the Set of Identifications, Measurements, and Bibliography for Astronomical Data), which is based at The Centre de Données Astronomiques de Strasbourg (CDS) in France. Catalogers read new astronomy publications as they appear, creating metadata records for each mentioned celestial object that can be identified (Genova 2013).

SIMBAD grows rapidly at the pace of publications and new discoveries, updating their statistics daily. As of this writing, SIMBAD contains about 18.2 million identifiers for 7.3 million unique objects that were mentioned in 285,000 papers, for a total of about 10 million references to unique objects (Centre National de la Recherche Scientifique 2012; SIMBAD Astronomical Database 2013; Genova 2013). Another way of representing these numbers is that each of these 7.3 million objects is known, on average, by about 2.5 different names—the 18.2 million identifiers. Each paper mentions an average of 35 celestial objects—the 10 million citations of objects in 285,000 papers. These objects are not evenly distributed in the astronomy literature. Most papers describe a few objects, and a few papers list large numbers of objects. Similarly, most objects have just one name (e.g., Jupiter) and some have many, such as their identification in surveys and catalogs created over a period of centuries. Each publication is thus richly tagged with metadata, adding value that can be used in discovering, combining, and distinguishing data about celestial objects.

Objects outside our galaxy are cataloged in the NASA Extragalactic Database (National Aeronautics and Space Administration, Infrared Processing and Analysis Center 2014a). Solar system and planetary data are cataloged in yet another service (National Aeronautics and Space Administration, Jet Propulsion Laboratory 2014). CDS is the coordination point for many of the metadata repositories for astronomy, and provides searching and mapping tools such as Aladin and VizieR (Centre National de la Recherche Scientifique 2012, 2013).

Data Archiving Massive amounts of astronomical observations are available in data archives, also known as repositories, databases, or information systems. While extensive, they are not comprehensive. Observations from government-funded astronomy missions, especially those collected by telescopic instruments launched into space, are most often made available as public resources. Most repositories are organized by mission, such as observations from the Spitzer Space Telescope, Chandra, and Hubble missions (Harvard-Smithsonian Astrophysical Observatory 2013a; NASA Spitzer Space Telescope 2013; HubbleSite 2013a).

Data also are organized by wavelength, such as the set of archives hosted by the Infrared Processing and Analysis Center (IPAC). IPAC organizes data by missions and also by types of celestial objects, such as the NASA Exoplanet Archive (National Aeronautics and Space Administration, Infrared Processing and Analysis Center 2014b). Each major sky survey, such as the SDSS,

Pan-STARRS, and LSST, offers its own data repository. Well-curated older data, such as the Two Micron All Sky Survey (2MASS), for which data collection was completed in 2001, remain valuable indefinitely (National Aeronautics and Space Administration, Infrared Processing and Analysis Center 2014c).

Although astronomy data repositories are valuable resources, each archive is independent and each has its own user interface, search capabilities, and underlying data model. Because archived astronomy data tend to be partitioned by observational wavelength and by the observatory that collected them, integration approaches are needed (Accomazzi and Dave 2011). Some repositories such as MAST curate data from multiple missions and spectra, and also accept contributions of data and models (National Aeronautics and Space Administration, Mikulski Archive for Space Telescopes 2013). The Data Discovery Tool, SkyView, and WorldWide Telescope are among the growing number of tools available for searching across data archives and integrating data sources (Goodman and Wong 2009; International Virtual Observatory Alliance 2013b).

Astronomers have a growing number of options for sharing data that they collected themselves or were derived from public sources: archives that accept contributions, university repositories, project and personal websites, and personal exchange. A small study of astronomers indicates that their sharing practices are much like other fields. The most common form of data sharing is to e-mail data to colleagues on request. Only a small proportion (about 20 out of 175) had put data into an institutional archive. Data handling remains largely in the hands of the people who collected or analyzed them. One respondent compared his team's data practices to those of the SDSS, saying that instead of SDSS Data Release 1.0, 2.0, and so on, "we have more like: Graduate student 1, 2, and 3" (Pepe et al. in press).

Publications Bibliographic control is much more comprehensive in astronomy than in most fields. The Harvard-Smithsonian Astrophysical Observatory–NASA Astrophysics Data System (ADS) is largely a bibliographic system, despite its name. ADS, operational since 1993, contains records on core astronomy publications back to the nineteenth century, as well as extensive coverage of gray literature in the field (Kurtz et al. 2000, 2005; Harvard-Smithsonian Astrophysical Observatory 2013c). ADS plays a central role in the knowledge infrastructure of astronomy by curating not only bibliographic records but also the links between publications, records of celestial objects, and data archives (Accomazzi and Dave 2011; Accomazzi 2010; Borgman 2013; Kurtz et al. 2005).

Provenance   Astronomers rely on this extensive array of knowledge infra-structure components to determine the provenance of data. Researchers must be able to trust the data, knowing that many people, many instruments, and many software tools have touched the observational bit stream. Those bits are calibrated, cleaned, transformed, and reduced at many stages in the pipeline processing. Provenance concerns vary by research question and circumstance. Data taken for one purpose, in one region of the sky, at particular times and wavelengths, may or may not be useful for a particular purpose later. For example, provenance may be much harder to determine on older data taken by individual astronomers than on data from sky surveys. Legacy data that are converted to digital form may not be documented adequately for some kinds of future uses.

The provenance of sky surveys and other large datasets are documented in the aforementioned *data papers,* such as those for individual data releases of the SDSS (Ahn et al. 2012) and COMPLETE (Ridge et al. 2006). *Instrument papers* also may be published to give credit to instrument developers and to provide more detailed documentation of decisions made. These papers document the instrumentation, calibration, and processing decisions. Data papers are among the most highly cited articles in astronomy because they aggregate references to the data sources.

Provenance in astronomy also is maintained by the use of common analytical tools and services. The International Virtual Observatory Alliance (IVOA) is a coordinating entity to develop and share data and tools (Hanisch and Quinn 2002; International Virtual Observatory Alliance 2013a). Partners meet regularly to address interoperability issues and to coordinate national efforts on scientific infrastructure for astronomy research.

While far from complete, astronomy has made more progress establishing relationships between publications and data than have most fields. SIMBAD provides links between celestial objects and the papers reporting research on them, which are in ADS. Less well curated are metadata to link publications to observations and to link celestial objects to observations. Efforts are under way to coordinate multiple systems and activities, with the goal of better semantic interlinking of these complementary resources (Accomazzi and Dave 2011). Coordination involves IVOA, ADS, CDS, astronomy libraries, data archives, and systems such as the WorldWide Telescope that can integrate disparate data sources (WorldWide Telescope 2012). The role of these coordinating efforts in data sharing and reuse are discussed in chapter 8.

External Influences   Astronomy is no less influenced by external matters of economics and value, property rights, and ethics than are other domains of the sciences. The creation and use of data in astronomy depends upon international agreements and an array of governance models. These underpin the knowledge infrastructures of astronomy in ways that are both subtle and profound.

Economics and Value   One reason that astronomy data are attractive for research in computer science is that they have no apparent monetary value. A second reason is that their great volume and consistent structure make them useful for database research. Third, no human subjects are involved, so ethical constraints on reuse are minimized (Gray and Szalay 2002; Hey, Tansley, and Tolle 2009b; Lynch 2009; Szalay 2008).

Although it is true that no market exists to buy and sell astronomical observations or the output of numerical models, telescopes, instruments, and large data archives such as the SDSS, Hubble, and Chandra, most are better understood as common-pool resources. Those that constitute infrastructure investments of public and private agencies have governance models in place to ensure the quality of the resources and equity of access. Sustainability and free riders are continual threats to these common-pool resources. However, many astronomical instruments and data resources are not part of these common pools. Data in the local control of individual astronomers and teams may be considered raw materials or private goods, depending upon the circumstance. Some instruments and archives are club goods, available only to partners. Software necessary to analyze astronomy data and to interpret files may be open source or commercial products.

Property Rights   Property rights in data vary by project, funding agency, and other factors. Whether research funding is public or private, investigators usually have exclusive rights to data for some period of time. Proprietary periods, also known as embargoes, tend to range from three to eighteen months or so, counted from the time the observations are taken by the telescope (National Optical Astronomy Observatory 2003, 2013a) or from the time that "scientifically usable data" are available from the processing pipeline (Spitzer Science Center 2013). Investigators may have discretion to make data available sooner, but special permission is required to lengthen the proprietary period. Distinctions about whether the proprietary period begins with the time of observation or the time of scientifically usable data can result in months or years of difference in the time that investigators have to control their data while writing publications. Data obtained from

privately operated telescopes may never be released, although legacy data from important telescopes have since become available.

For those missions whose data are destined for archiving, which is the case with most major space telescopes, data are made available via repositories once pipeline processing is complete and proprietary periods have ended. When astronomers wish to collect their own observations from these or other instruments, their rights to data are coupled to the governance of the instruments. Telescopes are owned, under various arrangements, by the universities, consortia, governments, and other entities that fund them. Responsibility for policies governing the use of instruments such as the Hubble Space Telescope may be delegated to the scientific mission. Most public telescopes are available to qualified astronomers who must submit proposals for their use. Other instruments are dedicated to synoptic surveys, assembling large data collections that will be open to all. A declining number of telescopes remain available only to the elite few associated with the private institutions that own them.

Data rights policies of these governing bodies make fine distinctions in the rights to use or control certain kinds of data. For example, the National Optical Astronomy Observatory (NOAO) data rights policies distinguish between scientific data subject to proprietary periods and other kinds of data that are available to the community "immediately upon ingest of the exposure in the NOAO Archive," such as metadata on individual exposures, including the time, duration, location, and instrument configuration. Internal calibration data similarly is considered public. NOAO staff have access to all data from the instruments for purposes of monitoring the health, safety, calibration, and performance of the instrument. NOAO is located at Kitt Peak in Arizona and operated by the Association of Universities for Research in Astronomy (AURA), Inc. under cooperative agreement with the National Science Foundation (National Optical Astronomy Observatory 2013a).

Ethics   Ethics issues arise in astronomy around access to data and to instruments, which are scarce and expensive resources. Who has access to which telescope, when, for how long, and with what resources for collecting and analyzing data is determined by the moral economy of astronomy (McCray 2000, 2001, 2003). Access became more equitable and merit-based in recent years with the growth in public funding for the field, but ethics and politics always will play a role. Telescopes are funded by a complex array of partners, including universities, to ensure that their members have access to necessary facilities.

Access to astronomy data can be delayed due to issues involving pipeline processing, proprietary periods, governance, and such. Data from the Planck mission to study cosmic microwave background, for example, was made available much later than initially promised. The investigators released about thirty papers all at once, along with the data, on the grounds that the data were not valid for use by others until fully calibrated (Planck Collaboration et al. 2013).

Astronomy observations can be sensitive, owing to their value for navigation and defense. For example, Pan-STARRS is partly funded by the US Air Force to monitor near-Earth objects; thus, data deemed sensitive are not available for astronomy research. Pan-STARRS distinguishes between its primary science mission and its role in defense (Pan-STARRS 2012, 2013b). "Working in the open" usually implies data release at the time of article publication, rather than subjecting one's day-to-day activities to public scrutiny.

Conducting Research in Astronomy

Most astronomers live in a data-rich world, with a wealth of tools and services to select and analyze those data. They also live in a world of constraints, with a very long time frame to plan missions and dependence on international coordination for funding, infrastructure, and access to instruments and data. Access to telescopes and to observing time is more equitable than in generations past, but those at wealthier institutions who are members of major instrument consortia still have more resources than those at lesser universities and those in poorer countries. Decisions about what entities become data and what data are shared, reused, or curated, and how are influenced by access to these resources and to constraints on time, technology, and infrastructure.

This case study follows one team, based at the Harvard-Smithsonian Center for Astrophysics (CfA), through a multiyear project known as the COMPLETE Survey as they developed research questions, collected and analyzed their data, and published their findings in more than forty papers. It explores the knowledge infrastructures on which they depend, how they represent data, when and how they share them, the array of stakeholders involved, and their publication practices.

The COMPLETE Survey The *COMPLETE* (*CO*ordinated *M*olecular *P*robe *L*ine *E*xtinction *T*hermal *E*mission Survey of Star Forming Regions) Survey, based at the CfA, is a large dataset created from public repositories of astronomical observations and from new observations in the same regions of

the sky. The Survey mapped three very large star-forming regions in our galaxy in their entirety. Observations covered the electromagnetic spectrum from X-ray to radio. The team then mined these data to address an array of research questions. The Survey is valued for its comprehensiveness, its diversity of data sources, and its size—estimated to be about a thousand times larger than what was available as a coordinated resource a decade earlier (COordinated Molecular Probe Line Extinction Thermal Emission Survey of Star Forming Regions [COMPLETE] 2011).

Over the course of seven years or so, many people with many kinds of expertise were involved in conducting the survey. The team has ranged in size from about a dozen to twenty-five members, including faculty, senior researchers, postdocs, graduate students, and undergraduates. Research using the Survey dataset continues, largely focused on observational and statistical work to understand the physics of star-forming regions.

Research Questions   Research questions of the COMPLETE Survey team concern how interstellar gas arranges itself into new stars. The overarching question in star-formation research is what distributions of stars form as a function of time, for interstellar gas with given conditions. They broke this question into smaller units, some parts of which had to be answered before the next parts of the puzzle could be addressed. Among the major findings to date are the discovery of "cloudshine" in the near infrared (Foster and Goodman 2006); development and implementation of a structure-finding algorithm to describe real (Pineda, Rosolowsky, and Goodman 2009; Rosolowsky et al. 2008) and simulated (Beaumont et al. 2013) star-forming regions; a reinterpretation of the meaning of temperature in maps of interstellar gas (Schnee, Bethell, and Goodman 2006); and an assessment of the role of self-gravity in star formation (Goodman et al. 2009).

Collecting Data   To identify data in existing archives, the team used coordinate-based and object-name–based searches in repositories to extract data for the three star-forming regions being studied (Perseus, Ophiuchus, and Serpens). They also used metadata in SIMBAD and ADS to identify prior papers that studied celestial objects and phenomena in these regions. However, metadata in archives are known to be incomplete, so the team relied on their professional knowledge of the field and on sources mentioned in papers to determine where to search for available data in archives. More than half of the COMPLETE Survey is new data resulting from multiple proposals for observational time on telescopic instruments. These new data were processed through the pipelines associated with each telescopic

instrument. While a complex process to accomplish, it is noteworthy that the knowledge infrastructure for this area of astronomy supports the ability to reconcile old and new observations from multiple instruments.

Analyzing Data The first steps in data analysis were to get all the datasets into a common FITS format, whether acquired from archives or via observing proposals. Reconciling these files requires an intimate knowledge of the FITS standard. Decisions had to be made about how to merge files. The datasets do not have identical footprints on the sky, thus more data are available for some areas of the star-forming regions than others. While the available metadata on sky positions and spectra are essential to merge datasets, considerable expertise is required to reconcile differences in calibration, instrument characteristics, data models, and other factors (Goodman, Pineda, and Schnee 2009). When the datasets were merged into a common file, the team could employ a suite of tools, both open source and commercial, that take FITS files and other common formats as input.

To gain a competitive edge, astronomers sometimes write new software tools or new scripts in existing tools. Creating new tools and validating new methods can themselves be scientific contributions (Rosolowsky et al. 2008). For example, in their *Nature* article about the role of gravity at multiple scales, Goodman et al. (2009) explain how they implemented dendrograms as a new technique to measure structures over a range of spatial scales. Their 3D visualizations separate self-gravitating from non-self-gravitating regions in the dendrogram to show the superiority of the dendrogram algorithm over a previous algorithm called CLUMPFIND. Their paper was the first to be published as a 3D PDF enabling three-dimensional views to be manipulated and rotated within the article (see figure 2 in Goodman et al. 2009) using a particular version of the Adobe PDF reader.

Publishing Findings COMPLETE yielded a cumulative body of research for the team, with each study producing findings that informed the next. Individual papers are based on subsets of the Survey assembled for a specific purpose, such as the exploration of the role of self-gravity in star formation mentioned above. Because multiple papers are drawing on the same large dataset, they document the research protocols only to the extent necessary for the specifics of each paper. The necessary provenance information for building the Survey is provided in the data paper, which has seventeen authors from the partner institutions (Ridge et al. 2006). The *Nature* article (Goodman et al. 2009) is only four pages in length because that is the maximum allowed by the journal; an additional twelve pages of supplemental

material is published online. Yet further documentation is on the project's website and referenced in papers.

Papers based on the COMPLETE Survey were published in astronomy journals; thus, the papers are cataloged in SIMBAD and ADS, making them discoverable by object, region, and bibliographic characteristics.

Curating, Sharing, and Reusing Data The COMPLETE Survey team is distributed across multiple institutions and countries, each of which has its own practices for sharing, curating, and reusing data. The core team, based at the Harvard-Smithsonian Center for Astrophysics, maintains the Survey datasets and website. They make the survey data available for download in multiple parts and formats, each with extensive documentation (COordinated Molecular Probe Line Extinction Thermal Emission Survey of Star Forming Regions [COMPLETE] 2011). A suggested citation to the datasets is provided, but the team does not attempt to track usage or citations. Derived datasets are being released via Dataverse, newly adapted for astronomical data. The dataset remains in active use; thus, they can add new releases, new documentation, and corrections as needed. They have not contributed the survey data to MAST or other repositories, which would relieve them of long-term curation responsibility.

The Harvard CfA team that conducted the COMPLETE Survey and exploited it for a series of research projects is far more concerned with data curation than are most scholars in most fields. They are actively involved in data sharing and infrastructure development in astronomy. The team developed a Dataverse site for depositing and sharing astronomy data, are principals in the ADS All Sky Survey to integrate data and publications in the field, are principals in the WorldWide Telescope, and have studied data sharing and reuse in astronomy (Goodman and Wong 2009; Goodman 2012; Goodman et al. 2013; Pepe, Goodman, and Muench 2011).

Despite their extensive documentation of the COMPLETE Survey, the team acknowledges they still have the "graduate student 1, 2, 3" problem that is endemic to long-term collaborative research (Edwards et al. 2011; Pepe et al. 2013). When questions arise that involve fine-grained decisions about calibration, transformations, or similar analytical processes that occurred years earlier, they sometimes have to locate the departed student or postdoctoral fellow most closely involved. These interpretations, in turn, can depend on decisions made by other parties earlier in the development of instruments, pipelines, and data products. This is the "building the house problem:" the provenance of data can be traced only as far back as the beginning, and data may have many beginnings.

As with most digital data, astronomy data are inseparable from the software code used to clean, reduce, and analyze them. Data in the form of FITS files, which are already reduced through pipeline processing, can be analyzed with standard suites of tools, whether commercial or open source. Many kinds of software code associated with astronomy data may not be subject to release, however. Astronomers may write their own pipelines for data they have collected via their own observing proposals or instruments. They may write specialized tools or scripts to analyze public data. In other cases, code in computational simulations is closely protected, but code associated with the analysis and interpretation of output is released. In yet others, outputs of simulations may not be released if they are not considered to be data. These are but a few of the many forms of data scholarship found in astronomy.

Sensor-Networked Science and Technology

By the late 1990s, science and technology researchers began to deploy embedded sensor networks to collect research data at higher volumes, densities, and qualities than were previously possible. In the environmental sciences, for example, sensor networks are used to study plant growth, wind and weather patterns, chemical and biological activity, animal activity, and sources of contamination in soil and water. Ten years of collaborative research on data practices in the Center for Embedded Networked Sensing (CENS), in which such sensing systems were developed, tested, and deployed for scientific applications, yielded a rich set of material for this case study. The social science methods by which this CENS case was developed are explored in chapter 6.

CENS was a National Science Foundation Science and Technology Center, funded from 2002 to 2012 and devoted to developing sensing systems for scientific and social applications through collaborations between engineers, computer scientists, and domain scientists. By partnering across disciplinary boundaries, participants had to articulate their research practices, methods, and expectations explicitly.

Size Matters

Sensor-networked science, in the field research areas of CENS, is a canonical example of "little science," in Price's (1963) terms. While Price might view this type of science as less mature than the big science of astronomy owing to the inconsistency of research methods, it is best viewed as adaptive. These are rigorous methods that meet the standards of evidence for

their respective fields. Such data may be high in validity but are not readily replicated.

CENS launched in 2002 with a core of investigators located at four universities in California, with a fifth added later. These investigators, in turn, had collaborators at other institutions. Membership varied from year to year as projects began and ended, and as the rosters of students, faculty, postdocs, and staff evolved. The Center had about three hundred participants at its peak, with a diverse array of data practices. On average over the life of the Center, about 75 percent of CENS participants were concerned with the development and deployment of sensing technologies; the rest were in science, medical, or social application domains. Technology researchers were developing new applications for science or other applications, whereas the scientists sought new technologies to advance their research methods.

The data collected in CENS field deployments were big in variety, if not in absolute volume or velocity. As volume and velocity increased, however, science teams experienced scaling problems. Sensor networks produced far more data than did the hand-sampling methods that dominated these domains. In a biology study of root growth, for example, scientists had collected and manually coded about one hundred thousand images in a period of seven years, using cameras in clear plastic tubing that were placed in the ground near the plants of interest. By automating the cameras and sending the images over the sensor network, they could capture up to sixty thousand images per day, totaling about ten gigabytes (Vargas et al. 2006). Transferring the manual methods to automated coding was problematic for several reasons. Manual coding relied on the expertise of graduate and undergraduate students, some of whom coded for hours on end. Coding was difficult because the roots were very small and grew slowly. When roots first touched the tube, they appeared only as tiny dots. Once they grew enough to be visible along the tube, coders could study prior images to determine when the roots might first have appeared. Identifying the origins of some of those observations required digging through field notebooks, videotapes of root growth, and other records. They did some testing of inter-coder reliability, but the margins of error made it difficult to codify the practices algorithmically. In the marine biology studies, science teams usually captured water samples three to four times in each twenty-four-hour period. Those observations were correlated as time series. Sensor networks, however, sampled the water at five-minute intervals. Simple correlations and time series analyses did not suffice for these data rates, which led to the adoption of complex modeling techniques (Borgman, Wallis, and Mayernik 2012; Borgman et al. 2007; Wallis , Borgman, Mayernik, Pepe, et al. 2007).

When Are Data?

The notion of data in CENS was a moving target throughout the ten years of the Center's existence. Each investigator, student, and staff member interviewed offered personalized descriptions of his or her data. These descriptions evolved in subsequent interviews, site visits, and examination of their publications. Individuals on the same team had differing explanations of what were the team's data, varying by their role in the team, experience, and the stages of research activity. Notions of data also evolved as the sensor-network technology improved and as the collaborations and research methods matured (Borgman, Wallis, and Mayernik 2012; Mayernik, Wallis, and Borgman 2012; Wallis et al. 2008).

CENS research as a whole was a mix of exploratory, descriptive, and explanatory research methods. Scientists might formulate a hypothesis in the laboratory and test it in the field, and vice versa. Technology researchers could test some theories in the lab and others in the field. Theoreticians, such as the electrical engineers who were modeling sensor networks, similarly could test theories in field deployments of sensor networks (Cuff, Hansen, and Kang 2008; Wallis et al. 2007).

Scientists in biology, seismology, environment, and other areas brought their research questions and methods with them to CENS. Particularly in the biological and environmental applications addressed in this case study, their science practices exhibited characteristics of ecology identified by Bowen and Roth (2007): (1) research design has a highly emergent character; (2) tools and methods are developed in situ, often from locally available materials, and are highly context-specific; (3) studies are not easily replicable because of the dynamic nature of ecological systems; and (4) social interactions between members of the community are highly important.

Researchers in computer science and engineering similarly brought their research questions and methods to CENS. Few of the technology researchers had experience in designing hardware or software for scientific applications, particularly for field-based research that took place in unpredictable real-world settings. Technology design was particularly daunting when requirements and evaluation criteria remained fluid, adapting to scientific questions (Borgman, Wallis, and Mayernik 2012). Teams had to learn enough about the domain area of their partners to design, deploy, and evaluate the technologies and resulting data.

CENS research often combined commercially purchased and locally developed equipment. Decisions made in the design of sensing technologies, both hardware and software, influence the types of data that can be acquired. As with telescope instruments in astronomy, design decisions

made long before field research takes place may determine what can become data.

Although science and technology teams worked together in the field, neither had a full grasp of the origins, quality, or uses of the data collected jointly. Some of the data collected in field deployments were of exclusive interest to the science teams, such as physical samples of water, whereas others were of exclusive interest to technology teams, such as proprioceptive data from robotic devices. Thus data from the sensors were of mutual interest, but applied to different research questions. Because these were new scientific applications of research-grade technologies, "ground truthing" the data against real-world benchmarks was a continual challenge.

Sources and Resources   CENS researchers collected most of their own data, having few repositories or other external sources on which to draw. The teams gathered an array of data from sensor networks and physical samples. Software code and models were essential to the design of instruments and interpretation of data. These sometimes were treated as data.

Embedded Sensor Networks   Embedded sensor networks were not new technologies even at the time that CENS was founded in 2002. Sensor networks are used to run industrial processes such as chemical and petroleum plants and to monitor water flow and water quality. What was new about CENS was the use of embedded sensor networks to ask new questions in science, and for science and technology researchers to collaborate on the design of technologies with real-world applications (Committee on Networked Systems of Embedded Computers 2001). CENS was able to combine commercially available technologies with new devices and new research designs to collect new kinds of data.

A generation earlier, remote-sensing technologies revolutionized the environmental sciences (Kwa and Rector 2010; Kwa 2005, 2011). The ability to view the Earth from satellites, at levels of granularity that continue to improve, made possible a far more integrated view of environmental phenomena than was ever before possible.

Sensor networks could be deployed on land and in water, depending on the technology. As shown in figure 5.1, sensors could be buried in soil, hung from buoys or boats in water, attached to poles or other fixtures, or hung from cables to be moved in three dimensions over land or soil. Sensors were used to detect indicators of nitrates in water, arsenic in rice fields, wind speed and direction, light levels, physical movements of earth or animals, and various other phenomena. Data were collected from the sensors

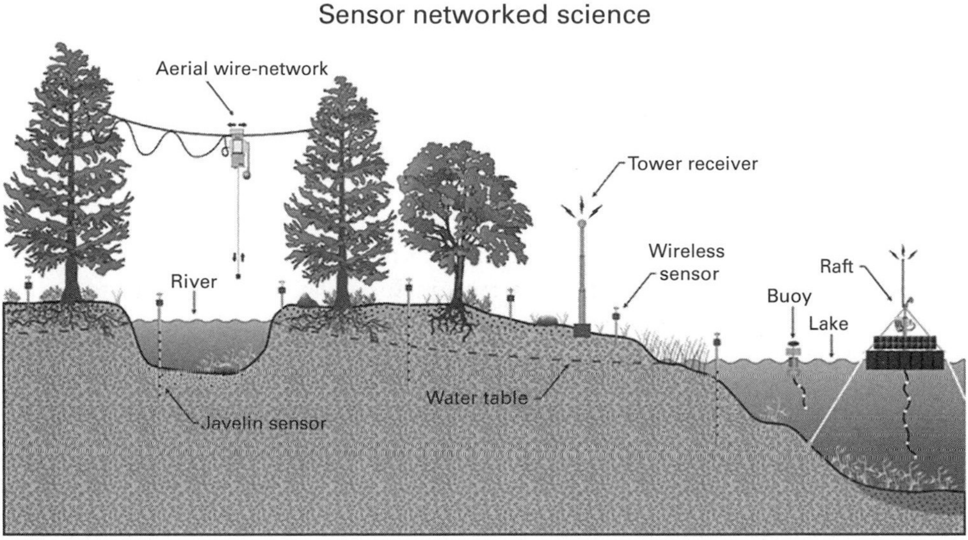

Sensor networked science

Figure 5.1
Sensor network technologies used in CENS. *Credit:* Jason Fisher.

either by hand, such as copying them to a flash drive, or by sending them to a node with Internet access. The uses of sensor data and the means by which they were captured varied by the application, choice of technologies, and remoteness of location. Some deployments took place in urban areas with ready access to wireless networks, but many were in remote mountains, islands, and deserts.

CENS technology researchers used sensor data for multiple purposes: (1) observations of physical and chemical phenomena, including sounds and images; (2) observations of natural phenomena used to actuate or to guide the robotic sensors to a place in the environment; (3) performance data by and about the sensors, such as the time that sensors are awake or asleep, the faults they detect, battery voltage, and network routing tables; and (4) proprioceptive data collected by the sensors—data to guide robotic devices, such as motor speed, heading, roll, pitch, yaw, and rudder angle (Borgman, Wallis, and Mayernik 2012).

Differences between the participating disciplines were most apparent in their criteria for evidence. Biologists, for example, measured variables such as temperature according to established metrics for their field. Engineers and computer scientists tended to be unaware or unconcerned with those international standards. For their purposes, a local baseline of consistent

measurements might suffice for calibration. When asked about measurement practices, one technology researcher stated simply, "temperature is temperature." When a partner biologist was asked independently about how to measure temperature, he gave a long and nuanced response involving the type of instrument, when and where the measurement was taken, the degree of control over the environment, the accuracy of the instrument, and calibration records. The latter biologist installed three types of temperature instruments side by side at a field site, recording measurements for a full year before he trusted the instruments and their resulting data (Wallis et al. 2007).

Physical Samples   CENS science teams continued to collect physical samples of water, sand, and soil. These included observations of living organisms such as the distribution of phytoplankton and zooplankton in a lake. Samples were tested in wet labs on site, and some were tested further on campus, after the deployment.

Software, Code, Scripts, and Models   Sensors do not measure wind, arsenic, nitrates, or other scientific variables directly; rather, they measure voltage and other detectable indicators. Most sensor outputs are binary signals that must be interpreted through statistical models. Some are images from cameras. Statistical models of physical or chemical phenomena were used to interpret these indicators (Batalin et al. 2004; Deshpande et al. 2004; Hamilton et al. 2007; Wallis et al. 2007).

The technology teams sometimes used external information resources such as software code repositories. Code, software, and models tended to be viewed synonymously as data among the computer science and engineering researchers studied (Wallis, Rolando, and Borgman 2013).

Background Data   The scientific teams used some data from external resources to plan their collection of new sources at specific field sites. Because teams tended to return repeatedly to the same field sites, they needed extensive baseline data and background context about those sites. Data collected by public agencies such as the Department of Fish and Game were important resources, as were data the team collected on earlier visits to the lake. Valuable background information about the lake included peak months for algae, a topology of the lake bed, phytoplankton and zooplankton species they were likely to see, and nutrient presence and concentration. Engineering teams sometimes obtained calibration data from external sources (Wallis, Rolando, and Borgman 2013).

Knowledge Infrastructures   Whereas astronomy has accrued a sophisti-cated knowledge infrastructure to coordinate data, publications, tools, and repositories over the course of many decades of international cooperation, CENS was at the opposite end of the infrastructure spectrum. The Center itself served an essential convening function to assemble researchers with common interests. It provided technical infrastructure in the form of equip-ment, networks, and staffing, but made little investment in shared informa-tion resources. Their publication records were contributed to the University of California eScholarship system, forming one of its largest repositories (Center for Embedded Networked Sensing 2013; Pepe et al. 2007).

The CENS research trajectory, as originally proposed, was based on auton-omous sensor networks and "smart dust" technologies. Had that trajec-tory continued, standardized structures for data and metadata would have been far more feasible. As the Center matured, participants gained a better understanding of the science and technology issues involved in explor-atory research of this nature. Experimental technologies were deemed too fragile and temperamental to be left unattended in field conditions. CENS research shifted toward "human-in-the-loop" approaches that were adapt-able on site (Mayernik, Wallis, and Borgman 2012).

Metadata   Scientific investigations using sensor networks is a research area, not a field with a history comparable to that of astronomy. Each of the part-ners brought their own disciplinary practices, including their uses of meta-data, to the collaboration. With the exception of seismology and genomics, few metadata standards existed for the data being produced by CENS teams. Those that did exist were not necessarily adopted by the scientific commu-nity or by local research teams—a characteristic of small science research (Cragin et al. 2010; Millerand and Bowker 2009). Formal XML-based stan-dards existed for environmental data and for sensor data, for example, but were not used (Knowledge Network for Biocomplexity 2010; Open Geospa-tial Consortium 2014; Higgins, Berkley, and Jones 2002; Ruixin 2002).

Some teams assigned metadata for their own purposes, although not from these XML standards. Researchers created records that described the context of data collection, including precise times, locations, local condi-tions, position of sensors, which sensors (make, model, serial number, and other characteristics), and scientific variables. File-naming conventions were the most common form of metadata. Rarely were teams satisfied with the degree of quality of metadata they used to manage their data, and often were concerned with the difficulty of locating or reusing their older data (Mayernik 2011).

Provenance   Each CENS team maintained its own records of the origins and handling of their data. Teams often used data from prior deployments or from laboratory studies for comparisons. CENS science teams tended to return repeatedly to the same field research sites, often over a period of many years. They developed cumulative knowledge and cumulative data about a site, enabling them to make longitudinal comparisons. Technology researchers were far less dependent on authentic field sites or longitudinal comparisons. Initial testing of their instruments could be conducted in bathtubs, swimming pools, backyards, and open spaces on campus.

Lacking a common data pool as in astronomy, researchers in the fields affiliated with CENS had no equivalent of data papers to establish the provenance of a dataset. Rather, provenance information was locally maintained, as were the associated data. Those wishing to reuse CENS data usually contacted the authors of papers in which data were reported (Wallis, Rolando, and Borgman 2013).

External Influences   Sensor-networked science attracts scholars from many different academic backgrounds. Each individual and group brought its own set of economic values, property rights concerns, and ethical issues to the collaboration. Some of the most interesting and unexpected issues arose in dealing with data at the intersection of research domains.

Economics and Value   The ways in which data were obtained and exchanged in CENS varied by domain and by the circumstances of each project. Researchers in seismology and marine biology had some common-pool resources for data. Those in environmental research drew on local, state, and US government records for meteorology, water flow, and other aspects of field conditions. To the extent that these were investigators working inside the United States, most of these records would be public goods. The same records may be licensed for use outside the United States, in which case they may become toll goods or common-pool resources, depending on how governed. CENS scientists collected observational data in many other countries, and their access to background data on local conditions varied accordingly. Computer science and engineering researchers sometimes obtained software from, or contributed code to, open software repositories such as GitHub and SourceForge, which serve as common-pool resources for this community (Boyle and Jenkins 2003; Kelty 2008; Uhlir 2006; Wallis, Rolando, and Borgman 2013). In other cases, as explored below and in chapter 8, data exchange consisted of informal agreements between individuals.

The seismology community in the United States is supported by the Incorporated Research Institutions for Seismology (IRIS), a consortium of universities that operate science facilities for the acquisition, management, and distribution of seismological data (Incorporated Research Institutions for Seismology 2013). Seismic data are used not only for scholarly research and education but also for earthquake hazard mitigation and for verification of the Comprehensive Nuclear-Test-Ban Treaty (IRIS Data Management Center 2013). Data resulting from National Science Foundation grants must be made available in the IRIS repository within a specified period after the last piece of equipment from a grant project is removed from the field. While rules on proprietary periods were respected, researchers had considerable flexibility about when to remove all remaining seismic equipment from a field site. Researchers might delay removing sensors to gain additional time to analyze their data (Wallis, Rolando, and Borgman 2013).

CENS collected very little genomic data, but some of the research in harmful algal blooms and in water quality included DNA analyses. When required by funding agencies or journals, these data were contributed to GenBank, the Protein DataBank, or other archives (Wallis, Rolando, and Borgman 2013). Some environmental data collected by remote sensing on satellites have great commercial value, such as tracking schools of fish or weather conditions that predict crop yields (Kwa 2005). Most of the CENS projects in environmental sciences collected small amounts of data about individual research sites. Few of the data were organized in ways that they could be readily combined or compared. In the aggregate, however, the potential existed for such data to be valuable to others (Borgman et al. 2007; Wallis et al. 2010).

Property Rights   As with astronomy, property rights in sensor-networked science and technology are associated more with instruments than with data. Whereas astronomers share large instruments, CENS scientists and technology researchers tended to purchase or build their own small devices for data collection. Equipment purchased through grant funding usually becomes the property of the university to which the grant was given.

Several companies partnered with CENS, providing expertise, equipment, and additional funding. A few small companies were formed to sell some of the equipment, algorithms, and methods developed in CENS research. None became major commercial successes; their goal was largely technology transfer. The Center's overall approach was toward open science, preferring to release software as open source code. Among the most successful continuing ventures is a nonprofit enterprise founded by CENS

alumni to design networked sensor technologies for environmental, health, and economic development applications (Nexleaf 2013).

Ethics   Ethics issues in the creation of scientific and technical data from sensor networks arose in decisions about what, where, and how phenomena were studied, and in how precisely the findings were to be reported. For example, some CENS researchers studied endangered species or habitats. Published findings included sufficient detail to validate the research but not enough for others to identify the exact location of the sites. Research that took place at protected natural reserves often was sensitive. Research reserves usually are in isolated locations, although some may be open to the public for educational activities. Recreational and research visitors alike were expected to respect the habitats and ecosystem to ensure that flora, fauna, and phenomena could be studied under natural conditions.

Computer science and engineering researchers in CENS were presumed to respect the ethical standards of their fields. The code of ethics of the Association for Computing Machinery (ACM), the largest professional organization for computer science, covers general moral imperatives (respect for others, do no harm, be fair and honest, respect privacy, honor confidentiality, etc.), professional responsibility (high-quality work, know and respect applicable laws, evaluate systems and risks, etc.), leadership, and compliance with the code (Association for Computing Machinery 1992). IEEE, which is a large professional organization for engineering, has a similar but less detailed code of ethics that mentions responsibilities such as "making decisions consistent with the safety, health, and welfare of the public," "to acknowledge and correct errors," and to avoid injury to others (Institute of Electrical and Electronics Engineers 2013).

Per these guidelines, researchers are to collect data responsibly, but notions of "responsibility" varied by domain. Engineers and biologists worked together to repurpose weapons-targeting algorithms to identify the location of bird sounds. Scientists who had avoided involvement with military applications found themselves deploying weapons technology for peaceful purposes. A team of computer scientists adapting sensor cameras to visualize the movement of birds and animals in the field mounted their cameras in campus hallways for testing purposes—then found themselves challenged on human subjects grounds for capturing people's behavior in hallways without consent (Wallis et al. 2007).

As CENS expanded into other applications of sensor networks, expertise in scientific usage of these technologies turned to social uses of mobile devices. Cell phones became an important platform for data collection and

for the study of network topology. When participants began tracking their own behavior via applications on mobile devices for food intake, commuting routes, bicycle usage, and other purposes, privacy concerns became paramount. Computer scientists and engineers faced a challenging set of decisions about what data they could collect versus what data they should collect. CENS became the site of a multiyear study on building values into the design of mobile technologies (Shilton 2011).

Conducting Research with Embedded Sensor Networks

CENS supported many independent projects at any one time, although some people, equipment, and practices were shared between projects. These collaborations took researchers out of their comfort zones: technologists had to test new equipment in highly unpredictable field settings, and scientists had to rely on technologists to ensure that field excursions were successful (Mayernik, Wallis, and Borgman 2012).

Small teams of researchers—a mix of students, faculty, and research staff from multiple research areas—would conduct research together on a field site for periods ranging from a few hours to two weeks. These events were known as "deployments," since the technology was deployed to collect data of various sorts. Participation varied from day to day, with a maximum of twenty or so people in total.

The following composite scenario of a typical CENS field research deployment, published in more detail elsewhere (Borgman, Wallis, and Mayernik 2012), illustrates a set of activities commonly associated with the collection, management, use, and curation of these types of data. This scenario involves a harmful algal bloom (HAB), a phenomenon in which a particular algae suddenly becomes dominant in the water, and can occur in fresh water and in oceans. The bloom creates toxic conditions that kill fish and other animals such as sea lions by consuming the available dissolved oxygen that fish need or by releasing domoic acid, a harmful neurotoxin that affects large mammals. HAB are an important phenomenon to study because they can cause severe damage, potentially killing tens of thousands of fish in a day. The HAB deployments were sited at a lake known for summer blooms.

Sensor networks enable marine biologists to study more variables than possible with hand-sampling techniques and to collect a much larger number of observations. Data collection can be adapted to local conditions through the choice and location of sensors. Sensor network studies of HAB enable computer scientists and engineers to test the ability of physical and

biological sensors to collect large numbers of variables. Roboticists find HABs of particular interest because the flow of observations can be used to trigger sensing systems on robotic boats, buoys, helicopters, cameras, and autonomous vehicles.

Research Questions   The overall goal of CENS research was the joint development, or co-innovation, of new instruments that would enable new kinds of science (Center for Embedded Networked Sensing 2012; Committee on Networked Systems of Embedded Computers 2001; Estrin 2008). Science and technology efforts were symbiotic, as in Licklider's metaphor of the wasp and the fig tree (Borgman 2011; Licklider 1960; Waldrop 2001). One could not proceed without the other; they were mutually interdependent and influencing.

Despite the interdependence of the science and technology teams, the long-term goals of their research were aligned with their respective disciplines rather than with the Center. The biology researchers continued their study of biological phenomena associated with HAB before, during, and after CENS, and the technology researchers continued to improve their instruments, algorithms, and models for targeting phenomena before, during, and after CENS. Their choices of data, how to manage their data, and where to publish their findings were more aligned with their respective research agendas, despite their substantial commitment to mutual participation (Borgman, Wallis, and Mayernik 2012; Mayernik, Wallis, and Borgman 2012; Wallis, Rolando, and Borgman 2013).

In the HAB field research, the science team studied the distribution of phenomena in the lake, whereas the technology team studied robotic vision (Borgman, Wallis, and Mayernik 2012). The science team's requirements provided a means to conduct technology research on algorithms for robotic guidance, network health, sensor fault detection, and the design of sensor technology interfaces. The computer science and engineering researchers relied on discussions with the science team to guide their choices of equipment, specific sensors, and the time, place, and length of deployment of each.

Collecting Data   The number of people and distribution of skill sets varied considerably from deployment to deployment. In the four-day lake deployment to study HABs, participation varied from day to day. On the first day, students and research staff arrived to set up equipment. On the second day, faculty investigators arrived to guide the data collection. In this example, about twenty people came and went over the course of the four days. These

included about eight to ten from electrical engineering who built the sensing system, about four or five from the robotics team, two from statistics, and six to eight members of the marine biology team. Responsibilities overlapped; thus, the figures for participation are approximate (Borgman, Wallis, and Mayernik 2012).

Although all parties came to the site with a set of research questions and associated instrumentation, data collection depended heavily upon local field conditions. Researchers chose and placed sensors carefully, as each sensor is suitable for certain types of conditions and can gather data at certain densities (Akyildiz et al. 2002). The placement of sensors is itself a topic of research (Younis and Akkaya 2008). Factors such as soil moisture and pH levels of the lake would influence where to place sensors. Sensors might be moved multiple times during the deployment based on interim findings. Some positions were based on conditional probabilities, such as the ability of roboticists to move sensors automatically to positions where HABs were predicted.

For the HAB research, both teams needed observations of chemical and physical phenomena (e.g., nitrate concentrations by time, location, and depth in the lake) and observations of natural phenomena (e.g., distribution of phytoplankton and zooplankton) that could be used to guide robotic sensors. The science teams also needed physical samples of water that contained living organisms; these were tested in wet labs on site and some were tested further on campus, after the deployment. The technology teams also needed performance and proprioceptive data about the sensors (Borgman, Wallis, and Mayernik 2012).

Sensors varied considerably in reliability, which was a source of much frustration in the early years of CENS. Sensors would function erratically, cease to function, or reboot themselves seemingly at random. In the latter case, time clocks would be reset, making it impossible to reconcile data collection from sensors across the network. Sensor networks for field-based science of the form conducted in CENS were much less reliable as autonomous networks than expected. After a devastating loss of data from a field site on another continent, the Center shifted its research focus to human-in-the-loop methods. The latter approach was more suitable to assessing data quality in real time (Mayernik, Wallis, and Borgman 2012).

In practice, the sensor technology was always research grade, continually adapting to new science questions and new technical capabilities. It never stabilized sufficiently to employ standardized data collection procedures. These were among the small science characteristics of CENS research (Borgman, Wallis, and Enyedy 2006, 2007).

Analyzing Data Data were processed before, during, and after field deployments. CENS teams devoted considerable effort to ground truthing the sensor instruments and data to ensure that they were trustworthy. Roughly speaking, ground truthing is the use of known measurement methods to test the validity of new measurement methods.

The science teams had full control over the physical samples of water, soil, and other materials they collected in the field. Some of these materials were processed on site, others back in campus labs. Technology teams had little interest in these data. Making scientific sense of sensor data requires scientific models, which are rendered as statistical algorithms. These scientific models, which were developed jointly by the science and technology teams, were considered to be among the most important products of CENS research.

In field deployments, such as those for harmful algal blooms, sensor data went to the computers of the technology teams that operated the sensor networks. These teams calibrated and cleaned the sensor data, which included reconciling variant time stamps among sensors, removing artifacts such as sensor restarts due to computer faults, and adding notes for field decisions such as when, how, and where a sensor was moved (Wallis et al. 2007). Cleaned and calibrated data were provided to participating science teams. The scientists then compared those sensor data to their models and to other trusted data sources, such as the calibration curves they had established in laboratory and field testing (Borgman, Wallis, and Mayernik 2012). Most data from a field site were retained, if at all, only by the team that collected them.

Differences in long-term goals of the science and technology teams were most apparent in the processing of their data. Frictions arose in areas such as conflicting standards, data-sharing practices, and availability of support for managing data (Edwards et al. 2011; Mayernik, Batcheller, and Borgman 2011; Mayernik 2011). In science-only and technology-only deployments, the teams that collected the data also processed them. In joint science-technology deployments, handling and disposition varied by the type of data.

Publishing Findings The research from CENS field deployments was published in the journals and conferences of each participating field. In many cases, the scientific findings and the technological findings of field deployments were published separately, each aimed at the audience of their respective fields. In other cases, findings were published jointly with authors from multiple fields. A study of the authorship and acquaintanceship patterns of CENS researchers showed how new collaborations formed and how they evolved over the decade of the Center's existence (Pepe 2010, 2011).

Participants in CENS research activities included faculty, postdoctoral fellows, graduate and undergraduate students, and full-time research staff. Students and staff involved in the design and deployment of research equipment were considered part of the team, although staff did not always receive publication credit for their roles. Authorship was a particularly sensitive topic for those who designed and maintained instruments for the project. Instrumentation in CENS changed continually, since co-innovation of science and technology was central to the goals of the Center.

Curating, Sharing, and Reusing Data At the end of a field deployment, teams dispersed, each taking the data for which they or their team were responsible. As a result, data from joint field deployments were widely distributed and unlikely ever to be brought back together again. Few provenance records exist that could be used to reconstruct or replicate a particular field deployment (Borgman, Wallis, and Mayernik 2012; Wallis, Rolando, and Borgman 2013).

Each team documented their data sufficiently for their own use. Some teams, especially in the sciences, maintained data for future comparisons. Others, more often in engineering, had little need for data from deployments after papers were published. CENS teams made minimal investment in metadata creation (Mayernik 2011). File-naming conventions were often the most elaborate form of data management employed by individual research teams. Spreadsheets tended to be the lowest common denominator for data exchange within and between groups.

The adaptive nature of CENS data collection methods led to datasets that were local in use and not easily combined with other datasets. Few researchers contributed their data to repositories, partly because of lack of standardization and partly the lack of repositories to which they could contribute their data. Responsibility for data tended to be addressed as part of the assignment of roles for writing papers (Wallis 2012), as discussed further in chapter 9 (Chang et al. 2006; Wallis et al. 2010; Wallis 2012).

In principle, existing metadata standards could be used individually or in combination to describe much of the Center's data. Ecological observations being collected by sensors or by hand sampling could be described with a common structure and vocabulary. Similarly, characteristics of sensors could be captured automatically if these XML standards were embedded in the algorithms for data collection.

However, formal metadata structures do not fit well into these local and adaptive forms of research activities (Aronova, Baker, and Oreskes 2010; Millerand and Bowker 2009; Ribes et al. 2005). Metadata languages

intended for use by professional catalogers and indexers are not easily adapted to lightweight use by researchers. The Ecological Metadata Language, for example, is accompanied by an instructional manual more than two hundred pages in length (Knowledge Network for Biocomplexity 2013). A vocabulary identified for water research had more than ten thousand entries, with four hundred entries for nitrates alone. CENS researchers found the scale of these metadata languages to be daunting. They could not justify the effort that would be required to implement them, even on a small scale. The Center was not staffed to support the level of professional data management that would be required. Efforts to build a data repository that would support the interdisciplinary research with sensor networks were only minimally successful, largely due to the heterogeneity of data and variety of local practices for data management (Wallis et al. 2010).

Despite the informal nature of data management in most of CENS teams, researchers were generally willing to share their data. Conditions under which they were comfortable releasing data varied considerably, ranging from releasing all the raw data immediately to requiring coauthorship on papers resulting from the data. Most were willing to release data after the resulting papers were published (Borgman, Wallis, and Enyedy 2006). Some data and some software code were contributed to public repositories, but the most common form of data sharing by the researchers was personal exchanges upon request (Wallis, Rolando, and Borgman 2013).

Conclusion

Astronomy and embedded sensor networks are contrasting cases that illustrate the diversity of scholarship, research practices, and data. Astronomy is a long-established field with a core of journals and conferences. Scientific applications of embedded sensor networks are more a problem area than a field, but they too have several journals and conferences. Scholars in astronomy and sensor network research rely on shared instrumentation. However, telescopes and data archives are large infrastructure investments, governed with the expectation of spawning thousands of papers, shared knowledge, and data that may be valuable indefinitely. By comparison, infrastructure investments in sensor-networked science and technology are minimal.

The use of embedded networked sensing technologies to study emergent phenomena in field conditions represents an opposite extreme of scientific data scholarship from astronomy. Sensor networks deployed by CENS were largely research-grade technologies. Some instruments were too delicate to

be left unattended. Others were moved frequently to adapt to field conditions, based on human-in-the-loop research designs. The convening function of CENS, which brought together the necessary scientific and technical expertise to address these research problems, was a component of their knowledge infrastructure. Part of the convening function is to provide additional technical expertise, administrative support, and collaborative spaces. Otherwise, participating scholars relied on the infrastructures of their home departments or domains.

Despite the infrastructure investments in the Center, participating researchers lacked data standards, archives, and classification mechanisms to facilitate and integrate the exchange of data resources. Data management responsibility fell to the investigators, with little apparatus on which to build. This is a chicken-and-egg problem, however. Sensor network projects tend to be exploratory, problems are emergent, and field situations are inherently dynamic. Research teams may have little need to reconcile their own data from one deployment to the next, since each field trip may address new problems with new instruments. Although they do make comparisons between places and over time, rarely do they have data integration demands of the sort faced by the COMPLETE Survey.

These contrasts are readily aligned with the provocations set out in chapter 1. Differences in the data scholarship of these two scientific domains contribute mightily to differences in who owns, controls, has access to, or sustains research data. Common-pool resources dominate astronomy, whereas privately held data will be the norm in embedded sensor network research for the foreseeable future. Within the domain areas of CENS, demand for common-pool resources exists only in specialized areas such as seismology and genomics.

These differences in data scholarship also underlie the contrasting ways in which data are exchanged, if at all. Common-pool resources, both instrumentation and information systems, rely on shared standards and on institutions that support interoperability such as the Astrophysics Data System, CDS, SIMBAD, and NED. Celestial objects are linked to the publications in which they are mentioned; linking papers and datasets occurs much less frequently. Data exchange in sensor network research relies largely on personal contacts and no formal means exist to link publications, data, and other research objects. However, both domains invest extensive human labor in making these knowledge infrastructures work effectively.

Temporal characteristics of these domains also influence the evolution of their knowledge infrastructures and relationships among stakeholders. Astronomy is among the oldest and most established fields in the sciences.

Today's infrastructures span space and time, allowing legacy data to be integrated with observations taken today and far into the future. Astronomers today are less dependent upon private patronage than in centuries and decades past, but the support of wealthy donors is still sought for major instrumentation endeavors. The growth of public funding contributed to the internationalization of the field, investments in common-pool resources, and greater equity in access to instruments and to data. Astronomy is the rare field that speaks with a unified voice, via the decadal survey.

Sensor-networked science and technology, in contrast, is a crossroads where scientists in need of better technology meet technology researchers in need of worthy application domains. Participants come from fields old and new, keeping a foot in each world for the duration of the collaboration. While the problem area is exciting and has reached critical mass with conferences and journals, prospects for hiring, tenure, and promotion are centered elsewhere. Motivations to build a more extensive knowledge infrastructure or common-pool resources for sensor-networked science and technology have yet to emerge.

6   Data Scholarship in the Social Sciences

Introduction

The social sciences encompass research on human behavior in the past, present, and future. Despite their long traditions of social inquiry, these fields are embattled on campus and off. Debates about the "two cultures" of the sciences and humanities, triggered by C. P. Snow's essay (1956), raged throughout the 1960s but left the social sciences largely out of the dichotomy. Despite the growth of interdisciplinary collaborations and curricula in recent years, divisions between disciplines have deepened with changes in funding and reward structures (Hollinger 2013). Political science lately has become the most politicized of the social sciences, with the US Congress halting public funding for the field with the exception of research that can be certified as "promoting national security or the economic interests of the United States" (Prewitt 2013). Responses from the United States and abroad express deep concerns about political meddling in the allocation of individual grants in any field. At risk are peer review and expert judgment, along with pressure for short-term outcomes rather than long-term theory building (P. Boyle 2013; Prewitt 2013).

Some of the problems in social sciences research can be attributed to the challenges of data handling. Computational errors, for example, were found in an influential economics paper when a graduate student attempted to replicate the research. These errors, and the response by the authors, became front-page news in scholarly and business journals alike, contributing to concerns about accuracy in economics research (Marcus 2013; Monaghan 2013; Wiesenthal 2013). A case of fraud by a Dutch social psychologist went undetected for many years, raising similar concerns about research in the field and about the effectiveness of peer reviewing (Enserink 2012a; Shea 2011). While the rate of retractions in economics, business, and other areas of the social sciences is much lower than in the

sciences, that does not ensure greater research integrity. Rather, differences may be due to the ways in which publications in each field deal with papers that may contain errors, plagiarism, or academic dishonesty (Karabag and Berggren 2012; Oransky 2012).

Traditional methods of sampling populations, such as those that use postal mail or randomized calling of telephone landlines, became less reliable as communication activity moved online. Some argue that surveys and other established methods of social research have reached their limits of utility and that much different approaches are needed (Savage and Burrows 2007, 2009). Also shifting are policies for protecting research subjects. Locked file cabinets do not suffice to protect digital records about human subjects; new methods that reflect the reality of privacy protection, data mining, and reidentification are necessary. Conducting research on sensitive issues such as terrorism and conflict is essential for public policy, but doing so while protecting the confidentiality—and lives—of subjects has difficult trade-offs (Jackson, Bikson, and Gunn 2013). Establishing causality in the social sciences is often very difficult, given the complexity of human behavior and social institutions. These fields are searching for new sources of data and new methods, encountering the promises and pitfalls of data scholarship along the way.

Research Methods and Data Practices

The data practices of a domain are part of its research methods, and the social sciences articulate their research methods more explicitly than do most fields. Methods texts abound to support required courses on research design, statistics, quantitative and qualitative research, and visualization. Fundamental to these methods is balancing the richest possible description of human behavior with the need to respect the rights of the individuals, groups, or institutions being studied.

Although reductionist, a few basic dichotomies suggest the range of methods possible. These dimensions are not mutually exclusive; they can be combined in various ways. The first is idiographic versus nomothetic explanation. Idiographic studies are those that are distinct to a particular place, condition, or event. This mode of research seeks to identify and explain a case as fully as possible. Nomothetic studies, in contrast, are those that identify a few causal factors influencing a larger class of events or conditions (Babbie 2013). The second dichotomy is to classify those methods that primarily use counting or computational techniques to study social problems as "quantitative" and those primarily using interpretive approaches as "qualitative." A third is between obtrusive or unobtrusive

methods. Obtrusive data are those from studies in which some intervention is involved; the research subject is aware of being studied, preferably with consent. Unobtrusive methods are those in which no intervention is involved; the researcher draws on records of human activity or observes behavior without interference.

Reliability and validity are dimensions that cut across these dichotomies. Reliability is consistency, or the likelihood that the same result would be achieved in repeated observations of the same phenomenon. Validity is the truth value, or the degree to which a measure captures the concept it is intended to measure (Babbie 2013; Shadish, Cook, and Campbell 2002).

Scholars may balance these considerations differently for each study. Surveys, for example, are usually nomothetic, quantitative, and require large samples to achieve adequate reliability. Ethnographies, in contrast, usually are idiographic, qualitative, obtrusive, and concerned more with validity than reliability. Studies using big data require statistical methods and perhaps computational modeling. These methods are most likely to yield data that can be anonymized and reused by others. Studies that depend on close analysis are most likely to yield rich descriptions of phenomena, but the data may be impossible to anonymize or to share. Most often, hard choices must be made about what data can or should be acquired, how and why, and the ways in which they can be reported and released.

Social Sciences Cases

Data scholarship in the social sciences is as diverse as in the sciences; hence, no attempt is made to be comprehensive. The case studies in this chapter address how and why people use information technologies, illustrating the methods dimensions outlined above. The first set of cases, on Internet surveys and social media, contrasts studies of how people say they use the Internet with records of what they actually do with Internet technologies such as Twitter. OxIS, as the Oxford Internet Survey of Britain is known, has been conducted biannually by the Oxford Internet Institute since 2003 using in-person interviews. Several studies using Twitter feeds and other microblogging services as data resources suggest the ways in which decisions about evidence and methods influence data practices and findings.

The second case study in this chapter explores how information technologies are designed, deployed, and used in science and technology research. Sociotechnical methods were employed to study data practices in the Center for Embedded Networked Sensing (CENS). The findings of these studies are reported as the CENS data practices case in chapter 5. In this chapter, the methods employed in a decade of sociotechnical research

are summarized, examining the implications for data scholarship. Methods were largely idiographic but also involved social network analysis and the design and evaluation of technologies. Together, these two case studies examine how scholars in the social sciences are coping with new methods and new problems, and the implications for knowledge infrastructures.

Internet Surveys and Social Media Studies

Internet studies draw on methods from other areas of social science research. Surveys are the usual way to ask the same questions of large numbers of people. They can be conducted in person, by postal mail, e-mail, or by using technologies such as web-based survey forms and mobile applications. Social network analysis, a method commonly used in Internet research, long predates the Internet and today's online social media such as Twitter, Facebook, LinkedIn, Flickr, and Pinterest. Sociologists have modeled relationships among individuals and groups since the 1920s or so, using whatever indicators were available: postcards, phone calls, membership lists, and other social ties (Freeman 2004; Wellman and Haythornthwaite 2002).

For any research method, scholarly expertise is necessary to design the study, to select the appropriate population and sampling methods, and to clean, analyze, and interpret the resulting data. The dangers of using big data in social sciences and elsewhere lie in mistaking their ease of acquisition for ease of analysis. Conducting surveys and social media studies well is much more difficult than it may appear. Some Internet studies are very sophisticated, carefully accommodating the limits of the reliability and validity of these data. Other studies are naive, mining data streams as interesting new sources of evidence without an adequate understanding of their limits (Boyd and Crawford 2012).

Size Matters

Big science in the sense of Weinberg (1961) and Price (1963) is concerned with the maturity of a field and with the sophistication of research methods. Survey research is arguably among the most mature areas of the social sciences, with a long history of documenting social trends. Archives such as the Inter-University Consortium for Political and Social Research (2013) have collected survey data for more than fifty years, first on paper and later in digital form. Social science data archives vary in focus by funding source, type of study, region, and other criteria. University-based research centers such as the Institute for Quantitative Social Science at Harvard and the Social Science Data Archive at UCLA support data repositories, tutorials and

instruction, development of tools, and other services (Institute for Quantitative Social Science 2013; Social Science Data Archive 2014).

Surveys can be done on a one-off basis, but are particularly valuable when conducted over long periods of time. Surveys of public opinion on politics, higher education, and general social attitudes have been conducted at regular intervals for many decades. By asking the same core set of questions each time, comparability is maintained. They are updated to address current social issues by adding or adapting a few new questions on each round. Once deposited in data archives, others can reanalyze the data, compare data between studies, or replicate the research design on different populations, in whole or in part. Reusing these data, however, requires considerable investment in learning how and why each study was conducted, interpreting findings, and determining what components can be reused or compared.

Social media data are large in absolute volume and can yield orders of magnitude—tens, hundreds, thousands, or millions—more observations than are possible from surveys, interviews, or laboratory studies. Tracking people's daily communication activities through diaries and other manual means, for example, yields only a trickle of records. While reliable figures on social media transactions are difficult to obtain, the volumes can be huge. A leading commercial provider of social network data for business analytics claims to offer a stream of three billion activities per day (Gnip 2013b).

When Are Data?

The deluge of data resulting from the digital capture of human activity can be a treasure trove for social science researchers. The surfeit of sources and resources, both contemporary and historical, brings its own set of challenges. Finding that treasure may be like following a pirate's map—a path with trap doors, land mines, misdirection, and false clues. The scholarly quest is to determine what entities can be deemed valid evidence of what phenomena. Often, scholars are torn between collecting the data they want and taking the data they can get. The best research is that which matches the methods to the question most effectively. Clever new designs may lead to powerful findings, but can be difficult to replicate or to explain to those outside the field. New methods also may yield data that are harder to document, share, reuse, and curate than data resulting from traditional research designs.

Sources and Resources   When scholars collect their own data they have more control over their research designs. To achieve greater scale, they often must assemble data from external resources. Many will combine approaches,

conducting interviews or ethnographies complemented by records of social media, economic transactions, census, or other phenomena.

Surveys are usually nomothetic in nature, controlling a few variables in ways that comparisons across large populations can be drawn. Scholars control as many sources of variance as they can, specifying precisely the questions to be asked, the population to be sampled, and the sampling plan. They know what they are asking, of whom, and what they expect to learn from each question. They also control how questions are asked by training interviewers to be consistent in how they approach participants, the exact wording of questions, and in the recording of responses. The research design should balance internal and external validity—the degree to which the study can control variables to isolate phenomena versus the degree to which the study is generalizable to larger and more diverse populations (Shadish, Cook, and Campbell 2002). These method choices influence the ability to trust data sources, determine provenance, employ available analysis tools, and interpret results.

Online, web-based surveys can reach much larger populations than can personal interviews, but consistent sampling is difficult to achieve and response rates tend to be low. Reliability and validity tend be higher in surveys that use human interviewers to talk to respondents in person, but these studies are much more expensive to conduct. When researchers collect their own data, they can sometimes control variance by comparing their sources to the resources of others. Public opinion pollsters usually interview about 1,500 people, and may do so by telephone rather than face-to-face contact. Surveys may be calibrated against known sources such as these, just as instruments in telescopes and in sensor networks are calibrated.

Twitter became popular for technology research because its use is widespread internationally and the system has been available for more than five years, making some longitudinal analyses possible. Twitter allows users to send short messages—up to 140 characters—known as "tweets." The 140 characters can carry more content by means of abbreviations and links; links can be condensed via another layer of URL-shortening services. Tweets carry additional information such as time stamps and geospatial coordinates, if sent from mobile devices with those features enabled. Photos and images can be attached to tweets. Twitter accounts can be named or anonymous. Many accounts belong to public figures, companies, or agencies large and small. The content of tweets knows few bounds: individuals make observations about their day, scholars comment on new findings, companies announce new products, activists rally their supporters, and libraries announce changes in their hours and services. Twitter data are

used to study communication relationships, public health, political events, linguistics, and the stock market, among many other topics (Bollen, Mao, and Zeng 2010; Bruns and Liang 2012; Collins 2011; Eysenbach 2011; Murthy 2011; Ozsoy 2011; Shuai, Pepe, and Bollen 2012; Simonite 2013; Thelwall et al. 2013; Zappavigna 2011).

The array of entities in Twitter streams and individual tweets that can be used as data is their attraction as a resource. However, the difficulty of obtaining valid and reliable data is their weakness. As the business value of Twitter content became more apparent, and as privacy concerns rose, Twitter feeds became less available to researchers. Access to the full "fire hose" of tweets is limited, making sampling difficult. Twitter accounts and activity are not evenly distributed by age, sex, race, country, political orientation, income, or other demographics; thus, any sample of Twitter users or tweets may not be an accurate representation of the population a scholar wishes to study. Yet more threatening to the validity of tweets as indicators of social activity is the evolution in how online services are being used. A growing portion of Twitter accounts consists of social robots used to influence public communication. Followers quickly can flock to accounts in vast numbers, for a price. As few as 35 percent of Twitter followers may be real people, and as much as 10 percent of activity in social networks may be generated by robotic accounts (Furnas and Gaffney 2012; Urbina 2013).

Knowledge Infrastructures   The diversity of data resources and instrumentation in the social sciences make it unlikely that a knowledge infrastructure comparable to that of astronomy would arise. Human behavior does not lend itself to standardized descriptions comparable to celestial objects or the electromagnetic spectrum, nor are projects coordinated on the scale of space telescopes. Knowledge infrastructures in this realm incorporate shared expertise and tools, however. Consistent training in research methods across graduate programs in the social sciences is essential for sharing methods and data. Methods courses typically include instruction in the use of analytical tools such as statistical packages, geospatial mapping software, and qualitative coding systems.

Among the richest data resources available for survey research are the social sciences archives discussed earlier. The tradition of gathering and curating social records long predates Internet research (Boruch 1985). Census records, for example, become more valuable with age, since they are observations of a place and time. The *Domesday Book*, which is the record of the census conducted in Britain in 1085 and 1086 by William the Conqueror, is now considered "Britain's finest treasure" by their National

Archives (2013). In 2011, the book was made openly available online with the ability to search for names and places mentioned. Modern census records and a vast array of other social and institutional records can be used for research.

Archiving social media is a major challenge, as the Library of Congress is learning. In 2010, they agreed to take and to curate the entire Twitter archive. By October 2012, about five hundred million tweets per day were being sent. At present, the library has 133 terabytes of data, which takes two days to search (Alabaster 2013; Allen 2013). They have not yet succeeded in making the data searchable. Making the data interpretable is even harder. The forms, content, and usage of social media are changing much more swiftly than scholars' understanding of how to use them. Finding ways to incorporate new media into knowledge infrastructures is a daunting challenge. These are valuable resources, but in what ways, how, and for whom are open questions.

Metadata   The diversity of data and questions in Internet research undermines the ability to establish common metadata schema that support interoperability and data exchange. For surveys, the metadata standard most widely agreed on is the Data Documentation Initiative (DDI), which is expressed in XML. As noted in chapter 2, DDI is widely adopted by social sciences data archives, to be applied to whatever digital objects the DDI user considers to be data (Data Documentation Initiative 2012). Among its goals is to facilitate the reuse of metadata (Vardigan, Heus, and Thomas 2008). DDI is more flexible and less prescriptive than FITS files in astronomy. However, like most standards, DDI has extensive documentation. Users must invest time in learning the standard and implementing it as a means to structure and document their data. Once done, DDI-documented datasets are readily submitted to data archives or exchanged with collaborators who use the standard.

Because each survey may stand alone, DDI does not standardize variable names, codebooks, and other forms of documentation that are essential to analyze data or to interpret them for later reuse. Naming conventions and documentation practices tend to be locally developed in the social sciences. Even basic conventions such as how to code gender and age in a survey vary between research projects and datasets, including those contributed to data archives. One survey may code male and female respondents as (0,1) respectively, others will use the reverse notation (1,0), and yet others (1,2) or (2,1). Similarly, age might be coded as age in years or as birth year, and might use two or four digits. Thus an entry of "45" in the "age" field means

"subject's age is 45" in one study and "subject born in 1945" in another study. Datasets are of minimal value if they lack variable names, codebooks, and other documentation.

Social media data are particularly complex, given the array of sources and the unstructured and dynamic forms of most communications. More standardization tends to occur with data taken from commercial services, especially if they provide application programming interfaces (APIs). Commercial sources of Twitter data, for example, publish the format in which Twitter streams are provided (Gnip 2013a). These formats, in turn, are based on published standards for data interchange, such as JavaScript Object Notation (JavaScript Object Notation 2013). As with DDI, these formats are but a starting point for how scholars may select units of social media activity for use as data.

Provenance Establishing provenance in Internet studies is difficult because of the adaptive nature of methods, the variety of data resources, the multiple origins of data, and lack of documentation about decisions made in handling them at each stage of processing. The best provenance information is usually found in surveys for which reuse was part of the initial design. The General Social Survey (GSS), which is part of the International Social Survey Programme (ISSP), is among the best known of these. Conducted since 1972, the data, codebooks, and other documentation are publicly available (General Social Survey 2013; International Social Survey Programme 2013). To those well schooled in survey research and in the use of these data, determining how a question was asked in a given year and the distribution of results is fairly straightforward. More sophisticated uses require deeper exploration to determine how the questions on a topic such as political orientation changed from year to year, how variables were coded, how variables were combined into indexes, and so on. See figure 6.1 from the General Social Survey as an example.

Despite the explicit provenance documentation in the General Social Survey, considerable expertise and labor are required to use these data reliably, as is apparent from the cross-references in the table caption. Questions changed slightly from survey to survey, adapting to the circumstances of the time. Aggregations also changed, shifting the footprint of each dataset, analogous to the mapping problems of the COMPLETE Survey discussed in chapter 5. Early decisions on data reduction and cleaning—whether in surveys, economic indicators, or astronomical observations—can have profound influences on the ability to track provenance or to make later interpretations of datasets (Blocker and Meng 2013).

56.   Generally speaking, do you usually think of yourself as a Republican, Democrat, Independent, or what?

[VAR: PARTYID]

RESPONSE	PUNCH	YEAR											COL. 240
		1972-82	1982B	1983-87	1987B	1988-91	1993-96	1998	2000	2002	2004	2006	ALL
Strong Democrat	0	2197	143	1271	151	864	1050	370	414	408	455	700	8023
Not very strong Democrat	1	3482	109	1655	89	1282	1542	597	507	515	504	738	11018
Independent, close to Democrat	2	1768	44	904	51	578	887	349	325	267	281	527	5981
Independent (Neither, No response)	3	1736	30	855	32	721	1031	477	566	528	471	997	7444
Independent, close to Republican	4	1106	8	743	9	571	698	244	261	199	239	327	4405
Not very strong Republican	5	2011	8	1259	15	1170	1318	484	399	449	425	637	8175
Strong Republican	6	1009	8	751	2	662	808	239	285	315	396	495	4970
Other party, refused to say	7	243	0	75	1	44	104	63	48	48	29	65	720
Don't know	8	10	0	0	0	0	0	0	0	0	0	0	10
No answer	9	64	4	29	3	15	64	9	12	38	12	26	274

REMARKS: See Appendix D: Recodes, for original question format and method of recoding. See Appendix N for changes across surveys. If planning to perform trend analysis with this variable, please consult GSS Methodological Report No. 56.

Figure 6.1

General Social Survey table comparing political party affiliation over time. *Credit:* National Opinion Research Center.

Provenance documentation is essential in social media data, and even harder to establish. The origin of a tweet, blog post, or other communication can be treated as an indicator of its value, trustworthiness, or validity. Provenance may include context about senders, receivers, content of the communication, and the chain of relationships associated with each of these elements. Some studies are concerned with relationships and others are concerned with the content of communications. Tweets frequently mention online resources and link to them. These links break quickly and resources disappear, making the provenance of tweets difficult to track (Salaheldeen and Nelson 2013).

Concerns for provenance and interoperability have led to the dissemination of open tools for research with social media (Social Media Research Foundation 2013). These tools, in turn, may depend on technical standards for documenting provenance relationships in the semantic web (Groth and Moreau 2013). However, most social media are not yet based on semantic web technologies, so researchers using these data still may need to construct their own provenance relationships (Barbier et al. 2013). Given the rate of change in social media, tools, methods, and expertise, establishing provenance to a sufficient degree so that datasets can be compared or reused is unlikely anytime soon.

External Influences   Because the social sciences study human behavior, they are the most constrained by external influences of any domain. Many privacy, confidentiality, and property rights problems are intractable. Others can be addressed imaginatively within the constraints of what can be asked or observed, the costs of obtaining data, and the use of property controlled by others (Brady 2004).

Economics and Value   The value in social sciences data, and particularly in Internet research, is often in the packaging. Social surveys can be common-pool resources if available through archives open to most researchers, such as the UK Data Archive. Others may be club goods, if available through archives in which data are available only to members of the consortium, such as ICPSR (Inter-University Consortium for Political and Social Research 2013; UK Data Archive 2014). They can be private goods, if exchanged only between individual scholars, or public goods if openly posted for anyone to use. Survey data can be costly to acquire. Sending trained interviewers into the field, for example, requires a considerable investment of money, time, and expertise. Reusing surveys can save money and expand the array of resources available for comparative and longitudinal research.

Similarly, the economics of social media data depend on sources and packaging. Commercial companies such as Facebook, Twitter, and Google own the largest resources. These resources have huge commercial value and are sold to other companies for use in business analytics. To acquire sets of these data, researchers often must pay for them; thus, they are toll goods. Some data can be obtained by "scraping" websites and other means. Internet activity in chat rooms and other public sources may be available without fee, but other restrictions may apply. Independent of whether fees are paid, social media content is usually subject to license restrictions about what can be done with them and the extent to which they can be released to others.

Surveys, social media, and other observations of Internet activity are analyzed with software tools. Many of these tools are commercial; some are open source. Once ingested into these tools, predefined routines can be run and custom scripts can be applied. Considerable custom programming may be required to analyze social media data. Datasets are usually output from these tools. Subsequent use of these datasets depends on access to analytical software, and often a particular version of that software, plus access to custom scripts or programs. Thus, no matter what license conditions may apply to a dataset, access to the tools may be the constraint that determines how and whether it can be used.

Property Rights   Rights in data and tools such as software are particularly complex in Internet research. When data are available, they may or may not be released with documentation that specifies associated software tools and versions. Customized software is not necessarily released. Software needed to reuse and interpret datasets may be expensive, no longer available, unavailable for the hardware and operating systems in use, or not released in full. When researchers collect information about people, rights in the data may belong to the researcher, to the research subjects, or to information providers. The ability of companies to sell data about their customers and the ability of customers to control data about themselves can vary by country and jurisdiction. The ability and responsibility to release data vary accordingly. Property considerations such as these influence choices for Internet studies and many other kinds of social science research. Scholars often prefer to collect their own data as a means to avoid these problems.

Ethics   Ethical issues in social sciences research, including Internet research, are about respect for the people being studied and the rights of those people, whether individuals or aggregates. Data about people are subject to many rules and regulations about what data can be collected and under what circumstances. In the United States, the basic ethical principles for treatment of human subjects are codified in the Belmont Report as respect for persons, beneficence, and justice (US Department of Health and Human Services 1979). Implementation of these rules varies by field, funding agency, jurisdiction, and other factors. Most countries have similar guidelines for research about human subjects.

A morass of conflicts arises around human subjects data. On the one hand are the proliferating volumes of personal information that people release on social media and through other social and economic transactions. These are subject to debates about privacy and ownership of data. On the other hand are established principles to protect the identity of research subjects because disclosure risks physical, psychological, or economic harm. In between are concerns that rules on informed consent are too rigid, preventing data sharing that could benefit the individuals involved. Biomedical data are on the front lines of these conflicts. Some patients' rights groups want tighter controls to prevent reidentification, and others want to give patients the right to opt in to sharing data about themselves (Field et al. 2009).

Ethics rules on human subjects are most clear for traditional methods such as surveys. Investigators determine what questions to ask, how to ask them, and how to report the data in ways that maintain confidentiality. The ability to release data from surveys often depends upon the ability to

code the data in ways that preserve anonymity. Data archives have procedures and policies to ensure that data are provided and released in forms that maintain confidentiality. However, as more human subjects data becomes available online, the ability to identify people by combining datasets increases. More layers of controls sometimes are necessary, for example, by providing access only to metadata and only to certified investigators. As more personally identifiable data are collected and maintained in digital form, the risks are changing, as are the means to mitigate those risks (National Research Council 2013).

Data that are public, or behavior that is performed in public such as tweeting, blogging, and posting, is not freely available for research under most human subjects guidelines. The Association of Internet Researchers has taken a lead role in this area by laying out principles for gathering data from online activity (Association of Internet Researchers 2012). By using social media services, individuals are not necessarily opting in to become research subjects. Although informed consent is difficult to obtain for such studies, other means exist to protect subjects' rights and privacy. Social media companies have been under intense regulatory scrutiny for their privacy policies, which has led to greater limitations on access to data from Twitter, Facebook, and similar sources (Bruns and Liang 2012; Schroeder 2014).

Questions about the ethical uses of data may arise after findings are published. Scholars are concerned about how their findings are used and potentially misused. The questions become more complex when the accuracy of papers is challenged, whether or not the papers later are retracted. The spreadsheet error in the Reinhart-Rogoff economics paper was found only when a third party attempted to replicate the findings, and the authors had to devote considerable effort to determining what error occurred and at what stage in the processing. Other questions were raised about choices of data, how the data were weighted, and the use of spreadsheets rather than statistical analysis packages (Marcus 2013; Wiesenthal 2013). Another influential writer chided policy makers for relying too heavily on a single statistical result, encouraging them to examine a broader array of data, methods, and theories to inform significant decisions (Summers 2013).

Conducting Internet Surveys and Social Media Research
Individuals and small teams can conduct a small interview study, experiment, online survey, or social media analysis. Surveys on the scale of OxIS require substantial human resources and financial capital. Social media studies require a theoretical and methodological framework, computational and statistical expertise, access to computational resources, and access to data.

The Oxford Internet Survey (OxIS) was first conducted in 2003 as part of an international study of Internet use (World Internet Project 2013). Based upon its initial success, OxIS was conducted again in 2005, 2007, 2009, 2011, and 2013 (Dutton, Blank, and Groselj 2013; Dutton, di Gennaro, and Millwood Hargrave 2005; Dutton, Helsper, and Gerber 2009; Dutton and Blank 2011). The OxIS principal investigator has provided continuity through six rounds of surveys, with other staff changing every round or two. OxIS has accumulated more than a decade of comparative observations on who uses the Internet in Britain, how, with what devices, and how Internet use compares to uses of other communication media. The survey also asks questions about social norms, such as attitudes toward politics and government, which enable comparisons with other studies.

Despite the common use of Twitter content, studies using them vary so greatly in theory and method that they are difficult to compare. Choices of phenomena to study lead to the choices of entities selected. As a result, the same content can yield many kinds of data. Meyer, Schroeder, and Taylor (2013), for example, compared theory, method, and findings of three studies of Twitter in which computer scientists addressed social questions. One study asked whether Twitter is used more as a communication medium or as a social network, with 1.47 billion Twitter relations (Kwak et al. 2010); two studies asked who influences whom (Bakshy et al. 2011; Cha et al. 2010) using, respectively, 1.6 million users and 1.7 billion tweets among 54 million users. Ralph Schroeder (2014), in a further examination of the social aspects of the Kwak et al. paper, notes that the scope of Twitter data on which they relied is no longer available to researchers.

Research Questions   In Internet surveys and social media alike, it is difficult to separate research questions from theory and method. Studies are designed to capture information about particular phenomena, in particular populations, at specific times, perhaps at specific places, and measured in ways that reflect theories and hypotheses.

The OxIS surveys are broad in scope, documenting Internet use in a single country over a long period of time, but designed in part to be used in comparison with similar questions asked by collaborating institutions involved in the World Internet Project. Researchers at the Oxford Internet Institute (OII) design the studies in great detail, carefully crafting each interview item, the sequence of items, the sampling plan, and instructions to interviewers. To provide continuity, a set of core items is repeated in each study, occasionally with refinements to keep up with technological change. Data analysis decisions are embedded in the design of survey research,

determining in advance how each item will be coded to achieve the maximum statistical power. Some survey items provide demographics and descriptive data about the Internet-using population; others are intended to explore theoretical questions about who uses the Internet, when, how, and why.

The ways in which research questions drive the choice of evidence is particularly notable in social media studies. For example, Kwak et al. (2010) are interested in the topology of the network. To ask whether Twitter is a social network or a news medium, they compared the follower-following distribution in the entire Twitter site in mid-2009 to patterns of activity in other human social networks. A contrasting study is that of censorship in Chinese microblogging networks (King, Pan, and Roberts 2013). These investigators, who are well known in quantitative social sciences, combined network analysis with interviews.

Collecting Data   The proportion of research effort and resources devoted to data collection also varies widely. In surveys, the fieldwork to conduct interviews can take weeks or months, followed by a comparable period of data analysis. Each of the six Oxford Internet Surveys reports responses from in-person interviews with more than two thousand individuals (Dutton, Blank, and Groselj 2013). Although designed and analyzed by researchers at the Oxford Internet Institute, interviews are outsourced to a commercial field research service. OII receives anonymized data files coded to their specifications.

In social media studies, determining what data are desired, what data can be collected, and how to collect them can be more labor-intensive than obtaining the dataset. Data collection might be accomplished algorithmically over a period of hours or days. Such forms of data collection are preceded by the development and testing of algorithms and may be followed by long periods of data analysis. Among the attractions of Twitter data are their relatively simple structure, standard format, and broad scope—despite the minimal amount of information conveyed in each tweet. If APIs are used to collect data, records are acquired with a standard syntax for time, date, location, and other variables that can be treated as metadata. However, learning to use the Twitter API is a nontrivial investment, judging by the availability of guidebooks that are more than four hundred pages in length (Makice 2009).

The Kwak et al. (2010) study used the Twitter API to collect profiles of all users during a three-week period. For two months thereafter, they collected profiles of users who mentioned popular topics. An array of ancillary

information about popular topics and related tweets also was collected. The King, Pan, and Roberts (2013) study used a very different set of methods to acquire their data, obtaining 11.3 million posts from more than 1,400 microblogging and other social media services in China. They devised their own algorithms to collect and code data, since their goal was to capture posts quickly before censors could identify and remove them.

Analyzing Data   Quantitative methods yield complex data that are difficult to clean, calibrate, interpret, and curate. Large numbers of small decisions are made in processing and analyzing data. The ability to reuse data later may depend critically on the accuracy of correcting errors and anomalies, the consistency with which these decisions were made, the degree to which they were appropriate for the goals of the study, and the clarity and completeness with which they were documented.

The OII receives datasets from the interviews as a file in STATA, a software package for data analysis and statistics that is widely used in the social sciences (STATA 2013). Per OII's specifications to the company conducting interviews on their behalf, each interview question response in the dataset is coded with specific variable names. OII analysts treat these names as metadata for use in their data analysis. Their first pass is to clean the dataset, looking for anomalies or errors, returning to the survey company with questions as necessary. In the 2011 survey, OII staff went back to the company with questions three times before publishing its initial report. To analyze the data in more depth for subsequent journal articles, the staff contacted the company several more times with finer-grained questions.

Most anomalies could be recognized only by people with an intimate knowledge of the relationships and the trends to expect in the data. Unexpected relationships might represent significant findings or might be caused by inconsistent coding. When young people were exhibiting behaviors more typical of the old and vice versa, OII researchers questioned the coding of the age fields. Although the OII had specified that interviewers ask for the year of birth rather than age, close inspection revealed that some interviewers asked a person's current age and coded accordingly. Thus some persons aged 22 were coded as 22, which meant 1922 as the birth year in the STATA file.

Kwak et al. (2010) frame their research problem in terms of network topology, using the social network data as a test bed. Accordingly, their data collection and analysis focused on link relationships. They collected as much context information about each tweet as was available. These

investigators experimented with different techniques for identifying spam tweets and multiple thresholds for treating them as bad data. Ultimately they removed more than twenty million tweets and almost two million user accounts from their initial dataset. Information flows were measured by the number of followers of each Twitter user and by the degree to which these relationships are reciprocal. The researchers concluded that Twitter is more a mechanism to disseminate information than to build or maintain a network of social relationships.

The King et al. (2013) study, in contrast, is based on theories of censorship and government actions. Their discussions of theory, data collection, coding, and analysis are tightly intertwined, consuming almost half of the paper's narrative. Each coding decision is carefully explained from the perspective of social theories. Some posts were hand-coded to interpret the content and intent of the message. They conclude with a discussion of the social and political implications of the censorship patterns identified.

Publishing Findings   The findings of these Internet studies are published in an array of venues, reflecting differences in theory, method, and audience. Reports of each OxIS survey are widely disseminated to the general public, with release events aimed at policy makers. The overview report, available online and in print, includes summary data on each of the major variables, cross-tabulations, and a summary of data collection methods. Further method details and the interview instrument are published online. Once the report is released, OxIS investigators mine the survey data more closely for theory and policy research. Journal articles are a better venue for addressing fine points of method and interpretation and for making comparisons to other studies (Di Gennaro and Dutton 2007; Dutton and Shepherd 2006). These appear in journals and proceedings in communication research, political science, sociology, and related areas.

Social media studies are reported in every domain, from the social sciences to computer science, science, medicine, the humanities, and the popular press. The two studies discussed here (King, Pan, and Roberts 2013; Kwak et al. 2010) were published in venues well recognized in their respective fields; both are highly cited. However, the theory and method vary so widely that making comparisons across social media studies may be pointless—or lead to groundbreaking insights. Studies such as these draw on common resources for their data, but the entities selected may become much different evidence for different phenomena. These scholarly domains are intersecting in new ways. However, political scientists and computer scientists generally do not search each other's literature for theory or method.

Curating, Sharing, and Reusing Data   The Internet studies cases highlight the trade-offs between conventional and innovative methods. Innovation may yield more powerful findings but lead to greater difficulties in documenting, sharing, and reusing data. Practices for curating, sharing, and reusing data appear to vary from project to project. The size and length of projects, continuity of staff, external requirements for standards or deposit, and expectations of reuse are among the factors that may influence data practices.

The OxIS surveys are designed to document Internet use in Britain in ways that can be compared to counterpart studies of other countries. Although many of the core questions are the same, the sampling plan, questions, and interpretation will differ in important ways. Whereas OxIS covers urban and rural areas of Britain, studies of developing countries are largely urban. Wealthier countries have more broadband connectivity, poorer countries rely more heavily on mobile access, and so on.

Expectations of reuse influence the ability to interpret data later. The first OxIS, in 2003, was launched quickly in response to the availability of funding and collaborators. Although intended as a continuing study, research staff for the initial project created only minimal documentation about the data collection, handling, coding, and analysis. The questionnaire and dataset of the 2003 survey were the basis for the 2005 OxIS study. Over the course of the OxIS studies, staff developed increasingly more elaborate and detailed documentation procedures to support longitudinal comparisons. The cumulative datasets become more valuable with each subsequent round of observations.

The OII releases OxIS data and documents its datasets extensively for reuse. These are separate processes, however. Since their funders do not require the OII to contribute their data to a repository, they release datasets directly to qualified researchers for noncommercial purposes, retaining a two-year embargo period. For example, when the 2011 report was published, the 2009 dataset was released. Instructions for access and licensing conditions are provided on their website. The shared dataset is the version obtained from the company conducting the interviews, available as a STATA file. Online documentation includes names of variables and the interview questions from which they were derived, plus the basic methods and descriptive statistics published in the survey report. While the OxIS staff will release more information about the datasets upon request, few inquiries have been received from the two hundred or so parties who have acquired the dataset. Reusers of the dataset can apply their own transformation and coding on the "raw" STATA dataset. The OxIS team is familiar

with DDI but has not implemented it. The overhead is not justified by their uses of the dataset, nor do they have external requirements to implement the DDI standard.

Findings reported by the OII are documented to the standards of their respective publication venues. Internal documentation developed to maintain reliability, validity, and continuity over the course of the surveys are considered proprietary materials for their own use, similar to the way that many forms of locally developed software are treated. Local information includes details on choices made in transforming variables, combining variables into indexes, validation checks between items, or other data cleaning and analysis done by the investigators. These sets of local documentation support continuity and provide a competitive edge for the team.

The specificity and timeliness of social media studies is their strength but is also their weakness in terms of reuse and replicability. The temporal nature of social media data, combined with the rapid decay of sources to which they refer, limits their value for reuse. In principle, social media studies could be replicated at regular intervals. However, the data collection and analysis methods have less continuity than do survey approaches since they rely on rapidly changing tools. As these media become more mainstream forms of communication, their characteristics change. The emergence of social robots, messages that self-destruct, and other innovations makes comparability difficult. Lacking stable metrics, validating and calibrating these methods is problematic. Both the computer science (Kwak et al. 2010) and political science (King, Pan, and Roberts 2013) papers conclude with remarks about how widely their findings can be applied to other areas. The papers are not explicit about how, where, or whether the datasets are available. Whether or not the datasets and algorithms can be reused or the conditions can be replicated, each study provokes research questions that can be explored in different domains.

Sociotechnical Studies

Sociotechnical studies, the focus of the second case in this chapter, are those that study problems that are part social and part technical. The case study developed in this chapter—research under way since 2002 on data practices and knowledge infrastructures in the Center for Embedded Networked Sensing (CENS)—combines idiographic and nomothetic approaches, applying a wide range of research methods in the process.

Idiographic methods applicable to sociotechnical research include ethnographies, interviews, oral histories, formal and informal observations,

and analyses of records of human activity. Technologies can be studied as human-computer interaction, whether to explore cognition or phenomena associated with specific contexts. They also can be studied as interventions in work practices, as in areas of computer-supported cooperative work. Projects in any of these areas can be small, local, and short term. They also can be large, distributed, and long term.

What unifies idiographic explanations are their focus on close study and interpretation. Interpretivist approaches bridge the social sciences and humanities, where multiple points of view are explored and compared. Although these methods have a long tradition, they remain subject to contentious debates about epistemology, standards of evidence, and philosophies of knowledge. Such debates are acknowledged here, without attempting to address or resolve them (Garfinkel 1967; Geertz 1973; Glaser and Strauss 1967; Latour and Woolgar 1986; Latour 1987; Levi-Strauss 1966; Lofland et al. 2006; Roth and Mehta 2002).

Size Matters

Most sociotechnical studies are small science, exploring problems that are emergent and messy. They can be done with small teams of researchers or even by sole investigators, depending upon the scope of the project. Months or years of labor may be required to transcribe, compile, code, analyze, and interpret qualitative data. Social networks of the research communities, whether through analysis of publications or other sociometric indicators, may provide quantitative comparisons. Similarly, text mining of publications can reveal patterns of research topics and how they change over time. The goal is usually to combine multiple methods. By applying approaches with differing degrees of reliability, internal and external validity, and scale, findings can be triangulated.

When Are Data?

The CENS research reported in this case study builds on a growing body of sociotechnical research on field practices, much of it in the environmental sciences. These are largely qualitative studies using a mix of ethnography, interviews, participant observation, and document analysis (Aronova, Baker, and Oreskes 2010; Cragin et al. 2010; Cragin and Shankar 2006; Jackson and Buyuktur 2014; Jackson et al. 2011; Karasti, Baker, and Halkola 2006; Olson, Zimmerman, and Bos 2008; Zimmerman 2007). As with Internet research, scholars may have a plethora of data resources from which to choose. Sociotechnical researchers must be clever in identifying sources of data and in assessing their credibility, independence, and relationships to other forms of data.

Sources and Resources Despite the deluge of data from and about scientific practice, sociotechnical research on data practices tends to be site-specific. As a consequence, scholars are more likely to collect their own observations than to draw heavily on external sources. However, records produced by research subjects, including their publications, can be essential ancillary sources. The categories of data sources and resources discussed below are common to the research on field practices previously cited but do not constitute a list of all possible sources of evidence.

Field Observations and Ethnography Sociotechnical studies take place in a research site, which may or may not be a single physical location. Multi-sited ethnographies are those that make comparisons across sites (Marcus 1995). Observations also can occur online, using methods of "virtual ethnography" (Hine 2000). Scholars can observe activities from afar and can conduct interviews via video or voice communications. While extending the scale and distance of the research project, the latter approaches forfeit some amount of contextual information.

Any research that involves studying individuals or communities in situ requires permission to do so. This is known as "getting in." Once in, "staying in" the research site can be equally challenging (Lofland et al. 2006). The goal of observational field research in the social sciences is to study phenomena without disturbing the environment more than absolutely necessary. Once in, researchers introduce themselves and their reasons for being there in more detail, then try to be unobtrusive, disturbing the environment as little as possible. Among their concerns are the "Hawthorne effect," named for a famous study at a Western Electric plant in which productivity improved in experimental interventions to increase and to lower light levels, then declined when the study ended. The very fact of being observed changed people's behavior (Landsberger 1958).

One way to minimize these risks to the validity of field observations is to stay long enough that the researcher's presence becomes part of the usual day-to-day environment. This process may require weeks, months, or years on site. Anthropologists may spend their entire careers studying one community, whether particle physicists or urban gangs. Among the ways to become part of the environment is to participate actively and thereby learn more about the site. When studying scientific data practices, for example, researchers might assist in collecting or analyzing the team's data, running errands to acquire needed supplies or equipment, or in physical tasks such as hauling batteries to field positions. Participation in the activities being studied has its own risks. Researchers are concerned about being too subjective, "going native," and speaking for their research subjects rather than about them.

Scholars apply many techniques to gather observations and to turn those observations into data. In field situations, it is often better to participate and to make notes later. Depending upon the circumstances, researchers take notes, capture audio or video recordings, or take photographs, with the permission of those being observed. Audio records may be transcribed, but transcriptions are time-consuming and expensive to produce. Recordings remain valuable for the nuances of voice and visual cues. Notes, transcripts, interviews, and other documents will be coded for themes, events, and other indicators of the phenomena being studied. Coding may be simple and manual or complex and technology assisted. Commercial and open source analytical tools are available to code events, persons, themes, and other categories. Once coded, these tools simplify aggregation and visualization.

Interviews In idiographic sociotechnical research, interviews tend to consist of open-ended questions. An interview of five to ten questions can provoke a conversation of an hour or more. Although the questions are general, they can draw out explanations of activities such as how participants select field sites or technologies and the particular challenges they encounter in curating their data. By asking the same questions of multiple people, researchers can compare practices between individuals, teams, research areas, field sites, and other factors.

Random sampling rarely is feasible in qualitative research. If the site is small, it may be possible to interview every participant. More often, the site population may be too diverse for any set of interview questions to be relevant to all participants. For example, topics of concern to team leaders may be irrelevant to instrument builders, and vice versa. An alternative approach is to stratify the sample by theoretical categories of the phenomena under study, balancing the number and distribution of participants in each category.

Records and Documents Records and other forms of documents associated with a research site can be very useful data resources, but records do not stand alone as forms of evidence, as historians and archivists well know. Records of human activity are understood differently depending upon the time, place, and circumstance of their use (Furner 2004a). Researchers must acquire as much information about the context of each record as possible, ultimately knitting together the many threads of information gathered. Differences in the data logs of two laboratory researchers, for example, may be due as much to their record-keeping habits as to the data they are collecting. Similarly, differences in available biographical information about

people reflect the form and frequency with which they choose to represent themselves.

Sociotechnical researchers use public sources to learn as much about potential sites as they can. Public information about grant funding, personnel, equipment, events, research activities, and publications is often easily found. While details of public documents are usually verified with study participants, advance knowledge about local activities allows researchers to make better use of their time in situ. When observing or interviewing, researchers often gather as many relevant internal documents as participants are willing to share. Records such as laboratory notebooks can provide detailed insights into how research is conducted. Some of these may be sensitive materials that researchers will protect as part of confidentiality agreements.

Building and Evaluating Technologies   Part of studying a research site is examining how people use technologies in their work. Studies of digital libraries, data archives, instructional technologies, collaborative tools, climate models, word processing systems, e-mail, and many other technologies have provided essential insights into how work is accomplished (Blomberg and Karasti 2013; Bowker and Star 1999; Edwards et al. 2007; Edwards 2010; Karasti, Baker, and Halkola 2006; Olson, Zimmerman, and Bos 2008; Ribes and Finholt 2007, 2009).

Some sociotechnical researchers build systems as interventions in community practices. In digital libraries, small systems can be constructed to test better user interface designs, information retrieval capabilities, pedagogical theories, or cognitive processes. The Alexandria Digital Earth Prototype Project, for example, was a joint effort of geographers, computer scientists, psychologists, and information scientists to employ earth science data in teaching undergraduate courses (Borgman et al. 2000; Janee and Frew 2002; Smith and Zheng 2002). The Science Library Catalog was an early graphical user interface to study the cognitive and developmental skills of children aged eight to twelve in searching for science information. The system was built incrementally, making improvements in response to children's abilities. Over the course of several years of research, hypotheses were tested about age differences in ability to manipulate hierarchies, to categorize information, to search alphabetically, to search graphically, and to persevere at information tasks (Borgman et al. 1995; Hirsh 1996).

Knowledge Infrastructures   Sociotechnical research is more a problem domain than a field. Scholars converge on a problem that has social and technical aspects such as data practices, each bringing his or her own theories, methods, and perspectives. They also bring with them the knowledge

infrastructures of their respective fields, to the extent those exist. Similar to Internet research, the shared expertise, methods, and tools are more central to the infrastructure than are shared archives. Data resulting from mixed methods are particularly difficult to organize, share, or curate. Few repositories or common standards exist that can be applied to field notes, websites, audio and video recordings, data files, software, photographs, physical specimens, and myriad other types of data that might be collected in these kinds of studies. Releasing data may mean dispersing them by genre and subject matter, which is counterproductive to goals of replication.

Metadata   Given the mix of data sources, naming conventions and documentation practices tend to be developed locally. Some researchers do construct codebooks to promote consistent coding over long periods of time and among multiple coders. In principle, the DDI can be used to structure qualitative data and metadata (Data Documentation Initiative 2012; Vardigan, Heus, and Thomas 2008). In practice, only large projects with multiple collaborators may have sufficient incentive to invest in formal metadata practices.

Because the array of data sources may vary widely from project to project and site to site, practices for encoding qualitative data are difficult to standardize. The iterative nature of field observations and coding also discourages standardization. In grounded theory, for example, researchers are encouraged to enrich and revise their coding structure as they collect more data and gain more context about the data they do have (Anderson 1994; Glaser and Strauss 1967; Star 1999). Hypotheses are developed through coding and then tested on other parts of the corpus. Iteration improves consistency and thus reliability of the methods. However, as internal validity increases, external validity may decrease.

Provenance   Documenting provenance for mixed methods requires records about each type of data and relationships among those data. For example, suppose that a certain photograph was taken at a particular time and place as part of a particular interview. Some set of documents also was acquired as part of that same interview. The photograph is useful in comparison to other photographs of the same laboratory taken at different times and to photographs of different laboratories taken at about the same time. Each set of interviews, photographs, recordings, documents, and other forms of data may have multiple lineages. Provenance in mixed methods and other forms of interpretive research may involve many threads of relationships.

Replication, per se, is rarely a concern, because idiographic explanation is tightly bound to people, places, times, and situations. Veracity is as much a concern in sociotechnical research as in other areas, however. Scholars acquire information from multiple independent sources when possible. Provenance information may serve the investigator's needs, rather than reuse by others. The scholar may retain data for a lifetime, ensuring that his or her observations can be verified. In other cases, human subjects review panels may require that confidential data about individuals be destroyed at the end of a project. Confidentiality of records and anonymity of individuals in reporting of data are paramount. The more detailed the provenance of any record on an individual participant, the more difficult it may be to release the datasets.

External Influences   Sociotechnical research involves human subjects and therefore is constrained by a comparable array of economic, property, and ethics issues as are other areas of the social sciences. Because idiographic research tends to be based on close working relationships between researchers and their subjects, these kinds of data can be more sensitive than those in Internet surveys or social media studies that capture public traces of activity.

Economics and Value   The packaging of data products influences their value. Data resulting from mixed methods research can be combined in so many ways that it is difficult to assign them to the quadrants of economic goods. Sociotechnical researchers may draw on common-pool resources associated with their research sites, such as data archives or repositories of publications on which participants are authors. Information about research subjects may be public or private, depending upon how obtained. Once obtained, however, sociotechnical data products may become private goods that cannot be shared, lest the identity of subjects be revealed. For example, a list of the home pages of research subjects may consist of links to public information, but the list itself constitutes the participant pool and must be kept confidential.

Property Rights   Sociotechnical researchers gain access to information that they can mine for evidence, but access does not mean they can release or reproduce those materials. For example, laboratory notebooks usually remain the property of the lab and publications remain the property of the copyright holders. Each of the data sources in sociotechnical studies may be encumbered with property rights, whether hardware, software, documents, specimens, or other materials.

Ethics   Sociotechnical research generally falls under human subjects over-sight. However, rules for consent, anonymity, confidentiality, and control of records may vary slightly for each of the methods applied. Risks and liabilities may be somewhat different for ethnographies, field observations, interviews, technology evaluations and other methods. Ethical issues arise in how data are collected, records are protected, and how findings are reported. In publishing research, for example, the degree of detail provided may depend upon the risks to the subjects. Identification practices can vary by journal and community. In most cases, research sites are concealed by obscuring local details and by assigning pseudonyms to people; in others, sites and people are identified by name. Findings are aggregated to large enough groups that individuals cannot readily be identified.

Observations may include long narratives in the participant's own words, biographical details, and video capture of faces. Any research that relies on great detail about individuals and groups involves considerable investment in protecting confidentiality and the rights of human subjects. Among the proposals for new national rules for human subjects protection in the United States is a four-part framework for protecting confidentiality: "safe data, safe places, safe people, and safe outputs" (National Research Council 2013, 50). In the proposed model, studies can be designed to keep data safer before, during, and after data collection. One approach is to collect data at multiple sites, making location harder to discover. Confidential data can be shared via "safe places" by means such as "virtual data enclaves." Data are maintained in a data center where researchers can submit requests and manipulate the data, but cannot transfer them to their local computers. Investigators who release data and those who reuse them can be made "safer people" through training and certification. Outputs can be made safer by categorizing data by degrees of harm. For data with low risk of harm, simple terms-of-use agreements may suffice. For data that are "really radioactive," much more rigid rules on release should apply (National Research Council 2013, 52). Although these rules would apply to all categories of human subjects data, the most profound changes may be to qualitative research. Some of the proposed rule changes are intended to promote more sharing and reuse of data about human subjects.

Conducting Sociotechnical Research in CENS

The Center for Embedded Networked Sensing provided a rare opportunity for long-term study of how collaborations formed and how data were collected, analyzed, managed, and published. As explained in chapter 5, CENS was a National Science Foundation Science and Technology Center

founded in 2002 with an initial five years of funding. The second five-year grant extended CENS to 2012. The lead investigator for the data practices research was one of the founding co-investigators of the Center. The data practices team, which later became part of the statistics and data practices team, was a research unit of CENS. Like many of the other units, the data practices team also had collaborators from universities outside of CENS.

Much of the CENS data practices research was participant observation because the research team was embedded in the Center. Faculty members, students, and staff members on the team participated in formal and informal activities, spending as much time on site as possible. Over the course of CENS existence, the team conducted ethnographies and open-ended interviews; observed pilot testing in lab and field; participated in field deployments ranging from a few hours to several weeks in length; went to countless team meetings; presented findings at colloquia, research reviews, and retreats; and analyzed documents such as lab and field notebooks, data files in many software formats, and publications. Data collection continues as the team studies the legacy of CENS in the several years after its official closing (Borgman et al. 2014).

Participant observers rarely are official members of the organization being studied. In this case, the social sciences research team had responsibilities to participate in the administration of CENS on a par with other research teams. They also contributed to the Center by developing technologies to aid in scientific data collection and management, including an open access repository site for CENS publications.

As with any set of research methods, trade-offs in scale, scope, and objectivity were continual. As full members of CENS, the team had far more access to individuals, research sites, and documentation than would be available to most social scientists. As insiders, the team was aware of the risks of subjectivity. Simply being aware of these risks helped to mitigate them, as did having outside collaborators to ask critical questions about methods and interpretation. The CENS science and technology researchers usually were asked to verify descriptions of their activities prior to publication by the data practices team. They were gracious in correcting and improving research descriptions, and did not attempt to alter the interpretations.

Research Questions The data practices team launched its study of CENS with questions about how individual investigators and research teams were creating data and how those practices varied by team and research domain. By being members of the community from the start, the possibility existed of following data from initial conception through iterations of cleaning,

analysis, reporting, and final disposition. As the context of data scholarship became better understood, questions evolved to address collaborative work of research teams, control and ownership of data, metadata and provenance, sharing and reuse, and educational applications of CENS data. Several doctoral theses, one master's thesis, and many student projects on data practices and collaboration in the Center further expanded the research questions addressed from 2002 onwards.

Research questions and funding iterated throughout the course of the projects. Startup funding from CENS supported the initial framing of data and data practices concerns. Those findings led to grant proposals, and subsequent findings led to more grant proposals and publications. Most of the grants involved multiple collaborators, enabling comparisons between data practices in CENS and other research sites (Borgman, Wallis, and Enyedy 2006, 2007; Borgman, Wallis, and Mayernik 2012; Borgman et al. 2007; Borgman 2006; Edwards et al. 2011; Mandell 2012; Mayernik, Wallis, and Borgman 2007, 2012; Mayernik 2011; Pepe et al. 2007, 2010; Pepe 2010; Shankar 2003; Shilton 2011; Wallis et al. 2008; Wallis, Borgman, and Mayernik 2010; Wallis et al. 2010, 2012; Wallis, Rolando, and Borgman 2013; Wallis 2012; Wallis et al. 2007).

Collecting Data   The sociotechnical researchers' site was wherever CENS researchers were located. CENS teams were based at any of the five participating universities and might have partners at yet more institutions. Data were collected in laboratories and public spaces on campus, and in research sites around the United States and in other parts of the world. Multiple methods were applied concurrently, with a team ranging in size from two to eight members. Some members focused on observing field sites, others on conducting interviews, analyzing documents, building and evaluating technologies, and identifying social networks within CENS. Everyone on the team participated in at least two methods of data collection to ensure cross-training and to facilitate combining data from multiple methods.

Among the data practices team's first activities was to identify metadata standards and formats that were appropriate for the research endeavors of this nascent interdisciplinary community. This proved to be a far more difficult task than anticipated and one that guided early years of research. Because CENS researchers had little experience with metadata standards, direct questions to them about their preferences did not yield useful guidance. The next set of tasks in this endeavor was to identify the range of data that were being collected. Field observation, interviews, and analysis of the Center's publications were essential sources for this information. The team

assessed what data these science and technology researchers acquired, and which of those data they most often retained for analysis and for later reuse.

Once a general set of requirements for metadata were identified, they were matched to existing or emergent standards. Several standards for environmental data and for sensor data were promising candidates. In principle, these metadata standards could be used individually or in combination to describe much of CENS data. Ecological observations being collected by sensors or by hand sampling could be described with a common structure and vocabulary. Similarly, characteristics of sensors could be captured automatically if these XML standards were embedded in the algorithms for data collection.

These metadata standards were then presented to the CENS researchers for consideration, explaining the perceived strengths and weaknesses of each. Although appreciative of the data practices team's efforts to assist them in managing their data, the CENS researchers did not find the available standards to be suited to their needs. Understanding the reasons for this lack of adoption required several more years of close study, as explored further in chapter 8 (Borgman, Wallis, and Enyedy 2006, 2007; Borgman 2006; Pepe et al. 2007; Shankar 2003; Wallis et al. 2006).

As CENS grew from a few dozen to several hundred participants, the need for better provenance records became apparent. The oral culture was breaking down. Research teams would travel to a deployment site, often several hours distance by road, only to find that they were lacking an essential item of equipment or an essential type of expertise that was held by one or a few individuals—typically a graduate student. The data practices team attempted to fill this gap with a simple software tool, dubbed "The CENS Deployment Center" (Mayernik, Wallis, and Borgman 2007). CENS DC, as it was known, was populated with descriptions of sets of equipment and personnel from past deployments—data gathered earlier by the data practices team. The system had template functions that could be used to generate plans for upcoming deployments and to create records of deployments while in the field, such as what worked and did not, what was missing or particularly useful, and so on. These functions were intended to make deployments more efficient and productive, based on findings from observing earlier ones. The system also captured categories of information that these researchers typically included in their publications; thus, the system was intended to help in writing papers about the field research. CENS DC was pilot tested with the teams on whose work practices the design was based, then deployed. It was moderately successful in serving these functions, as a few teams integrated the system into their activities (Mayernik 2011; Wallis 2012).

Analyzing Data   Like the OxIS surveys, the CENS data practices research began as a small endeavor. As the team grew in size and the possibilities for larger and longer studies became apparent, data analysis became more formal. Interviews were audio recorded and professionally transcribed. Codebooks were developed to maintain consistency over the course of multiple surveys and many field observations. NVivo, a commercial data analysis software package for qualitative and mixed-methods research, was employed to code people, events, themes, and other categories in notes and transcripts (NVivo 10 2013). In each round of data collection, two graduate students would code some of the same interviews independently. They then compared and discussed their coding, focusing on reconciling differences in interpretation. This process was repeated until adequate inter-coder reliability was achieved. Codebooks were annotated to explain interpretations, contributing to consistency of interpretations. The challenge was to build and test hypotheses with these data, while remaining open to unanticipated findings.

Interview transcripts were more amenable to assessing inter-coder reliability than were other kinds of data. Although multiple team members conducted interviews, they were working from a common set of questions to ask CENS researchers. When working in the field, each team member took extensive notes on his or her observations. These notes had to be coded by the observer who took them. If coded quickly and regularly, observers could fill in gaps in their notes or determine if something missed might be acquired through other means. Observers were encouraged to take copious notes and to take photos when possible. Note-taking skills increased with experience. However, individuals vary considerably in their attention to detail and knowledge about what they are observing. The graduate student with a background in biology gathered great detail on the species being studied, whereas the graduate student with a degree in engineering was more attentive to the instrumentation being deployed. Having multiple observers in the field with complementary backgrounds expanded the breadth of information that could be acquired about the Center's data practices.

Data coded with NVivo could be aggregated by themes, events, and various other categories. Subsets of data could be extracted, enabling comparisons across multiple studies. The more data collected, the richer the comparisons and interpretations that could be made. NVivo files, summary memos, photos, and other records became the input to data practices team discussions that framed the publications, presentations, and posters.

Publishing Findings   The first stage of sharing findings from the data practices research often was within CENS itself. The Center held poster sessions and demonstrations as part of regular public events. These events included annual site visits by the National Science Foundation, annual research reviews open to the public, and research retreats. The data practices team made posters from its own work and participated in posters with other CENS teams. Visitors might mingle among thirty to eighty posters in these events, providing ample opportunity for discussion and feedback. The Center also held weekly lunchtime seminars to report on current research. The data practices team attended these events regularly and presented findings periodically.

Findings of the CENS data practices research were published in an array of venues to reach multiple audiences. Since the core funding of the Center was from computer science, many papers were submitted to ACM conferences. These are prestigious publication venues with low acceptance rates. Presenting at ACM conferences was an important opportunity to present sociotechnical findings to a technical audience. Other publications were aimed at information studies and social studies of science and technology communities. A few publications were targeted at the education community, particularly in the reuse of data for learning applications. In addition to publications, many talks resulted from this body of research, reaching an even broader array of audiences in the sciences, social sciences, technology, and humanities.

The identity of CENS as a research center is revealed in these publications but individual participants are not named. When quoting individuals, they are labeled by category (e.g., scientist, technology researcher) or assigned a pseudonym. The Center's identity is revealed for several reasons. One reason is that the specifics of the embedded network sensing research are essential to explaining their data practices; thus, the site is too distinctive to obscure easily. To anonymize the Center, so much context would be removed to render the findings meaningless. Another reason is to promote the work of CENS since the data practices team was part of that community. The National Science Foundation recognized the Center's social sciences contribution in addition to its scientific and technical accomplishments. By making CENS an exemplar site for research about data practices, other centers were encouraged to host social science studies. However, because the research site was named, even more care was required to aggregate findings at a level that obscured the identity of individuals.

Curating, Sharing, and Reusing Data   The data from the data practices team, consisting of audio recordings, transcripts, field notes, NVivo files, and an array of public and private records, are stored securely under the control of the investigators and team. Following Institutional Review Board (IRB) guidelines, paper records and other documents are kept in locked file cabinets in locked offices. Digital records are stored on secure servers. Whereas IRBs sometimes require data to be destroyed at the end of projects, this team renews IRB approvals annually, continuing to analyze data and compare them with subsequently collected data. Under current guidelines, project data can no longer be analyzed once the IRB approval lapses.

For the data practices grants that involved multiple universities, each investigator had to obtain IRB approval for the data his or her team was collecting. Although university policies varied in the specifics, the ability to share data between universities was limited. Generally speaking, investigators could share coded and anonymized data across universities, but not transcripts and other records containing personally identifiable information about subjects. Rather than pooling the data of collaborators, each participating university team managed its own data in isolation. As new graduate students and postdoctoral fellows joined each team, they had to be certified and added to the IRB protocol for datasets they would use.

To date, the funding agencies have not required that these data be released, nor have investigators outside the group of collaborators requested access to them. They are a trove of valuable resources to the team and are being used for comparisons to data practices studies of other fields. When the funding ends and if the IRB approvals are allowed to lapse, reusing them may be difficult, even by the investigators. Research subjects signed consent forms to participate in these studies. Those consent forms, which are several pages long and subject to close scrutiny by the IRB, promise confidentiality of personally identifiable data in the analysis and reporting of findings in return for participating in the studies.

In sum, these data are being curated for the continuing use of the research team. They cannot be released to anyone not named on the approved IRB protocol. It is possible that some parts of the data might be releasable in the future, such as records obtained from public sites. Documents obtained as part of interviews fall under the confidentiality agreements in the consent forms, unless specifically designated otherwise. Some field notes might remain useful to others even if stripped of personal names and other identifying information. Releasing audio recordings, interview transcripts, records created by research subjects, or other information that is tightly

coupled to personal identity is unlikely, due to ethical concerns and the terms of consent under which those data were obtained. Taken as a whole, the dataset has multifaceted information about the activities of CENS over its ten years of operation, along with continuing studies of its legacy. Taken piecemeal, context and provenance can never be reconstructed.

Conclusion

Internet research and sociotechnical studies are exemplar topics of the social sciences. Both apply innovative methods, ask questions about human behavior, and attract scholars from multiple fields. Their knowledge infrastructures are characterized more by shared knowledge than by shared technical infrastructures or information resources. Agreements on research methods, as embodied in academic courses and textbooks, form a substrate of shared expertise in the social sciences. These methods, in turn, employ common sets of technical tools, such as software for data analysis and computational modeling.

Survey research, whether about Internet use or any other topic of human behavior, draws on a long tradition of methodological expertise. These practices balance the richness of information that can be collected about people, precision control of variance, and confidentiality of data. Evidence is reported with detailed explanations of sampling plans, populations, questions asked, distribution of answers, and inferences about findings, all while ensuring the anonymity of the participants. Data from studies that achieve appropriate levels of quality assurance may be contributed to data archives or released directly by investigators.

Social media studies, such as the microblogging examples presented here, also may draw on long traditions of research methods such as those for social network analysis. Scholars from other fields bring their own traditions, such as network topology methods of computer scientists. These contrasting approaches to the use of common data resources may contribute to the transfer of expertise between fields. Alternatively, the approaches may have so little in common as to render them opaque to scholars in other fields. What is most striking about the comparison are the differences in what each scholar may deem to be data. A link between Twitter accounts, for example, may be treated as evidence of influence, graph structure, illicit communication, a personal relationship, or other phenomena. The content of a tweet or other message can be treated as evidence of a multitude of phenomena, depending on the research question and method. Determining

which messages were intentional exchanges between humans, which were exchanges between humans and social robots, which were robotic exchanges—and when these categories matter—requires sociological and technological expertise about the environment under study.

Sociotechnical research, as embodied in the decade-long studies of the Center for Embedded Networked Sensing, applies a range of complementary research methods to a problem. In this case, the problem was to understand the data practices of the Center's many participants and to develop tools and services to support those practices. Research questions and methods evolved as the data practices were better understood, as technologies were designed and tested, and as the research of CENS matured. The knowledge infrastructure of CENS incorporated shared expertise in the science and technology of embedded sensor networks, shared collaborative space, and other forms of administrative and collegial support. Investment in shared information resources was minimal, however, since technologies formed the common ground rather than data. The team that conducted the sociotechnical studies maintains its own internal repository of data. These data remain useful for comparison to other research environments and for continuing study of the legacy of CENS. However, their richness and the diversity of their genres make them difficult to share. The more comprehensive the information about individuals and groups, the less amenable they are to anonymization. Even if these challenges could be overcome, finding a common home for audio recordings, transcripts, photographs, field notes, coded interviews, publications, posters, an innumerable array of documents in paper and digital form acquired from research subjects, and assorted technological objects is unlikely, and dispersing them by form or subject matter would make them less valuable.

In reference to the provocations in chapter 1, these social science cases exhibit the variety of ways in which the same entity could be treated as data, the variety of research methods that can be applied to a common data source, and the variety of knowledge infrastructures that arise to support these kinds of scholarly work. In reference to the first provocation, ownership and control of data differ across these cases. The Oxford Internet Institute collected the OxIS survey data and retains control of them. The survey cannot be reproduced, as these are observations at specific times and places, but it can be repeated with new samples at later times. The OxIS data are released after a two-year embargo, but are not contributed to social science repositories. The microblogging studies are less amenable to reproducibility or to sharing. They also are observations of times and places,

some from public and some from proprietary sources. The sociotechnical studies of CENS are not replicable, but the protocols have been applied to other research sites at other times for the purposes of comparison. Those data remain under the control of the investigators, with sharing limited by human subjects regulations.

Transferability, the second provocation, also plays out differently across these case studies. While agreements on research methods provide common ground across the social sciences, specific data handling techniques— cleaning, interpolating missing values, removing outliers, and so on—vary sufficiently that analysis and interpretation of datasets diverges. Shifts in the functions of scholarly communication, as framed in the third and fourth provocations, appear more gradual than radical in these exemplar cases in the social sciences. These scholars remain far more concerned with publishing their findings than with releasing their data. They draw on a greater volume and variety of data sources than in the past, intersecting with research questions addressed in the sciences, technology, and humanities. Despite the common data sources across these domains, differences in methods, questions, and representations may limit the discovery and reuse of resulting datasets.

These case studies also exemplify the shift in expertise necessary for social science research, the fifth provocation. The mix of qualitative and quantitative skills employed varies by study. Some degree of software expertise is necessary in each of these areas, whether developing new tools, writing scripts within existing tools, or exploiting complex statistical routines. The ability to reuse these data is constrained by access to those tools, scripts, and routines.

Lastly, relatively little new investment in knowledge infrastructure aimed at data sharing is being made in domains covered here. The strongest support exists for the discovery and curation of survey data, and that infrastructure is far from comprehensive. Social media is the fastest-moving research front addressed. The objects of study and the tools to study them evolve too quickly for effective sharing. Combining data from multiple studies or conducting meta-analyses requires substantial investment in data integration. The methods and tools for sociotechnical studies are more stable, but confidentiality concerns limit the release of these forms of qualitative data. In all the case examples, datasets tend to remain in researchers' control, whether due to preference, lack of alternatives, intractable problems of confidentiality, or combinations of these. As a result, these social science scholars have few incentives to invest in metadata or classification schema that

would facilitate the transfer of their data to other domains. A longer view of knowledge infrastructure requirements for the social sciences will need to address the acquisition and management of data resources within these disciplines, between these and other scholarly domains, and between public and private resources. Given the diffuse data sources, fuzzy boundaries between fields, political sensitivity of topics, and the array of stakeholders, knowledge infrastructure investments in the social sciences will be contentious for the foreseeable future.

7   Data Scholarship in the Humanities

Introduction

The humanities are unified by their study of human culture and the human record, drawing on all imaginable sources of evidence. They are divided in most other respects, including the scope of the discipline. Any lumping of disciplines or domains as "the humanities" is problematic. History and archeology, for example, are sometimes considered part of the humanities and sometimes part of the social sciences. The arts may be part of the humanities, may stand alone, or be conjoined with programs in theater, architecture, or design. Academic programs under the humanities umbrella may include departments large and small, from classics to languages and literature to Near Eastern cultures. Within any of these departments may reside scholars with advanced degrees from yet other fields. UCLA, for example, has more than 150 departments and programs of study at the undergraduate and graduate levels, and their faculty members may have multiple affiliations. The digital humanities program lists about thirty-five affiliated faculty members, whose home departments span the humanities, social sciences, sciences, and professional schools.

For the purposes of discussion here, the humanities are those fields that study human culture and the human record. The scope includes scholars who self-identify as being part of the humanities no matter what their official affiliation may be. Humanities scholars are clever in finding new sources of evidence, whether material or digital, static or dynamic, on the ground or under the ground, very old or very new. As more parts of the world became open to travel, the geographic scope of their inquiries expanded. As more material objects began to be represented in digital form—texts, images, audio, and so on—the genres of available evidence also expanded. The humanities are experiencing as much of a data deluge as other fields but are less likely to call it by that name. To cope with the scale of content

available to them, scholars are borrowing technologies and methods from related fields and developing some of their own. In the process, they are beginning to think in terms of data, metadata, standards, interoperability, and sustainability. Borrowing techniques usually requires borrowing concepts. They too need ways to represent information in computationally tractable forms.

Data, as defined in chapter 2, refers to entities used as evidence of phenomena for the purposes of research or scholarship. *Data scholarship,* as defined in chapter 3, is the set of relationships between data and scholarship. This set of relationships in the humanities is particularly complex and not always a comfortable framework for the scholars involved. Exploring the ways in which these scholars identify sources of evidence they can use as data, and coping with those data, sheds light on the challenges they face and the components of knowledge infrastructures that they may need.

Research Methods and Data Practices
Humanities scholars observe human activity via products left behind, whether physical artifacts, images, texts, or digital objects. Their methods tend toward idiographic explanation, closely exploring individual texts, objects, communities, and cultures. As they work with larger amounts of data, nomothetic explanation may become more feasible, enabling the same questions to be explored across more contexts.

The digital humanities can be dated to 1949, when IBM partnered with Roberto Busa, a Jesuit priest, to create a concordance of the complete works of St. Thomas Aquinas. A thirty-year text-digitization project, it is now available online. Tools, services, and infrastructure for scholarship in the humanities continue to expand, along with the volume and variety of digital content available. Technologies are now so embedded in research practice that some scholars consider "digital humanities" to be a tautology. To others, the term remains useful to signify the expanding array of research methods and sources of evidence (Alarcón 2000; Borgman 2007, 2009; Burdick et al. 2012; Wouters et al. 2012).

Humanities scholars rely heavily on unique materials—letters, memos, treaties, photographs, and so on—that exist only in physical form. Many of the sources are housed in archives at universities, museums, government agencies, and public and private institutions. Archivists organize these materials to provide context, usually trying to maintain as much of the original order as possible. Finding aids, which may be available in print or online, provide hierarchical access to collections, boxes of materials, and individual items. Researchers must visit the archive, identify the boxes of

interest, and request some small number of boxes. Within the boxes, materials may be organized within folders. Users of archives often are allowed to view only one folder at a time to ensure that the materials remain in the order in which they are arranged. Archives vary widely in their polices about the use of personal technologies. A few allow users to bring their own digital scanners. Many allow them to take photographs of items with digital cameras and to take notes on laptop computers. In many archives, however, pencil and paper remain the only technologies permitted.

Making comparisons between research objects is essential for many forms of humanistic inquiry. Objects being compared may be widely dispersed, whether in one archive or in public places around the world; hence, comparisons often must be based on representations of those objects. Scholars represent objects by many means, such as making notes about their features, taking photographs, or making sketches. They also draw on others' representations. If the original object no longer exists or cannot be observed directly, scholars may be entirely dependent on representations as sources of evidence. Digitization of objects and their representations has transformed research methods that rely on such comparisons. Texts, images, sounds, and other entities—or portions thereof—can be compared in ways never before possible, whether side by side on a screen or through computational modeling.

Some humanities scholars collect observations such as recording spoken language or excavating archeological sites. In these cases, representations of observations may become irreplaceable forms of evidence. Recordings of rare or lost languages are resources for studying linguistics and culture. Excavations disturb the earth in ways that the sites never can be restored to their prior form. Artifacts are unearthed from their resting places, and may be removed for conservation and security. Many kinds of documentation are captured, such as photographs, 3D digital scans, weights, detailed notes, and precise locations. Less destructive means—for example, imaging technologies such as light ranging and detection, known as LIDAR—also can be used to capture observations about sites.

Humanities scholars, often in partnership with scholars from other domains, are combining many data sources and methods to ask new questions. Some are using geographic information systems to map cultural heritage sites. Others are modeling social activities in cities and places over periods of decades and centuries. Yet others are experimenting with digital forms of text, poetry, and publishing (Burdick et al. 2012; Fitzpatrick 2011; Frischer et al. 2002; Presner 2010). Research methods in the humanities are as fluid as are their sources of data. Although scholars trained in the

humanities learn methods specific to their domains, they do not have the common substrate of research methods courses and practices that span the social sciences. Often their expertise is developed through long mentorships and independent research. The average time to the doctorate in the humanities is much longer than in most sciences and social sciences fields.

Humanities Cases

The case studies of data scholarship in the humanities explore the creation and use of digital collections and their relationship to the study of physical artifacts. These were selected to illustrate the transition from material to digital objects as sources of evidence, how data scholarship is changing, and how, when, and why scholars choose particular entities for use as data. The first case study spans two areas of classical art and archeology. One exemplar is the CLAROS project at the University of Oxford, a multidisciplinary collaboration to create a technology test bed for cultural heritage sites, monuments, and objects. The second exemplar focuses on the archaeo-metallurgical analysis of the Pisa Griffin, a historic bronze sculpture. In the latter example, scholars with complementary expertise collaborate to write "biographies of artifacts" such as the Griffin.

The second case is in Buddhist studies, exploring how a lone scholar in Chinese Buddhist philology uses digital collections in combination with physical texts and artifacts. The digitization of texts, some dating to the third century CE, have transformed the conduct of his research.

Classical Art and Archaeology

Classical art and archeology are intersecting areas of research. Together they draw on methods, theories, and expertise from the humanities, social sciences, and sciences. Artifacts unearthed in archeological excavations may be studied for their cultural and artistic value (Wiseman 1964; Yoffee and Fowles 2011). Social scientists also study these objects for what they reveal about the societies that created and used them (Smith et al. 2012). Archaeo-metallurgists and materials scientists study these objects to identify metals, ores, ceramics, dyes, and other physical characteristics that can be used to date them and to trace their origins (Northover and Northover 2012). Zooarcheologists study animal remains and the use of animals in societies, bringing the life sciences to the study of ancient objects (Crabtree 1990).

Archaeological excavations are major sources of scholarly evidence. The forms of data that excavations yield vary by form of inquiry, professional

practices, and when collected. In the nineteenth-century heyday of archeology when the Roman Forum and other major sites first were excavated, objects often were dug from sites and then piled together for examination. Only selected items were cataloged; many may have been looted. No complete inventory was conducted, nor were the original positions of artifacts carefully recorded. Well into the twentieth century, information about the location of artifacts was minimally documented. Archivists continue to receive boxes of unlabeled photographs, slides, and other forms of evidence about important sites such as Easter Island. In current best practice, the location of each object is meticulously recorded, as are many details on the circumstances of the excavation. Recording absolute and relative positions of each item found is now considered essential to understanding the context of individual objects. When cultural heritage artifacts are found serendipitously, detailed documentation on the "find spot" is less likely. Bronze age swords, for example, continue to be found by farmers plowing their fields or cutting peat bogs (Faoláin and Northover 1998).

Many of the world's great museum collections were assembled with little regard for the rights of countries to control their cultural heritage. Until the latter twentieth century, archeologists and adventurers could return home with loads of cultural heritage artifacts. When these cultural artifacts gained in monetary value as art and collectable objects, illicit trade grew. In 1970, UNESCO adopted a convention to control the trade of cultural property. Legal specifics vary by country and apply differently to art objects, manuscripts, specimens, human remains, and so on (UNESCO 1970, 2013). Scholars now return home with digital records, notebooks, photographs, laser images, and other representations of their observations. These are the data from which they write their research publications and plan their next investigations.

Size Matters
Although they represent mature fields with centuries of scholarship, most humanities research projects still involve only one or a few investigators. Their data sources can be big in volume, very big in variety, but usually are small in terms of velocity. Many scholars work with small subsets of objects and records, spending months or years on close inspection and on drawing together disparate sources of evidence. Records from individual excavations may be dozens or thousands in number. Digital collections can contain many millions of records. High-resolution scanning of artifacts in three dimensions can yield digital files gigabytes and terabytes in size.

When Are Data?

The humanities are in a position similar to the social sciences in determining what or when something might be used as data. Research areas that long were data-poor, in Sawyer's (2008) terms, now are drowning. Instead of coveting a single rare manuscript, scholars may have access to vast collections of digitized manuscripts. Choosing what to use as evidence, and of what phenomena, now may be harder rather than easier. Scholars gain competitive advantage by identifying entities that could be used as data. Those entities might be obscure or be hiding in plain sight. Objects used as data in other fields may be repurposed for humanistic study, becoming new forms of data. To astronomers, Galileo's observations of Jupiter's moons are evidence of celestial objects. To historians of science, religion, or politics, those observations may be evidence about the culture of the time.

Several characteristics of the humanities distinguish them from the sciences and social sciences with respect to data scholarship. One is their focus on interpretation and reinterpretation. The Higg's boson can be discovered only once, but Shakespeare's Hamlet can be reinterpreted repeatedly. A second characteristic is the vast variety of data sources and the expertise required to interpret them. For many kinds of humanistic inquiry, scholars must speak or read multiple languages, be familiar with multiple scripts and character sets, and be versed in the cultures of many parts of the world. Only by knowing the context of each object being studied can they be compared. As a result of these two qualities, data sources can be reused repeatedly, often becoming more valuable as they cumulate over time. Conversely, because the same objects can be represented and interpreted in so many ways, it is difficult to apply classification mechanisms that transcend the array of possible uses of collections.

Sources and Resources   Because almost anything can be used as evidence of human activity, it is extremely difficult to set boundaries on what are and are not potential sources of data for humanities scholarship. Museums, libraries, and archives navigate those boundaries in determining what to collect. The roles of these three "memory institutions" overlap substantially, especially with regard to digital objects. Each institution will represent and arrange its objects according to its mission. Libraries are the most consistent in representation and arrangement because they largely collect published materials that exist in many copies. While not identical around the world, cataloging and classification mechanisms are sufficiently harmonized that the same book is similarly described in any research library that owns a

copy. The same is not true for museums and archives, however. Two similar objects, such as sculptures of a dancer by the same artist, will be treated differently when collected by a museum of fine art, a museum of dance, an archival collection of materials by the artist, or a cultural museum about the artist's country or region. Digitized images of the sculpture could be represented and arranged in yet more ways in other collections. Whether something becomes a source or resource for data in the humanities may depend on its form, genre, origin, or degree of transformation from its original state.

Physical versus Digital Objects   Scholars who study material objects—paper, papyri, bindings, notations, inks, imagery, technique, structure—need to observe, handle, or test the artifacts. However, few libraries, archives, or museums allow scholars to touch objects that are rare, precious, or fragile. If touching is allowed, then it may be only briefly and in certain ways. Rare books often are left open to one page at a time to limit light exposure. Testing of paper, metals, and other materials requires the cooperation of the owners of the objects.

For scholars studying the content of documents, digital representations may be as good or better than the original. Digital images can be compared side by side and closely examined—browsed, compared, printed, and annotated. Page sections and images can be magnified, providing microscopic analytical techniques. Text and images also can be enhanced, revealing details not visible to the naked eye.

Digital versus Digitized   Digital collections may consist of content that was "born digital," such as books and journal articles that were written on computers, and digitized records, which are representations of documents, images, sound recordings, or other objects that originated in physical or analog form. The majority of humanities collections consist of digitized representations of physical and analog materials. As more content is born digital, the balance is expected to shift.

Surrogates versus Full Content   Until the 1980s advances in automation, scholars relied on paper catalogs and on postal correspondence to inquire about the locations of books, records, and artifacts. As digital surrogates, whether bibliographic records, thumbnail-sized images, audio or video clips, or other representations of objects, became available online, scholars could identify easily what existed and where, saving substantial travel time and human resources. Although online catalogs and other finding aids

offer speed, scale, and convenience for searching and retrieval, surrogate collections rarely lead to fundamental changes in scholarly practice.

Digitizing full content was the next transformation in humanities research, enabling materials to be disseminated online. Depending upon how materials are digitized, they can be mined, combined, modeled, and exploited as data resources. Massive numbers of books have been scanned and posted online, as have historical documents, images, and sound and video recordings. The growing availability of old or obscure materials is a boon for readers in countries and institutions without access to large research library collections, thus democratizing scholarship in unexpected ways.

Surrogates often remain necessary to describe, locate, retrieve, and authenticate digital content. The use of nontextual content depends most heavily on information in surrogate records. An image or sound clip, for example, rarely is valuable for research purposes without evidence of the artist, date, origin, ownership, and other contextual information.

Static Images versus Searchable Representations   The next transformation in humanities research practices occurred when searchable representations of text, images, audio, and video became widely available. Exploitation of digital content is a matter of degree, ranging from static images to semantically enriched objects. These distinctions are most easily explained with examples of text conversion. The earliest method to represent documents by mechanical means was to capture as perfect a visual representation of each page as the available technology allowed. Photographs and digital images of pages are more readily disseminated than paper copies but have little more functionality than the printed book. Users can only locate pages of interest by consulting the table of contents (if one exists) or by browsing. Large portions of scholarly materials remain available online only as page images, scanned into early versions of PDF (portable document format) or other formats, some of which are proprietary.

To be searchable, individual letters and words in texts must be identifiable. Text can be converted through manual typing or by optical character recognition (OCR) technology. OCR techniques date to early-twentieth-century telegraphic systems. Although these technologies are much improved, they remain most effective with typed text in modern fonts on clean white paper or backgrounds. Historic books and records often fail to meet those criteria, however. Converting text that was printed in centuries past remains a great technical challenge and an active area of research in lexicography and computer science.

The adoption of Unicode in 1992, a standard that now is incorporated into all major operating systems, displays, and printing technologies, ensures that born-digital text in modern languages and character sets is searchable. For text conversion, modern OCR technologies can recognize characters and convert them to Unicode if mappings exist (Unicode, Inc. 2013; ISO 10646 2013). Mass digitization of texts such as the Million Books Project and Google Books became feasible with Unicode and OCR, although whether conversion is sufficiently accurate for scholarship remains a matter of some debate (Duguid 2007; Nunberg 2009, 2010).

Scanned text not easily converted by OCR methods is being interpreted through crowdsourcing. CAPTCHA (Completely Automated Public Turing test to tell Computers and Humans Apart) is a clever technique used in website security. People requesting new accounts, passwords, or other privileges are asked to transcribe a string of letters presented as a puzzle. About two hundred million CAPTCHA puzzles are solved per day, representing about 150,000 hours of human labor. ReCAPTCHA creates the puzzles from text for which OCR conversion failed. More than forty thousand websites are using ReCAPTCHA to transcribe old text. Thus those annoying puzzles are helping to achieve greater accuracy in text transcription, putting human labor to effective use (von Ahn et al. 2008; reCAPTCHA 2013).

Text that long predates Gutenberg is yet more difficult to interpret, requiring human intervention. Scholars are employing crowdsourcing for assistance in converting large caches of rare material. Ancient Lives, for example, is a Zooniverse project to transcribe text on papyri that was written in Egypt more than a thousand years ago. Volunteers are presented images of papyri and asked to identify individual characters by marking their center and matching them to a table of known characters. Identifying even a few characters or other features of a papyrus such as its dimensions aids the scholarly project in determining the content of the document (Ancient Lives 2013).

Searchable Strings versus Enhanced Content   A yet more radical transformation of research methods becomes possible when materials are enhanced for fuller exploitation. The humanities pioneered the structured representation of digital documents through efforts such as the Text Encoding Initiative (TEI) in the mid-1980s. Text digitization projects continue to follow TEI standards and associated tools with variations for Latin and Greek, music, and other types of materials (Text Encoding Initiative 2013).

In the humanities and sciences alike, the ability to treat an entire corpus of texts as digital objects opens up new options for inquiry. Searchable

strings of letters, spaces, and punctuation already are more useful than page images. When semantic information about words, phrases, headings, chapters, page breaks, personal names, places, quotations, and other units is represented, far richer analysis is possible. In plain text, for example, words such as *Paris* and *brown* can be identified, whereas in semantically encoded text, uses of *Paris* as the city, the Greek god, and the form of plaster can be distinguished, as can *brown* as a color or as a surname. Similarly, images, audio, and video can be enriched with tags and encoding.

Once characters in text, notes in music, and other sequences can be treated as digital objects, the computational possibilities expand. BLAST, the basic local alignment search tool mentioned in chapter 5 for matching sequences of DNA, turns out to be valuable in the humanities. It is being used to identify similar historical texts, whether in eighteenth-century French or in papyri, similar sound strings in music collections, and many other forms of content (Altschul et al. 1990; Ancient Lives 2013; Olsen, Horton, and Roe 2011).

Images also can be enhanced with laser and x-ray imaging techniques. Palimpsests, which are documents that have been overwritten, are notoriously difficult to decipher. With imaging technologies, layers of writing can be separated and worn carvings in stone and wood can be enhanced and distinguished. Ancient materials have become a frontier in scientific areas such as optics (Knox 2008; Miller 2007; Salerno, Tonazzini, and Bedini 2007).

Knowledge Infrastructures   The array of collections available to humanities scholars is vast, considering the scope of the world's museums, archives, libraries, monuments, excavations, cultural heritage sites, and materials available outside of institutional contexts. Similarly, they have a long and rich history of methodological expertise. Bringing all these resources and expertise together into a knowledge infrastructure to support scholarship is a difficult challenge, however. The diversity of resources, their wide distribution, and the multiplicity of access arrangements are the strengths and the weaknesses of the humanities. Even when constraining the discussion to scholarship in classical art and archeology, the boundaries of collections and expertise are unclear.

Knowledge infrastructure concerns for the humanities in general, and classical art and archeology in particular, differ from the cases in the sciences and social sciences in important ways. One is the distinction between research collections and general public collections. Grant funding for research collections comparable to those in the sciences is minimal. Scientific

research collections that are successful and attract a larger community may become resource collections and eventually reference collections, such as the Protein Databank or the Sloan Digital Sky Survey (National Science Board 2005). Rarely do research collections in the humanities make this transition. General public collections, such as those of museums, archives, and libraries, are of great value for scholarly research. However, each institution has its own mission, community, and governing body. Most serve a broad public, of which scholars are only a part. Knitting together the collections and services of these disparate entities into a common infrastructure is unlikely. Some interoperability can be achieved with agreements on standards and classification mechanisms, but multiple overlays are needed to serve the disparate array of potential users.

The second distinction, which is largely a consequence of the first, is that little direct investment is made in infrastructure for the humanities compared to the sciences and social sciences. Far less funding is available for their research, resulting in grants that are smaller and shorter in duration. The diversity of collections, questions, and methods contributes to difficulties in developing common tools, making sustainability a continual challenge (Borgman 2009; Burdick et al. 2012; Zorich 2008). Academic departments in the humanities also tend to have less technical support and scholars with less technical expertise. The exceptions are many, with pockets of deep technical expertise in some universities and a growing number of digital humanities centers that provide infrastructure support, at least on a local basis (Parry 2014).

Whereas knowledge sharing in the sciences often is coupled with shared collections, online communities and collections tend to be more independent in the humanities. Scholars do share expertise and build communities through social networks such as H-Net (Humanities and Social Sciences Online). These sites support discussions, reviews, job postings, conference announcements, and other information exchange (H-Net 2013b).

Metadata Metadata provide context, but the question of whose context is particularly contentious in the humanities. For the same reasons that the "Western canon" of literature and "great books" approaches to education (Bloom 1994) are being supplanted by a much more diverse array of content, classical methods of organizing knowledge are being supplemented by "postcolonial" approaches. The more classical methods are those whose purpose is to establish common ground across collections and professional practices. Among the best known of these are the classification mechanisms developed and maintained by the Getty Trust and partners such as

the *Art and Architecture Thesaurus, Union List of Artist Names, Getty Thesaurus of Geographic Names,* and *Cultural Objects Name Authority.* These provide metadata for such features as names, places, objects, and styles, and relationships among them. The *Art and Architecture Thesaurus* is used widely in the classical art and archeology communities, but use of terminology and relationships varies from application to application (Baca 1998, 2002; Borgman and Siegfried 1992; Getty Research Institute 2013; Harpring 2010). Several decades in development, the CIDOC conceptual reference model is now being deployed for information exchange and integration within the museum community to encode object descriptions. Classical art and archeology projects are among the early adopters (Binding, May, and Tudhope 2008; International Council of Museums 2013).

Formal mechanisms such as these promote standardization and interoperability between systems. They provide the rigorous structure necessary for curatorial databases of museums, archives, and libraries. However, the terminology used by experts to provide detailed representations of unique objects is often a foreign language to museumgoers—or to scholars asking questions from different perspectives. Alternative approaches are to represent cultural heritage materials using the language of those who create and use them. These approaches include crowdsourcing descriptions through image tagging and developing classification mechanisms from the bottom up. Although valuable to engage the public and add value to the collections, efforts to "decolonize" the language of cultural heritage may come at the expense of standardization (Marshall 2008a, 2008b, 2009; Srinivasan, Boast, Becvar, et al. 2009; Srinivasan, Boast, Furner, et al. 2009; Srinivasan 2013; Steve: The Museum Social Tagging Project 2013).

Provenance   Provenance is a core concept in the humanities, but whose provenance may be a research question. Scholars document the origins, ownership, location, and uses of objects, documents, texts, or other cultural heritage materials as part of their research. In classical art and archeology, distinctions are made between where something was made, where it was found, how it was used, and how those uses changed over time. Provenance can involve tracing the composition of the object, such as the origins of its paint, stone, metal, wood, or the instruments used to construct it. Others may attempt to reconstruct the manufacture of an object based on known methods and materials of the probable time period. In classical art and archeology, research objects may be associated with few, if any, documentary records—and may predate writing altogether.

Provenance, metadata, and ontologies are notoriously difficult in classical art and archeology because the same item can be understood in so many ways. An early Chinese teapot, for example, may be important for its ceramics, its design, its manufacture, its age, or its role in the history of tea making. It could be important because it was traded along the Silk Road, or belonged to a certain person, or where it was found, or because of other artifacts with which it was associated. These are but a few examples of how provenance might be documented or studied for any given object.

Curatorial records in museum collections provide basic information about dates of acquisition or origin if known, but sensitive details about ownership, transfers, and associated dates and prices rarely are included in public records. Auction catalogs from major art houses such as Christie's and Sotheby's include detailed descriptions and other documentation that can assist in establishing provenance. Provenance can be a complex legal matter also since all parties must abide by the UNESCO conventions and other applicable laws (UNESCO 1970). As in astronomy, provenance of objects in classical art and archeology can be an infinite regress.

When ownership of artifacts is contentious, provenance often comes to the fore. Amid decades of legal battles with Greece, the British Museum claims rightful ownership of the marble sculptures from the Parthenon frieze it has on display. Near the sculptures, the museum displays records documenting the legal authority by which they acquired the materials in the nineteenth century. They juxtapose Greek sculptures with those of other ancient civilizations such as Egypt, Assyria, and Persia (British Museum 2013). The Acropolis museum in Athens sets its portions of the Parthenon frieze in the context of the ancient history of the city. In 2009, the museum expanded into a new building with ten times more exhibit space than was available at the Acropolis site, hoping for the return of materials long held in London (Acropolis Museum 2013).

Collections Collections, both material and digital, are essential components of the knowledge infrastructure in any field. Classical art and archeology offer illustrations of the degree to which collections are developed for research, for general public use, or as components of an infrastructure.

Funding agencies do support the development of some research collections, whether as the main goal or as a by-product of research. To be competitive, researchers often propose projects that take deliberate risks with new media and new forms of argument. However, agencies rarely are in a position to make strategic decisions about what content should be

digitized for the greater good of the community. Rather, they usually must make funding decisions in a responsive mode, awarding grants to the best proposals received in each cycle. As a result, the development of digital collections tends to be driven more by supply than by demand. Rarely do communities speak with a unified voice about their needs for collections and infrastructure, as in astronomy.

Those with strong community support sometimes do make the transition from research to reference collections. The Cuneiform Digital Library survived the transition from a grant-funded digital library project in the 1990s to an operational system with continuing institutional support. Tablets once physically adjacent are now scattered in collections around the world. Individual tablets are cataloged by type, genre, location, period, and other characteristics. Scholars now can study individual objects or reconstruct related objects digitally by using the tools and resources of the digital library (Cuneiform Digital Library Initiative 2013).

CLARIN (Common Language Resources and Technology Infrastructure), a European Union project for corpus linguistics research, also addresses collections, infrastructure, and community building as a whole. Their goal is "easy and sustainable access" to "digital language data in written, spoken, video or multimodal form." Efforts include technology development, user involvement, data resources, and interoperable services from a federation of data repositories across Europe (CLARIN European Research Infrastructure Consortium 2013).

Funding agencies in the arts and humanities began to focus more explicitly on infrastructure and sustainability concerns after some notable failures. The UK Arts and Humanities Research Council (AHRC) established the Arts and Humanities Data Service (AHDS) to archive data from funded research projects and to make them available for reuse. The system supported the creation and deposit of digital resources, providing several best practices guides. The AHDS focused on preserving underlying data resources rather than on sustaining online environments with searching capabilities. Funding ceased in 2008; the website and much of the documentation remain, but the collections are no longer searchable. Shuttering the AHDS raised alarm about the commitment of the agencies and the research community to maintain such resources. Questions arose about choices of sustaining back-end content in dark archives, sustaining active websites and services, academic versus technical sustainability, preservation versus curation, and the uses and demand for these collections (Arts and Humanities Data Service 2008; Robey 2007, 2011).

Another promising infrastructure effort that failed to survive was Project Bamboo, funded from 2008 to 2012 by the Andrew W. Mellon Foundation. The project was a significant investment in building community, tools, and services for the humanities. At this writing, it is officially on hiatus, with the website and wiki archived and the source code released through a public repository (Project Bamboo 2013).

The infrastructure and sustainability concerns of funding agencies in the humanities are reflected in new requirements for data management plans or technical plans. Investigators must specify how data and associated technologies will be maintained for access and reuse, and for how long. While not all collections or technologies are expected to be of indefinite value, planning for continuity or closure has become a part of grant proposals (Arts & Humanities Research Council 2012; McLaughlin et al. 2010). Efforts such as ConservationSpace, funded by the Mellon Foundation, are assisting in areas such as documentation management for conservation of materials (ConservationSpace 2013).

A brief review of early digital collections illustrates some of the infrastructure lessons learned. Project Gutenberg, the Beazley Archive, the Perseus Project, and Valley of the Shadow began in the 1970s and 1980s. Each of these began as research collections led by one or more scholars. Michael Stern created the first "e-books" in 1971 by launching Project Gutenberg to provide free online access to books, using computers at the University of Illinois and volunteers to type the texts. Although scholarly in intent, Project Gutenberg could digitize only out-of-copyright materials. These often were not the authoritative versions on which scholars relied. Project Gutenberg now promotes itself primarily as a source of free e-books and is supported by donations, grants, and other partnerships (Hart 1992, 2013).

The Beazley Archive, led by Donna Kurtz and others at the University of Oxford, began in 1979 on mainframe computers, focusing on digital representations of classical art objects. Designed to serve schools and the public, in 2009 it was among the collections awarded the Queen's Anniversary Prize. With continual growth and enhancement, the Beazley Archive became the core of the CLAROS project, which addresses infrastructure as much as collections (Burnard 1987; Hockey 1999; Kurtz and Lipinski 1995; Moffet 1992; Robertson 1976).

The Perseus Project, led by Gregory Crane at Tufts University since 1985, started as an Apple Hypercard database of Greek and Roman classics texts. By 1994, they had subjected the system and services to sociotechnical evaluations (Marchionini and Crane 1994), and by 1995, it had moved to the

nascent World Wide Web. Many generations of technology later, it is now known as the Perseus Digital Library and includes art, archeology, and history materials spanning many languages and time periods. Crane and his colleagues continue to conduct research in classics with Perseus resources and technology research on digital libraries (Crane and Friedlander 2008; Smith, Mahoney, and Crane 2002; Perseus Digital Library 2009).

The Valley of the Shadow was developed by Edward Ayers from 1993 to 2007 as support for his research on the US Civil War and as a public resource for research and learning. The system offers digital access to archival materials, enhanced by new forms of searching and presentation. Ayers, his colleagues, and his students wrote publications from these materials, including a Bancroft award–winning book, but few other scholars drew on these as resources for research (Ayers and Grisham 2003; Ayers 2003, 2007). Although Ayers long since moved to another university, the University of Virginia has invested two years and about $100,000 to curate these materials so that they remain accessible and useful for scholarship (Howard 2014).

Two strategic efforts to build infrastructure by aggregating disparate digital collections are Europeana and the Digital Public Library of America (DPLA), both focused on cultural heritage materials (Europeana 2013; Digital Public Library of America 2013). They include content from libraries, museums, and archives, have multiple sources of funding, and are broad in scope. Europeana assembles resources from European countries and DPLA from US-based collections; both have international partners. The European Union is a major funder of Europeana, whereas DPLA is a nonprofit organization supported by public and private foundation grants. They contain important collections that can be used for research, but neither is intended primarily as a research collection for a specific community.

External Factors   Access to data resources in the humanities is particularly constrained by external factors. Classical art and archeology can be a minefield in which to work. Artifacts often are old, valuable, and subject to ownership disputes. An array of laws and policies govern their handling, often in conflict between jurisdictions. The stakeholders are many and competing: scholars, universities, schools, libraries, museums, archives, governments, private owners, dealers, and the public at large. Some of their economic, property, and ethical issues are intractable, and others are subject to negotiation.

Economics and Value   As in other fields, the value of specific resources in the humanities often depends on their packaging. Some objects in the

realm of classical art and archeology have high scholarly value, some have high monetary value, some have both, and some have neither. These scholars function in multiple, competing economies. Collections developed for scholarly purposes and open to all, such as the Perseus Project, Beazley Archive, Valley of the Shadow, Arts and Humanities Data Service, Archaeological Data Service, and the language resources in CLARIN ERIC, can be considered common-pool resources. They are governed by members of the community to varying degrees and are subject to concerns for sustainability and free riders. The same is true for collections developed for the general public, such as the DPLA and Europeana. Substantial portions of these collections are digital surrogates for material objects or for texts that may be under copyright. Those material objects and texts may be owned by public or private institutions or by individuals, and those parties will determine who has access to them and under what conditions. Scholars are gaining more access to representations of objects but not necessarily greater access to the objects themselves. How satisfactory that may be depends upon their research methods and questions.

Archaeology is making faster strides toward open access to data than are most other areas of the humanities. Notably, the Archaeological Data Service, originally a component of the AHDS, was not closed in 2008, which reflects the demand for these collections. Some UK funding agencies require that data be contributed to the service and others recommend it. The international archeological research community has developed guidelines for data management and deposit, and scholars are contributing research materials to these and other collections (Archaeology Data Service 2013; The Digital Archaeological Record 2013; *Journal of Open Archaeology Data* 2013; Open Context 2013; Kansa 2012; Kansa, Kansa, and Schultz 2007).

Access to data, material collections, and digital objects is uneven, however. Many resources of interest to scholars in classical art and archeology can be considered club goods, available only to those individuals who meet certain criteria. Countries often reserve access to excavations, sites, artifacts, and documents for native scholars, researchers, and government staff or for teams led by their citizens. Embargoes, whether implicit or explicit, may last indefinitely until locals are ready to publish their findings or are otherwise finished with their research. Getting access to research reports on archeological sites can be very difficult; gaining access to the artifacts may be even harder.

As in any other area of scholarship, access to the software necessary to interpret, analyze, or reuse data can be problematic. The generalizability

of tools is limited by the wide array of resources and the variety of ways in which they can be used. Each collection and each project may build custom software. Even if scholars do release their code, sustaining the software can be even harder than sustaining the underlying collections. The challenges of curating disparate data, associated software, and interoperability mechanisms appear to have contributed to the demise of the Arts and Humanities Data Service, Project Bamboo, and other worthy endeavors (Borgman 2009; Robey 2007, 2011, 2013; Unsworth et al. 2006; Zorich 2008).

Property Rights   Scholarship in the humanities in general and in classical art and archeology in particular is deeply embroiled in property rights concerns. Data rights in these areas of the humanities are tied to the ownership of material objects and sometimes to ownership of representations of the objects. Scholars may control their observations of an object or phenomena, for example, but be unable to reproduce images of that object in a publication. Multiple property rights can be associated with an individual object. Rights in a photograph could involve the owner of the object, the owner of the reproduction rights, the photographer, and the publisher of the photograph. Reluctance by some museums to allow scholars to reproduce images has constrained the move to digital publishing in the art world (Whalen 2009). Recent moves to put more images in the public domain may assist scholars greatly (Getty Trust 2013). As notions of data come to the fore in the humanities, rights in data and representations may be the next frontier of property disputes.

Ethics   Ethical concerns in classical art and archeology are of several types, one of which is legal. Researchers are responsible for knowing applicable regulations and for negotiating ethically with museums, curators, owners, local authorities, and other stakeholders. A related concern is respect for the objects. Scholars are expected to minimize damage to research sites and to the objects. Testing metals, for example, requires careful sampling in unobtrusive locations.

De facto "proprietary periods" are not unusual in the areas of the humanities that study rare texts and cultural artifacts. Once scholars obtain access to materials, they may wish to mine them in private until they are ready to publish. Governments may be complicit, preferring that their own scholars have first rights to local heritage before it is available to the international community. The Dead Sea Scrolls episode is a well-known case of local control, albeit one often viewed as hoarding. Discovered in the Judean

desert in the 1940s, they were held by Israeli scholars until 1991, and only released then under the pressure provided by opening access to a microfilm copy that had been made for preservation purposes (Schiffman 2002). The scrolls are now open to wider study but their interpretation continues to be subject to rancorous debate (Leland 2013).

Conducting Research in Classical Art and Archaeology

These case studies provide a contrast between creating infrastructure for classical art and archeology and conducting research in an area where minimal information resources are available in digital form. CLAROS, "The World of Art on the Semantic Web," builds infrastructure through tools, technologies, and digital collections intended for research, education, and use by the public. Originally an acronym for *Classical Art Research Online Services*, its roots are in the Beazley Archive, which began digitizing its classical art collections in the late 1970s. CLAROS is based at the University of Oxford, home to four of the world's finest university museum collections—the Ashmolean, Natural History, History of Science, and Pitt Rivers—and is a test bed for research on multimedia databases. Based on open source software, it includes data integration tools developed for zoology, image recognition tools from engineering, and artificial intelligence tools for Internet services. Collections are drawn from museums, monuments, and other cultural heritage institutions in Europe and Asia. CLAROS also is testing the CIDOC conceptual reference model from the museum community to achieve interoperability across these collections (University of Oxford 2013b; Kurtz et al. 2009; University of Oxford Podcasting Service 2011; Rahtz et al. 2011).

The Pisa Griffin is a scholarly detective story that illustrates the difficulties that can impede the discovery of information about a material object. The Griffin is a large bronze statue of a mythical beast that was atop the cathedral in Pisa, Italy, for at least three centuries (see figure 7.1). An art historian tracing its provenance found a visual reference to it from the late fifteenth century. Other evidence indicates that the Griffin was removed from its pedestal in 1828 and ultimately replaced with a modern copy. The original is now housed in a museum near the Pisa Cathedral. Despite several centuries of scholarship in art, history, archeology, and other fields, the Griffin's origins, provenance, and function continue to be disputed. The Pisans may have obtained it from local craftsmen, or as war booty, or by some other means (Contadini, Camber, and Northover 2002; Contadini 2010; The Pisa Griffin Project 2013).

Figure 7.1
The Pisa Griffin. *Credit:* Gianluca de Felice of the Pisa Griffin Project.

Research Questions Humanities scholars more often problematize an object or phenomenon rather than pose research questions or testable hypotheses. However, their research activities do have iterative phases comparable to those of the sciences and social sciences.

Although CLAROS has a broad scope, the central research goal is to develop a technology platform that can serve a diverse array of cultural heritage collections. It is a federated system, making it readily expandable to more partners. Most CLAROS records include images and short textual descriptions, including the unique identifier assigned by the institution. At present, each subcollection is independent. Linking related objects within the CLAROS collections and in external collections are planned features.

The goal of research on the Pisa Griffin is to understand its origins, provenance, cultural value, and functions over the course of its existence. Simply put, what is it, where did it come from, and how did it get there? Antique artifacts such as the Pisa Griffin are not static in form, function, or role. The Griffin may be Islamic or Christian in origin, and possibly a sacred object. The most likely, and most fascinating, assessment of its function was to "emit eerie and fascinating sounds" while atop the cathedral as the wind blew through its internal vessel (Contadini, Camber, and Northover 2002, 69). Metallurgical analyses of the Griffin are used to test hypotheses and to generate new ones. It appears to have been used for target practice, bearing bullet holes, so ballistic analyses are planned. Using carbon dating, the year of creation has been narrowed to the range of 1020 to 1250 CE. The copper almost certainly came from Cyprus, but the sculpture may have been manufactured in southern Italy, Egypt, or Spain. Interest in the Pisa Griffin was renewed when a lion of similar style appeared on the New York art market in the early 1990s (Contadini, Camber, and Northover 2002; Contadini 2010). Among the reasons that the Griffin is difficult to study is that it is hard to classify. Similar objects are scattered across museums of fine arts, applied arts, archeology, natural history, local history, and anthropology.

Collecting Data   Many activities could be considered data collection in classical art and archeology. One aspect of data collection for CLAROS is to acquire content for the databases, another is to collect information about the current and potential user communities for the collections, and a third is to gather information about technologies that might be applied to these collections for these communities. These aspects interact in several ways.

CLAROS can only collect records that each partner is willing to contribute. Records vary widely in form, content, and completeness. Some of the participating institutions have accumulated their collections over the course of several centuries. The process of converting those records to digital form spans a period of thirty years, during which time standards, practices, and technologies have evolved considerably. Accordingly, those records include varying amounts and types of information on the origin, acquisition, and curation of objects. Record structure and classification mechanisms also vary widely. Starting with about two million of these records, CLAROS mapped them onto CIDOC, the data structure and ontology developed by the international museum community. It is among the first projects to implement CIDOC at scale (International Council of Museums 2013; Kurtz et al. 2009).

User studies and system evaluation of the sort done in sociotechnical studies is uncommon in the digital humanities, although such research is planned for later stages of CLAROS. Lacking those studies, the user interface for the test bed was based on knowledge of how the collections currently are used. In addition to the usual keyword searching, for example, the ability to search Greek vases by shape and color adds value to the Beazley collection. Partners from zoology, computer science, and engineering adapted their technologies to the starting collections and the anticipated audiences. The project goals were to keep the design open enough to adapt to other content and audiences as needed.

Research on the Pisa Griffin combines methods and expertise from art history and archaeo-metallurgy. Data collection in each realm informs the other. The art historian assembles evidence about the sculpture from historical records and earlier studies. Her sources include drawings, wood carvings, engravings, translations of the inscriptions, and stylistic analyses (Contadini, Camber, and Northover 2002; Contadini 1993). The archaeo-metallurgist took discrete and distributed samples of the sculpture to identify the metals in each section of the object and the methods by which sections were joined. His work draws on the art historical analyses to determine what samples to take and how to test them.

Much of the information the archaeo-metallurgist seeks is related to the use of metals in these time periods and regions. His searching is constrained by the lack of online digital resources and by the proprietary status of many relevant records. Metallurgical analyses are not done routinely but may be performed as part of conservation, valuation, provenance, or challenges to authenticity. When records of analyses exist, they may be only on paper or microfilm. Records on similar objects that would inform his research are held in the personal collections of private owners, dealers, and scholars, including archaeo-metallurgists who have taken the samples. Information sharing relies heavily on personal exchanges among colleagues. The archaeo-metallurgist studying the Pisa Griffin contacted experts by e-mail, phone, and other means to identify and locate relevant metals analyses on similar objects. He also traveled widely to examine records on paper and microfilm.

Analyzing Data   It is in the analysis stages that competing methods of representing, classifying, and organizing information become most apparent. The CLAROS project mapped the diverse array of records from participating institutions into a common structure, developed ontologies to organize the semantic descriptions of objects, and built technologies to exploit

the resulting data. The advantage of encoding object descriptions with the CIDOC conceptual reference model is that it can support as much metadata as exists, rather than reduce all records to the lowest common denominator. The "data web" architecture of bioinformatics was implemented by partners in zoology who specialize in taxonomy. They found the semantic problems of objects in biology and in classical art to be similar. Museums differ in the use of terms such as *artist* or *creator*; biology collections tend to use *insect* rather than *bug*. Some classification systems distinguish clearly between *Paris* as the city or the plaster, whereas biologists distinguish between *fly* as an insect or an action (University of Oxford 2013b; Kurtz et al. 2009; Rahtz et al. 2011). CLAROS encountered technological barriers to interoperability due to the disparate array of legacy formats they were ingesting. Records already converted to XML and SQL database formats were most readily ingested. More difficult were records intended for specific uses, such as a relational database used to drive the typesetting of printed volumes.

In analyzing data about the Pisa Griffin, it became apparent that this one material object was better understood as a set of objects. Ornamentation and other elements appear to have been added or removed over the centuries since the sculpture was first made. Accordingly, metals from many sources may be incorporated in the Griffin as it exists today. The art historian traces mentions of the Pisa Griffin and similar objects through time, attempting to situate it in multiple and changing contexts (Contadini 2010). Metals analyses test the microstructure of samples to reveal individual ores and the composition of alloys. These help to determine the mine from which the ores were dug, patterns of impurities that reveal how much scrap metal was incorporated, the approximate time period when an object was made, and the probable method of manufacture. Other analyses of the Griffin include two- and three-dimensional visualizations from digital scanning.

Once in the metallurgy laboratory, samples are mounted, polished, and subjected to testing for hardness and composition. The choice of tests and microscopic analyses are determined by hypotheses about the metals composition and by the detection limits of each method. Some methods are destructive; others retain the sample for future analysis. Less destructive methods are preferable, since samples can be retested for new hypotheses or with later technologies. Current technology already is sub-nanoscale, and some analyses can be done to picoscale or angstrom resolution.

To establish the origins of the materials as precisely as possible, further analysis is based on research in archives, patent records, museum records, curatorial and conservation records, and auction catalogs. Knowing the

mine from which the metal originated is necessary but not sufficient. Also important are knowledge of the trade in metal from those mines in the likely time period, uses of the metal by craftspeople in the likely region where the object was made, social and political influences on the exchange of objects during the period, such as trade routes and war booty, and any other contextual information about the object that can be found. With each advance in technology and with better access to information resources, better data can be obtained about the object. Thus cultural artifacts such as the Griffin can be reinterpreted indefinitely as more becomes known about them.

Publishing Findings   Classical art and archeology has distinctive publication practices. While collaborators report their findings to their respective communities, the structure of their coauthored publications is unusual. Coauthored works in most fields have a single narrative. The overview article about CLAROS, which is a conference paper, is divided into sections with individual authorship. Each of five sections is signed by one of the authors; only one author lacks his own section. Other collaborators are mentioned by name in the first section, rather than in an acknowledgments section at the end of the paper or in footnotes (Kurtz et al. 2009).

Research on the Pisa Griffin is reported in multiple papers with different combinations of authors. The initial survey of evidence on the Griffin's origins was authored by Anna Contadini, the lead art historian on the project, and published in Italian in an exhibition catalog. Her several papers on the Pisa Griffin appear in English and in Italian (Contadini 1993, 2010). An overview paper comparing the Pisa Griffin and the New York Lion follows the same partitioned format as the one describing CLAROS (Contadini, Camber, and Northover 2002). The first three sections discuss the art historical context; two are sole authored, one coauthored. The last section, signed by Peter Northover, reports the metals analysis in detail, listing the composition of samples from individual parts of the two objects and of samples from a third object thought to be related to the Lion and the Griffin. Acknowledgments are listed in footnotes of individual sections of the paper, with a combined bibliography. Also included are images of the objects discussed. In both of these cases, credit for collaborative work is carefully divided, perhaps a legacy of the sole-author traditions of the humanities.

Curating, Sharing, and Reusing Data   Difficulties in curating, sharing, and reusing data in classical art and archeology stem from the diversity of entities that could be considered data in each of these situations and from the competing interests of stakeholders.

CLAROS is more a test bed than a collection. As a test bed, it is designed to be open and interoperable, using semantic web technologies in ways that other parties can add classification mechanisms, user interfaces, and other capabilities. As a collection, it is open so that others may repurpose records. Sustainability of CLAROS depends on continued funding, continuing commitments from current partners, and development of new partners, all of which have proved to be challenging. Recognizing that partners were not likely to change their internal data structures to join CLAROS, their approach is to export data from each partner system into the CIDOC conceptual reference model. While appropriate for an infrastructure test bed, this approach may not motivate the partner institutions to harmonize their systems. Local systems usually must interoperate with internal systems such as finance, personnel, and library and archive collections, and with external facing systems such as public websites, virtual museum tours, federated collections such as CLAROS, and broadly federated services such as Europeana and the Digital Public Library of America.

Information about the Pisa Griffin is shared far more widely than is typical for these areas of scholarship. As a large, unique, and historically important object, the Griffin has its own website that includes project documentation. Scholarship on the Pisa Griffin can inform studies in many related areas of art, archeology, architecture, history, religion, culture, trade, and metallurgy. Publications about the Pisa Griffin are the lasting record of the scholarship. Historical records on which the scholarship is based remain in the libraries, archives, curatorial offices, and other places where they were found. Digital records created by the project are voluminous. CT scans, laser imaging, and high-resolution photography can yield files that are gigabytes and terabytes in size. These are not readily released, nor are such sharing practices common in this community (Contadini, Camber, and Northover 2002; Contadini 2010; The Pisa Griffin Project 2013).

Data from the metals sampling of the Griffin are reported in the publications in the form of tables, following practice in the metallurgy field. These are open in the sense of being freely available to the reader, but not in the sense of being structured data that can be discovered or mined computationally (Murray-Rust and Rzepa 2004). Ownership and release of the physical samples of objects is a relatively unexplored area. The miniscule samples remaining after testing remain in the possession of the archaeometallurgist, following community practice. Although he views his samples as the property of the museums or the other owners of objects he has studied, documenting them sufficiently to be of use to others is a major endeavor—one he plans as a retirement project.

Buddhist Studies

Buddhism originated about 2,500 years ago and continues to be practiced widely in Asia, with disciples, clergy, and scholars in all parts of the world. Buddhist doctrine is well documented, from early manuscripts to modern digital collections. It is conjectured that Empress Wu of the Tang Dynasty printed and distributed one hundred thousand copies of a Buddhist text, ca. 705, thus advancing the dissemination of paper and printing (Barrett 2008). Advances in paper and printing were closely related in East Asia. Wood block printing on paper matured in Asia centuries before Gutenberg perfected his combination of ink and movable type, about 1450.

Buddhist texts date back more than two thousand years. As words of scripture, the earliest texts were transmitted orally in prose and verse. Some texts are sacred religious objects; others serve devotional or scholarly roles. Manuscripts on birch bark, bamboo, bricks, clay tablets, and other media preceded paper. Texts were later recorded in many different writing systems and languages and were translated from one language to another. Buddhism spread quickly through translation, whereas early doctrines of Christian, Muslim, and other religions often forbade translations of sacred texts from their original language. Martin Luther's radical act of translating the Bible into German, for example, spread Protestantism throughout the German-speaking world in the sixteenth century.

The ethic of disseminating Buddhist texts widely continues today, with massive digitization projects conducted to the highest scholarly and technological standards. Scholarly practices are being transformed as more texts become available and as the tools to study them become more sophisticated. Because these texts can be studied in so many fields, and for so many different questions, scholars have a multitude of ways in which to select entities that they can treat as evidence of phenomena. This case study in Chinese Buddhist philology encompasses textual analysis, the creation of large digital collections of sacred and scholarly texts, comparisons between the use of physical artifacts and digital objects, and the role of these collections in supporting new methods of inquiry. Philology is a domain that combines linguistics, literary studies, and history to study written historical sources.

Early Buddhist texts can be studied for their historical, cultural, artistic, linguistic, and religious value. Countries where Buddhism has flourished historically include China, Japan, India, Sri Lanka, Thailand, Mongolia, Tibet, and Burma/Myanmar. Buddhism continues to be the majority religion in Japan and many other parts of Asia. In the West, Buddhism tends

to be more a topic of study than a field around which university programs are organized. Western scholars of Buddhism are located in departments of religion, history, languages, world culture, and in area studies. Although Buddhist scholarship is centered on canons of sacred texts, the questions, methods, and publication venues of individual scholars may be aligned with the fields in which they were trained or they currently teach.

Many important Buddhist texts appear to have originated in Sanskrit and related Indic languages. Sanskrit, an Indo-European language of culture long used in India, is written in several modern scripts and in many ancient scripts. Sanskrit and Indic texts later were translated into Chinese and other languages for dissemination and study. The Chinese writing system, which is used in multiple languages, was standardized about the third century BCE. Chinese was the common cultural language of East Asia, serving a role comparable to that of Latin in early Europe. Given the way these texts were communicated over the centuries, extensive expertise in language, history, and culture are necessary to study them. To study Buddhist texts that were translated into Chinese between the second and fifth centuries CE, for example, a scholar must be familiar with Chinese, Sanskrit, and other languages of the period. Ideally, he or she also should be familiar with the scripts in which these languages were written at the time.

Size Matters

The community of Buddhist scholars is small and widely distributed around the globe. The largest centers are in parts of the world where the religion is most active, primarily in Asia. Their materials are big in variety, spanning many languages, writing systems, geographic regions, and time periods. Scholars typically work alone or in small groups. Their methods involve close and meticulous readings of texts, yielding small numbers of observations. However, as digital collections of Buddhist texts grow in size and sophistication, automated analysis becomes feasible. Buddhist philologists are starting to explore technologies for text analysis. Tools from CLARIN for corpus linguistics, mentioned previously, may be applicable. Similarly, BLAST, already adapted from string matching in DNA to historical texts in French, would support some of the research questions of this community.

When Are Data?

Buddhist texts are religious in origin. Choices of evidence from these texts may depend on whether they are studied for religious or for other scholarly reasons. Dissemination of sacred texts is a basic tenet of Buddhism, thus adherents are motivated to translate, edit, and make these materials widely

accessible. This process has had multiplicative effects for centuries. Each text that is copied or translated can be leveraged to create yet more copies in more languages. Scholarship and commentary about the texts also are of research interest; these too have been copied and translated. That multiplicative effect is accelerating with increased imaging and digitization. Each text that is captured in digital form can be leveraged to create yet more digital products. Digitization also aids scholars in treating different units as discrete entities. Once digitized, the texts can be studied as a whole or phrases, characters, strokes, punctuation, or other units can be examined. These entities can be mined and combined in many ways to explore different phenomena.

Sources and Resources   The distinction between sources and resources in Buddhist studies is particularly problematic, given the extremely long period over which these works have evolved. Digitized collections of early texts clearly are resources. Whether something is a source depends on what is considered original—another contentious concept in this area of the humanities. A few distinctions will help to illustrate the challenges in determining when and how something might be treated as data.

Primary versus Secondary Sources   Distinguishing between primary and secondary sources is somewhat helpful, but even this boundary is blurry. In Buddhist philology, for example, an original Sanskrit text or an early Chinese translation is considered a primary source, whereas modern translations and scholarly writing about the early texts usually are considered secondary sources. In books and journal articles, bibliographies sometimes provide separate lists of primary and secondary sources. Critical editions usually are considered to be primary sources because they present consensus forms of texts. The critical editions may bring together multiple sources, presenting the text in a readable format that is as close to the original texts as scholars can construct.

These distinctions often rest on deep expertise in the domain. Early Buddhist texts can be far more difficult to interpret than Western materials. In Greek and Roman philology, for example, certain assumptions can be made about practices during the period of time that the empire was united. In Buddhism, fewer cultural assumptions can be made. Practices associated with these texts vary by ruling government, language, geographical region, time period, script, and many other factors. A scholar working with these texts also must consider the role of the translator or transmitter. In certain periods in India and sometimes in China, the person who translated the

document had implicit authority to change the text or to choose not to change it. Even a sacred text has a different meaning in each translation, which is far from the literalism typical of translating Christian texts. Critical editions also have a long history and can include corrections to texts. Some critical editions from the thirteenth century are considered primary sources today.

Static Images versus Enhanced Content   Buddhist studies in general and philology in particular depend on the ability to compare texts, in whole or in part. Scholars study how texts were understood in different temporal, geographic, linguistic, and cultural contexts. Comparing original material objects side by side is nigh unto impossible for those who study texts of the fifth century or earlier. Few texts survived as physical entities; they are known only by later translations or mentions. Those that do remain are rare, precious, fragile, and scattered around the world. The distribution of static images on microfilm, facsimile editions in print, and on CD-ROM enabled scholars to compare many texts side by side for the first time. Next was the distribution of static page images online, which increased the scale of access.

Over the last decade or so, the conversion of these texts to searchable representations and to enhanced content has accelerated, leading to radical advances in the exploitation of these historical materials. Instead of viewing a page, a folder, or box of documents at a time, scholars can now compare, combine, and extract information from these digital texts. As found in early studies of how classics scholars adapted to using the *Thesaurus Linguae Graecae,* their relationship with the texts changes in subtle and complex ways (Ruhleder 1994).

Knowledge Infrastructures   The community of Buddhist scholars is united by their interest in these texts. They come from many disciplines, apply diverse methods and theories, read numerous languages and scripts, and work in various parts of the world. To the extent that they have a common knowledge infrastructure, it centers on the means of access to Buddhist texts. Rarely do they obtain grants for purposes other than travel. They do not have ready access to public funding agencies that would support the digitization of collections, creation of repositories, technologies, tools, standards, or the hiring of student assistants. To the extent possible, they rely on sources obtained from libraries or available online without fee. What the Buddhist scholarly community does have as institutional support for knowledge infrastructure is the religious community that keeps these

texts alive. Monasteries and other centers of religious activity are actively engaged in digitization and dissemination of texts, often in concert with the scholarly community.

Buddhist scholars share expertise through conferences, social media, and Internet technologies. H-Buddhism, for example, is part of H-Net, which serves humanities and social sciences scholars internationally. This active website includes discussion lists, reviews, announcements, jobs, and other postings (H-Net 2013a, 2013b). Scholars in areas such as Chinese Buddhism convene online meetings in which they employ video technologies to read, interpret, translate, and discuss Buddhist texts. Their publications include extensive acknowledgments to others who have provided materials, commentary on earlier drafts, and other assistance.

Metadata   Questions of metadata are important in Buddhist studies as they are in most areas of the humanities. Scholars disagree on which texts are authoritative, on who authored which text, and even on the notion of authorship. No common classification mechanism such as the *Art and Architecture Thesaurus* is available for Buddhist studies, nor are reference models such as CIDOC applied to their texts in digital form.

To the extent that organizing mechanisms exist, they appear to be associated with specific collections of texts. The authoritative digital version of the Chinese Buddhist canon is based on the authoritative printed version of the canon developed in the 1920s and 1930s. Known as the Taisho edition, the printed version was created to serve religious and scholarly purposes. It is a massive text, consisting of fifty-five primary volumes and eighty supplemental volumes. Although expensive to acquire, it became a necessary addition to research library collections for Asian and Buddhist studies. Most subsequent scholarly quotations of the Chinese Buddhist canon refer explicitly to this source, often by page number (Takakusu and Watanabe 1932). In 1998, the Chinese Buddhist Electronic Text Association (CBETA) released the first digital version of the Taisho edition, closely emulating the print version. They maintained the same pagination in the print and digital editions to ensure the historical continuity of the scholarship. CBETA editors enhanced the content by correcting punctuation, which is an important scholarly contribution. Punctuation marks can identify whether a Chinese word is a noun or a verb, for example, profoundly influencing the interpretation of the text. The system includes syntactic and semantic markup for use with tools to select and compare portions of text but does not establish a metadata vocabulary or other classification system (CBETA Chinese Electronic Tripitaka Collection 2013).

In some sense, the methods of these Buddhist scholars yield metadata about the texts they study. Philological descriptions are interpretations of texts, which are metadata to the extent that they aid others in locating and interpreting those texts. The boundary between data and metadata is unclear since much of the scholarship consists of creating thick descriptions of thin phenomena, akin to ethnography (Geertz 1973).

Provenance   The older the sources, the more complex the questions of provenance may become. The initial Buddhist texts from which others emanate cannot be established precisely, because scholars have been unable to agree on the dates of the Buddha's lifetime. Current approximations are that he lived in a period four to five centuries BCE. Texts were transmitted orally, with the first written texts appearing about the first century BCE. An Indic Buddhist manuscript from the first century CE was recently discovered. Temporality was determined by a combination of paleographic analysis and carbon dating (Falk 2011). Indic manuscripts predate the earliest known written Chinese texts; the latter date from about the third century CE.

The ambiguity of the provenance of early manuscripts is part of the scholarship of Buddhist studies. Scholars compare texts in multiple languages from the same and different time periods, attempting to determine the identity of authors, editors, translators, and other parties involved in the creation and communication of these texts. Some scholars are interested in the transmission of ideas, others of language, and others of physical objects. Buddhist texts can occur not only in familiar media such as bamboo and paper, but on everyday objects such as the Gopālpur bricks held by the Ashmolean Museum. Even the provenance of the bricks is disputed (Johnston 1938).

Collections   Collections such as CBETA and the holdings of libraries, archives, and museums are parts of the knowledge infrastructure for Buddhist studies. Materials are widely scattered around the world, but their representations can be brought together through the use of digital technologies. By the tenth anniversary of CBETA's launch, Buddhist scholars lauded its transformative influences on their work (Goenka et al. 2008). CBETA is not a static system; they continue to add content and to incorporate new technologies. The current version is enhanced with modern text encoding, including XML and Unicode. Searching and text-mining apparatus enable CBETA users to explore the collections, export results to other analytical tools, and transfer excerpts to word processing software with all characters, punctuation, and other metadata intact. The system is usable not only on

computers but has applications for all the major mobile devices, operating systems, electronic book readers, and social networks.

The CBETA edition of the Chinese Buddhist canon continues to grow beyond the scope of the printed edition by digitizing other important records related to Buddhism. At present, CBETA contains more than 2,370 sutras and over seventy million Chinese words. The collection is a resource of unprecedented scale for scholars conducting linguistic analyses of Chinese Buddhist texts. The CBETA edition, in turn, is being leveraged for new online collections. For example, the Vietnamese combined machine translation of the CBETA corpus with Vietnamese electronic dictionaries as a basis for their own vernacular edition. Vietnamese Buddhist scholars are correcting and editing the computer translations (Nguyên and Nguyên 2006).

Another example of how collections can serve as infrastructure for Buddhist studies is the International Dunhuang Project (IDP), established in 1994 by the British Library and now including partners from around the world. Dunhuang, China, was an important trading post on the ancient Silk Road. Early in the twentieth century, a large cache of Buddhist documents was found in one of the Mogao caves nearby, having been sealed safely for about a thousand years. The fifty thousand or so documents were dispersed to libraries, archives, and collectors around the world by various means, with contentious results. Among those documents is the famous *Diamond Sutra,* now held by the British Library. An important Buddhist sacred text, it is the first complete printed book that is clearly dated: 11 May 868 (The British Library Board 2013). The IDP is a project to catalog and to digitize manuscripts, paintings, textiles, and other artifacts from Dunhuang and archeological sites of the Eastern Silk Road. As of this writing more than four hundred thousand images are available on the site (International Dunhuang Project 2013). They are freely available for research and educational purposes.

External Factors The external factors that influence access to scholarly sources in Buddhist studies are highly specific to the domain. While perhaps less of a minefield than classical art and archeology, this community has its own set of economic, property rights, and ethical constraints on what they might treat as data.

Economics and Value Due to the tenets of the religion, Buddhist texts are more openly disseminated than many other historical resources. Not all are open or free, however. The massive printed edition of the Chinese Buddhist canon is expensive to acquire. These volumes can be considered private

goods, available for sale. Once acquired by libraries, they may be viewed as common-pool resources whose use is governed by the libraries and the communities of which they are a part. Each library, archive, museum, and historic site has its own rules about who can study its materials and under what conditions.

CBETA, the digital counterpart of the Taisho edition of the Chinese Buddhist canon, is an online open access system, free to use. CD-ROM versions also are available. CBETA is a common-pool resource owned and governed by the association that developed and sustains it. The Buddhist religious community is investing in these resources for the use of adherents and scholars alike. Sustainability and free riding are less of a concern than in domains that depend upon grant funding.

Many important materials remain in the hands of private collectors, some of whom make their collections available to scholars. Scholars themselves can acquire important collections over the course of their careers. Their papers and private libraries become valuable resources that may be donated or sold upon death or retirement.

Property Rights   Property issues are most commonly associated with the control of material artifacts and the dissemination of representations of the texts. These may be matters of ethics as much as matters of law. Buddhist texts have surfaced in the twenty-first century as isolated parts of Asia— especially Afghanistan, Pakistan, and Tibet—have become more open. Some of these are rare finds, including texts assumed to be long lost as they were known only through references in other texts or translations into other languages. Precious documents occasionally fall into the hands of private collectors who may or may not provide access to scholars. Individual leaves of some texts have been sold on the black market; thus, these texts are not likely to be reconstructed. Substantial portions of recently discovered texts have disappeared underground. Others have been controlled in secret for many years, known only to a select group of scholars and revealed only when they are ready to publish their scholarship about the texts (Allon 2007, 2009).

Ethics   Ethical concerns in Buddhist scholarship are subtle and complex. Religion, scholarship, culture, and politics are inextricably intertwined. For example, the communication of texts has been supported or restricted by governments at different periods over the centuries. CBETA is a Taiwanese project, available to readers of Chinese around the world. Relations between Taiwan and China are delicate and Buddhism is a source of tension within

China and between the Chinese and other governments. The Dalai Lama, who won the Nobel Peace Prize in 1989, is in exile from Tibet, a province of China that seeks independence. Scholars are well aware of past, present, and potential future tensions between religious and political institutions and their influence on access to materials (Vita 2003).

The Buddhist religious community affirms the value of their texts as cultural, historical, and linguistic artifacts, encouraging scholarship on them. Scholars, in turn, respect the religious traditions on which the sacred texts are based. Some material objects warrant religious reverence, whereas most serve scholarly study. Texts are substitutes for the Buddha's presence. Artifacts that evoke the Buddha are enshrined in an area of the temple. Inscriptions on bricks might be built into the wall of a building as blessings. Interesting ethical questions arise with digital technologies; for example, how Buddhist monks might view texts that are enshrined in a computer or other technical device.

Conducting Research in Buddhist Studies

This case study describes recent work by a scholar of Chinese Buddhist philology. One of his projects compared texts in different languages, presenting an argument about the commonality of their origins. This led to one journal article, and the scholar continues to study these texts (Zacchetti 2002). Another of his other projects is a critical synoptic edition of an important early Chinese Buddhist sacred text (Zacchetti 2005). His subsequent work relies heavily on CBETA, which has led to new questions, methods, and sources of evidence for his scholarship.

The depth and breadth of expertise required for scholarship in Chinese Buddhist philology is daunting. This scholar has academic training in Chinese studies and in philology, similar to the dual training in archeology and metallurgy of the scientist in the previous case. Of particular note is the number and variety of languages in which this scholar works, while teaching and publishing most of his scholarship in English. Whereas classical philology requires knowledge of Latin and Greek, these are linguistically close to English; this scholar learned Latin and Greek as part of his education in philology. On that foundation, he learned Chinese, Sanskrit, Tibetan, Pali, and Japanese. The latter languages and their associated scripts are not widely studied by Western scholars. His first language is Italian, in which he also teaches and publishes. When teaching advanced courses in Chinese history and culture, he lectures in Chinese. His extensive language skills are a means to an end, being necessary to study the history, culture,

and language of Buddhism as documented and understood by ancient cultures across Asia.

Digital collections and their associated apparati have revolutionized linguistic research in Chinese Buddhist studies. This scholar refers to CBETA as his telescope because he can use it to see farther than ever before possible. To explain the metaphor, he invokes his fellow Italian, Galileo, who described how his new technology (a better telescope) enabled him to see phenomena never before visible. He also refers to CBETA and similar collections as his microscope, because he can examine each text much more closely. He can produce his own concordances of portions of text, mine them, and make new types of comparisons.

Research Questions   This scholar examines relationships among texts that can reveal how those texts were communicated and understood by different cultures at specific times and in particular places. The questions explored in the journal article arose when he was studying a printed version of an early Chinese Buddhist text and recognized a similarity to a text he had read in Pali, an ancient Indian language. If a geographical or cultural relationship between these texts could be established, it would be a significant historical discovery because these texts were presumed to be independent. The Chinese text is the shorter of the two. The Pali text is a chapter of a longer scripture. His hypothesis was that this Chinese Buddhist scripture was translated from an earlier Indic text from which the existing Pali text also was translated. Thus, one Indic text spawned the Chinese and Pali texts, illustrating the complex paths by which these ideas were communicated between cultures (Zacchetti 2002).

Critical editions attempt to establish as much of the original intent of a text as possible. They do so by documenting the provenance of each text, by comparing translations and variations, and by explicating what is known about the context in which these texts were written, circulated, and used. Critical editions become primary sources if accepted as authoritative scholarship in their field. This scholar's critical edition is a comprehensive analysis of similar texts in two languages. He devoted years of scholarly labor to comparing three chapters of an important Chinese Buddhist text with their Sanskrit counterparts. The relevant section of the Chinese canon is a single text, whereas the comparable Sanskrit parallels are tablets from multiple texts, including a hitherto unpublished portion of a manuscript. By comparing four Sanskrit texts to the Chinese translation, he interpreted how the texts were translated into Chinese many centuries ago and how

the concepts in those texts were understood in these two cultures at that time (Zacchetti 2005).

Collecting Data   *Data* was not a term in this scholar's usual vocabulary until discussions began for this case study. His methods involve meticulous selection of terms, phrases, concepts, and characters from texts, which are readily construed as data collection. Because he makes pair-wise comparisons, he constructs two-column tables using a word processor. When working with material artifacts, he searches manually and then enters a description of his observations into the table. When entities are selected from CBETA, he captures the entities in digital form, copying and pasting into his document. CBETA apparatus carries the metadata for the text selection along with the text, increasing both the speed and the accuracy of data selection. Some comparisons are line by line and others are clause by clause. Each entry is heavily annotated with information about its source and the ways in which the paired items are similar or different. He manages his tables with simple file-naming conventions such as the chapter number of the Chinese text.

In the journal article and the monographic critical edition, his purpose was to interpret texts, specifically the use of language within each text. His research depends on a variety of digital tools and resources, some widely available and some being tools custom-built by other scholars. One obscure tool of particular value to him is an online lexicographical source for historical variants of Chinese characters (Ministry of Education, Republic of China 2000).

The Chinese text with which he worked was a printed copy, whereas the counterpart was found in a digital collection of Pali texts. He draws on histories of these documents and related scholarship to make his arguments, acknowledging the difficulty of establishing their origins absolutely. For instance, he notes the "putative originals" of important terms (Zacchetti 2002, 79). To gather evidence, he searches print and digital sources, some in libraries, some online or CD-ROM, and some from the substantial collection of reproductions of texts that he has accumulated over the course of his career. He identifies earlier translations and the historical catalogs and bibliographies in which these texts first are mentioned (Zacchetti 2002, 75).

Analyzing Data   Analysis, in this scholar's approach to Chinese Buddhist philology, consists of interpreting the evidence in his notes and tables to build an argument. The journal article presents his analysis as a

series of tables with the Chinese text on the left and the Pali text on the right. Although the article is written in English, much of the commentary includes phrases in Chinese and in Pali to explain the comparisons. Some comments explain obscure expressions; others compare literal and metaphorical interpretations of the texts. Like law reviews, some pages devote more space to footnotes than to the main text; like journals in the social sciences, the article begins with a literature review to situate the argument and ends with a discussion of the evidence and a conclusion.

His monograph is referred to as a critical synoptic edition because of the line-by-line and clause-by-clause comparisons. The main body of the work is the comparison of the texts in a two-column table, one page of which is shown in figure 7.2 (Zacchetti 2005, 157). As in his journal article, the comparisons are heavily annotated with commentaries in English and with references in Chinese and Sanskrit. Some of these explain how definitions of terms compare or how concepts are enumerated. The tables compare sources, variants, and translations, providing evidence of how the language evolved and where texts may have originated. His sources often contain older variants of characters in Chinese, Sanskrit, and their associated scripts. These variants are difficult to render properly in digital form if they do not exist in Unicode. Part of his analysis is to transliterate text from original scripts to modern characters when necessary, making the content more accessible to the contemporary reader. The critical edition also includes extensive narrative discussion of the provenance of these texts (Zacchetti 2005).

Publishing Findings   Chinese Buddhist scholars publish their work in journals, books, and conference proceedings. Publications in philology rely heavily on textual quotations. These quotations are much more extensive than the few words typical of fair use or fair dealing rules of copyright, and are thus a distinctive scholarly practice. In both of the publications discussed, the text is presented in modern character sets, whereas some of the original Chinese characters from which the scholar worked are written in ancient scripts that cannot be represented in Unicode. Unicode is now implemented in all mass market software and hardware, so his writing in English, Chinese, and Sanskrit is rendered properly on computer screens and printers, at least for modern scripts. Problems can occur with different keyboards and browsers, but interoperability is improving. Although this scholar works in Microsoft Word, some humanities scholars who work with multiple scripts prefer the LaTeX typesetting language. Most publishers accept either of these or PDF formats for submissions.

SYNOPTIC EDITION OF THE *GUANG ZAN JING* – CHAPTER 1: 光讚品

karmāntājīvā
virahitākuśalakāyavāṅmanas-
karmāntājīvāś[109] ca bhavanti sma

§ 1.66
(147c 28-148a
1)
一切眾生得平等心，展轉相瞻如父、如母、如兄、如弟、如姊、如妹，各各同心，等無偏邪，皆行慈心。

PG 4r 4-5 (Ś 18, 22-19, 1; PD 10, 1-2; PSL *kā* a 4-5): sarvasatvāś ca sarvasatveṣu samacittā abhūvan* yad uta[110] mātāpitṛbhrātṛbhaginīsamacittāḥ mitrajñātisahāyasamacittāḥ[111]

§ 1.67
(148a 1-2)
一切群萌悉修十善，清淨梵行，無有塵埃。

PD 10, 2-3 (PG 4r 5-6; Ś 19, 2-3; PSL *kā* a 5): daśakuśalakarmapathasevinaś ca bhavanti sma[112] / brahmacāriṇaḥ śucayo nirāmayagandhāḥ[113]

§ 1.68
(148a 2-4)
一切黎庶悉獲安隱，所得安隱猶如比丘得第三禪。于時眾生而致智慧，而悉具足善快調定，離於卑劣，逮得和雅。

PG 4r 6-8 (PD 10, 3-8; PSL *kā* a 5-6; Ś 19, 3-8): sarvasatvās tasmin samaye sarvasukhasamarpitā abhūvan* evaṃrūpeṇa sukhena samanvāgatās[114] tadyathā {s} tṛtīyadhyānasamāpannasya bhikṣoḥ sukhaṃ sarvasatvāś ca tasmin samaye evaṃrūpayā prajñayā samanvāgatā abhūvan* yad evaṃ jānaṃti sma[115] • sādhu dānaṃ sādhu damaḥ sādhu saṃyyamaḥ[116] sādhu satyaṃ • sādhv apramādaḥ sādhu maitrī sādhu karuṇā sādhv avihiṃsā prāṇibhūteṣu[117] •

---

[110] sarvasattvāś … yad uta: not in PD & PSL.
[111] PG wrongly repeats verbatim this latter compound. PD 10, 2 and PSL have at this point a longer reading: mitrāmātyajñātisālohitasamacittā. Note that Ś has all the words construed as one compound.
[112] PG 4r 5-6 & Ś 19, 2: daśakuśalakarmapa(tha)samanvāgatā [Ś without daśa-] abhūvan.
[113] PG 4r 6, Ś 19, 3 and PSL *kā* a 5: nirāmagandhāḥ, which seems to be the correct reading; after this word, PG & Ś + sarvākuśalavitarkavigatāḥ.
[114] PD 10, 4 & PSL *kā* a 5: idṛśaṃ sukhaṃ pratilabhante sma.
[115] yad … sma: PD 10, 6 & PSL *kā* a 6: yad anyabuddhakṣetrasthā buddhā bhagavanta evam [PSL + udānam] udānayanti sma.
[116] Ś 19, 7: saṃyamaḥ.
[117] sādhu dānaṃ … prāṇibhūteṣu: PD 10, 7-8 & PSL *kā* a 6: sādhu damaḥ [PSL + sādhu śamaḥ] sādhu saṃyamaḥ sādhu cīrṇo brahmacaryyāvāsaḥ sādhu prāṇibhūteṣv avihiṃseti.

Figure 7.2

Page 157 from *In Praise of the Light: A Critical Synoptic Edition with an Annotated Translation of Chapters 1–3 of Dharmaraksa's Guang zan jing, Being the Earliest Chinese Translation of the Larger Prajnaparamita* by Stefano Zacchetti (2005). *Credit:* Used with permission of Stefano Zacchetti, Numata Professor of Buddhist Studies, University of Oxford.

His journal article is twenty-three pages in length, including 134 footnotes and three pages of references (Zacchetti 2002). His critical synoptic edition is 469 pages in length, consisting of three parts, each with several chapters, plus multiple appendices and an extensive bibliography (Zacchetti 2005). The latter work was published as a monograph in Japan by a major center of Buddhology. While remaining under copyright, the monograph is published online without charge as a PDF document and has been incorporated into other online collections of Buddhist materials. A print edition also is available. Both publications include extensive acknowledgments to other scholars who read drafts, provided commentary or materials, or assisted in other ways.

Curating, Sharing, and Reusing Data   This scholar's research methods and work practices have evolved considerably with advances in information technology. His options for curating, sharing, and reusing his data have expanded even further. A brief historical overview of his methods and technologies illustrates this transition. He submitted his bachelor's thesis in Chinese studies in 1994, only two years after the official adoption of Unicode. Unicode was not yet widely implemented in word processing software, printers, or displays. Other software to capture and represent Chinese, Japanese, and Korean character sets was available in Asia; some versions already were in use by research libraries in the West.

As a student lacking access to these early technologies for representing Chinese characters, the budding scholar wrote his thesis in Italian on a common word processing system, leaving blank spaces for the Chinese characters. He wrote the characters by hand on the final printout submitted for his degree. Thus, no digital copy of his thesis exists that contains the Chinese characters.

He adopted an early generation of Chinese word processing for the critical synoptic edition. The resulting document, a product of several years of labor, was converted to PDF for publication. Although readily disseminated online, this early version of PDF could only represent static page images. Consequently, the publication is not searchable and does not include any computer-readable semantic structure. The 1990s-era word processing system with which he produced the synoptic edition rendered the Chinese and Sanskrit character sets properly, but the files are not readable by current technologies. The word processing system was not widely adopted and the files were not migrated. The lack of migration may be due to text encoding in a format other than Unicode, software that was no longer supported, being stored in physical formats that no longer are supported, or some

combination of these. Whatever the reason, the result is that he does not have a computer-readable version that maintains the syntactic and semantic structure of this major work. The monograph is open in the sense of being freely available, but not in the sense of having its contents discoverable or minable by computers. His situation is not uncommon in the humanities and is particularly problematic for a reference work. To correct or to update the text would require producing a full new edition.

In his current work, he is concerned about capturing and curating his data and metadata in computer-readable forms. His data come from many and varied sources. These sources are labor-intensive to mine, and only a few scholars at a time may be working on any particular text. By curating his data as he works, he will be better able to reuse them later. He also can share his data and analyses with others. While personal exchange is most common in this community, some digital repositories are acquiring materials in Buddhist studies, such as the one that ingested his open monograph.

Conclusion

The humanities are the most difficult to characterize of the disciplines because their boundaries are the least well defined. Any grouping of fields or domains within the humanities also will raise objections. It is the diversity of their objects of study, their questions, and their research methods that embody the challenges of characterizing their data. The same object can be studied in many ways, for many questions, at many different places and times. Each scholar can represent his or her findings in a distinctive way. In doing so, those representations become entities that are evidence of some phenomena. Each object, and even each representation of an object, can be reinterpreted multiple times. The ability to interpret or reinterpret— whether artifacts from an archeological excavation, Greek vases, Buddhist texts, the transmission of knowledge in third-century China, or any other aspect of human culture—in light of new perspectives or evidence is the essence of scholarship in the humanities. However, the ability to reinterpret depends on a different kind of infrastructure from that for fields where knowledge is more cumulative. Developing standards for describing objects or provenance leads to questions of who has the authority to establish classification mechanisms or provenance documentation. These characteristics of their research, combined with limited funding and competing stakeholders, have constrained the ability of humanities scholars and funding agencies to develop much shared infrastructure.

The first provocation, that addressing matters such as who owns, controls, has access to, and sustains research data will determine how their value can be exploited, and by whom, is especially problematic in the humanities. Resources needed by scholars in classical art and archeology and in Buddhist studies are scattered widely around the world, each collection governed and sustained—or not—by its own community. Efforts to build infrastructure, such as the CLAROS test bed, demonstrate what can be accomplished by aggregating collections on a common platform and augmenting them with new technical features. Similar approaches to federate collections underlie the infrastructure efforts such as CLARIN, Europeana, and the DPLA. All face sustainability challenges. CBETA, developed by the Buddhist religious community, appears to have the most enduring infrastructure support.

Transferring knowledge across contexts and over time, the second provocation, also is difficult in the humanities. However, some of the features that matter are becoming apparent. In the cases presented here, the ability to compare objects and to inspect them more closely are essential. For many research projects, comparing representations of objects can serve scholarly purposes as well or better than comparing material objects. CLAROS enables images of Greek vases to be compared side by side, rotated, and expanded. CBETA enables Chinese Buddhist texts to be searched and compared at scale for the first time. Images of characters written in ancient scripts can be enlarged. Three-dimensional visualizations of the Pisa Griffin provide details not visible to the human eye. While these technologies serve similar scholarly purposes, they are not transferrable across scholarly contexts. CLAROS offers little to the archaeo-metallurgist, even though it covers collections of interest, because records do not include the metals information he needs. The apparatus developed for CBETA is a powerful set of tools for scholars who can work in the Chinese language and are experts in the scripts and culture. The knowledge infrastructure challenge is to generalize features in such ways that they can be transferred across domains.

With respect to the third and fourth provocations, the forms and genres of publication in these areas of the humanities are distinct from those of most other fields. In both exemplars of classical art and archeology, publications are divided into short sections signed by individual authors. The example publications in Buddhist philology are a cross between scientific practice, providing long tables of data, and law, with footnotes that can be more extensive than the main body of text. Although data release is not common in these areas of scholarship, some portions of their work are open. CLAROS provides open source code and builds collections of records

made available by partner institutions. Metals data about the Pisa Griffin are presented in tabular form in publications about the object. The Buddhist philology publications provided detailed evidence for the arguments, presented as tabular comparisons of entities. None of these actions would likely be considered data release in the sciences, yet they serve the scholarly communication functions of these communities.

Last, it is important to emphasize the history of the knowledge infrastructures for these domains of scholarship. Although reinterpretation is continual, their work relies on collections and expertise accumulated over a period of many centuries. Knowledge does transfer over time and across contexts, but not always easily or well. Scholars of classical art, archeology, archaeo-metallurgy, and Buddhist studies have adapted their practices to many new technologies—papyrus, printing, and paper, to name a few. They navigate minefields of economics, property rights, ethics, and competing stakeholders. Many are making innovative new uses of information technologies, gaining competitive advantage over other scholars. They also are encountering the risks of new technologies, especially the Buddhist philologist who cannot recover his data from the previous generations of software in which he invested his labor. Cultural records captured only in digital form will not survive by benign neglect. Unless substantial infrastructure investments are made, they will disappear, unlike the papyri, cuneiforms, Greek vases, and metal sculptures that continue to be studied today. The knowledge infrastructures that are most resilient in these domains are the personal networks of scholars. They exchange knowledge via old and new media alike. They share ideas and develop evidence through long and regular discussions. They provide entry points to information resources that cannot be discovered through the Internet, library catalogs, or other sources. Whereas big data usually comes to the desktop, these scholars often must go to their data. Their knowledge infrastructures must somehow adapt to this complex mix of intellectual, material, and digital resources and provide the means to exploit them effectively.

III Data Policy and Practice

8   Sharing, Releasing, and Reusing Data

Water, water, every where,
And all the boards did shrink;
Water, water, every where,
Nor any drop to drink.

—Samuel Taylor Coleridge, *Rime of the Ancient Mariner*—Part II

Introduction

Galileo (1610) in the seventeenth century and Cavendish (1798) in the eighteenth century famously provided their full datasets in support of their scientific arguments. Galileo's work on the moons of Jupiter and Cavendish's work on the density of the Earth remain scientific landmarks because their data, methods, and arguments can be examined today (Goodman et al. 2014). When present-day researchers are asked whether they are willing to share their data, most say yes, they are willing to do so. When the same researchers are asked if they do release their data, they typically acknowledge that they have not done so (Tenopir et al. 2011; Wallis, Rolando, and Borgman 2013). Willingness does not equal action, thus "data, data, every where, nor any drop to drink" is the norm in most research areas. Would Galileo and Cavendish release their data today?

Another way to ask the question is whether, indeed, "the value of data lies in their use," and whether that implies that "full and open access to scientific data should be adopted as the international norm for the exchange of scientific data derived from research" (National Research Council 1997, 10). Oft-repeated policy statements such as these promote the idea that data are an end in themselves. If they have inherent value, then they should be captured, curated as assets, and sustained for indefinite reuse. An alternative view, also oft-repeated, is that research objects are malleable, mutable,

and mobile (Latour 1987). Data are not "natural objects," as explained in chapters 1 and 2. Rather, they are a means to an end, inextricable from the research process. From this perspective, data can be discarded at the end of a research project or after a paper is published. They are liabilities, as well as assets, and not necessarily worth the investment to keep them. The truth, no doubt, lies somewhere in between. Some data are worth sharing, and many are not.

Despite several decades of policy moves toward open access to data, the few statistics available reflect low rates of data release or deposit. A survey conducted by the *Science* staff (2011) of their peer reviewers found that only 7.6 percent contribute their data to a community repository; 88.7 percent store their data in university servers or laboratory computers, out of the immediate reach of other scientists (*Science* Staff 2011). Only about 1 percent of ecological data are accessible after the results have been published (Reichman, Jones, and Schildhauer 2011). Even when journals have data availability policies, compliance is low. A study of research papers in fifty high-impact journals, most of which required some form of data release, found that only 9 percent of the papers deposited the full data online. When the policies applied (about 70 percent of papers), 59 percent adhered partially to the journal instructions, whereas papers not subject to the requirements never released all of their data (Alsheikh-Ali et al. 2011).

The ability to release, share, and reuse data—or representations thereof—depends upon the availability of appropriate knowledge infrastructures to do so. That, in turn, depends on agreements among the many and competing stakeholders. Who should invest in infrastructure and who should benefit? As is evident from the case studies, data and their uses vary by context and over time. The kinds of investments these communities need in collections, tools, and policies vary accordingly, as do their relationships with other stakeholders.

This chapter provides three contrasting analyses. The first examines the degree to which stakeholder interests in releasing and reusing data are matters of supply and demand. The second considers scholars' motivations to release and to reuse data, setting data practices in the larger context of scholarly communication. The third analysis assesses the implications of these two perspectives for the design and sustainability of knowledge infrastructures. These analyses draw on the case studies; on reports of who shares data, how, when, why, and to what effects; who reuses data, how, when, why, and to what effects; and on conversations with researchers and scholars in many fields.

Supply and Demand for Research Data

The National Research Council (1997) *Bits of Power* report is but one of many policy reports that promotes open access to research data. A decade later, the Organisation for Economic Co-operation and Development (OECD) promulgated international principles for access to research data from public funding. The thirteen principles explicated in that short policy document are openness, flexibility, transparency, legal conformity, protection of intellectual property, formal responsibility, professionalism, interoperability, quality, security, efficiency, accountability, and sustainability. Despite their wide application, these principles are narrowly drawn. Their definition of research data includes only "factual records" ... "used as primary sources" ... "that are commonly accepted in the scientific community as necessary to validate research findings." The definition specifically excludes "laboratory notebooks, preliminary analyses," and "physical objects" such as laboratory samples (Organisation for Economic Co-operation and Development 2007, 13–14). Most later reports and policies promote sharing a broader array of data types (Australian National Data Service 2014; Ball 2012; Wood et al. 2010). Of these, the OECD document is among the most specific in identifying the many constraints on data release and how those vary by data type, jurisdiction, and other matters.

Supply and demand might be a chicken-and-egg problem. Lacking demand for reuse, few data are released. Lacking data release, demand is insufficient to build the infrastructure necessary to facilitate reuse. Most data-sharing policies attempt to increase supply by mandating or encouraging investigators to release their data. Policy makers, funding agencies, scholarly journals, and other stakeholders have focused on sticks—enforcing data management plans, data deposit, and similar requirements—because they have few carrots to offer. These policies include surprisingly little mention of any expected demand for data or the infrastructure necessary to support release and reuse.

Declaring that data should be released does not make it so. Data-sharing policies appeal to the better nature of investigators with historical arguments for openness. Less often acknowledged are the highly competitive nature of scholarship, incentives for reward and credit, mismatch of labor and benefits, investment in research practices, diversity of practices among domains and researchers, the disparity of resources between communities, difficulties of interpreting shared data, and the scale of resources necessary to share or to sustain data. Policies such as those of the OECD are aimed at governments, similarly appealing to openness and transparency.

Governments also are competitive with each other, and national policies differ in the degree to which information defaults to being open or closed. Many mechanisms exist to increase the data supply, all of which are considered data release for the purposes of discussion here. These include data released by investigators; research data available in repositories, observatories, or other types of collections; and data collected for purposes other than research.

The Supply of Research Data

The origins of data-sharing policies are many. One factor was the increasing commodification of information associated with 1970s and 1980s changes in intellectual property regimes (Schiller 2007). Attempts to patent and commodify the human genome in the early days of sequencing provoked a firestorm about the control of scientific information. These "anti-commons" moves contributed to the development of more common-pool resources for research. Establishing policies for open access to human genome data was a turning point in scientific data-sharing practices (Hamilton 1990; Hess and Ostrom 2007b; Koshland 1987; *Science* Staff 1987; Roberts 1987, 1990; Watson 1990).

Arguments for sharing data come from many quarters: funding agencies—both public and private—policy bodies such as national academies and funding councils, journal publishers, educators, the public at large, and from researchers themselves. Four rationales for sharing data that were developed earlier (Borgman 2012a) are reformulated here: (1) to reproduce research, (2) to make public assets available to the public, (3) to leverage investments in research, and (4) to advance research and innovation. While not an exhaustive list, they provide a framework to examine supply-side interactions of policies, practices, and stakeholders involved in sharing research data.

Reasons, rationales, arguments, motivations, incentives, and benefits often are conflated. A *rationale* is an explanation of the controlling principles of opinion, belief, or practice. An *argument,* in contrast, is intended to persuade; it is the set of reasons given for an individual or an agency to take action. Underlying these rationales are motivations and incentives, whether stated explicitly or left implicit. A *motivation* is something that causes someone to act, whereas an *incentive* is an external influence that incites someone to act. A *beneficiary* in this case is an individual, agency, community, economic sector, or other stakeholder who receives a benefit from the act of sharing data, such as the use of those data for a particular purpose.

To Reproduce Research Reproducibility is often claimed to be "the gold standard" for science (Jasny et al. 2011). As a rationale for sharing research data, it is powerful yet problematic. Although fundamentally research-driven, it can also be viewed as serving the public good. Reproducing a study confirms the scholarship, and in doing so confirms that public monies were well spent. However, the argument applies only to certain kinds of research and rests on several questionable assumptions.

Defining Reproducibility The most fundamental problem with this rationale is the lack of agreement on what constitutes "reproducibility." A special issue of *Science* devoted to replication and reproducibility highlights the competing concepts of reproducibility across fields. Particularly challenging are the "omics" fields (e.g., genomics, transcriptomics, proteomics, metabolomics), in which "clinically meaningful discoveries are hidden within millions of analyses" (Ioannidis and Khoury 2011, 1230). Fine distinctions are made between reproducibility, validation, utility, replication, and repeatability, each of which has distinct meaning even within individual "omics" fields. The variation in use of these terms across the sciences and social sciences is even greater (Ioannidis and Khoury 2011; Jasny et al. 2011; Peng 2011; Ryan 2011; Santer, Wigley, and Taylor 2011; Tomasello and Call 2011).

A new twist on reproducibility is for scientists to pay to have their research and associated data validated by a third party, either before or after publication. Discussions of the Reproducibility Initiative revolve around what problem, if any, it would solve, whether the initiative is attempting to reinvent science, and whether it would divert resources from new research. Response from publishers has been tepid out of concern that paired studies and replications would only clutter the literature (Bamford 2012; Science Exchange Network 2012).

Determining What to Reproduce The difficulty of distinguishing between concepts such as reproducing, repeating, replicating, validating, or verifying research become apparent when considering what unit is to be reproduced and for what purpose. Some approaches attempt exact replication with the same observations, materials, conditions, instruments, software, and so forth, whereas others attempt to obtain comparable results with similar inputs and methods. The first approach validates a specific paper, whereas the latter approach may yield more valid scholarship by confirming the hypothesis being tested.

Reproducibility may have several levels, such as the precise duplication of observations or experiments, exact replication of a software workflow, degree of effort necessary, and whether proprietary tools are required. Computational science is the most promising area for reproducibility, since it may be possible to repeat processes exactly, given sufficient access to data and software (Stodden 2009a, 2009b, 2010; Vandewalle, Kovacevic, and Vetterli 2009). Scientific workflow software that maintains detailed records of research tasks often have reproducibility as a goal, or at least the ability to maintain provenance records (Bechhofer et al. 2010; De Roure, Goble, and Stevens 2009; Goble, De Roure, and Bechhofer 2013; Hettne et al. 2012).

Clinical trials of drugs and medical procedures are concerned with replication and verification, but the costs of reproducing a full trial are prohibitive. A successful trial with one population might be replicated on a different population, however. Rather than reproducibility per se, evidence-based medicine depends on systematic reviews of multiple trials, validating results via comparisons of populations, methods, and findings (Chalmers 2011; Cochrane Collaboration, 2013; Goldacre 2012; Thomas 2013). Biomedical companies often attempt to replicate the results reported in a journal article as a first step in determining whether a line of research is likely to be productive. Companies may spend tens or hundreds of millions of dollars to reproduce published research, often without success. Stakeholders disagree whether this is money well spent to avoid errant investments or whether it reveals flaws in the scientific method. The *Wall Street Journal* took the latter view (Naik 2011). However, journalistic accounts of science frequently simplify methods and results to a degree that is misleading, if not contradictory to actual findings (Goldacre 2008).

Detecting Fraud   Whenever published articles are withdrawn from major journals, questions are raised regarding what the reviewers knew—or should have known—about the data and procedures (Brumfiel 2002; Couzin and Unger 2006; Couzin-Frankel 2010; Normile, Vogel, and Couzin 2006). After a high-profile case of fraud in psychology research, a group of academic psychologists started a project to replicate recent articles in leading journals of the field. Tensions quickly developed over whether the replication effort would strengthen research in psychology or whether those applying innovative methods would be unfairly indicted (Carpenter 2012; Doorn, Dillo, and van Horik 2013; Enserink 2012a).

Questions of what constitutes valid, appropriate, or reasonable data review are only now being formulated, with few answers in sight (Borgman 2007; Lawrence et al. 2011; Parsons and Fox 2013). Identifying faulty

findings does not necessarily require access to data. In many cases, fraud can be detected only after publication, such as when the same images or figures are found in multiple articles (Couzin and Unger 2006; Wohn and Normile 2006). Distinguishing between fraud, misconduct, and error are harder problems. Peer review is an imperfect mechanism to validate scholarly work, but a better system has yet to be found. Reviewers, also known as referees, are expected to assess the reliability and validity of a research report based on the information provided. Peer review rests on expert judgment rather than on reproducibility (Arms 2002; Fischman 2012; Fitzpatrick 2011; Harnad 1998; King et al. 2006; Shatz 2004; Weller 2001).

Resolving Disputes   Most ambitious of all is to view reproducibility as a means of resolving scientific or scholarly disputes. If a result can be confirmed or disconfirmed, then the answer should be clear, or so it would seem. However, efforts to reproduce results often reveal the epistemological disagreements on which these disputes are based, cutting to the core of scholarly inquiry. Theories of plate tectonics were proposed by Albert Wegener early in the twentieth century, but not widely accepted until the 1960s when advances in technology to map the ocean floor confirmed his model. Wegener drew on corroborating facts from a diverse array of fields, lacking sufficient depth in each specialty to convince scientists of the advantages of his theory (Frankel 1976). Similarly, attempts in physics to resolve whether gravitational waves existed failed due to disagreements about validation methods. Some scientists believed that only the experiments that detected these waves were performed appropriately, whereas other scientists only trusted the experiments that failed to detect such waves (Collins 1975, 1998).

To Make Public Assets Available to the Public   Another common rationale for data release is that products of public funding should be available to the public. This rationale is found in arguments for open government, open access to publications, and open access to data (Boulton 2012; Lynch 2013; Wood et al. 2010). For example, the UK policies combine open access to publications and data (Research Councils UK 2011, 2012c; Suber 2012b). Australia incorporates data management in its research ethics code (National Health and Medical Research Council 2007; Australian National Data Service 2014). US policies vary by funding agency. The National Institutes of Health established open access to research publications through PubMed Central before it addressed data management plans. The National Science Foundation addressed data-sharing and data-management plans

without addressing open access to publications. US policies may converge under new federal policies for research information, but these are early days (Burwell et al. 2013; Holdren 2013a, 2013b).

The consequence of conflating these policies is that open access to publications and to data become equated, raising the problems identified in chapter 3. Open access to publications benefits all readers, whether scholars, practitioners, students, or the general public. Open access to data has direct benefits to far fewer people, and those benefits vary by stakeholder. Early reports on open access to clinical trials data, for example, indicate that the majority of requests are coming from drug companies, lawyers, and consultants, and only a few from academic researchers (Bhattacharjee 2012; Cochrane Collaboration, 2013; Fisher 2006; Goldacre 2012; Marshall 2011; Rabesandratana 2013; Vogel and Couzin-Frankel 2013).

To Leverage Investments in Research   A third rationale for data release is that others should have the opportunity to exploit them. Here, too, the difference in the interests of stakeholders is apparent. Scholars' motivations to release their data are influenced by whom they perceive to be the beneficiaries. This rationale supports the need for more repositories that can accept and curate research data, for better tools and services to exploit data, and for other investments in knowledge infrastructure. It also supports the arguments of stakeholders in the private sector who wish to "unlock the value" in the data being produced by universities (Biemiller 2013; Thomson Reuters 2013). However, this rationale conflates investments in research with investments in data, which serve different roles in scholarly communication.

Examples of unanticipated uses of old data often are used to buttress the argument for keeping as much as possible. Minute traces of DNA from Louis XVI, who died at the guillotine in 1793 along with his wife, Marie Antoinette, were compared to DNA from a direct ancestor. Analyses revealed that King Louis's genetic risk factors included diabetes, obesity, and bipolar disorder. The findings contribute new information to debates on the sources of the king's indecisiveness (*Science* Staff 2013). Progress on decoding ancient DNA was among the 2012 "Breakthroughs of the Year" named by *Science* (Gibbons 2012; *Science* Staff 2012). Anticipating future applications is a classic problem for libraries, museums, and archives, but even they cannot keep everything.

To Advance Research and Innovation   The last rationale is that sharing data will advance research and innovation. It differs from the prior two by

addressing the benefits for scholarship. This rationale is implicit in statements such as "Science depends on good data" (Whitlock et al. 2010, 145) and "scientific data curation is a means to collect, organize, validate and preserve data so that scientists can find new ways to address the grand research challenges that face society" (Data Conservancy 2010). It is an argument for investing in knowledge infrastructure to sustain research data, curated to high standards of professional practices. Not all data are worthy of curation, but data worth keeping should be kept well, becoming assets for the research community.

The Demand for Research Data

The four rationales for sharing data are based on assumptions of reuse: if data are shared, then users will come. That assumption is implicit in claims that sharing data will enable others to "unlock their value" (Thomson Reuters 2013). However, research data are complex sociotechnical objects that exist within communities, not simple commodities that can be traded in a public market. If scholars actively sought data for reuse, then more data would be shared. The heaviest demand for reusing data exists in fields with high mutual dependence, as discussed in chapter 4. These are domains that have invested heavily in knowledge infrastructures to share instrumentation, collections, and other resources. As discussed in the case studies, many aspects of data scholarship appear to influence when, how, and whether scholars release or reuse data.

In some fields, scholars are actively discouraged from reusing data. To paraphrase Jamie Callan and Alistair Moffat (2012), data reuse is like looking for lost keys under the streetlamp, because that is where the light is—the interesting data and questions lie elsewhere. Careers are made by charting territory that was previously uncharted. Asking new questions with new data is the most reliable way to break new ground. Asking new questions with old data also can lead to new findings, but it can be difficult to convince editors and peer reviewers that reanalyses are worthy contributions. Asking the same questions by replicating studies reaps little recognition and is especially difficult to get published.

Studies in the sciences and social sciences suggest that private exchange of data may be more common than public exchange via repositories. Researchers report that they rarely seek data from other investigators and that they rarely are asked for their own data (Faniel and Jacobsen 2010; Pienta et al. 2010; Wallis et al. 2013). When data are requested, researchers may or may not comply, depending upon factors such as the resources required to share the data, their relationship to the requestors, and the

elapsed time since the data were created (Campbell et al. 2002; Hanson, Surkis, and Yacobucci 2012; Hilgartner and Brandt-Rauf 1994; Hilgartner 1997). Mayernik (2011) found that data were not released because investigators could not imagine who might want them or for what purposes they might be useful.

The greatest difficulty in assessing practices for data reuse is the lack of agreement on what constitutes "reuse." In turn, reuse depends on what is meant by "use" of data or other forms of information. Information seeking, needs, and uses are old and thorny problems in information science. No satisfactory definition of "information use" applies across disciplines and contexts, so the lack of agreement on "use" or "reuse" of data is unsurprising. After many years of analysis, astronomy archivists reached international consensus on telescope bibliographies but without establishing a clear definition of what is meant by "using the data" from a given telescope (IAU Working Group Libraries 2013). The definitional problem cascades: archives differ on what they consider to be "refereed" publications and on how they measure core concepts such as "observation." Although metrics for astronomy data usage are more commensurate across their field than most, those metrics are not transferrable to nearby fields, and are not comparable across scholarly disciplines.

In sum, a supply-and-demand model does not adequately characterize the challenges of releasing, sharing, and reusing data. A much deeper analysis of scholarly practice is required to shed light on the motivations, incentives, and stakeholders involved in these activities.

Scholarly Motivations

Data sharing is difficult to do and to justify by the return on investment. Few scholars appear to conduct their research with data reuse in mind. Data are a means to an end, which is usually research findings to be reported in publications, rather than an end in themselves. Treating data as products to be released or shared requires changes in methods and practices of research. In some cases, practices are adaptable, but intractable problems of ownership, ethics, resources, and community norms are common. In most fields, scholars have minimal resources to invest in making their data sharable, and even if they do share, no repositories exist to take their data. The success of policies to promote data release may depend upon far more radical investments in knowledge infrastructure than funding agencies, journals, libraries, archives, or scholars acknowledge.

Publications and Data

Data play very different roles in scholarship than do publications, as introduced in chapter 3. Attempts to equate open access to literature and to data obfuscate the complex relationship between data and publications. These relationships are evolving, albeit slowly, as explored in chapter 10.

Communicating Research   The communication of research long predates books and journals. Discussions by the Greeks from the days of Aristotle, "often precariously preserved in repeatedly copied manuscripts" (Meadows 1998, 3), influence scholarly thinking to this day. Scholarly communication gradually became more formalized and more professionalized. Books, as a long form of communication, emerged first. Journals were established in the seventeenth century to formalize the exchange of letters between scholars. Genres gradually evolved into the current forms of publication. Articles have a formal structure that includes statements of authorship, titles, abstracts, references to other publications, figures, tables, and so on. These have diverged into parallel structures for each field, but core elements remain the same for articles dealing with any area of scholarly inquiry. Furthermore, the genre differs little between print and online formats.

Books, journal articles, conference papers, and other publications make research findings inspectable by the community. Publications include sufficient details on the arguments, methods, sources of evidence, and procedures to support the conclusions, but rarely enough detail to reproduce the results. Journals in some fields publish detailed tables and figures. In other fields, articles consist largely of argument with minimal explanation of the sources of evidence.

Publications necessarily simplify research activities, leaving out details deemed unnecessary for the intended audience to understand the argument and evidence. Among the omitted details may be machine settings, calibrations, filters, and protocols in the sciences; methods of statistical analysis, data reduction, interview design, and fieldwork protocols in the social sciences; and methods of searching archival materials, translating between languages, and obtaining access to field sites in the humanities. While not necessary for understanding the article, these details may be necessary for understanding the data.

Thus, publications are not simply containers for data. Scholars formulate their narratives to convince others of the validity and importance of their work. Publications are arguments backed with evidence. They are fixed products at the end of a long process of negotiation with collaborators, funders,

peer reviewers, editors, publishers, program chairs, and colleagues. Findings from any given study are crafted strategically to appeal to the readership of the journal to which an article is submitted, to the editors at the publisher for which a book manuscript is aimed, or to the attendees of the conference. The same or similar findings may be adapted for multiple audiences. Authors choose their terminology, research questions, data, tables and figures, length and organization of the manuscript, and their arguments for each publication. Even the format of references differs from article to article (Bowker 2005; Kwa 2011; Latour and Woolgar 1979, 1986; Lynch and Woolgar 1988a; Merton 1963b, 1970, 1973; Star 1995; Storer 1973).

Identifying what are "the data" associated with any individual article, conference paper, book, or other publication is often difficult. Investigators collect data continually, over long periods of time, with multiple methods, to explore an interrelated set of problems. They draw on cumulative sets of data, which may be documented to varying degrees, to make different arguments in each publication. They may or may not extract a discrete dataset for any given article. Explaining how a dataset was derived may require explaining the methods in a series of prior papers and prior phases of data reduction. The general rule on publications is that they should be sufficiently discrete that each can be understood alone, acknowledging that a fuller interpretation may require reading other publications that are referenced.

Once published, those fixed products take on lives of their own. Each reader brings his or her own knowledge to the document and takes away his or her own meaning. One person reads an article for the findings, another reads it for the methods, another for a specific figure, and yet another for the literature review. A reader in the same specialty reads the preprint for breaking news of the findings. A reader in a related specialty reads the article a year after publication, comparing its findings to recent developments in his or her area. A reader in a different field reads the article in search of methods or findings that might be transferrable. Five or ten years later, a doctoral student assesses the publication for a dissertation, by which time it may have been deemed a landmark, a fraud, or a spurious finding that sent the field down an errant path (Brown and Duguid 1996, 2000; Latour and Woolgar 1986).

Publishing Research Releasing datasets with each publication never became the norm in scholarly communication. From a publisher's perspective, the arguments for incorporating datasets in the publishing process differ between print and digital dissemination. In a print world, the cost of reproducing large datasets is prohibitive. Authors are constrained to a fixed number of pages, which are usually devoted to explicating the argument

with the minimum necessary supporting evidence. Methods sections often get short shrift for reasons of space and because readers are presumed to be sufficiently expert in the field not to need much detail.

In a digital world, the economics change. Printing and page constraints cease to be a major concern. However, journals that publish in both print and digital versions, such as *Science* and *Nature,* tend to maintain identical scope for each article. Thus a four-page limit in print translates to a digital article of the same length. These constraints are partially overcome by requiring "supplemental information" that is published only online and which may include essential information about the methods and data. Supplemental information is largely a characteristic of science publishing and never became as popular in the social sciences or humanities. Peer reviewers may ask for more evidence of how an experiment worked, for example, and authors must satisfy those requests within the constraints of the journal's editorial policy. Some journals have strict rules about what information goes in the main text, what in the supplemental information, what should be stored elsewhere and linked, and how these relationships must be identified. As datasets and other forms of evidence become more voluminous, publishers are concerned about committing to long-term storage and curation costs. More problematic from a data reuse perspective is that datasets behind journal pay walls or posted on authors' websites are not easily discoverable.

Data as Assets and Liabilities

Requirements to release data at the time of publication presume that the authors are "done" with the dataset. Data release is most common in fields such as genomics where the match between a publication and a dataset is relatively clear and in which "datasets are relatively simple, homogeneous and well-defined" (Shotton 2011). In cases where a research career is based on long-term study of a specific species, locale, or set of artifacts, data become more valuable as they cumulate. These researchers may never be done with their data. They are reluctant to release data associated with a specific publication because it might mean releasing many years of data. Similarly, reproducing the data associated with any single publication is problematic because the set of observations reported may depend heavily on prior studies and on interpretation of much earlier data.

Datasets also are assets that can be traded with other researchers, used as leverage in collaborations, and brought as a dowry. Scholars in the humanities may bring troves of material to new jobs or new collaborations. If data are released, they lose their value as assets to barter. Unless researchers get something of value in return, it is difficult to convince them to relinquish

these assets, especially if great effort and expense was involved in acquiring them (Borgman 2007; Edwards et al. 2011; Hilgartner and Brandt-Rauf 1994). Timing is another factor in data release. Researchers protect their collaborations and their investments in their work by not releasing data any sooner than necessary. If data are released too soon, partners may be reluctant to devote the overhead labor and costs necessary for collaboration. Embargo periods are intended to balance the publication priority of investigators with timely dissemination.

Data also are liabilities. Depending upon their types, storing data requires physical space and computational resources. Managing them requires human resources. Time spent on preparing data for release is time not spent on other research activities. Similarly, funds included in grants for data management are funds not available for conducting research. The rights to release data may be inextricable from the responsibility to keep them; hence, legal and economic issues pervade the problem of data sharing. Data often are not released because it is not clear who has the rights or responsibility to do so. Researchers may not know if their data are "owned" by themselves, their university, their laboratory or department, their funding agency, their publisher, or some other entity. The answer may not matter until issues of data release arise. The more collaborators and the more jurisdictions involved, the more difficult it is to ascertain the rights to release data (Arzberger et al. 2004; Berman et al. 2010; Birnholtz and Bietz 2003; Hirtle 2011; Reichman, Dedeurwaerdere, and Uhlir 2009; Stanley and Stanley 1988).

Researchers also are concerned about legal liability and risks to their reputations if data are misused or misinterpreted. Misuse may appear to be a minor concern since researchers are painfully accustomed to their work being misconstrued by the mass media (Goldacre 2008). However, selective extraction of data points, reidentification of human subjects or experimental animals, and other forms of misuse—whether due to lack of expertise, lack of documentation, or malice—are legitimate problems. Global and comparative research on climate change depends on open access to data, yet the politicization of climate research makes scholars in these domains wary of data release (Costello et al. 2011; Gleick 2011; Overpeck et al. 2011; Santer et al. 2011; Servick 2013).

Releasing Data

Scholars often have great difficulty managing their own data for present and future exploitation. Having the means to manage data effectively is a prerequisite to releasing them in ways that they become interpretable by other scholars.

Representation and Mobility The difficulty of extracting data from research context is known as the "mobility" problem. Making data mobile requires separating them from the situation in which they became data. As a result, some amount of meaning is lost. Documenting provenance can restore some of that meaning, but the precise context is never fully transferrable. Data can be "boundary objects" that demarcate the edges of communities. They take on different meaning as they are used, described, documented, and interpreted from field to field and researcher to researcher (Bishop and Star 1996; Bowker 2005; Kanfer et al. 2000; Star, Bowker, and Neumann 2003; Star and Griesemer 1989; Star 1983, 1989).

As explicated in chapter 2, data are entities used as evidence of phenomena for the purposes of research or scholarship. Rarely can those entities be separated from their representations. Whether scholars study a child in a park or phrases in a Chinese Buddhist text, they represent their data in a particular way as evidence of a particular phenomenon of interest. Once those representations become part of a file in STATA, Word, R, or other tool, they are stripped of the reasons why they are evidence of particular phenomena.

Software tools can be sources of friction in data exchange. In CENS, for example, some groups used R, a popular open source statistical package, and some preferred Matlab or other tools. To exchange data, groups exported their data to Excel spreadsheets as a lowest common denominator solution. Others shared data via Google spreadsheets and similar methods. Although CENS is at the small science end of data scholarship, Vertesi and Dourish (2011) encountered the same problem in astronomy, when groups had to reduce their data to a lowest common denominator software to exchange them. Similarly, qualitative data can be exported from analytical tools such as NVIVO and Atlas.ti into spreadsheet or word processing software by forfeiting structure. Such reduction results in considerable loss of analytical power. The use of spreadsheets to exchange data is sufficiently ubiquitous, however, that they have become a common form for data deposit (California Digital Library 2013).

Common standards make possible suites of tools to analyze, visualize, document, share, and reuse data. Standards trickle down to interoperability among hardware, software, tools, protocols, and practices within and between communities. Conversely, these same standards create silos of data and systems that do not interoperate with each other. Lowest common denominator formats may be the only means to exchange data between the parties involved. Silos are a canonical problem of the information sciences. Many translation mechanisms exist, both human and technical, but

they always are translations (Busch 2013; Lampland and Star 2009; Libicki 1995; *Nature* Staff 2012; Star 1991).

Sharing data with the expectation of immediate reuse, as in exchanges between collaborators, is easier than releasing them for unknown future users at unknown times, which could be many years hence. In the latter case, the documentation and representations are the only means of communicating between data creator and user. The future user may be another researcher or may be a computer. Data miners, or bots, have their own criteria for what to "read," index, and extract. The greater the distance from the authors in time, disciplinary expertise, language, and other factors, the more difficult it may be to interpret the argument, methods, data, findings, and context of a study or a dataset.

Data-sharing policies differ between digital data and material objects. Some policies for data sharing refer explicitly to samples and specimens. Physical samples are shipped through the post as a form of data sharing between bioscience labs. Data sharing is sometimes accomplished by sending staff to the laboratory, archive, or field site where the data are located. Material transfer agreements usually govern these types of sharing.

Provenance   Questions of provenance, in the archival sense of "chain of custody" and in the computing sense of "transformations from original state," arise in interpreting data that have evolved through multiple hands and processes (Buneman, Khanna, and Tan 2000; Carata et al. 2014; Groth et al. 2012). Data and their representations tend to be closely aligned with software and often with hardware, too. Sensor networks, pipeline processing in astronomy, and scanning electronic microscopes for metallurgy are but a few examples for which hardware and software processing are deeply intertwined. Replicating the processes or interpreting the output requires access to the software. Whether open source or proprietary, software changes continually. Documenting data may require records of each software version and configuration of the platforms on which the data were handled. Interpretation of outputs can be difficult because processing and analysis tools such as statistical, mathematical, and workflow software rarely maintain a precise record of the systems or data at each transaction (Claerbout 2010; Goble and De Roure 2009).

Some of the software necessary to interpret data may be custom tools that scholars have developed to collect, process, analyze, and document their data. Researchers write code to model the phenomena under study, whether climate models or symbol sequences in papyri. Sometimes code is a major investment requiring programming staff, but often it consists of

scripts written in statistical, visualization, or other tools. In computer science, software is sometimes "the data" that results from a project.

Researchers tend to be even more reluctant to release their code than to release their underlying data. The reasons for reluctance are several. One is a concern for the "messiness" of the code. Research-grade code often is poorly documented and execution may be inefficient. As in one-off research projects, code intended only for immediate use is rarely documented for reuse. A second concern is for control over the software. The researcher's intellectual investment in code transcends the individual dataset or publication. Models of phenomena or other analytic code are a researcher's competitive advantage. Output from models and model parameters are sometimes shared without releasing the underlying code.

An underexplored aspect of data release and reuse is the influence of early processing decisions on later interpretations of a dataset. Initial decisions about how to clean and reduce data may determine how completely the provenance of data can be recovered. In domains such as astronomy, biology, and the "omics" fields in which reuse is common, researchers clean and reduce their data to build a database. As Alexander Blocker and Xiao-Li Meng (2013) explain, preprocessing decisions "can be quite treacherous" from a statistical perspective because most are irreversible. Initial assumptions constrain analyses in all subsequent phases. Reuses made by researchers downstream therefore rest on those assumptions. Each inference is only as valid as the assumptions on which processing in prior phases was based—and these can be impossible to know. Many scientific disagreements can be traced to the statistical problem of multiphase inference. Even collaborators working together can overlook these assumptions. Reuse is even riskier for scholars outside the collaboration or in nearby domains, since they are less likely to know what questions to ask about preprocessing decisions (Blocker and Meng 2013; Meng 2011).

Decisions on preprocessing and other forms of data cleaning and reduction are done with particular sets of research questions and phenomena in mind. When those data are reused for different questions, different preprocessing decisions may be necessary. For example, new theories about cancer suggest that responses to treatment are highly individualized. Cases when drugs or other treatments are exceptionally effective on only a few patients may be excluded from data analysis because observations at the extreme ends of the curve usually are treated as statistical outliers. A new effort will examine these outliers by mining old data to generate new hypotheses about why some drugs work on some people but not others (Kaiser 2013). However, these decisions come at a price. NASA maintains data at multiple levels

of processing, as explained in chapter 2. Few researchers are able to maintain their data resources at multiple levels of processing or with sufficient documentation that each stage of processing could be reanalyzed or reused.

Provenance of datasets is better understood as a network than as a linear sequence of relationships. Depending upon the domain, an individual dataset may be related to research objects such as software tools, instruments, protocols, laboratory notebooks, technical documentation, and one or more publications. Linking these objects together makes each of them more useful and aids in discovery. Linking publications to associated datasets is particularly useful because they add value to each other. Papers are the primary means by which most datasets are discovered and may be their only public documentation. Creating such links is an investment in data management since each research object must be described and relationships between objects must be specified. Technologies such as linked data can aid in recording and discovering these relationships but are an incomplete solution (Bechhofer et al. 2010, 2013; Borgman 2007; Bourne 2005; Parsons and Fox 2013; Pepe et al. 2010).

Acquiring Data to Reuse

Enchantment with the possibilities for reusing old DNA samples, climate records, transportation flows, and mobile phone traffic, and determining patterns of exploding manhole covers (Anderson 2006, 2008; Mayer-Schonberger and Cukier 2013), too often obscures the risks of reusing data. The majority of effort in repurposing old data is devoted to cleaning, coding, and verification. As danah boyd and Kate Crawford (2012, 668) comment, "bigger data are not always better data." Increasing the size of the haystack does not make a needle easier to find; hence, researchers are cautious in deciding when to acquire data from other investigators, repositories, or other external resources (J. Boyle 2013; Eisen 2012; Kwa and Rector 2010).

Background and Foreground Uses   Data resources may not be referenced in scholarly publications, irrespective of whether datasets are attached to those publications. The lack of referencing does not mean that no data were used in the study; it merely means that no use or reuse of data was mentioned. Data acquired for purposes such as calibrating instruments, verifying measurements, or assessing site conditions may not be deemed worthy of mention, nor deemed a "use" within the scholarly practices of a field. Searching for information in the researcher's personal files, libraries, museums, archives, digital repositories, attics, and warehouses or by asking friends and colleagues is part of scholarly activities. These aspects of

gathering evidence tend not to be documented explicitly in publications, although practices vary. Findings may depend on many searches, sources, resources, uses, and reuses that are not mentioned because they are not deemed necessary to the narrative.

These are among the reasons that use and reuse of data are hard to document in practice. Those who collect new data in support of their research questions may also seek other information for background purposes. In studies of CENS and of astronomers, for example, these types of information were drawn from data repositories, sky surveys, government records on weather or land use, or occasionally from other researchers. Although essential to interpreting the findings of the study, those sources tended not to be mentioned in papers or to be cited explicitly. New data sources collected by the investigators were in the foreground of their work and were mentioned (Borgman, Wallis, and Mayernik 2012; Wallis et al. 2012; Wynholds et al. 2012).

These early findings on foreground and background uses of data suggest that reuse—in the sense of using data that were not collected by the investigators—may be higher than reported. Comparing data to external sources may be considered good practice and be the sort of tacit knowledge about methods that need not be reported in publications. As discussed in chapter 9, the rate of data citation appears to be increasing in some fields. Whether the actual reuse of data is increasing or whether citing data sources is gaining greater acceptance as good practice is not known and probably cannot be known. These appear to be issues of when something is considered to be data, what kinds of evidence are considered appropriate for reporting, and what parts of the research process are appropriately left as tacit knowledge within a community. They may be matters of figure and ground, in the psychological sense. Some objects come to the fore as data and others remain in the background as context or simply as noise.

Interpretation and Trust The ability to trust others' data is crucial since investigators are staking their reputations on their choices of data. Publications and personal networks are primary means of data discovery, particularly outside of fields that rely on shared repositories. When possible, researchers contact investigators to discuss the methods by which the data were created, cleaned, processed, analyzed, and reported (Faniel and Jacobsen 2010; Wallis et al. 2013; Zimmerman 2003, 2007). Communities working on related problems may contribute data to different repositories. Their data may be hidden from each other because of differences in metadata, classification mechanisms, or the lack of awareness of resources outside the

community's boundaries. When a search for something as specific as a protein structure leads to a paper describing it, researchers may contact the paper's authors rather than look for archives in which the structure may have been deposited.

Given the great interest in data sharing and reuse, surprisingly few studies have examined the circumstances, motivations, or practices associated with reusing data. Faniel and Jacobsen (2010, 357), in studying earthquake engineering researchers, identified three questions used to assess data reusability: "1) are the data relevant, 2) can the data be understood, and 3) are the data trustworthy." These engineering researchers usually are seeking technical parameters to which they can compare their own observations. They appear to be seeking "background data" for purposes similar to those found in astronomy and sensor-network research (Wallis et al. 2012; Wynholds et al. 2012).

Knowledge Infrastructures

Strategic investments in knowledge infrastructures, such as data repositories, human resources with expertise in data management, better tools, and methods to provide credit for data sharing, may increase the release and reuse of data. To be effective, knowledge infrastructures must be able to accommodate the many kinds of data that might be released, the many ways in which they might be used, and ways to transfer knowledge about those data between contributors and users. They must also support curation and access to information resources for appropriate periods of time.

The lack of infrastructure to support release and reuse was acknowledged in some of the earliest policy reports on data sharing. A 1985 report from the US National Academies of Science, entitled *Sharing Research Data*, made recommendations that would require changes in the practices of funding agencies, investigators, researchers, journal editors, peer reviewers, data archives, universities, and libraries (Fienberg, Martin, and Straf 1985). Similarly, the long list of OECD principles published in 2007 reflects the infrastructure concerns of many stakeholders. Building information systems—or knowledge infrastructures—that people want to use is much harder than it may appear (Markus and Kell 1994). Infrastructures are not things that can be built all at once, nor are they static. They are complex ecologies with many moving parts. They must adapt to changes in practice, policy, technologies, and stakeholders. Major components of knowledge infrastructures can be identified, even if all the relationships among those components cannot.

Repositories, Collections, and Archives

Asking scholars to release their data begs the questions of how and where those data will be made available and for how long. The most obvious, if incomplete, response is to develop more repositories to which scholars can contribute their data. Whether known as archives, collections, data systems, databanks, information systems, or repositories, the technology is but a starting point. These are common-pool resources that need governance models—collection development policies, rules for contribution and access, standards for classification and data structures, and plans for sustainability. Collections and governance are associated with communities, but the boundaries of scholarly communities are porous and overlapping.

Repositories often grow from the bottom up, originating as research collections that serve small research teams or communities, as introduced in chapter 2. These kinds of collections facilitate sharing for the duration of the collaboration, but may not be sustained. Those that attract larger communities may become resource collections. The most successful become reference collections that attract longer-term funding and can set standards for their communities (National Science Board 2005). Other collections are established from the top down, as a strategic goal of large projects. This is the case with astronomy missions, especially for space-based telescopes. Data archiving consumes a relatively small amount of the budget of major telescope missions and makes possible the long-term use of the data. Data remain valuable long after the instruments have been decommissioned.

Data can be represented in multiple ways concurrently and over time. Researchers can submit their datasets to several repositories or to none at all. Their choices may depend upon the requirements of their funding agencies, journals, and institutional contracts, and the collection policies of each repository. Some collect within a research domain, others by type of material, and others by geographic region. Some will accept contributions from anyone, while others accept data only from members of their consortium. University libraries are beginning to acquire data from research projects based at their institutions. However, most libraries are able to accept only smaller datasets that do not otherwise have a home or to operate a registration service that aids in the discovery of data.

Repositories for data also vary widely in their commitments to curation. Backing up data in their submitted form can be expensive, but sustaining them over long periods of time requires much larger investments in migration to new technologies and formats as they appear. Each repository specifies quality and format standards for what they will accept. The degree to which they invest in verifying data content and structure, augmenting

datasets with metadata and provenance documentation, or providing other value-added services varies considerably. Some accept data that meet technical standards, leaving most of the scientific or scholarly validation to the contributor. Others will audit the data for quality standards before accepting for deposit. Once deposited, responsibility for maintaining and providing access to the data usually is transferred from researcher to repository. Repositories may commit to keeping data indefinitely or for fixed periods of time. They may be subject to certification for standards of quality and for sustainability planning, but certification is often voluntary (Consultative Committee for Space Data Systems 2012; Data Seal of Approval 2014; Jantz and Giarlo 2005; Digital Curation Centre 2014).

To the extent that researchers are willing to release data at all, they may be more willing to release them to trusted repositories that will curate their data and make them available indefinitely. Repositories can add value to data through metadata, provenance, classification, standards for data structures, and migration. They can also add value by making data more discoverable and by making them more usable through tools and services. These are substantial investments to be made by communities, universities, and the agencies and governments that fund them.

Repositories are an essential part of the knowledge infrastructure, and a primary component for the release and reuse of data. They are far from a panacea, however. Design considerations will vary by community and circumstance. It is easier to organize collections by the structure of their content than by how people will ask questions of that content. Individual systems attempt to be internally consistent, using criteria that suit the content and the perceived uses of the community. Because repositories serve distinct purposes, few effective means exist of searching across repositories. Each person, and each computational agent, may ask a different question of those data. People's queries change over time. Robots also learn and adapt. Repurposing data for unanticipated questions is an even higher goal than simply reusing data for the same purposes for which they were created. Federation mechanisms are needed and those too must be governed.

Some scholars argue against the development of collections on the grounds that they drain resources away from other forms of research, from smaller grants, and from the creation of other kinds of data. Large data-intensive initiatives may be viewed as counterproductive if they appear to discourage new lines of discovery-driven research. Others argue that data are being aggregated on the wrong scale, either too large or too small, for effective reuse (J. Boyle 2013; Eisen 2012; Kwa and Rector 2010).

Granularity and representation are fundamental challenges in the design of any information system. The set of structures, tools, and classification that accelerates the exploitation of data for one community will create barriers for another. One size does not fit all, especially when the information is as malleable as research data. In designing knowledge infrastructures in general, and data repositories in particular, accommodating multiple levels of granularity, multiple tools to exploit content, and flexibility in means of access are essential.

Private Practice
Repositories are only one means by which data might be released for reuse by others. Data also are released as part of supplementary information, by posting on a website, or only upon request. Studies of journal practices reflect how difficult it is to say definitively how much data are released along with articles (Alsheikh-Ali et al. 2011). Even when journals state that data associated with articles must be made available, journal editors are unlikely to keep detailed statistics on compliance. Types, formats, and amounts of data and documentation vary widely. A data registry identifier may be provided to certify deposit in a community collection, or a statement that the data are available upon request may suffice. Any of these means of release might satisfy the requirements or recommendations of funding agencies.

As noted earlier, private sharing of data may be more common than acquiring data from repositories (Faniel and Jacobsen 2010; Pienta et al. 2010; Wallis et al. 2013). These forms of data sharing are difficult to identify and to document; hence, studies and statistics are few. Private communication can be very effective because scholars can discuss the content, context, strengths, limitations, and applicability of a particular dataset to a phenomenon.

Data sharing between individuals, although a common and effective mechanism for reuse, does not scale. Scholars will invest time and effort making their data useful to others only in specific circumstances. These may depend on how well they know and trust the requestor, what is being requested, and the uses for which the data are intended. If requests are frequent or onerous, they may decline. Data sharing by posting datasets or information about datasets on websites relieves some of the burden of documentation but relinquishes most controls over how the data are reused and by whom.

While imperfect, each of these methods increases the availability of data for reuse and should be accommodated in knowledge infrastructures.

Private sharing and public website posting may satisfy data release requirements but do little to foster discoverability, provenance, usability, or sustainability. Private sharing works only for contemporaneous reuse during the period that the scholars still have the data and remain familiar with their context. Similarly, datasets posted on websites usually are static files associated with specific versions of software. Knowledge about research data decays quickly as students graduate and postdocs leave the team. Access to those data declines as software evolves, computers are replaced, storage is purged, and memory of the specifics fades.

Human Infrastructure

The ability to release, share, and reuse data depends heavily on human infrastructure. Data can be released as unprocessed datasets—strings of symbols with minimal documentation—but they are of little value for reuse without adequate representation and documentation. Few scholars have the expertise to document their data to archival standards. Concepts such as metadata and provenance are not core concepts included in graduate courses, at least outside the information professions. The time required to learn these skills is often viewed as time not spent on research. Data documentation, to the extent it is done, is commonly delegated to graduate students and other research staff. These often are the people closest to the data; they do most of the collection and analysis, especially in the sciences. Researchers may be willing to delegate some of these activities to librarians and archivists, depending on the amount of time required to work with them, the perceived payoff, and the perceived beneficiaries.

Investments to make data releasable and reusable are infrastructure issues. They should be viewed as community matters, not solely the responsibility of individual scholars. Institutions that invest in the human resources necessary to manage data are more able to reuse those data. People who curate data and who maintain standards, classification systems, and associated tools are mediators between those who create data and those who might reuse them. Much of this work is done—when it occurs—by information professionals in data repositories and other institutions (Lee, Dourish, and Mark 2006; Mayernik, in press).

All too often this is invisible work, as explained in chapter 3. Those who benefit from the labor of researchers and information professionals to represent data in ways that they can be made mobile may be blissfully unaware of those investments. The invisibility of the work required to keep all the components interacting smoothly is a defining characteristic of infrastructure. The invisibility of this labor also highlights the tensions

between stakeholders. Those who make the investments in repositories, in local work to manage data, and in other parts of the infrastructure are not always the direct beneficiaries. Stakeholders in other communities, other countries, and other sectors may be substantial beneficiaries. Therein lie the challenges of governing these common-pool resources, which include sustainability and the ready access to free riders.

Intractable Problems

Governance of common-pool resources such as data repositories is possible, but the methods to do so are far from formulaic (Ostrom and Hess 2007). Continual negotiation is necessary. Some problems appear to be intractable, including those arising from the external influences identified in the case studies. They cannot be solved, but some negotiation may be possible. For example, ownership, licensing, and rights to data vary by domain, practice, policy, and jurisdiction. Agreements made early in collaborations may reduce friction but will not necessarily eliminate it.

Some forms of data are not sharable because of confidentiality or ethical concerns. Most social science research on human subjects is conducted under regulations that limit data release. When human subjects data are released they are anonymized to the extent possible. If these data are used alone, basic techniques such as replacing names with identifiers may suffice. Other methods, such as those used for taking a national census, aggregate data in large enough units that individuals cannot be identified. However, people who are anonymous in one dataset often can be identified when several datasets are combined. Reidentification is surprisingly easy by combining such information as age, sex, geographic location, date of hospital release, and number of children. Anonymous DNA donors have been reidentified with public genealogy databases (Bohannon 2013b; Gymrek et al. 2013; Rodriguez et al. 2013). Finding ways to anonymize data securely while keeping them useful for research is a technical and policy challenge (Ohm 2010; Sweeney 2002). One approach is to release human subjects data only to qualified researchers and only under conditions ensuring that reidentification will not be attempted. Models such as these require institutional oversight.

Disciplinary Knowledge Infrastructures

The case studies provided rich detail on the data scholarship in many domains of study. A brief summary of how each of these domains manages their data, their motivations to do so, and the stakeholders involved

illustrates the ways in which their knowledge infrastructure requirements may vary.

Sciences

The sciences are far from homogeneous in their handling of data, their data-sharing practices, and investments in knowledge infrastructures.

Astronomy The data supply in astronomy is largely top down—major national and international missions develop and deploy telescopic instruments in space and on the ground. Space missions invest most heavily in data collections, streaming data from instruments to ground stations to data repositories where they are processed through a pipeline. Once cleaned, calibrated, and verified, they are released to the community.

Each data release from astronomy missions such as the Sloan Digital Sky Survey, Hubble, Chandra, and Planck is usually accompanied by a data paper to document the science and the provenance of the dataset. Data papers are submitted to astronomy journals for publication, bearing the names of all the team members responsible. These are among the most highly cited papers in the field and are the means by which researchers get credit for sharing the data.

Astronomy has the most extensive knowledge infrastructures of the domains covered in the case studies. Their common-pool resources include telescopes, data repositories, classification systems, and many other resources. The community has agreed on standards for data structures, metadata, and ontologies. They have suites of software tools for analyzing data in these standard forms. Since the early 1990s they have coordinated international publishing efforts, contributing the bibliographic records of astronomy to the Astrophysics Data System. ADS covers astronomy literature back to the nineteenth century. Celestial objects that are mentioned in these publications are cataloged in SIMBAD, NED, and related systems. These systems are tightly cross-referenced so that publications link to celestial objects and records on celestial objects are linked to publications in which they are mentioned. The WorldWide Telescope combines data and literature from these and other sources to create a platform for visualizing data. Experts and novices alike can contribute "tours" of objects, phenomena, and regions of the sky. The WWT is being integrated into scientific tools for astronomy to serve as a scientific and educational platform (Accomazzi and Dave 2011; Accomazzi 2010; Eichhorn 1994; Genova 2013; Goodman, Fay, et al. 2012; Hanisch 2013; Norris et al. 2006; Pepe, Goodman, and Muench 2011; Udomprasert and Goodman 2012; White et al. 2009; WorldWide Telescope, 2012).

Despite their extensive knowledge infrastructure, the astronomy community has not expected investigators to release their own data, whether derived from repository data or obtained by other means such as observing proposals. A few data repositories exist to accept data; most are mission support archives. Some investigators post data on their team websites, as done with the COMPLETE survey in the case study. University repositories such as Dataverse are building astronomy-specific archiving capabilities (Goodman, Muench, and Soderberg 2012). Relatively few astronomy publications include links to the data sources although the rate of data citation is increasing (Pepe et al. in press).

The Chandra X-Ray Observatory offers an example of how astronomy data can become more valuable over time through intensive investments in stewardship. The Chandra team has documented usage since inception of the mission in 1999, developing metrics and means to add value to the data. Chandra data archive staff search the astronomy literature for mentions of Chandra, then read the publications carefully to determine if their data were used, and if so, how. Their metrics require that a paper has an unambiguous link to a specific observation, and that some property was derived from that observation. They distinguish between a Chandra science paper, a Chandra-related paper, and an instrument-development paper. Qualifying uses of data are added to the Chandra archive, to ADS, and to SIMBAD, linking datasets, publications, and celestial objects with added metadata. This process adds value to the data by providing additional scientific documentation, and makes datasets more readily discoverable by providing new points of entry. The Chandra team creates the links because authors rarely cite the data source explicitly (Becker et al. 2009; Blecksmith et al. 2003; Lagerstrom et al. 2012; Rots and Winkelman 2013; White et al. 2009; Winkelman and Rots 2012a, 2012b; Winkelman et al. 2009).

These stewardship efforts also reveal the difficulty of defining a "use" of the data. As Rots, Winkelman, and Becker (2012) found, the notion of an "observation" differs between observatories and may differ within an astronomical mission. As a result of these and other ambiguities in comparing metrics across repositories, an international working group established a set of best practices for statistics on usage of astronomy data archives (IAU Working Group Libraries 2013).

Sensor Networked Science and Technology Efforts to standardize data collection at CENS and to adopt metadata standards were at odds with the exploratory, hypothesis-generating nature of this research community. When reuse did occur, it often involved private sharing to ensure that context information was transferred with datasets. Data most likely to be

contributed to repositories were those from standardized practices and protocols, such as genomic and seismic data. Some software was contributed to repositories of code. Teams often had good intentions to release data, but failed to resolve which team member should be responsible for doing so (Borgman et al. 2012; Wallis and Borgman 2011; Wallis 2012).

CENS researchers did not need to reconcile data over the long term, except within individual teams. Most CENS researchers were more concerned with consistency of their own observations than with comparability across research sites. Comparability on a global scale is necessary to assess climate change and loss of biodiversity, but this is a different kind of research program than CENS. The exceptions were the participating natural reserve sites, which collect synoptic observations of flora, fauna, and climate (James San Jacinto Mountains Reserve 2013, Natural Reserve System 2013). These served as background data for some types of CENS research.

Few repositories exist to take exploratory data such as those being generated by CENS field research. Little demand for repositories existed in CENS either, since researchers could not imagine who might use their data (Mayernik 2011). CENS developed a small data-archiving facility to encourage sharing and reuse, but contributions were low (Wallis et al. 2010). The environmental and ecological science communities began to implement repositories and data-sharing requirements only in the latter days of CENS (Dryad 2013; Reichman, Jones, and Schildhauer 2011; Whitlock 2011).

One of the many situations in common between CENS and the Long Term Ecological Research Centers (LTER) was the effort to adopt the Ecological Metadata Language (EML) standard as a mechanism to improve data sharing, reuse, and comparison. Millerand and Bowker (2009) identified competing narratives of how EML was accepted at LTER sites. The narrative of the EML developers was that the standard was adopted by the entire LTER community and was therefore a success. Another narrative was told by information managers involved in implementing EML at their research sites: EML is a complex standard, difficult to understand in its entirety, and the tools provided were incompatible with local practices. In their view, EML was only partly successful. The CENS experience is comparable to the latter narrative. EML was the best match to research activities of several CENS teams, so it was proposed as a standard for use in a common data repository. However, the two-hundred-page EML manual daunted these small teams. They rejected EML on the grounds that it was too "heavyweight" a solution for their needs. Most continued to organize their data with hierarchical file folders and other local conventions for naming data elements and variables (Wallis et al. 2010).

CENs collaborations formed around research problems of mutual interest rather than around shared data. The scientists needed better tools to conduct their science. The computer science and engineering researchers needed real-world applications in which they could develop and test technologies. Each team might be able to reconstruct the provenance of its respective series of data collection efforts, but the joint deployments cannot be reconstructed fully. This is not a bad outcome. Rather, it represents the great effort invested by the teams to learn enough about each other's domains to be able to address problems jointly. Despite their interoperability problems, they still were able to collaborate (Edwards et al. 2011; Mayernik, Batcheller, and Borgman 2011; Olson, Zimmerman, and Bos 2008; Wallis et al. 2008; Wallis et al. 2007).

Genomics   Genomics, although not developed as a full case study, provides contrasting examples to knowledge infrastructures from the other science cases. Because researchers in genomics need to reuse their own data, the data supply is created from the bottom up as teams sequence genomes and contribute them to repositories. These scientists have massive resource investments in laboratories, hardware, software, and staff. They are motivated to standardize their procedures, leading to standardized forms of data that are more readily shared. These are highly competitive research areas. Teams race to find cures for cancer, Alzheimer's, pandemic influenza, and other dread diseases. Lives and money are at stake, as they see it. The early threat to patent and control the human genome, combined with a deluge of genomic data, led to historic agreements on data sharing (Watson 1990). In the time since those agreements, the success rate of clinical trials for new drugs has declined and the cost of conducting trials has increased. Public pressure to release the results of clinical trials also has mounted. Among the promised outcomes of sharing genomic data are to increase the speed of drug discovery, reduce the duplication of trials, enroll fewer research subjects, reduce costs, and provide more benefits to patients and clinicians.

Despite the intense competition between stakeholders, common-pool resources are being developed. Multiple drug companies and academic consortia have begun to share data on clinical trials, genome sequences, and protein structures. Not all parties are willing to participate, and each party may impose its own conditions for sharing and reuse (den Besten, Thomas, and Schroeder 2009; Bhattacharjee 2012; Check Hayden 2013; Corbyn 2011; Couzin-Frankel 2013b; Edwards et al. 2009; Edwards 2008b; Goldacre

2012; Howe et al. 2008; Nelson 2009; Rabesandratana 2013; Weigelt 2009; Williams, Wilbanks, and Ekins 2012).

Despite releasing their protein structures, the research team that conducts the studies still has advantages in using those data to explain scientific functions. They have spent weeks or months generating, cleaning, and reducing their data. Only the final, cleaned, and calibrated data are reported and released. Although records of protocols and interim processing are kept, so much data are generated and reduced that the exact steps are unlikely to be replicable. The precise conditions of each experiment cannot be reproduced because minute differences in temperature, humidity, and other laboratory conditions affect the observations. They release their protocols along with their data to aid others in reusing them. They do find, however, that as others attempt to replicate their results, small deviations from the protocol can yield very different results. Even when high scientific standards are applied, stepwise processes such as the crystallization of proteins can be stochastic.

While the pooling of these data represents a remarkable merger of competitive interests, it is fraught with challenges, some foreseen and some not. Two large collaborations on the front lines of data sharing and reuse for genomics and other biomedical data are the Structural Genomics Consortium (2013) and Sage Bionetworks (2013). They are funded from multiple sources, including research grants and drug companies. To recruit and retain top talent, their researchers must be able to publish their findings in top journals such as *Science, Nature,* and *Cell.* Here the porous boundaries between data and findings become apparent. If data are posted prior to submitting an article about them, journals sometimes consider that to be "prior publication" and refuse to consider the manuscript. Yet the novel research finding may be the ability to explain the biological functions of the protein and model. Releasing the data is thus a different scholarly act than reporting the findings. A drug company can pursue a new drug based on correlations between gene expression and protein at the same time that an academic research team pursues the biology that explains the correlation.

Complex biomedical ethics issues are entangled in the release of human genetic information. For example, proposals to release "incidental findings" reveal sharply divided opinions of bioethicists, biomedical researchers, policy makers, clinicians, and patients. Some believe that unanticipated genetic results must be released to patients, and others believe that patients or clinicians should decide whether findings unrelated to the condition for which the patient was tested should become part of the record (Couzin-Frankel 2013a; McGuire et al. 2013; Wolf, Annas, and Elias 2013).

Social Sciences

Research in social sciences has a similarly mixed array of data-sharing practices, as evidenced by the case studies. These influence the ability to release, interpret, and reuse data.

Internet Research As participants in the World Internet Project, the researchers conducting the Oxford Internet Survey need to compare data across times and places, thus are motivated to maintain internal consistency to ensure comparability. They embargo each dataset for one survey cycle while they exploit the data for journal publications. The datasets they release to qualified researchers are the "raw" observations provided by the survey company and in a form for ingest by STATA, a popular statistical package.

By releasing datasets through their website, with a simple license to ensure noncommercial use, the Oxford Internet Institute has a record of requests and downloads. They have no way of tracking actual use, however. Lacking many inquiries about detailed characteristics of the data from those who have downloaded, they presume that the data are serving background purposes for research or educational purposes such as teaching survey methods courses. Because they are not contributing the datasets to an archive, they need not assign metadata or provenance documentation beyond that needed for internal use.

Twitter feeds and other social network data can be obtained from the companies that own the services. If data are obtained through contracts with the providers, those contracts may govern whether investigators may release them. If data are gathered by scraping sites, they are harder to control, although service providers attempt to limit distribution. The ability to control and release information about oneself or about other people falls into a gray area of Internet policy (J. E. Cohen 2012). Journals are concerned about publishing articles based on proprietary data that cannot be released. Information retrieval researchers are similarly concerned about conducting research on datasets that cannot be released for replication by others.

Sociotechnical Research The sociotechnical research team whose work is discussed in chapter 6 adapts interview questions, protocols, codebooks, and other methods in ways that findings can be compared over time and across research sites. Reuse of instruments, codebooks, interviews, and field notes requires annual approval by human subjects committees. Research subjects can opt in or out of data reuse provisions. For collaborative projects involving multiple universities, human subjects protocols must be approved by each participating university and pairwise between universities.

Open-ended interviews and ethnographies can be harder to anonymize than surveys or medical records, especially in cases when people are known within their communities. Audio recordings of science and technology researchers, as in the case studies, cannot be anonymized. Voices are distinctive and recognizable; transcripts are only slightly less recognizable. Details of research interests, choices of metaphor, and distinctive speech patterns can reveal identities. The work to redact these materials for anonymity in ways that they would retain enough information to be reusable by others would be a research project in and of itself. Reporting findings from these kinds of data requires scholarly craft. Explanations are edited carefully to be as descriptive as possible, retaining nuanced interpretations of communication, but not providing enough detail to reveal the identities of the persons involved. Using these data is difficult. Reusing them is even harder.

Humanities

Data in the humanities are the most amorphous of all, yet reuse appears to be increasing. These scholars are finding new ways to exploit their data, and to ask new questions.

Classical Art and Archaeology The CLAROS project is as much infrastructure as it is collection building. They are repurposing curatorial records to allow them to be reused by scholars, learners, and the public-at-large. They add new capabilities such as image searching and cross-museum searching. Such collections are useful to multiple audiences. The governance challenge is to be "all things to all people" while serving communities well enough for them to stake a claim in the system's survival. These are complex systems that could be sustained in several ways. One approach is to maintain an interactive system; another is to maintain a dark archive of its contents. Efforts to archive the "back-end data" independent of the full operational system were among the contributing factors in the demise of the Arts and Humanities Data System (Reimer, Hughes, and Robey 2007; Robey 2007, 2011).

For the Pisa Griffin research, art historians and an archaeo-metallurgist gather data from archives and secondary sources around the world. They also inspect the object itself. The scientist provides tabular data in a form that enables comparison of the metals in this bronze object to similar objects. Publications about the Pisa Griffin include references and footnotes to publications and other documents where information was found. Sometimes people who provide specific information to the researchers are named. Rarely mentioned are the archives visited or the collections

in which evidence was found. These may be considered background data within these fields. The archives and collections from which material was obtained may never know how their collections were used or how the evidence obtained was reused. Publishing interpretations is more important to the community than is the release of data. Only in the rare cases when scholarship is challenged on grounds of accuracy or fraud do notes and other records tend to be released (Wiener 2002).

Buddhist Studies   The scholar of Chinese Buddhist philology has accumulated a large collection of materials over the course of his career, which he continues to mine. Until recently, these were mostly collections on paper. Now that it is possible to capture, disseminate, and reuse representations of very old texts in non-Western languages, he is accumulating more digital records of his observations. Only a few years ago, these were unimaginable capabilities for this small and close-knit community of scholars. His motivations are to maintain those resources in ways he can mine and combine them in the future. Similarly, his access to CBETA gives him a far larger set of digital resources on which to draw. He reports the details of his analyses in his publications in the form of long tables.

CBETA and other collections supported by the Buddhist religious community are a special case of common-pool resources. This community has promoted the dissemination of their texts for many centuries as a tenet of their religion; thus, sustainability of these digital resources does not appear to be a worry for these scholars. The collection, which continues to expand beyond the original 135 or so volumes, is of unparalleled scope and quality for scholars in this field.

Conclusion

The policies of funding agencies, journals, and other stakeholders in data scholarship have focused on increasing the supply of data available for reuse, with minimal attention to scholarly motivations for sharing or reusing data or to the knowledge infrastructure investments required. The rationales for promoting data sharing reflect the legitimate concerns of stakeholders, such as the ability to reproduce research, make public assets available to the public, leverage investments in research, and advance research and innovation. These rationales often lead to generic policies that fail to reflect the vast diversity of data scholarship within and between domains. Data are both assets and liabilities. When research depends on the ability to reuse one's own data and to pool those data with researchers within the community, incentives exist to release and reuse data. When research is local and

exploratory or when research depends on evidence accumulated over long periods of time, incentives to release are few.

Equating open access to data with open access to publications is to misunderstand scholarly communication. Publications are much more than containers for data—they are arguments backed with evidence, and the relationship of data to those arguments varies greatly. In the fields where datasets are discrete and can be matched one-to-one with a publication, data release may be feasible. In fields where publications consist largely of interpretation, data release may be irrelevant. Releasing data is rarely a simple step beyond publishing a journal article. Representing data in ways that they become useful to others can consume substantial resources, and those are resources not being spent directly on research.

Releasing, sharing, and reusing data are better understood as problems of knowledge infrastructure. Focusing on the supply of data begs the question of demand. In most fields, the demand for reusable data appears to be very low. However, defining uses and reuses is difficult because practices vary so widely. Making data mobile across domains, contexts, and over time is extremely difficult. Data are not natural objects that can be readily commodified and exchanged in a marketplace. They are entities used as evidence of phenomena. The same observations and objects can be represented in many ways. As a consequence, the same entity often becomes different data when transferred to another context. Slight changes in interpretation, method, or practice can result in those entities being assessed as slightly different evidence of somewhat different phenomena. Decisions made in the earliest stages of the research, such as preprocessing done before observations are considered data, ricochet through the remainder of the process.

Data often are inextricable from software, hardware, instrumentation, protocols, and documentation. Scholars have many ways to deal with these complexities in handling data. Often they involve decisions that are embedded deeply in research activities, part of the tacit knowledge that is difficult to document or convey to others. At other times they are details assumed to be known by the community and thus can be omitted from documentation and publications. Datasets may be extracted from their technological context, reduced to lowest common denominator tools for interpretation. Making data mobile requires dealing with these subtleties and acknowledging the loss of meaning in translation.

Knowledge infrastructures can facilitate the exchange of information within and between communities. Often, scholars' greatest challenges lie in managing their own data. The ability to exploit one's own data is a prerequisite to sharing them. Knowledge infrastructure developments in data management methods, tools, and human resources are likely to leverage data

release. Another useful capacity for many communities is shared means to represent research objects, such as metadata and classification mechanisms. When communities can agree on representations and on other standards for information exchange, they have a basis on which to build shared collections. Shared collections, in turn, are most likely to arise from communities that need to combine information resources. Those collections may serve communities large or small, for short or long periods of time.

The boundaries of research communities are porous and change continuously, however. Individual scholars may be members of multiple communities, and those memberships adapt to changes in research agendas and research fronts. Standards, practices, and representations that facilitate data sharing within a community can create barriers to sharing between communities. When these barriers can be bridged, it is often through private communication between individual scholars. Personal discussions and sharing of knowledge within groups are essential parts of the knowledge infrastructure. They do not scale, however. Each scholar can share data one-to-one with a limited number of other people. Private sharing does not scale over time. Data, and knowledge about them, decay quickly unless nurtured.

Most important of all is the need to recognize the level of investment that must be made in knowledge infrastructures if sharing, releasing, and reusing research data are to be effective. The value in any dataset or collection may not become apparent until much later. To realize that value, however, requires massive investments of monetary, technical, and human resources. Knowledge infrastructures require the involvement of multiple and competing stakeholders, often across international boundaries. The costs and benefits of investing in them are unevenly distributed. All need to be governed, to be sustained for appropriate periods of time, and to deal with free riders. To declare that researchers should release their data for the benefit of the common good is simplistic at best. These are community responsibilities. A broader conversation is necessary about what data sharing, release, and reuse are intended to accomplish. If two scholars want to learn more about each other's data scholarship, then private sharing is the most expeditious means. If data resources are to be stewarded for the benefit of generations to come, then major investments in technology, collections, workforce, and governance are necessary. The goals, no doubt, are a mix of these and many others. Stakeholders and vested interests abound, but so do great opportunities to make better use of the resources that exist already.

9 Credit, Attribution, and Discovery of Data

Introduction

If publications are the stars and planets of the scientific universe, data are the "dark matter"—influential but largely unobserved in our mapping process.
—CODATA-ICSTI Task Group on Data Citation Standards and Practices, "Out of Cite, Out of Mind"

Data will remain "dark matter" in scholarly communication unless they are described, curated, and made discoverable. Data citation is high on the agenda of libraries, publishers, scholarly societies, repositories, and funding agencies. Assigning credit for data has become an urgent problem for organizations concerned with research information, such as CODATA, the Research Data Alliance, the Board on Research Data and Information (United States), the Joint Information Systems Committee (United Kingdom), and DataCite. International task groups on data citation have been formed. Stakeholders have convened topical conferences and working groups. Manifestos have been issued and standards are being developed (Altman and King 2007; Crosas et al. 2013; Institute for Quantitative Social Sciences 2011; Research Data Alliance 2013).

On the surface, data citation appears to be a straightforward technical problem of adapting existing mechanisms for bibliographic citation. Efforts to do precisely that have unearthed long-standing debates about who, what, how, why, and when to give credit for any form of scholarly contribution. Scholarly practices for managing and assigning credit, attributing responsibility, and discovering publications have accreted gradually over a period of centuries. While imperfect, the resulting knowledge infrastructure is sufficiently robust to support these functions for publications old and new; thus, Galileo's works can be discovered and cited in today's distributed digital networks. Overlaid on this infrastructure are metrics to evaluate the

productivity of scholars; the influence of journals, publishers, and countries; and the flow of ideas between disciplines and over time (Borgman and Furner 2002; Borgman 1990; Cronin 1984, 2005; Kurtz and Bollen 2010).

Assigning credit for data is a far more complex challenge than it appears, even in the face of dedicated efforts to reach solutions. Technical mechanisms for citation are only surface characteristics of the knowledge infrastructures in which they are embedded. Social conventions underlie citation practice, whether to publications, data, documents, webpages, people, places, or institutions. For each publication, authors select the objects worthy of citing. Selection is based on practices that are poorly understood—who chooses to cite which items, when, how, and why? Methods for citing vary widely between fields, as exemplified by the disparate publication style manuals of the sciences, social sciences, humanities, and law. Citations accrue to a publication from many styles, with or without the full list of author names, the article title, page numbers, or numerical identifiers. Citations may be explicit or oblique; important sources of evidence may go unmentioned. Bibliographic references largely presume that objects are fixed, stable, and complete units. None of these conditions can be assumed with data.

Mechanisms for credit, attribution, and discovery of research objects are inextricable from scholarly communication, and yet theories about the social practices of citation are sorely lacking. Citation methods tend to be learned by example, rather than taught. Practices emerge and evolve independently within communities, often in isolation or in conflict with those of nearby communities. Allocation of authorship credit also varies widely between domains, leading to conflicts in collaborations and confusion across disciplinary boundaries. Determining who should receive credit depends partly on which products or processes are deemed worthy of credit.

Pragmatic decisions made by practitioners unfamiliar with the larger set of principles of scholarly credit, attribution, discovery, identity, persistence, and bibliographic control can wreak havoc on knowledge infrastructures. Database producers have been known to reorder the sequence of authors on papers to improve the efficiency of their sorting algorithms. Publishers have been known to change Digital Object Identifiers (DOIs) on articles for branding purposes. Authors drop middle initials of cited authors rather than verifying names in original sources. The possibilities for undermining the integrity of citations to publications and to data are endless. Small decisions can have large effects as they ripple across domains and over time.

Much is at stake in the choice of standards, policies, and implementations for assigning credit for data. The success of data citation methods depends upon adoption by the community—the scholars who write the publications and use data as evidence in those publications. Success also depends on investments in knowledge infrastructures to make data citation feasible and attractive. Considerable human labor may be required to describe and organize data in ways that they become discoverable. This chapter explores how citation practices are embedded in the theory and practice of scholarship, proposing a broader conceptualization of credit and attribution for data as part of knowledge infrastructures.

Principles and Problems

Among the concerns for data citation are how to distribute credit to the multiple parties involved with specific data objects; legal requirements for licensing, ownership, and control; granularity of objects to be cited; tracking provenance over long periods of time; maintaining integrity and verifiability of data; integration with existing mechanisms of bibliographic control; integration with extant standards and technologies of digital networks; discoverability by humans and by machines; management and stewardship of data; facilitating sharing and reuse; identity of individuals and organizations associated with data; utility of citation mechanisms for secondary uses such as evaluation and policy; and accommodation of the disparate practices among disciplines and stakeholders. This is a huge list of requirements for something that appears as simple as "data citation" (Borgman 2012b).

A fruitful starting point is to assess the scholarly communication system in which bibliographic citation is embedded, drawing out some of the theoretical thickets that plague current concerns with data citation. Those insights can be applied to credit, attribution, and discovery of data. Of the many issues that could be explored at this intersection, a few of the most salient are chosen: how to cite, why to cite, how to assign credit, how to attribute responsibility, how to identify people and objects, how to implement data citation, the role of citations in credit and attribution, differences between bibliographic and data citation principles, and the disparate concerns of stakeholders in scholarly communication.

Stakeholders concerned with science policy and infrastructure have formulated sets of requirements for data citation. The most comprehensive set of principles published to date was that promulgated by an international

task group (CODATA-ICSTI Task Group on Data Citation Standards and Practices 2013):

I. The Status Principle: Data citations should be accorded the same importance in the scholarly record as the citation of other objects.

II. The Attribution Principle: Citations should facilitate giving scholarly credit and legal attribution to all parties responsible for those data.

III. The Persistence Principle: Citations should be as durable as the cited objects.

IV. The Access Principle: Citations should facilitate access both to the data themselves and to such associated metadata and documentation as are necessary for both humans and machines to make informed use of the referenced data.

V. The Discovery Principle: Citations should support the discovery of data and their documentation.

VI. The Provenance Principle: Citations should facilitate the establishment of provenance of data.

VII. The Granularity Principle: Citations should support the finest-grained description necessary to identify the data.

VIII. The Verifiability Principle: Citations should contain information sufficient to identify the data unambiguously.

IX. The Metadata Standards Principle: Citations should employ widely accepted metadata standards.

X. The Flexibility Principle: Citation methods should be sufficiently flexible to accommodate the variant practices among communities but should not differ so much that they compromise interoperability of data across communities.

Immediately upon publication of the CODATA-ICSTI report, other groups began to discuss this set of principles and refine them further. As of this writing, representatives of libraries, publishers, science policy agencies, data repositories, and other sectors have achieved consensus on a similar but more concise set of eight principles: importance, credit and attribution, evidence, unique identification, access, persistence, versioning and granularity, and interoperability and flexibility (Datacitation Synthesis Group 2014). Implementation groups also are being formed.

Achieving consensus on these principles required several years of discussion. They are operational requirements arising from the need for workable mechanisms for credit and discovery that could be the many stakeholders responsible for the institutional arrangements of scholarly communication. The discussion herein, in contrast, begins from theory and evidence of scholarly behavior. Scholars pursue myriad lines of inquiry by myriad

methods, drawing on evidence new and old. Those evidentiary sources may be static or dynamic, clear or contested, singular or complex, and scarce or plentiful. Publications based on these sources may bear the name of one author or thousands. Criteria for authorship vary wildly from field to field, as do criteria for what acts or objects are worthy of citation. Technical frameworks for bibliographic citation are fragile at best, having evolved over the course of centuries to accommodate a diverse array of practices. Notably, the frameworks adapt to practice, not vice versa. Establishing a technical framework and then asking scholars to adopt it is a risky approach. Starting with scholarly practice for credit, attribution, and discovery of research objects is more promising.

Theory and Practice

The role of citations in scholarship sparked the interest of sociologists by the mid-twentieth century, spawning an extensive literature on scholarly communication and bibliometrics, including several dedicated journals and conference series. Bibliometrics, or the study of relationships in published literature, has much older roots. Some date bibliometrics to Talmudic scholars in the Middle Ages (Paisley 1990). Others date them as early as several centuries BCE, depending upon what textual analyses are considered analogous to bibliometrics. Modern use of citations for information discovery is usually traced to Shepard's citators in the field of law. Beginning late in the nineteenth century, Shepard's used stickers, and later a printed index, to link cases to subsequent decisions such as whether the case was upheld, overturned, or sustained. By the late twentieth century, these links were automated. Cases now can be "Shepardized" in LexisNexis to determine their present legal standing.

In 1955, Eugene Garfield conceived the *Science Citation Index (SCI)* by inverting the reference lists of journal articles to enable searching by citations received (Garfield 1955). By the mid-1960s, the machine-generated SCI was published in print form, and by the early 1970s it was an online database. The *Social Sciences Citation Index* and the *Arts and Humanities Citation Index* followed later. Citation linking, and following references from one object to the next, is one of the techniques used by modern search engines.

Substance and Style: How to Cite

Citation mechanisms are so deeply embedded in the practices of authors and readers that they are used without much consideration of the underlying principles and assumptions. Common parlance tends to conflate

distinct concepts. For example, references are made and citations are received. The referencing, or citing, document controls the form of citation that is received. The referencing author may describe the cited document completely and accurately with the style of reference most commonly used in the fields of the cited authors. Alternatively, the referencing author may misspell author names; leave out or reorder names; introduce errors in the title, date, volume, issue, page numbers, or other elements; and employ a different citation style. Authors who usually follow the style guidelines of the American Psychological Association, for example, may find their publications described differently when cited in legal, scientific, or humanities publications. Errors and variant forms, once created, tend to proliferate. Once a publication—or a dataset—is released into the wild, the authors have little control over how it is cited, used, or interpreted, as discussed in chapter 8.

When an author cites another publication in the reference list, footnotes, or bibliography, a relationship is created between the citing and cited documents. In a completely print world, the relation from citing to cited document is unidirectional. Not until *Shepard's,* and later the *Science Citation Index,* began to invert reference lists could citations be treated as a bidirectional relationship. In a completely digital world of publication, bidirectional relationships can become automated links. The efficacy of those links depends on the accuracy of the citation and on the ability to identify uniquely the citing and cited objects. It may also depend upon the participation of the publishing venues in the technical infrastructure that supports the linking. Underlying these technical infrastructures, in turn, are software engineering decisions about symmetric and asymmetric data structures that emerged from long debates in the computational sciences. None of these relationships is easy to establish, and the mechanisms by which linking is accomplished are largely invisible to their users. Authors and readers encounter links from citing to cited—or cited to citing—documents that work seamlessly. They also encounter links that are broken, misdirected, nonexistent, or that take them to a pay wall or other authorization page.

To understand why some links work and some do not requires sophisticated knowledge of the scholarly communication system and the technologies that support it. For the vast majority of users, the system is opaque. The invisibility of the infrastructure makes it easy to use but disguises its complexity. To transfer the principles and mechanisms of linking publications to linking data, some of this complexity must be revealed.

Also largely invisible to users are the agreements on metadata elements and on styles of presentation that underlie the citation process. Almost all bibliographic citation styles agree on the basic metadata elements of author, title of publication, and date of publication. Beyond those, metadata tends to vary by genre, such as volume, issue, and page numbers for journal articles and publisher and place of publication for books. These elements are aligned with the control systems of publishers and with the cataloging and indexing systems deployed by libraries, both of which are key stakeholders in the scholarly communication system. Metadata for location and identification, such as uniform resource names (URNs) and digital object identifiers (DOIs), came later, as did metadata specific to research areas, systems, and classification mechanisms.

The choice of metadata elements is distinct from the style in which they are presented in the citation. Common style manuals such as those of the American Psychological Association, Modern Language Association, law (*Bluebook*), and the Council of Science Editors, vary in matters such as the order of metadata elements, the use of full author names or initials, abbreviation of journal titles, and the inclusion of other metadata. Some styles require numbering in text and reference lists; others use in-line citations and are ordered alphabetically. Bibliographic management tools such as Zotero, Endnote, and Mendeley capture descriptive metadata and support tagging and note-taking. They can render these metadata elements as bibliographic references in thousands of citation styles. Technology for linking cited and citing documents, such as CrossRef, is agnostic to the style of citation (Council of Science Editors and the Style Manual Committee 2006; CrossRef 2009, 2014; EndNote 2013; Mendeley 2013; American Psychological Association 2009; Harvard Law Review Association 2005; Zotero 2013; Modern Language Association of America 2009).

These are but a few examples of the invisibility of the infrastructure that underlies bibliographic citation. Bibliographic citation has evolved over a period of centuries; its roots are visible only to the cognoscenti. Because the system is robust enough for most purposes, the fragility of its foundation is not readily apparent. It adequately supports information discovery, basic functions of giving credit for sources, and attributions of authorship. These foundations begin to break down when citations are used for second-order purposes, such as counting citations to assess the influence of authors, journals, publishers, and countries, for mapping the flows of knowledge across time, geographical location, and disciplinary boundaries—and for citing data.

Theories of Citation Behavior: What, When, and Why to Cite Objects
Questions of who chooses what to cite, when they do so, and their reasons
for doing so are the most problematic and least explored areas of the citation process. They also are a promising area for theory building in scholarly
communication. Research on the uses and reuses of data should inform the
design of a robust system for data citation.

Meaning of Links   Treating links between publications as the basis for discovery, credit, attribution, and evaluation metrics has been problematic
from the start. It assumes that the relationship has meaning and that the
meaning can be counted objectively. David Edge's (1979) critique of the
use of citations as quantitative metrics to map scholarship continues to
resonate today. His nuanced analysis, from the perspective of a historian of
science, reveals that citations are not an objective measure of the influence
on a scholar, a paper, or a project. The choice of documents to reference
in any given publication can be understood, if at all, by examining the
research process closely. Even retrospective accounts are suspect, as authors
can justify their choices post hoc.

Edge's article was a rallying call for bibliometricians, and many
responded (MacRoberts and MacRoberts 1989, 2010; McCain 2012; White
1990). Howard White (1990) recognized that conflicts about the validity of
citation metrics would not be settled empirically any time soon. He characterized the conflicting perspectives succinctly (p. 91): "On the one hand are
people willing to think only biographically, in terms of particular interests
and individual peculiarities. On the other are persons willing to trust, and
look for patterns in, highly aggregated data, which exist at a high degree of
abstraction."

White further characterized these distinctions as "ground level" versus
"aerial" views of reality. He found these views to be incommensurate. In
the aggregate view, patterns are visible that cannot be seen on the ground,
yet the risk is that those patterns cannot be interpreted without adequate
understanding of what is actually on the ground. Telescopes and microscopes both are necessary for viewing data, but they offer contrasting
perspectives.

A satisfactory model from the aerial perspective requires a better
theoretical understanding of local practices. However, despite several
decades of study, little is known about how authors choose what to cite
in each paper, article, book, or other document. To count and map citations as objective indicators of relationships, an implicit assumption is
that authors select references from the universe of all possible sources of

documentation, choosing all that are necessary and only those that are necessary. Thus the set of citations made by each article should be optimal: it should be the necessary and sufficient record of all sources relevant to the article. Also implicit is that references are accurate and complete descriptions of the cited objects. In practice, none of these assumptions is true or generalizable.

The aerial and ground views of citations are incommensurate not only because of differences in theoretical perspective but also in methodological approach. Citations in the aggregate are used to map flows of information between fields, communities, and countries. They also are used to assess the influence of journals, universities, and other large organizations. The problem arises when aggregate statistics are used to draw inferences about individuals within that group, known as the "ecological fallacy" (Babbie 2013; Robinson 1950). Citations or other indicators are distributed unevenly within any group. Influential communities do not consist of individual authors of equal influence. A few highly cited papers can skew the counts for any group. Good journals publish poor papers and vice versa. Using the aggregate statistics for any group as a proxy for the behavior or influence of individuals in that group is statistically invalid.

Selecting References   Social practices in selecting references are far from the objective ideal described above. References are employed in the narrative of the publication to support the argument. Although authors will reference publications that contradict their findings, overall they tend to cite supporting evidence more extensively than contradictory evidence or inconclusive findings. Authors read many things they do not cite. Authors sometimes cite things they do not read, whether canonical works of a field, items referenced in other papers, or works by department chairs or others in positions of authority.

What authors deem to be worthy of citation varies by publication venue, audience, and many other factors. Authors read most comprehensively when writing dissertations, annual reviews, and books. At other times, they may select what is most familiar or most readily at hand on desks or desktops, rather than conducting extensive literature reviews. They may oversample references from the journal to which they are submitting the paper as a means to position their argument for that community and set of peer reviewers. The obverse is coercive citation, where others expect explicit recognition by bibliographic reference (Cronin 2005). The choice of references may reflect only the reading of the coauthor who conducted the literature review rather than the reading choices of all of the authors. The length of

reference lists may be constrained by publication page limits or by specific numbers of references allowed by a journal.

Referencing practice is also a matter of personal style. Some authors apply Occam's razor, carefully selecting only those references that are necessary and are sufficient to support the argument of the paper. Others are effusive in their referencing, sprinkling citations to pique readers' interest in pursuing topics in more depth. Some cite defensively, fearing accusations of plagiarism or fraud.

References are made for many reasons, both positive and negative, yet each is counted as a single unit when used for evaluation purposes or when mapped in a bibliometric network. References to document facts, support arguments, refute arguments, provide background on methods, identify or validate prior work by the authors on which the present paper builds, give homage to a mentor, or identify related work in the target journal are all treated as equivalent acts.

Theorizing and Modeling Citation Behavior   The reduction of references to simplistic counts provoked calls for a comprehensive theory of citation behavior (Cronin 1981, 1984; Zhang, Ding, and Milojević 2013). Lacking general theories, many have attempted to categorize the reasons for which references are made. Ben-Ami Lipetz (1965) was among the first to categorize citations. His goal was to reduce the "noise" in using citations for retrieval, since some are more relevant to the content of the article than others. Lipetz proposed twenty-nine "relational indicators" to type the relations between citing and cited publications. These were grouped into four categories: the original contribution or intent of the citing paper, other type of contribution, identity relationship between the papers, and disposition of the cited to the citing paper. Data are mentioned in two categories: "data transformation" and "data cumulation." Thus the ability to distinguish data citations from other kinds of citations has been a concern since the early days of information retrieval.

The many attempts to categorize citations vary by the purpose of the study—some to develop theories of scholarly communication, some to improve retrieval systems—and by the body of literature on which they are based. Citation practices in the humanities are much different from those in the sciences, for example. Attempts to categorize citation behavior vary so widely in theory, method, research questions, and corpus of literature that no overarching theory of how, when, and why authors cite has been achieved. The many typologies cannot be merged, due to differences in scope, assumptions, and purposes. An overarching theory of bibliographic

citation behavior is unlikely, given how little is understood about how and why practices vary.

Authors, objects, data, and the relationships between them can be modeled formally. SCoRO, the Scholarly Contributions and Roles Ontology (Shotton 2013), for example, is based on semantic web standards and describes classes, object properties, data properties, named individuals, and other characteristics of scholarly contributions. More than one hundred categories of named individuals are included in the ontology, making fine distinctions between access provider, agent, analyzer of data, researcher, reviser of manuscript, rights holder, scholar, securer of funding, and so on. SCoRO did not originate from theoretical models of scholarly communication. Rather, its origins are technical, attempting to provide an exhaustive list of categories and relationships that can be used in semantic publishing. Similar, but simpler, classifications of citations are being developed by authors and publishers (Harvard University and Wellcome Trust 2012).

Categorization varies by who does the assigning: the author, a student, an indexer, an editor, a later reader who annotates the document, or a researcher studying citation practices. Indexers—whether human or automated—can categorize citations based on surface-level meaning, but cannot capture the intent of the authors. Authors cite what they consider relevant to the paper, but often have difficulty making finer distinctions about the purposes of individual references.

Authors can only select candidate citations from the universe of materials available to them, and that universe varies widely. Some authors have access to the world's great libraries, whereas others have minimal information resources and minimal access to current publications. The growth of open access to publications is creating more equity in the pool of resources available to scholars and students, and will likely change patterns of citation. The number of references attached to papers continues to grow. Rarely can the set of references in any given publication be assumed to be the optimal set of necessary and sufficient sources for the content presented therein.

Citing Data What is known about data citation is that data rarely are cited. Studies of data citation show that only a small percentage of papers include data in reference lists or footnotes, although the numbers have been growing in recent years. Here, too, the findings are difficult to compare because data citations may be formulated as bibliographic citations, URNs, mentions in text, or by other means. Comparing counts is problematic. Data often are reported in papers or included in papers as tables and

figures. Authors cite papers as proxies for the data within them. Some fields publish "data papers" and "instrument papers" to give credit for specific contributions. These are highly cited publications that serve as proxies for citing data per se. Conversely, authors use data they do not cite, as in the foreground and background examples discussed in chapter 8.

Determining what constitutes a data citation or a use of data is complex and contextual. As discussed in the Chandra X-Ray Observatory example in chapter 8, astronomy data archivists disagree on how to define an observation, which is the basic unit for classifying uses. The community eventually achieved an international consensus on best practices for statistics on data usage. Implementation depends on the work of information professionals to create links between papers and datasets, since the authors of papers rarely give explicit citations to the data they use.

Clear or Contested: Who Is Credited and Attributed?

The single metadata element on which all citation styles agree is *creator,* or the party responsible for the object that is being cited. In most cases, the creator is a personal author or multiple authors. In others, the creator may be a corporate body such as a committee, research collaboration, or agency, like the National Science Foundation. In yet others, the responsible parties may be contributors, editors, translators, performers, artists, curators, illustrators, and so on. Statements of responsibility have become so complex that some have suggested they be treated like movie credits, with long lists of individuals and organizations credited by category.

Naming the Cited Author   The most straightforward part of the citation process is creating the list of references to be included in a publication. Each reference gives credit to creators by naming them. To the citing author, the names of those who created the cited document may be clear: the statement of responsibility as it appears on the document. In contemporary journal articles and books, authorship statements are explicit and easily restated in citations. In other cases, citing authors must make judgment calls about who or what should receive credit. The well-known NSF report on cyberinfrastructure is variously cited as "the Atkins report," the "Blue Ribbon Panel Report on Cyberinfrastructure," by all or part of its long title, *Revolutionizing Science and Engineering through Cyberinfrastructure: Report of the National Science Foundation Blue-Ribbon Panel on Cyberinfrastructure,* or by the personal authors on the panel (Atkins et al. 2003).

To maintain consistent points of entry, catalogers refer to hundreds of pages of rules. Citing authors tend to make ad hoc decisions about credit,

although guidance is available in most publication manuals. When references are inaccurate, those variant forms proliferate in search engines and bibliographic databases. Despite consistency in authorship statements, references to the publications of Christine L. Borgman can be found with and without the middle initial and occasionally with the Germanic surname of Borgmann. Authors with common names become conflated when initials are omitted, merging Clifford A. Lynch and Cecilia P. Lynch into "Lynch, C." Variant forms of names, dates, page numbers, DOIs, URNs, and other publication details undermine information discovery. The accuracy of citation statistics varies accordingly.

Complicating matters further, the same person may publish under multiple names or be known by variant names, as discussed further below under questions of identity. Creators of documents and datasets often provide a preferred form of citation, which contributes to consistency but does not ensure it. Credit for the content of web pages and gray literature is even less consistent. Search engines can resolve some kinds of ambiguity in references, although forms of referencing may have so little in common that they are difficult to recognize as pointers to the same object.

Perhaps the ultimate honor is to have one's ideas referenced but not to be named in a bibliographic citation. Once ideas become part of accepted knowledge, citations may be incorporated by obliteration (McCain 2012), which muddies the intellectual trail. "Diffusion of innovations," for example, is often mentioned without reference to Everett M. Rogers, who coined the term (Rogers 1962). Such obliteration occurs throughout scholarship, sometimes intentionally and sometimes not. What is public knowledge in one field may be a new finding in another. Scholars and students alike may be unaware of early origins of an idea. In areas within the humanities, especially, authors make oblique references to the ideas of others, assuming that the readership is part of the continuing conversation within a community. Tracing the credit for ideas can be as much historical inquiry and forensics as bibliometrics.

Negotiating Authorship Credit   Far more complex is the process of determining the parties entitled to be named as authors of a publication or dataset. Authorship and other forms of responsibility are social conventions. These conventions vary by person, team, community, publication venue, and over time. Until the mid-1950s, most scholarly publications were sole-authored. As the number of authors per paper increased, responsibility for publications became more diffuse (Wuchty, Jones, and Uzzi 2007). By the late 1990s, papers often had several authors, and sometimes several

hundred; the rate of single authorship continues to decline (Davenport and Cronin 2001; King 2013).

Collaborators negotiate who is named as an author on each paper and in what order. As authorship credit and citations increase in value for hiring and promotion, these negotiations have grown more contentious. Authorship may or may not be credited for writing narrative, collecting data, compiling a bibliography, analyzing data, or building instruments. Courtesy authorship is sometimes given to heads of departments or labs who acquired the funding, independent of the person's involvement in the specific publication. Responsibility may be divided among papers, with some members of a collaboration being named on data papers, some on instrument papers, and some on science papers, as occurs in astronomy. In survey research, those who formulated the questionnaire may or may not be named as authors on each paper, yet they may be the critical people to contact when reusing data.

First authorship might rotate sequentially or be assigned based on who "needs it" for an upcoming tenure review, job search, or national evaluation exercise. In some fields, the first author position is most significant; in others, the last author position is most prestigious. Authorship may be in alphabetical order and possibly in two alpha sequences, first by the student authors and second by the faculty authors. The persons named as corresponding authors may be most significant, regardless of the order in which names appear.

Publications frequently include acknowledgments sections that identify contributions other than authorship. Acknowledgments rarely are counted in bibliometric assessments. The few studies of their role in scholarly communication confirm that specific acknowledgments can be important documentation of relationships among people and ideas (Cronin and Franks 2006; Cronin 1995). Sources of funding tend to be acknowledged but not given as citations or credited as authors. An ontology of funding sources, containing a taxonomy of more than four thousand standardized funder names, is being developed for authors and publishers to tag sources in publications (CrossRef 2013). By standardizing the form of reference, funders and publishers hope to improve the tracking of publications that result from specific funding sources.

When the number of authors is few, authorship for each paper usually is negotiated locally among collaborators. In fields with many authors on each paper, such as medicine, biology, and physics, publishers have issued ethics rules to specify conditions for authorship status (Committee on Publication Ethics 2013; International Committee of Medical Journal

Editors 2013). All authors may be asked to sign off on the final manuscript before publishing. Some journals require categorized statements that identify the contribution each author made to the research or the writing of the article. Contributions may include data collection, data analysis, writing, and so on, but are less discrete than the one-hundred-plus roles in SCoRO (Shotton 2013).

In fields such as high energy physics, authorship may be collective. For instance, the first Higgs boson paper from CERN states the author as "The Atlas Collaboration" and then lists 2,932 author names (Aad et al. 2012). Authorship criteria are specified explicitly by the CERN collaboration. It lasts for a set time period to ensure that those who contributed to early stages of research get credit for the findings. As a result, deceased persons can be authors (Mele 2013). The Aad et al. paper "is dedicated to the memory of our ATLAS colleagues who did not live to see the full impact and significance of their contributions to the experiment." Specificity does not eliminate controversy, however. Peter Higgs, for whom the boson is named, is but one of several theorists who proposed its existence (Cho 2012). The Nobel Prize in physics was awarded to Higgs and François Englert, but not to the ATLAS collaboration, as some had hoped.

The number of authors per paper has grown more slowly in the humanities, where sole authorship remains the norm in many domains. Coauthored papers may be an assemblage of individually authored sections. For example, in the areas of classical art and archeology covered in chapter 7, coauthored papers are organized into discrete units, each signed by one or two authors (Contadini, Camber, and Northover 2002; Faoláin and Northover 1998; Kurtz et al. 2009).

Responsibility Today's discussions about authorship revisit very old debates about responsibility for ideas or documents. Notions of individual and collective responsibility vary over the centuries, by culture and context (Eisenstein 1979; Fitzpatrick 2011). Early religious documents, works of art, and other artifacts of cultural heritage often are unsigned and undated. Subsequent scholarship seeks to identify their origins and provenance, which may remain contested for centuries. Scholars attempt to reconstruct texts that were copied, merged, divided, glossed, annotated, edited, and translated over long periods of time. Texts also were transferred through oral traditions, changing slightly with each retelling and writing, as in the Buddhist studies case in chapter 7.

Individuals who recorded ideas contributed to the documented history that survives. These include not just scholars but also the monks, scribes,

shopkeepers, and bureaucrats who created records. Work that might be considered plagiarism today is regarded as authentic scholarship in other contexts. Boundaries between authoring, editing, and copying have blurred over time. Many roles can be significant in interpreting the responsibility for documents. A "tradent," for example, is a producer of text who hands along spiritual truths, sometimes anonymously (Editors 2013; Mayer 2010). Scholars whose names have been obliterated through incorporation of their ideas in the modern canon (McCain 2012) are members of a large cohort of unknown contributors to knowledge. For all of these reasons and more, some prefer to reframe authorship as "contributorship" (Harvard University and Wellcome Trust 2012).

Credit for Data   The ability to discover and reuse data is enhanced when the parties responsible for those data can be identified. However, notions of responsibility for data are no better understood than is authorship of the Buddhist canon. Compilations of data such as navigational charts, tables of logarithms, and census records remain useful despite the anonymity of those responsible for their creation. The roles of authors, editors, compilers, contributors, and collectors are difficult to separate. Credit and attribution are distinct in some circumstances, as parties using data may have a legal responsibility to attribute the source with a certain citation (Pearson 2012). Distinctions between creating information and compiling facts have legal implications for what can be copyrighted.

Authorship of publications does not map well to data, for the reasons presented in chapters 3 and 8. Publications are arguments made by authors, and data are the evidence used to support the arguments. Those data may come from many sources, and many people, instruments, and processes may have touched them along the way. A publication is a singular object, understandable on its own by the intended audience. Data do not stand alone; they derive meaning from context and associated objects such as protocols, software, instrumentation, methods, and the publications in which they are described. It is often impossible to name precisely the set of people who are responsible for a dataset, much less to put them in an author sequence. When datasets are large, such as a sky survey, data papers are written to explain the data sufficiently that others may use them. Citations to those data accrue to the papers, not directly to the datasets.

When researchers in CENS were first asked about authorship of their data, it became clear that data authorship was not terminology that resonated with them (Wallis, Borgman, Mayernik, and Pepe 2008). Data were associated with publications, but the relationship was not one-to-one. A

single dataset might yield multiple papers and a single paper might draw on multiple datasets. Further exploration revealed that lack of agreement on responsibility within the team was a primary reason that data were not deposited. It was unclear whether the principal investigator, the student who handled data analysis, or some other team member should take responsibility for releasing or posting data (Wallis, Rolando, and Borgman 2013). Students and postdoctoral fellows who collected and analyzed the data were most intimately familiar with their characteristics and provenance. Investigators are legally responsible for the project and are the corresponding authors on most papers. The corresponding author may be the person with the most stable address, not the person with the most detailed knowledge of how the research was conducted.

Jillian Wallis's (2012) dissertation is the most extensive study to date on questions of authorship and responsibility for data management, albeit within one research center—CENS. She explored how researchers perceive responsibility for data, how data management tasks are allocated in a team, for what tasks individuals are held responsible, and to what standards. Although the specifics of the data management tasks varied by research topic and by team, she found different patterns of responsibility within each of the six teams studied. Responsibility sometimes changed over the course of the project as data were handed off from one person to another. Authorship on papers and data management responsibility were intertwined in many ways. In all cases, "responsibility for data" was a vague concept that often required long discussions to explicate (Wallis 2012, 174).

Assigning credit for data facilitates reuse if individuals responsible for data can be contacted. When data are discovered through publications in which they are described, the authors are the first point of contact. Credit for data is thereby associated with credit for the publication. Because scholars benefit from references to their publications, most appear to prefer citations to their publications rather than to their datasets.

When datasets are cited independent of publications, matters of provenance arise. Data provenance is a cascading problem as datasets are merged and mined. The multiphase inference problem discussed in chapter 8 occurs when later parties need to understand earlier phases of processing on the data. Provenance records should carry forward with the dataset for multiple generations, which requires considerable investment in curation. Provenance is also a matter of credit. Although some researchers will release data into the public domain without retaining rights, most data creators want credit for later uses. Provenance records can include legal contracts, such as data licenses that specify precisely what can be done with those data, who must be attributed, and how (Ball 2012; Guibault 2013).

Name or Number: Questions of Identity

References are made to specific objects, whether those objects are publications, datasets, people, places, web pages, records, software, workflows, or other entities. In the ideal case, objects should be identified uniquely so that a precise relationship between citing and cited entities is established. Identifiers and metadata records, which are the usual forms of representation for research objects, should enable people or machines to locate, discover, and retrieve cited and citing objects. Identification also should persist as long as the object persists so that the citation remains accurate and discoverable. In practice, neither identity nor persistence is absolute. People change names, documents change versions, digital objects change locations when transferred from one computer to another, and they change in form when migrated over generations of software, ceasing to be bit-for-bit identical. The document of record, as introduced in chapter 3, is far less stable in digital than in print environments, whether publications or data. As Herbert van de Sompel (2013) framed the problem, it may be necessary to build technical infrastructures not for the "version of record" but for "versions of the record."

Identifying People and Organizations   Identity and persistence are intractable problems with deep conceptual roots. Individuals have many roles and identities, despite the efforts of Facebook to conflate them: author, editor, student, teacher, employer, employee, parent, child, friend, colleague, supervisor, citizen, sibling, driver, member, and so on. Individuals carry many forms of identification, each with an identifier that is unique within a name space: driver's license, passport, employee ID, voter registration, insurance cards, credit cards, debit cards, frequent flyer cards, store loyalty cards, and health club memberships. Every attempt at universal identification encounters a common set of problems about how to identify people for a given purpose, who is eligible, and the conditions for which the identification is recognized. A driver's license is required to rent a car and a passport is required to cross international borders. These forms of identification are not interchangeable for these purposes, although either may be accepted to verify an airline boarding pass.

Establishing consistent and persistent forms of personal names is fraught with difficulty. The very notion of surname is highly contested, and name order is highly contextual. Collocating contemporary variants of names is difficult; collocating historical variants requires considerable domain knowledge. Legal names originate in character sets of their languages. When transliterated into English, Chinese characters and Hungarian

diacritics are left behind. In Asia and Central Europe, family name usually precedes given names. Hence, Berend Ivan in Hungary is the same person as Ivan Berend in the United States. Asian students studying in the West commonly adopt Western given names, as when Ding Jian became known as James Ding; Westerners may adopt Asian names for use in Asia. In Latin and Hispanic traditions, spouses and children acquire compound names to acknowledge parents and partners. In some regions, prefixes and suffixes are acquired for marriage and even for academic degrees. Spouses sometimes gain the honorifics of their partners. Individuals identify themselves using names appropriate for the occasion, whether authorship, legal records, or social events. These are but a few examples of how names and their purposes change over time, language, region, and context. Information systems that presume each person has a single and persistent name are doomed to failure. The challenge is to cluster multiple versions of names with sufficient reliability that systems can support their intended uses (Borgman and Siegfried 1992).

Each name space within which people are identified has rules for eligibility, identification, and application. Author names are no exception. Library cataloging rules include criteria for identifying authors, editors, illustrators, and other contributors. These rules create consistency within catalogs and between indexers. However, internal consistency can come at the price of conflicts between systems. Because cataloging rules arise from social practice, they reflect national and regional cultures, varying from country to country and continent to continent. Since library automation accelerated in the 1960s, international rules have become more harmonized, yet still reflect local variation. Author names are standardized within each country by their national libraries, although authors of books are covered more fully than are authors of journal articles.

Library name authority files establish a preferred, or authoritative, form of name and cross-references for variant forms. Authors who publish under pseudonyms, for example, may be entered under legal names with references from the pseudonym or vice versa, depending upon how well the person is known by each of the names. Samuel Langhorne Clemens published under the name Mark Twain. Catalog entries, at least in the United States, are under Twain with a cross-reference from Clemens. J. K. Rowling, author of the Harry Potter series, later published under pseudonyms she attempted to keep secret. Records for Harry Potter books are entered under J. K. Rowling, with cross-references from variant forms such as Joanne Kathleen Rowling. Later catalogers will determine whether to add cross-references from her secret pseudonyms.

Identity and Discovery   Information systems can be divided into two broad categories: those that organize information at the time of ingest and those that organize at the time of retrieval. Library cataloging systems are the first type, investing in the infrastructure to establish, coordinate, and maintain consistent forms of entry. These are expensive investments that pay off in discoverability and information management over a very long term. Search engines are the second type, attempting to disambiguate and reconcile variant forms at the time of retrieval. The latter approach has scaling problems, since forms that cannot be reconciled by machine are returned to the searcher. Long lists of records include duplicate objects due to variation in author names, article titles, dates, and other descriptors. These lists grow in length with the proliferation of scholarly journals and the increase in number of authors per article. Common author names are difficult to disambiguate, such as Smith, Jones, Garcia, Chen, Lee, or Nguyen. Another challenge is the growth of searching by machines, with no human in the loop to disambiguate similar names based on other clues.

As the scaling problem in name disambiguation accelerates, technical and policy solutions are being sought. Systems and services to establish unique identifiers for authors would organize material at the time of ingest, whether at record creation or conversion. VIAF, ORCID, and ISNI are loosely coordinated efforts to standardize name forms. VIAF, the Virtual International Authority File (2013), is an initiative led by national libraries and hosted by OCLC. ORCID, the Open Researcher and Contributor ID, is led by the publishing industry (Haak et al. 2012; Open Researcher and Contributor ID 2011). ISNI, the International Standard Name Identifier, is hosted by OCLC but is intended for identification well beyond authorship and contributorship. ISNI is an ISO standard also in use for artists, performers, and other kinds of rights holders (International Standard Name Identifier International Agency 2013).

VIAF is an institutional effort whereby libraries and other organizations use the established form of entry in their systems. Authors, living or dead, do not participate directly in VIAF and most are unaware of its existence. ORCID depends heavily on the participation of the authors and institutions identified. Individuals are encouraged to register for an ID and then to claim their publications as their own, creating an online bibliography of their work. Participating publishers are implementing ORCID by asking, or requiring, authors to include their ORCID number at the time of article submission. Universities and other organizations are encouraged to claim the publications of their authors, creating bibliographies and layering other services, such as databases of faculty expertise. ORCID is concerned

primarily with contemporary authors, whereas ISNI has focused more on establishing identifiers for historical persons and records in extant databases.

To the extent that VIAF, ORCID, ISNI, and other services are adopted and implemented, the infrastructure for managing information associated with personal names will be consolidated. Their success depends on how well they navigate intractable problems of name identification, trust, cooperation, and flexibility. No single entity can establish a trust fabric on its own. Many authors remain suspicious of efforts led by publishers or any other central authority. Some authors invest great effort in maintaining personal websites and managing their online presence. Others are unwilling or unable to do so. Many would prefer that librarians maintain the bibliographic presence of the institution.

Larger questions revolve around who has the authority to issue identifiers, who will maintain them, and who can edit them. Some of the challenges cut to the core of scholarly communication: Who has the authority to claim publications? Can persons not listed as authors claim a publication? Can universities claim for present or former faculty members, staff, and students? Who can claim the publications of deceased persons? How will disputes be resolved? Can individuals maintain multiple identities? Can the scientist keep her research publications distinct from her fiction writing? Adoption also depends upon who implements and maintains the identifier system. To the extent that publishers, universities, libraries, data archives, and other stakeholders concerned with operational systems invest the technical and human resources, it may succeed. To the extent that adoption depends upon the investment of scholars in maintaining their identity, it is less likely to succeed. The closest analogy is the adoption of institutional repositories, which have had a low rate of contribution by authors. Their success has depended largely on library investments in acquiring, cataloging, and depositing publications on behalf of affiliated authors.

Identifying Objects Research objects are no easier to identify uniquely than are persons or organizations. Information discovery depends upon identifying items uniquely and collating related ones. A search for Hamlet that retrieves hundreds of records rarely is useful, especially when the results include Shakespearean plays and small villages. Authors must determine which version of a work to cite and which translations, such as the references to Borges, Galileo, and Voltaire mentioned in earlier chapters. Each stakeholder and namespace has its own methods of managing relationships and cross-references. For instance, library cataloging principles are based

on a hierarchy of works, expressions, manifestations, and items that can be implemented in retrieval systems (Mimno, Crane, and Jones 2005).

Books might appear to be the most stable objects to identify. However, they exist not only in many copies but also in formats such as hardcover and paper, multiple digital editions, and translations, each of which is assigned a unique number in the namespace of International Standard Book Numbers (International Standard Book Number Agency 2013). Variants require new ISBNs; for example, a movie, a play, a children's edition, or acquisition by another publisher. Libraries catalog each work with sufficient metadata to distinguish it from related works. Circulating libraries further distinguish each copy with a local and unique number so that physical objects can be loaned to borrowers. Borrowers, in turn, have unique library card numbers that are local to the institution.

Similarly, journals are assigned an International Standard Serial Number that identifies them uniquely (International Standard Serial Number International Centre 2013). Journal titles sometimes change, which results in a new ISSN. For example, *American Documentation* became the *Journal of the American Society for Information Science (JASIS)*, then the *Journal of the American Society for Information Science and Technology (JASIST)*, and now the *Journal of the Association for Information Science and Technology (JASIST)*. Despite continuity in the scholarly society and editorship, the journal has four ISSNs. Citation metrics accrue separately to the journal by each of these names and numbers.

ISBNs and ISSNs, which originated for print publications, are not sufficiently discrete to manage individual journal articles. Digital Object Identifiers were established by the publishing industry in the late 1990s to assign a unique and persistent identifier to individual publications (Paskin 1997, 1999). They have been adopted widely for journal articles and assigned retrospectively to older items. A DOI is a particular instance of a Handle, which is a system of unique and persistent identifiers for Internet resources (Corporation for National Research Initiatives 2013). As the use of DOIs has proliferated, they are used less consistently, sometimes referring to an article, sometimes referring to individual tables or figures within an article, and sometimes to data. Variant forms of publications, such as preprints in repositories, may receive DOIs independent of the DOI of the published article. DOIs are being adopted in other sectors, such as the movie industry, which leads to less consistency of application. The merits of DOIs, URLs, URNs, and other systems for identifying digital objects are much debated (Altman and King 2007; Sompel and Lagoze 2009; Van de Sompel et al. 2012).

Buried beneath debates over the choice of object identifiers is the intractable problem of granularity. What unit should be cited? The unit of publication to cite is becoming less clear as articles appear online in multiple versions and as subsections of articles are cited individually, such as tables and figures (Cronin 1994; Nielsen 2011). Bibliographic citation addresses some of these issues by referencing full publications or by "deep linking" to page numbers through footnotes. References to full publications, as in the style employed in this book (*Chicago Manual of Style* 2010), create a single list of works cited at the end of the publication. Footnotes provide more discrete referencing, but can introduce multiple representations of the same cited object within a citing publication. Uses such as *ibid.* and *op. cit.*, common in citation styles of law and the humanities, describe the same object differently on the first reference, later references on the same page, and later references in the citing document. Bibliographies listing all the footnoted items may or may not be provided at the end of the publication. When footnotes refer only to portions of a document by selected page numbers, the full object being referenced may be unidentifiable. Page numbers, long a stable identifier in printed publications, often are meaningless in digital objects. The length of a page may depend upon the size and shape of the screen on which the digital object is displayed; page numbers, if any, are assigned by the local viewing device.

Supplemental materials attached to journal articles are another area where units of data are in question. Many journals, especially in the sciences, request supplemental information necessary to interpret, verify, or reproduce the research. The materials, which may include datasets, usually are available only online, linked from the article. As supplemental materials proliferated, concerns arose that their existence undermines the notion of a self-contained research report (Maunsell 2010). Complicating matters further, search engines rarely index these materials, making them difficult to discover. Best practices for supplemental materials, as promulgated by international standards organizations, distinguish between integral content, additional content, and related content (National Information Standards Organization 2013).

Each repository has its own rules about the scope of a dataset or other unit of deposit (Gutmann et al. 2009). Citing data in a repository is the low-hanging fruit, from the perspective of granularity, and the one first addressed by DataCite. DataCite is an international nonprofit organization to facilitate discovery, use, and reuse of data. Partners include national libraries, research libraries, scholarly and professional societies, standards agencies, and the DOI Foundation (Brase et al. 2014; DataCite 2013).

Data are especially problematic to identify since they may consist of many types of objects and versions: physical samples, digital records, datasets at multiple degrees of processing, laboratory notebooks, codebooks, field notes, archival records, photographs, annotations, and so on. The unit problem proliferates when these and other digital objects such as talks, slides, tables, figures, videos, tweets, and blog posts receive unique identifiers.

Relationships among these many objects rarely are hierarchical. Rather, the network of relationships is essential to understanding the provenance of any given dataset. Formal models of these relationships, such as Object Reuse and Exchange (ORE), can aid in linking and discovery, but are labor-intensive to construct (Pepe et al. 2010). Objects from research in CENS that can be represented by ORE are presented in figure 9.1.

Data exist in many units, in many places, and can be cited in many ways for many purposes. The granularity principle previously noted encourages authors to cite "the finest-grained description necessary to identify the data" (CODATA-ICSTI Task Group on Data Citation Standards and Practices 2013). Citing smaller units such as tables, cells in tables, figures, and subsets of compound figures may facilitate provenance tracking, especially if they can be set in the context of larger units. Citing streaming data, in which datasets are but a snapshot in time, is yet another challenge. The ability to identify units uniquely and persistently while facilitating the collocation of related items is a canonical problem in library cataloging, archival practice, information retrieval, and data citation (Agosti and Ferro 2007; Renear, Sacchi, and Wickett 2010; Svenonius 2000).

Theory Meets Technology: Citations as Actions

Citation methods are now embodied in technologies to create, discover, retrieve, mine, count, and map citations. A single click on a browser bar can create a bibliographic record with full metadata to render citations in the styles of individual journals. Zotero currently supports 6,789 citation styles (Zotero 2014). References from one article to another are clickable links. Citations are query terms to retrieve articles. Counts of citations to authors yield h-indexes, g-indexes, and other metrics of scholarly influence. Counts of citations to journals become journal impact factors (JIFs) that are used to rank publication venues and are reified as lists of places to publish for tenure and promotion. Maps of citations are used to model the flow of ideas and the influence of universities and of countries.

Some of these technologies draw on theories of scholarly communication. Others are engineering solutions to managing digital objects, developed

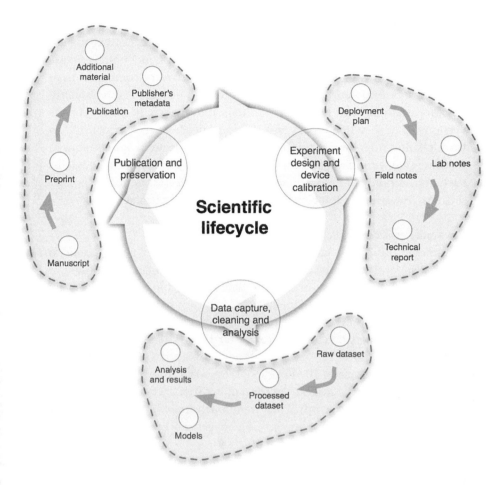

Figure 9.1
Scientific life cycle example from the Center for Embedded Networked Sensing (Pepe et al. 2010). Reprinted with permission.

without reference to the diverse origins or long history of bibliographic control. Either way, the result may be that software code determines what can and cannot be cited, how citations can be made, and what can be done with them. Lawrence Lessig explained how code can lock in practices and lock out other essential influences, such as social norms, markets, and the law (Lessig 1999, 2001, 2004). Early choices matter, and these are the early days in establishing practices for credit, attribution, and discovery of data. Early choices in technologies, such as typewriter keyboards, had long-term influences unimaginable to their inventors (David 1985; Mullaney 2012).

In a print world, citations are stable links between fixed objects. In a digital world, citations are links between mutable objects. Neither the citing nor the cited object may be fixed in form or location indefinitely. To use citations for purposes of credit, attribution, and discovery, some notions of fixity must be imposed on the infrastructure. Unique and persistent identifiers, for example, are essential to maintain provenance. If objects change versions, then new identifiers and links are needed. Version control, in turn, requires rules for what degree of change constitutes a new version. In software engineering, version control is codified. Big data research domains such as astronomy often codify versions as data releases. In most scholarly settings, however, version control is a matter of local practice.

Risks and Rewards: Citations as Currency

One of the principal arguments for data citation is that giving credit to researchers for data will be an incentive to share. Although oft repeated, it is an untested hypothesis. Citations to data may be appreciated, especially when datasets are widely used. However, credit for publications carries so much more value that some researchers discourage data citation. They prefer that their papers be cited as proxies for their data. Scholars' interests in data citation appear to vary by its intended purposes. For example, the team that tracks usage of the Chandra X-Ray data found that researchers were willing to assist in linking data and publications when those links add scientific value to the records. They were much less willing to spend time on citation and linking for purposes of managerial accountability (Winkelman and Rots 2012a; Winkelman et al. 2009).

The more that publication and citation metrics are used in hiring, promotion, and evaluation, the more closely they are examined. Any metric can be gamed, especially singular metrics such as citation counts. Colleagues can cite themselves, their colleagues, their students, and their mentors, and make fewer references to their competitors. Research output can be "salami sliced" into small units to increase the number of publications and citations. Honorary authorship and other methods of increasing citation rates can be hard to spot, which is one reason that publishing ethics have become more codified (Committee on Publication Ethics 2013). Data citation is similarly subject to gaming, especially given the granularity problem. Why cite one dataset when one hundred or one hundred thousand data objects can be cited individually?

The weaknesses of citation metrics are well known, having been studied from the time that impact factors and other indicators were first proposed. Citation metrics too often involve faulty reasoning, committing

the ecological fallacy of applying group characteristics to individuals within the group. Citations to journals are not distributed evenly across the articles in that journal; a few highly cited articles usually are responsible. When articles were bound together in journal issues, the correlation between article and journal citation was higher. As articles became units retrieved independently of the journal, that correlation has declined (Lozano, Lariviere, and Gingras 2012). Journal Impact Factors, as computed by Thomson Scientific (previously the Institute for Scientific Information; now Thomson Reuters), is among the metrics least predictive of scholarly influence (Bollen et al. 2009). However, it remains among the most commonly used metrics for evaluating journals and individual scholars—even over the objections of editors of highly cited journals (Alberts 2013; The PLoS Medicine Editors 2006). Originating in the sciences, the JIF is based on a two-year citation window. The citation lag in the social sciences and humanities tends to be much longer; hence, the JIF is even less valid in those disciplines (Borgman 2007).

Problems with bibliographic citation metrics led to Webmetrics or Webometrics, which apply bibliometric methods to documents and links on the Internet (Ingwersen 1998; Thelwall, Vaughan, and Bjorneborn 2005). Researchers well schooled in the reliability and validity problems of bibliometrics developed broader models of influence beyond those that could be computed from publisher databases. Others have sought to include counts of informal scholarly communication in the evaluation of scholars. The *Altmetrics Manifesto* proposed alternative indicators of scholarly influence and productivity (Priem et al. 2010). These include downloads, mentions in blogs, annotations and tagging, and appearances in social media such as Twitter and Reddit. A small industry has developed around altmetrics, providing counts to publishers and other venues who post them with articles. Authors and readers now can see how many times an article has been viewed, cited, mentioned, or shared, and follow those links (Chamberlain 2013; Fenner 2013; Thelwall et al. 2013; Yan and Gerstein 2011).

These discrete units of scholarly communication are useful for discovering related objects, but their validity as alternative metrics for scholarly productivity is questionable. Strictly speaking, a tweet announcing a new journal article is a citation to that article. Bibliographic citation, for all its flaws, is based on historical scholarly practice of giving credit to sources of evidence and influence. Far less is known about the meaning of mentions in informal communication or in citations to data. To model evaluation and credit practices for data on those of bibliographic control is to transfer the untested assumptions along with it.

The value of citation counts, especially those derived from journals indexed by Thomson Reuters and Elsevier's *Engineering Index,* has become so inflated that authorship is being bought and sold for large sums of money. An investigation conducted by *Science* found a "flourishing academic black market" in China, with authorship on papers being swapped just days before publication. In other cases, papers were self-plagiarized by translation from Chinese into English and resubmission to English-language journals. Authors, journals, editors, agents, and other players were involved in various schemes, with fees as high as the annual salary of a faculty member (Hvistendahl 2013). The *Science* investigation focused on China, where researchers may be richly rewarded for publishing in these journals, and where publications in the *Science Citation Index* have expanded six-fold since 2000. The extent of fraud elsewhere is unknown, but publishers and scholars alike acknowledge the opportunities to game citation counts.

Scholars became sufficiently threatened by the extensive use of citation and other metrics in the evaluation of research to launch the San Francisco Declaration on Research Assessment (DORA). Initiated by the American Society for Cell Biology, it has since been endorsed by many journals, professional societies, and scholars. Editorials about DORA have appeared in a wide array of scholarly journals and the press. DORA offers guidance to multiple stakeholder groups in scholarly communication, calling for broader based and more nuanced methods of evaluating scholars (Declaration on Research Assessment 2013). Projects such as Academic Careers Understood through Measurement and Norms (ACUMEN) are promoting more holistic approaches to the evaluation of scholarly productivity and influence, including the role of data (Research Acumen 2013).

Too many of these metrics merely count that which is easily counted. It remains surprising how often that scholars, funding agencies, research policy makers, publishers, libraries, and other stakeholders accept citation counts, altmetrics, and other indicators at face value, rather than holding these metrics to standards of scholarly evidence.

Conclusion

Data citation is a solution for a poorly defined problem. Mapping bibliographic citation to data citation on the grounds that publications and data deserve equal status is misguided. Making data discoverable is the real problem at hand. Publications are, and will remain, the stars and planets of the scientific universe. Methods to assign credit only need to shine enough light on data that they cease to be dark matter. Nodes in a network need

not have equivalent value. Clusters of tightly coupled stars will coexist with sparse regions between galaxies. The essential requirement is to have vehicles that can follow paths between related research objects, enabling those objects to be discovered, mined, and combined.

Data archives, publishers, and libraries are key stakeholders in data discovery because their services facilitate management and reuse. A robust infrastructure for data citation will depend on massive resource investments, including information professionals to represent data in ways that make them citable and discoverable. Few scholarly authors are purists in their diligence and accuracy of bibliographic citation. Even fewer are likely to become experts at data citation.

Bibliographic citation is seen as the gold standard to which data citation should aspire. In truth, bibliographic citation is a fragile knowledge infrastructure that barely supports the purposes for which it was intended. The infrastructure has evolved and adapted to changing practices and technologies for countless generations of scholars over the course of centuries. It functions better for discovery than for credit and attribution or for mapping the flow of ideas. With every new function imposed on the bibliographic citation infrastructure, it becomes more fragile. Citation metrics, when applied to scholarly productivity, never held up to rigorous standards of statistical inference, reliability, or validity. They are easily gamed and now subject to fraud, and yet they continue to be embedded deeply in the scholarly reward system. Data citation is a means to assign credit for selecting, collecting, compiling, cleaning, processing, analyzing, managing, interpreting, mining, combining, licensing, instrumenting, extracting, visualizing, presenting, and dancing with data. It is not an end in itself. The larger problem is to understand the many roles associated with data and to reach some consensus within communities for which of these roles deserve credit and the best ways to assign that credit. Credit, in turn, facilitates discovery and reuse. A robust knowledge infrastructure that incorporates credit for data activities must encompass the galaxies of varied and competing stakeholders, always bearing in mind the incentives and reward systems of those who collect, create, analyze, interpret, and present evidence based on data—the scholars themselves.

10   What to Keep and Why

Introduction

The concepts of big data, little data, and even no data remain poorly understood. Efforts to promote better data management, sharing, credit, and attribution are well intentioned, but stakeholders disagree on the starting points, the end goals, and the path in between. Lacking agreement on what entities are data, it remains difficult to establish policies for sharing, releasing, depositing, crediting, attributing, citing, and sustaining access that can accommodate the diversity of data scholarship across all domains. Sustaining access to data is a difficult and expensive endeavor, with costs and benefits distributed unevenly among stakeholders. Questions of what to keep and why are inseparable from questions of who, how, why, for whom, and for how long they will be kept. The individual scholar, student, librarian, archivist, research officer, or journal editor may have at best an ant's eye view of this elephantine conundrum.

Some data undoubtedly are worth keeping indefinitely, and their value is apparent at the time of creation. Other data may be worth keeping in case they become valuable later, whether alone or as part of larger aggregations. Many data have transient value that may or may not be apparent initially. It is difficult to distinguish among these cases, and to do so early enough that data can be captured and curated before they are lost. Even harder is to determine what those data are, as they lack an essence of their own. Their future use may depend upon how they are represented, with respect to what phenomena, and how those representations and phenomena change over time. Repurposing for unanticipated uses may bring the greatest value, but these are the most speculative investments. Individual scholars have few reasons to keep data just in case someone else might want them, for some reason, in some form, at some future time.

Building collections of data is the most obvious way to make them available to future users. Libraries, archives, museums, and data repositories have professional guidelines to select and appraise objects for their collections. As memory institutions, their holdings have long tail characteristics: about 20 percent of the materials receive about 80 percent of the use. Although tracking usage informs selection policy, the useful 20 percent changes continuously. Some objects are popular initially, with interest fading gradually over time. Others have little initial use, with surges of interest later. Usage of others has random patterns. A few objects remain untouched, awaiting their discoverers. Even the most prestigious institutions can fail to foresee future value. The Bodleian Library (University of Oxford) famously sold its copy of Shakespeare's *First Folio* because some librarian apparently viewed the third folio, published in 1664, as a replacement. Early in the twentieth century, they reacquired their seventeenth-century *First Folio* for a very large sum of money. On Shakespeare's 449th birthday, they released a digital facsimile of this treasured object (University of Oxford 2013a).

Sustaining access to research data is a knowledge infrastructure problem that involves all stakeholders in scholarly communication. Digital preservation, a problem that intersects with access to research data, has similar infrastructure and scaling characteristics. Four structural challenges were identified by an international panel charged with economic analyses of digital preservation: "(1) long time horizons, (2) diffused stakeholders, (3) misaligned or weak incentives, and (4) lack of clarity about roles and responsibilities among stakeholders." The panel made three policy recommendations: (1) "articulate a compelling value proposition," (2) "provide clear incentives to preserve in the public interest," and (3) "define roles and responsibilities among stakeholders to ensure an ongoing and efficient flow of resources to preservation throughout the digital lifecycle" (Berman et al. 2010, pp. 1–2).

These are daunting challenges when considering either digital preservation or research data. Preserving digital representations of data is only one aspect of sustaining their value. Digital or otherwise, data rarely stand alone. They are inextricable from research methods, theories, instruments, software, and context. Sustaining access to research data requires curation of individual objects and relationships among them. The ways and means of doing so vary by research domain, as is evident in the case studies. To restate the problem of big data, little data, and no data in terms of open data, the challenge is to make data discoverable, usable, assessable, intelligible, and interpretable, and to sustain those conditions for a reasonable period of time. A first step is to consider how these problems are distributed across individual scholars and communities. A second is to consider what kinds of data in any domain might be worthy of that degree of investment,

and for whom. A third step is to determine who may be willing to make those investments and where those investments might have the greatest benefits. The value proposition for access to data depends upon an intricately interconnected set of factors that vary by stakeholder. These challenges are assessed in terms of the provocations presented in chapter 1.

Provocations Revisited

What is worth keeping depends on where one stands. In a few fields, major research projects develop data collections as part of their mission. Observations not captured are considered data lost. Some fields have data repositories to which scholars can contribute their data, but many fields have none. In most cases, what to keep, how, and for how long are left to the discretion of individual researchers and teams. While some scholars would like to retain every note, record, book, paper, digital object, and physical specimen collected over the course of a career, most wish they had better ways to manage the data they do consider worth keeping. However, attitudes toward data release often shift as retirement approaches. To ensure their intellectual legacy, scholars may offer long-held collections to archives or repositories for long-term stewardship.

Many parties would benefit if more research data were kept and made available for exploitation in a timely manner. None of the stakeholders in scholarship—scholars, students, universities, libraries, archives, museums, funding agencies, publishers, companies, taxpayers, policy makers, patients, the general public, and so on—has much leverage on their own. These are collective challenges, best addressed as knowledge infrastructure issues. The more stakeholders who come to the table, the deeper the conversation is likely to be.

Rights, Responsibilities, Roles, and Risks

Responsibility for research data is diffuse, since many parties may handle them between origin and interpretation, as presented in the first provocation:

Reproducibility, sharing, and reuse of data are issues that have been discussed for decades, and in some cases for centuries. Addressing matters such as who owns, controls, has access to, and sustains research data will determine how their value can be exploited and by whom.

Those who conduct research do not necessarily own all the data they use. Legal rights for data may be associated with instruments, as in astronomy; with private companies, as in the use of social media; or with compilers and

editors, as in the digital version of the Chinese Buddhist canon. Within a research team, responsibility for initial collection and management may fall to graduate students, but maintenance is left to the investigator. By design or by default, care of data may fall to the parties with the most permanent addresses rather than to those most knowledgeable about their origins. Establishing legal ownership is an intractable problem due to the plethora of practices, parties, and jurisdictions involved. Whether or not ownership is clear in any given case, responsibility for collection, analysis, and management may fall to multiple parties. The legal expression "possession is nine-tenths of the law" is apt for research data. Those who possess something, whether land or data, are presumed to own it until proven otherwise. Owners can do what they wish with their property, within the bounds of ethics and the law. Few scholars are legally bound to keep or deposit all of their data.

Storing data is expensive, whether in physical or digital forms. By 2007, digital information already was being created faster than storage devices could be produced (Berman 2008). Researchers must be selective in what they keep, as must anyone who generates or uses information resources. Scholars typically are constrained by the physical space in their offices, laboratories, and homes. Universities and research consortia provide shared server space for digital storage, although costs may be recharged to research projects or academic departments. Cloud storage is an alternative model, but is not yet reliable for research data (Kolowich 2014). Although the cost of cloud storage has dropped, some projections indicate that long-term data storage costs are leveling off or increasing (Rosenthal 2010, 2014). Sustaining access to research data requires that the information necessary to interpret them also be sustained—protocols, codebooks, software, specimens, metadata, standards, and so on. These resources often are more voluminous than the data themselves.

Scholars are probably no better housekeepers than anyone else. Random visits to faculty offices reveal that "filing by piling" is more common than meticulous desktops, with most falling somewhere in between. Even the most elite cadre of scientists, such as peer reviewers for *Science,* store most of their data locally; only 7.6 percent of those 1,700 respondents archived most of their data in community repositories (*Science* Staff 2011). Few institutions have requirements for managing data, resulting in ad hoc approaches that vary by lab and often by individual. Scholars deposit data where requirements apply, such as genomic sequences, clinical trial records, and seismic records. They will keep data that they reasonably expect to

use again, but whether they can keep them well enough to be reusable is another matter. As students and staff depart from projects, expertise about data may be irretrievably lost. As software upgrades are installed and computers replaced, data files may cease to be interpretable, especially if data are not migrated to new generations of technology. Bits rot, links break, specimen refrigerators are purged, and records are lost in office moves and computer upgrades.

Data management is best viewed as an institutional concern, rather than solely the responsibility of the individual scholar. The degree of support available varies widely by domain and by institution. Researchers in some fields have ready access to suites of tools, technical standards, and repositories for acquiring and contributing data, whereas other fields have none of these. Universities and other research institutions may be well staffed with information professionals to aid in managing data, assigning metadata, migration to new platforms, deposit, discovery, and other types of coordination. These are the exceptions, however. The larger issue is the uneven distribution of costs and benefits. In many quarters, data stewardship is viewed as an unfunded mandate with few direct benefits to the institution. It is unclear who will pay the price for storing and stewarding digital assets. To university research officers, libraries, academic departments, and individual scholars, data may be as much liabilities as assets.

Data Sharing

Sharing information between humans or between machines is a complex activity, as framed in the second provocation:

Transferring knowledge across contexts and over time is difficult. Some forms and representations of data can be shared readily across disciplines, contexts, and over time but many cannot. Understanding what features matter and which do not is necessary to inform scholarly practice and policy and to guide investments in knowledge infrastructures.

Knowledge is most likely to be communicated intact when individuals interact directly and synchronously. They can ask questions of each other, clarifying intent. Tasks can be explicated, practices demonstrated, skills identified, and tacit knowledge made more explicit. With each step away from person-to-person interaction, more mediation occurs. Metadata and other forms of documentation become necessary to discover, interpret, and use data. That documentation will be more meaningful within a research community, improving internal exchange, but may create barriers between communities. Thus, the ability to share research data depends heavily upon who

is managing data for what intended communities and purposes. Returning to the economics discussion of chapter 4 and the examples in the case studies, some kinds of research data are amenable to being treated as common-pool resources while others will remain private goods. Some data will be released as public goods and some will be sold as toll or club goods. The differences are in the packaging or treatment of the data, not in characteristics of the data per se. The same set of observations could be available concurrently under each of these economic conditions, albeit represented differently.

An example from astronomy of how a given set of data might be differentially available illustrates some of the challenges of assessing the conditions for data sharing. Observations can be grouped into three general categories by how researchers acquire them: data collections, data collected anew by researchers, and derived data. NASA is the largest investor in common-pool resources in astronomy, partnering with many other US and international agencies. Creating and managing data collections are part the agency's mission. These repositories are staffed with scientists, data scientists, and software engineers. Investments are made in data migration, tools to exploit the data, and staff to assist users in discovering, acquiring, using, and interpreting data. Astronomers make heavy use of these repositories, mining them for many years after the observations were taken.

Data collected anew, the second category, are observations acquired directly by astronomy researchers. As in the COMPLETE Survey in chapter 5, some astronomers write proposals to obtain their own observations from telescopes. These observations may or may not be processed through the pipeline associated with the instrument. Other astronomers build their own instruments to capture observations and build their own pipelines. These data, once cleaned and calibrated, might go to repositories or to institutional collections. Some are released directly via project websites or upon request. However, the vast majority of data collected anew, even in astronomy, appears to remain in researchers' control.

Derived data, the third category, are those obtained from archives or combined from multiple sources. When scholars take data from curated collections such as the Chandra X-Ray Observatory or the Sloan Digital Sky Survey, they transform the data to address their own research questions. Often they compare them to data from other collections or to data collected anew. The COMPLETE Survey, for example, merged observations from multiple repositories with data collected anew. Derived data might go to other repositories, be released directly, or most likely, remain in the control of the researchers.

This tripartite model can be applied to other fields that maintain common-pool resources. Data repositories vary in the degree of investment in data curation and in the centralization of resources. Some of the common-pool collections emanate from one source. The Sloan Digital Sky Survey consists of observations from a single telescope, collected synoptically over a course of many years. CBETA began by digitizing a single body of texts from the Chinese Buddhist canon. Other collections rely on the quality assurance of the data creators, accepting data from disparate sources. Some repositories have sufficient staff to verify the content of datasets, accepting only those that meet their quality standards. Staff can add value through metadata, further documentation, migration to new formats, and help desks. Although some duplication exists between collections, the gaps are many. Scholars may not be aware of collections in nearby fields, and discovery remains a problem.

To derive data from repositories or other resources, scholars rely on available provenance information. Subsequent analyses, interpretations, management, and documentation of provenance lie in the hands of the scholar. Derived data appear no more likely to find a permanent home than are data collected anew. Few archives, data or otherwise, appear to solicit products derived from their resources, especially those merged with other sources. Archivists often are reluctant to take research objects for which they cannot verify the provenance or subsequent actions taken on them. A few data collections, such as the Sloan Digital Sky Survey, do accept derived data products after they have been vetted.

Notably, data sharing is even less systematic in domains where few common-pool resources exist. In areas such as sensor-networked science and technology, the partners had few choices but to maintain their own data resources. These were data collected anew, with research questions, technologies, and protocols varying from deployment to deployment. Teams pooled their own data resources when needed, but even these might be incommensurate from task to task or project to project. In social media research, scholars might derive data from a common stream but then transform them to address their own research questions. Whether or not the data of different teams are comparable, the legal contracts by which data were obtained may prevent sharing. When funding agencies mandate data management plans, scholars may become more aware of the potential value of their data. However, unless such plans are backed by effective means of data sharing, such as repositories, tools, and staffing, they may not have the intended results in promoting the sharing and reuse of data.

Publications and Data

The various analogies between data and publications tend to obfuscate, rather than illuminate, discussions of policy and practice, as stated in the third provocation:

The functions of scholarly publication remain stable despite the proliferation of forms and genres. Data serve different purposes in scholarly communication than do journal articles, books, or conference papers. Treating data as publications risks strengthening the roles of vested interests at the expense of exploring new models of scholarly communication. The functions of data in scholarship must be examined from the perspectives of diverse stakeholders.

As explored throughout this book, scholars write publications to make arguments, and data are evidence to support those arguments. Credit, attribution, and authorship are associated with publications, but do not map easily or well to data. Some publications are data-heavy, laced together with minimal narrative. Others are mostly narrative, with data mentioned in passing, if at all. No matter what the ratio of evidence to argument, publications are much more than packages of data. To extract data from publications as independent commodities is to remove much of their meaning. Publications are intended to be independent units, interpretable by readers familiar with the domain. They can be a means to discover data, and vice versa; thus, links between publications and data can enhance the value of each. However, the risk of focusing too heavily on data-publication links is to reify a one-to-one relationship between data and publications. Keeping data for the purposes of reproducibility may force datasets into publication-sized units, rather than representing them in ways in which they can be exploited more generally.

Open access to scholarly publications is viable for two reasons specific to scholarship, as Peter Suber (2012a) explained (chapter 3). Scholars own the rights to their publications, at least initially, and are motivated to distribute them as widely as possible, because they write for impact rather than for revenue. Neither is true with data, which has ramifications for many other aspects of data management and policy. Scholars welcome methods that enhance the discoverability of their publications, especially when the result is increased citations to those publications.

The business models for scholarly publishing have shifted radically over the last several decades. Most aspects of the publication process now are digital, from submission by authors through online dissemination and access. Unique and persistent identifiers such as DOIs are assigned at the time of publication and are assigned retroactively to older materials.

Repositories are assigning DOIs, Handles, and other identifiers to datasets. Unique and persistent identifiers such as ORCID—Open Researcher and Contributor ID—are being assigned to individual authors. These and other identifiers can be used to link digital objects with technologies such as Crossref, Object Reuse and Exchange, or ResourceSync, as discussed in chapter 9. These same technology advances have contributed to the open access movement, lowering the barriers to becoming a publisher. Publishers large and small are offering new data mining services, exploiting the integration of digital objects to provide customized reporting on the performance of journals, universities, academic departments, repositories, funding agencies, and individual scholars.

Libraries and archives are experts in building and managing collections. Libraries primarily focus on published materials and archives on unique items. Research libraries collect broadly across most areas of knowledge, with depth of collections matching the curricula of their universities. Following accreditation guidelines, doctoral programs are supported by more comprehensive collections than are undergraduate-only programs. Archival collections typically are much smaller and more concentrated by domain or type of material. Deep collections in a domain attract scholars and students to a university; these are core assets of each institution. Scholars in many areas of the sciences and technology want only digital services from their university libraries. Scholars in many areas of the humanities rely heavily on print and archival materials. They expect the library to sustain deep historical collections and provide physical spaces in which to use them. Scholars and students need both digital and physical materials, buildings in which to use them, and staff to assist in discovery and interpretation. All users depend on the expertise of information professionals to select, collect, organize, and make information resources available, whether or not that labor is visible to them.

Among the institutional challenges to address is the balance between preservation and access. The most effective forms of preservation, such as storing paper copies under a mountain, are poor for access. Conversely, effective forms of access, such as low-resolution images of pages, are poor for preservation. Institutions often do both, which requires dual systems for some types of assets. This distinction is even sharper when applied to research data. Digital files can be preserved in dark archives that can be restored in case of disastrous loss but provide little or no access. Providing access in ways that sustain their value for research requires online, interactive systems, technical apparatus appropriate to the domain, computational

power, and staff expertise to assist users in exploiting the resources. These activities require domain expertise and continual investment in curation.

Even setting aside the larger problems of digital preservation, which are many, most universities are better positioned to manage dark archives or small collections of specialized materials than to take responsibility for sustaining access to large domain collections. The latter requires infrastructure investments at the levels of research communities, university consortia, or entire countries. For most research areas, aggregation of data resources is the most viable means of exploitation.

Other distinctions between publications and data are relevant in considering what to keep and why. One is that publications may exist in many copies and in many collections, but need to be cataloged only once. Libraries began to share the burden of cataloging by the early twentieth century, later building on those partnerships to develop shared digital services (Borgman 2000). Research data are more analogous to archival materials, each set unique and requiring its own metadata and provenance records. More labor is required to describe unique items or to merge them into common structures. However, in both cases, collections gain in value as they grow. University libraries make consortial agreements about what each will collect, promoting the concentration of resources and providing access to community members. The same can be done with data collections.

Libraries and archives have complementary policies about what to acquire. In professional parlance, libraries select and archives appraise. Both acquire resources they expect to keep indefinitely. Libraries do more weeding or "deaccessioning" of materials as information goes out of date or as new editions appear. Determining when to discard or dispose of items can be harder decisions than those at time of acquisition. With published matter, libraries make "last-copy" agreements, such that one partner commits to curation so that others may dispose of their copies. However, last-copy agreements do not apply to unique objects such as data. Some data may cease to be useful in a matter of months; others in decades. Retention planning is particularly problematic with regard to data. Scholars and librarians often defer to each other in setting expiry dates, resulting in a standoff.

Differing investments in publications and data are notable throughout the case studies. Sustaining access to publications is common to all research domains. Sustaining access to data is uneven at best. In astronomy—which has the most comprehensive knowledge infrastructure of the cases presented—publications, classification of objects, and data are managed separately. The literature of the field is curated in the Astrophysics Data System (ADS), whereas CDS and NED catalog celestial objects named in the

publications. These three institutions are tightly coupled, and they create links between publications and objects. Observations from space missions are better curated than are those from ground-based missions, however. The most extensive linking between celestial objects, publications, and data is that done by information professionals at ADS, CDS, NED, and astronomy data repositories. Other links are provided by astronomy libraries, which add value to their local collections. The least consistent linking is that done by authors of astronomy publications, who cite other publications but rarely cite data (Accomazzi and Dave 2011; Pepe et al., in press). In astronomy and elsewhere, the robustness of knowledge infrastructures to link publications and data for discoverability depends on investments in information professionals to do the requisite work.

Data Access

Providing access to data is even more difficult than providing open access to publications, as framed in the fourth provocation:

Scholarly work is being disseminated more widely through movements such as open access publishing, open data, and open source software. The different purposes of data and publications in scholarship influence the incentives, means, and practices for dissemination. Providing open access to data has implications for scholars, libraries, universities, funding agencies, publishers, and other stakeholders that are poorly understood.

The ability to discover and gain access to data is greatest in fields that have invested in common-pool resources. In domains where data are readily pooled or aggregated, incentives exist to build such resources. Astronomy, biology, biomedicine, and the "omics" fields in the sciences, survey research in the social sciences, and textual corpora in the humanities are obvious examples. In all of these areas, data can be compared and combined. Scholars are willing to contribute their data to get access to the pool in return. As with any common-pool resources, they must be governed, however. Sustainability and free riders are continual challenges. Launching research collections is hard; building the institutional commitments to make them into resource or reference collections is harder. Not all of them survive. Even the most robust data repositories have succession plans that outline the disposition of their assets should funding cease. Converting free riders into active members requires clever management.

Most research data are likely to languish as legacy files until actively destroyed or left to fade away. The reasons are many, as illustrated throughout this book. If left to their own devices, most scholars will document their data just well enough to serve the purposes of their immediate and planned

research projects. To improve data access, more data must be kept in reusable forms, which requires a change in incentives. For most scholars, the fundamental problem is better management of their own data. They need tools, services, and assistance in archiving their own data in ways they can reuse them, which increases the likelihood that their data will be useful to others later.

Permission rules are important. Scholars need data management solutions where they can maintain control over their resources. Many types of controls may be needed, depending upon the research and the data. These may include compliance with embargo periods, licensing, collaborative agreements, and human subjects regulations. If scholars can archive their data in reliable and compliant systems, available to themselves as needed, they may be willing to expose those data publicly at a later time. Once stored in a repository, data could be made available to collaborators or to the public by changing permissions parameters. Systems such as Dataverse and SciDrive operate on the principle that archiving data reliably is a necessary first step to open access (Crosas 2011; Drago et al. 2012; Goodman et al. 2014; SciDrive 2014). Data documentation may be less than optimal, but these approaches offer means to curate data that otherwise would be lost and to increase the likelihood that the data will become discoverable. When data are more easily kept, the motivation to invest in making them more reusable may increase. Similarly, investments in curation may enhance discoverability. Data that are stored reliably are more readily cited. Publications may remain the primary path to discovering data, both because publications describe data more fully and because scholars prefer citations to publications over citations to datasets.

Data are both liabilities and assets. They are expensive to keep, yet the potential for misuse, misinterpretation, and legal liability are disincentives to release them. In a recent case, an official request for data release led to months of negotiation, extensive legal consultation, and more publicity than any of the parties would have liked. Earthquake engineering researchers at a major university studied concrete buildings in Los Angeles that were at risk of collapse. Publications resulting from their National Science Foundation grant explained their findings, but did not include the list of buildings. City of Los Angeles officials requested the list for use in assessing building safety. The researchers and university officials initially refused on the grounds of potential lawsuits by the building owners. The university distinguished between data collected for a scientific study and seismic assessments of individual buildings. Eventually the parties agreed on the release of a redacted list and on legal wording about the earthquake risks

(Lin, Xia, and Smith 2014a, 2014b; Smith, Xia, and Lin 2013; Xia, Smith, and Finnegan 2013). All stakeholders involved had legitimate concerns, albeit not aligned.

The use of earthquake engineering data for public policy is but one example of unanticipated repurposing of publications and data. A more general solution to the problem of reuse is to allow computational analysis, or mining, over large corpora of publications, data, and other digital objects. Rather than anticipating the questions that might be asked, later searchers can write their own algorithms, perhaps using application programming interfaces (APIs). The latter approach has been proposed in various guises (Bibliographic Services Task Force 2005; Bourne 2005; Bourne et al. 2011; Shotton et al. 2009). The weaknesses of this approach are the loss of context, loss of provenance, and the difficulty of maintaining the relationships among objects that are necessary to interpret the results. Open data in the sense of being free for reuse (Open Data Commons 2013) is a necessary but not sufficient condition for research purposes. Open data in the fuller sense of flexibility, transparency, legal conformity, protection of intellectual property, formal responsibility, professionalism, interoperability, quality, security, efficiency, accountability, and sustainability embodied in the OECD principles is a much higher bar (Organisation for Economic Co-operation and Development 2007).

Stakeholders and Skills

Scholars get more credit for collecting or creating new data than for exploiting existing data. If the reward system is to shift, even slowly, toward placing more value on reuse, new skills and new infrastructures are needed, as presented in the fifth provocation:

Knowledge infrastructures are evolving to accommodate open access, data-intensive research, new technologies, social media, and changes in practice and policy. Some stakeholders gain advantage and others lose. Costs, benefits, risks, and responsibilities are being redistributed. New kinds of expertise are needed but their application will vary across contexts and research domains.

Stakeholders have conflicting answers to basic questions about what data are worth keeping and why: Why should any set of data be kept? What are the criteria for determining which data to keep? Who decides which data are worth keeping? For whom should they be kept? What purposes or uses can be anticipated? In what forms, and with what ancillary information, should they be kept? How long should they be kept? Who should keep them? Who will invest in short and long term sustainability for data deemed worthy? Who should have access to the data? What policies should

be in place for access, use, and reuse? What tools, technologies, facilities, and human resources are needed to maintain the usefulness of any given data resource?

When data are collected anew or derived from available resources, as discussed above, responsibility for managing, curating, and disseminating them usually falls to the investigator. Data management requires a combination of expertise in the research domain and in the organization and curation of information. Considerable technical expertise also may be required, depending upon the specifics of the data, their context, and their uses. Being an expert in a research domain does not make one an expert at data management. Such skills rarely are taught in graduate programs within scholarly domains.

However, it is not clear how much of the data management burden scholars are willing to bear. Many, if not most, view time and resources devoted to managing their data as effort lost on their research. They may prefer to delegate these duties to library or archival staff, although such partnerships also take time to develop. Libraries are stretched to provide current services, and not all view data management as being within their purview. Publishers are more willing to index data and link to repositories than to curate data.

Academic programs in data science variously address data analytics, management, organization, curation, and access. A US National Academies study on the workforce for digital preservation reveals the difficulty of defining the array of skills required (Hedstrom et al. 2014). A core challenge for staffing is that most of the labor involved in data management is invisible work. Information professionals, software engineers, scientific programmers, instrument builders, and other technical experts underpin the foundations of scholarship. These skills often are undervalued and career paths are unclear. It is difficult to recruit talented people under "soft money" contracts that lack job security and routes for promotion. Investments in the human infrastructure will be crucial to the success of keeping and exploiting research data. Research communities must employ these professionals and provide career paths for them if robust knowledge infrastructures are to be sustained.

The necessary combinations of expertise in data management, curation, and digital preservation will vary by stakeholder. Universities, academic departments, libraries, and research teams need these kinds of expertise throughout their organizations. Data repositories, themselves supported by funding agencies, research communities, or other institutions, need professionals with skills in their domain areas, in data management, and in

technology. New players are entering this space, some public and some private. The European Union is investing in the Open Access Infrastructure for Research in Europe (OpenAIRE) that takes publications, data, and other content into its repositories. Zenodo, based at CERN, is a component of OpenAIRE that accepts research objects not held by other repositories. Australia incorporated data management into its code of research conduct and then began building a national infrastructure for data management that includes repositories, staffing, and various partnerships with individual institutions (Australian National Data Service 2014; National Health and Medical Research Council 2007; Open Access Infrastructure for Research in Europe 2014; Schirrwagen et al. 2013; ZENODO 2013).

Institutional repositories at universities and open access repositories such as arXiv and SSRN continue to focus on preprints, reprints, and gray literature. Some will accept datasets as supplements to text documents. Others, such as Dataverse, are intended specifically for datasets (ArXiv.org 2013; Crosas 2011; J. King 2013; Social Science Research Network 2014). Commercial companies such as SlideShare and FigShare ingest a wide array of research objects, assigning DOIs and making those objects more discoverable. Thomson Reuters has launched the *Data Citation Index* to register datasets in repositories, but does not ingest data. These are but a few of the many players offering value-added services for research objects. Some have short-term objectives and others are concerned with sustaining long-term access to research resources.

Knowledge Infrastructures Past, Present, and Future
Building knowledge infrastructures is a chicken-and-egg problem, as presented in the sixth and last provocation:

Knowledge infrastructures develop and adapt over generations of scholars. A long view of design and policy is needed, but research funding operates on short cycles. Substantial investments in infrastructure are necessary to acquire, sustain, and exploit research data today, tomorrow, and beyond. Those investments will be contentious, because choices that are made today will determine what data and other information resources will be available tomorrow and well beyond.

The tensions are many, especially in the "long now of technology infrastructure" (Ribes and Finholt 2009). Individuals, projects, and organizations function on different time scales, and conflicting goals may not become apparent immediately. Most research funding is on cycles of five years or less. Many grants are one to two years in length. Even data repositories are funded by research grants, facing renewals every few years. Assuming that "if we build it, they will come" can be a risky strategy. By the time

that proof of concept is achieved, the grant may be over. When research funding ends, collaborations may disband gracefully, taking resources and expertise to the next projects. Alternatively, those with the expertise may be stranded, leaving data to decay, technology to be dispersed, and critical parts of the infrastructure left untended. Too little is yet known about the beginning, middle, or ends of knowledge infrastructures (Cummings et al. 2008; Duderstadt et al. 2002; Edwards et al. 2007, 2011, 2013; Lee et al. 2006; Olson, Zimmerman, and Bos 2008; Ribes and Jackson 2013).

Funding research infrastructure is different from funding research. Convincing governments and funding agencies to invest in shared infrastructure of technology, people, and services can be a hard sell, as learned by the Cyberinfrastructure program in the United States, the eScience program in the United Kingdom, the National Data Service in Australia, and similar ventures elsewhere. Although the specifics of these ventures vary widely, many scholars favor these investments, recognizing that shared technologies and common-pool resources are beyond the reach of individual universities and researchers. Others are not supportive, resisting investments that appear to be top-down, centralized solutions. These are long-term initiatives that must navigate short-term funding cycles and political turnover. They have many moving parts, each of which evolves on different time scales. Technologies advance quickly. Universities and publishers move much more slowly. Startup companies can move quickly but may not be investing for long-term sustainability.

The ability to keep and exploit data also depends on institutional investments in data management. Researchers appear more motivated to curate data when those investments add research value than when the goals are managerial accountability. Scholars and others who would invest in data management can make joint decisions about what data are worth keeping. If the value of data is perceived to degrade quickly, fewer reasons exist to keep them. Legacy data, hardware, and software are difficult and expensive to maintain. Some data are recoverable only by running layers of emulations, which is usually hard to justify (Brooks 1975; Jackson and Buyuktur 2014; Lee et al. 2006; Mayernik, in press; Segal 2005; Winkelman and Rots 2012a).

Data useful only in the short term may be deposited or posted on sites that will disseminate them and provide access. Data and other research objects of long-term value are better entrusted to stable institutions, whether libraries, archives, museums, or well-funded repositories. Some scholars adopt and adapt new technologies quickly. Others are risk averse, adopting only technologies for which future support appears to be secure. Similarly, some will maintain their data in proprietary software; others will

only maintain data in open formats. Silos are everywhere and interoperability remains a distant goal.

Conclusion

No generic answer exists to the question of what data to keep because no generic answer exists to the questions of what are data. Despite the overall lack of agreement, most scholars would like better means to manage whatever they do consider to be their data. Better management is likely to lead to more sustainable data and in turn to better means of discovering and sharing data. These are expensive investments that cannot fall on the shoulders of scholars alone. Better access to data requires investments in knowledge infrastructures by research communities, funding agencies, universities, publishers, and other stakeholders. Technology, policy, and practices intersect in many ways. Knitting together the many moving parts of knowledge infrastructures requires investment in the people who hold those parts together through their invisible work.

Scholars can collect, discover, retrieve, analyze, and disseminate data at scales never before possible. Some of those data are worth keeping forever; others have transient value. Some are more readily recreated if needed than kept. Throughout human history, keeping everything was never an option. Future uses of information can never be fully anticipated. The ability to identify new evidence in old information is the essence of many forms of scholarship. Sustaining data is a much higher bar than simply storage and backup. The challenge is to make data discoverable, usable, assessable, intelligible, and interpretable, and to do so for extended periods of time. Stakeholders may disagree on what kinds of data in any domain might be worthy of that degree of investment or to whom those data might be valuable. The hardest part is to determine who may be willing to make those investments on behalf of the interested parties. The value proposition for access to data is the value proposition for knowledge infrastructures. A very long view is needed, which is difficult to do with the intricately interconnected set of stakeholders across research domains, communities, and countries. To restate the premise of this book, the value of data lies in their use. Unless stakeholders can agree on what to keep and why, and invest in the invisible work necessary to sustain knowledge infrastructures, big data and little data alike will quickly become no data.

References

Aad, G., T. Abajyan, B. Abbott, J. Abdallah, S. Abdel Khalek, A. A. Abdelalim, O. Abdinov, et al. 2012. "Observation of a New Particle in the Search for the Standard Model Higgs Boson with the ATLAS Detector at the LHC." *Physics Letters [Part B]* 716 (1):1–29. doi:10.1016/j.physletb.2012.08.020.

Abbate, Janet. 1999. *Inventing the Internet*. Cambridge, MA: MIT Press.

Accomazzi, Alberto. 2010. "Astronomy 3.0 Style." *Astronomical Society of the Pacific Conference Series* 433: 273–281.

Accomazzi, Alberto, and Rahul Dave. 2011. "Semantic Interlinking of Resources in the Virtual Observatory Era." *Astronomical Society of the Pacific Conference Series* 442: 415–424. doi: arXiv:1103.5958.

Acropolis Museum. 2013. "The Frieze." http://www.theacropolismuseum.gr/en/content/frieze-0.

Agosti, Maristella, and Nicola Ferro. 2007. "A Formal Model of Annotations of Digital Content." *ACM Transactions on Information Systems* 26 (1). doi:10.1145/1292 591.1292594.

Agre, Philip E. 1994. "From High Tech to Human Tech: Empowerment, Measurement, and Social Studies of Computing." *Computer Supported Cooperative Work* 3 (2):167–195. doi:10.1007/BF00773446.

Ahn, Christopher P., Rachael Alexandroff, Carlos Allende Prieto, Scott F. Anderson, Timothy Anderton, Brett H. Andrews, Éric Aubourg, et al. 2012. "The Ninth Data Release of the Sloan Digital Sky Survey: First Spectroscopic Data from the SDSS-III Baryon Oscillation Spectroscopic Survey." *Astrophysical Journal* 203:21. doi:10.1088/0067-0049/203/2/21.

Akyildiz, I. F., W. Su, Y. Sankarasubramaniam, and E. Cayirci. 2002. "Wireless Sensor Networks: A Survey." *Computer Networks* 38 (4):393–422. doi:10.1016/S1389-1286 (01)00302-4.

Alabaster, Jay. 2013. "Library of Congress Saves 500 Million Tweets Per Day in Archives." *Computerworld* (January 8). http://www.computerworld.com/s/article/9235421/Library_of_Congress_saves_500_million_tweets_per_day_in_archives.

Alarcón, Enrique. 2000. "Corpus Thomisticum." www.corpusthomisticum.org.

Alberts, Bruce. 2012. "The End of 'Small Science'?" *Science* 337 (6102):1583. doi:10.1126/science.1230529.

Alberts, Bruce. 2013. "Impact Factor Distortions." *Science* 340 (6134):787. doi:10.1126/science.1240319.

Allen, Erin. 2013. "Update on the Twitter Archive at the Library of Congress." (January 4). http://blogs.loc.gov/loc/2013/01/update-on-the-twitter-archive-at-the-library-of-congress.

Allon, Mark. 2007. "Recent Discoveries of Buddhist Manuscripts from Afghanistan and Pakistan: The Heritage of the Greeks in the North-west." In *Memory as History: The Legacy of Alexander in Asia*, ed. Himanshu Prabha Ray and D. T. Potts. New Dehli: Aryan Books International.

Allon, Mark. 2009. "Recent Discoveries of Buddhist Manuscripts from Afghanistan and Pakistan and Their Significance." In *Art, Architecture and Religion along the Silk Roads*, ed. Ken Parry, 133–178. Belgium: Brepols.

Alsheikh-Ali, Alawi A., Waqas Qureshi, Mouaz H. Al-Mallah, and John P. A. Ioannidis. 2011. "Public Availability of Published Research Data in High-Impact Journals." *PLoS ONE* 6:e24357.

Altman, Micah, and Gary King. 2007. "A Proposed Standard for the Scholarly Citation of Quantitative Data." *D-Lib Magazine* 13 (3/4). doi:10.1045/march2007-altman.

Altschul, S. F., W. Gish, W. Miller, E. W. Myers, and D. J. Lipman. 1990. "Basic Local Alignment Search Tool." *Journal of Molecular Biology* 215 (3):403–410. doi:10.1016/S0022-2836(05)80360-2.

American Psychological Association. 2009. *Publication Manual of the American Psychological Association*. 6th ed. Washington, DC: APA.

Ancient Lives. 2013. Home page. http://ancientlives.org.

Anderson, Chris. 2004. "The Long Tail." *Wired*. http://www.wired.com/wired/archive/12.10/tail_pr.html.

Anderson, Chris. 2006. *The Long Tail: Why the Future of Business Is Selling Less of More*. New York: Hyperion.

Anderson, Chris. 2008. "The End of Theory: The Data Deluge Makes the Scientific Method Obsolete." *Wired*. http://www.wired.com/science/discoveries/magazine/16-07/pb_theory.

Anderson, David P., Jeff Cobb, Eric Korpela, Matt Lebofsky, and Dan Werthimer. 2002. "SETI@home: An Experiment in Public-Resource Computing." *Communications of the ACM* 45 (11):56–61. doi:10.1145/581571.581573.

Anderson, Robert J. 1994. "Representations and Requirements: The Value of Ethnography in System Design." *Human-Computer Interaction* 9 (3):151–182. doi:10.1207/s15327051hci0902_1.

Archaeology Data Service. 2013. Home page. http://archaeologydataservice.ac.uk.

Arms, William Y. 2002. "What Are the Alternatives to Peer Review? Quality Control in Scholarly Publishing on the Web." *Journal of Electronic Publishing* 8. http://www.press.umich.edu/jep/08-01/arms.html.

Aronova, Elena, Karen S. Baker, and Naomi Oreskes. 2010. "Big Science and Big Data in Biology: From the International Geophysical Year through the International Biological Program to the Long-Term Ecological Research (LTER) Network, 1957–Present." *Historical Studies in the Natural Sciences* 40:183–224. doi:10.1525/hsns.2010.40.2.183.

Arts & Humanities Research Council. 2012. "Technical Plan." http://www.ahrc.ac.uk/Funding-Opportunities/Research-funding/RFG/Application-guidance/Pages/Technical-Plan.aspx.

Arts and Humanities Data Service. 2008. Home page. http://www.ahds.ac.uk.

ArXiv.org. 2013. "ArXiv.org e-Print Archive." Home page. http://arxiv.org.

Arzberger, Peter, P. Schroeder, Anne Beaulieu, Geoffrey C. Bowker, K. Casey, L. Laaksonen, D. Moorman, Paul F. Uhlir, and Paul Wouters. 2004. "An International Framework to Promote Access to Data." *Science* 303: 1777–1778. doi:10.1126/science.1095958.

Association for Computing Machinery. 1992. "ACM Code of Ethics and Professional Conduct." http://www.acm.org/about/code-of-ethics.

Association of Internet Researchers. 2012. "Ethics Guide." http://aoir.org/documents/ethics-guide.

Atkins, Daniel E., Kelvin K. Droegemeier, Stuart I. Feldman, Hector Garcia-Molina, Michael L. Klein, Paul Messina, David G. Messerschmitt, Jeremiah P. Ostriker, and Margaret H. Wright. 2003. "Revolutionizing Science and Engineering through Cyberinfrastructure: Report of the National Science Foundation Blue-Ribbon Panel on Cyberinfrastructure." Washington, DC: National Science Foundation. http://www.nsf.gov/cise/sci/reports/atkins.pdf.

Australian Law Reform Commission. 2014. "Defining 'Non-Consumptive' Use." http://www.alrc.gov.au/publications/8-non-consumptive-use/defining-%E2%80%98non-consumptive%E2%80%99-use.

Australian National Data Service. 2014. Home page. http://www.ands.org.au.

Ayers, Edward L. 2003. *In the Presence of Mine Enemies: The Civil War in the Heart of America, 1859—1863*. W. W. Norton.

Ayers, Edward L. 2007. "The Valley of the Shadow: Two Communities in the American Civil War." http://valley.lib.virginia.edu.

Ayers, Edward L., and Charles M. Grisham. 2003. "Why IT Has Not Paid Off as We Hoped (Yet)." *EDUCAUSE Review* 38 (6):40–51. http://www.educause.edu/pub/er/erm03/erm0361.asp.

Babbie, Earl. 2013. *The Practice of Social Research*. 13th ed. Belmont, CA: Wadsworth.

Baca, Murtha. 1998. *Introduction to Metadata: Pathways to Digital Information*. Los Angeles: Getty Information Institute.

Baca, Murtha. 2002. *Introduction to Art Image Access: Issues, Tools, Standards, Strategies*. Los Angeles: Getty Publications.

Bakshy, Eytan, Jake M. Hofman, Winter A. Mason, and Duncan J. Watts. 2011. "Everyone's an Influencer: Quantifying Influence on Twitter." In *Proceedings of the Fourth ACM International Conference on Web Search and Data Mining*, 65–74. New York: ACM. doi:10.1145/1935826.1935845.

Ball, Alex. 2012. "How to License Research Data." Digital Curation Centre. http://www.dcc.ac.uk/resources/how-guides/license-research-data.

Ball, James. 2013. "Verizon Court Order: Telephone Call Metadata and What It Can Show." *The Guardian* (June 12). http://www.guardian.co.uk/world/2013/jun/06/phone-call-metadata-information-authorities.

Bamford, Connor. 2012. "Solving Irreproducible Science." *The Scientist*. http://the-scientist.com/2012/09/26/solving-irreproducible-science.

Barbier, Geoffrey, Zhuo Feng, Pritam Gundecha, and Huan Liu. 2013. "Provenance Data in Social Media." *Synthesis Lectures on Data Mining and Knowledge Discovery* 4 (1):1–84. doi:10.2200/S00496ED1V01Y201304DMK007.

Bard, Jonathan. 2013. "The Living World." Unpublished manuscript. University of Oxford.

Barrett, Timothy H. 2008. *The Woman Who Discovered Printing*. New Haven, CT: Yale University Press.

Basken, Paul. 2012. "NIH to Begin Enforcing Open-Access Policy on Research It Supports." *Chronicle of Higher Education* (November 19). http://chronicle.com/article/NIH-to-Begin-Enforcing/135852/?cid=at.

Batalin, Maxim A., Mohammad Rahimi, Yan Yu, Duo Liu, Aman Kansal, Gaurav S. Sukhatme, William J. Kaiser, et al. 2004. "Call and Response: Experiments in

Sampling the Environment." In *Proceedings of the 2nd International Conference on Embedded Networked Sensor Systems*, 25–38. New York: ACM. http://cres.usc.edu/pubdb_html/files_upload/420.pdf.

Beaulieu, Anne, Sarah de Rijcke, and Bas van Heur. 2012. "Authority and Expertise in New Sites of Knowledge Production." In *Virtual Knowledge: Experimenting in the Humanities and Social Sciences*, ed. Paul Wouters, Anne Beaulieu, Andrea Scharnhorst, and Sally Wyatt, 25–56. Cambridge MA: MIT Press. http://mitpress.mit.edu/books/virtual-knowledge-0.

Beaumont, Christopher N., Stella S. R. Offner, Rahul Shetty, Simon C. O. Glover, and Alyssa A. Goodman. 2013. "Quantifying Observational Projection Effects Using Molecular Cloud Simulations." *Astrophysical Journal* 777 (2):173. doi:10.1088/0004-637X/777/2/173.

Becher, Tony. 1989. *Academic Tribes and Territories: Intellectual Enquiry and the Culture of Disciplines*. Buckingham, UK: SRHE & Open University Press.

Becher, Tony. 1994. "The Significance of Disciplinary Differences." *Studies in Higher Education* 19 (2):151–161. doi:10.1080/03075079412331382007.

Bechhofer, Sean, Iain Buchan, David De Roure, Paolo Missier, John Ainsworth, Jiten Bhagat, Philip Couch, et al. 2013. "Why Linked Data Is Not Enough for Scientists." *Future Generation Computer Systems* 29 (2):599–611. doi:10.1016/j.future.2011.08.004.

Bechhofer, Sean, David De Roure, Matthew Gamble, Carole Goble, and Iain Buchan. 2010. "Research Objects: Towards Exchange and Reuse of Digital Knowledge." *Nature Precedings*. doi:10.1038/npre.2010.4626.1.

Becker, Glenn, Arnold Rots, Sherry L. Winkelman, Michael McCollough, Aaron Watry, and Joan Hagler. 2009. "It's Not Just for Data Anymore: The Many Faces of the Chandra Data Archive." In *Chandra's First Decade of Discovery, Proceedings of the Conference Held 22–25 September, 2009 in Boston, MA*, 65. http://adsabs.harvard.edu/abs/2009cfdd.confE.65B.

Bell, Gordon, Tony Hey, and Alex Szalay. 2009. "Beyond the Data Deluge." *Science* 323:1297–1298. doi:10.1126/science.1170411.

Benkler, Yochai. 2007. *The Wealth of Networks: How Social Production Transforms Markets and Freedom*. New Haven, CT: Yale University Press.

Berlekamp, Elwyn. 2012. "Small Science: Radical Innovation." *Science* 338 (6109):882. doi:10.1126/science.338.6109.882-a.

Berman, Francine. 2008. "Got Data? A Guide to Data Preservation in the Information Age." *Communications of the ACM* 51:50–56. doi:10.1145/1409360.1409376.

Berman, Francine, Brian Lavoie, and Paul Ayris, G. Sayeed Choudhury, Elizabeth Cohen, Paul Courant, Lee Dirks, et al. 2010. "Sustainable Economics for a Digital

Planet: Ensuring Long-Term Access to Digital Information." San Diego: National Science Foundation, Andrew W. Mellon Foundation, Library of Congress, Joint Information Systems Committee of the UK, Council on Library and Information Resources, National Archives and Records Administration. http://brtf.sdsc.edu/publications.html.

Bhattacharjee, Yudhijit. 2012. "Pharma Firms Push for Sharing of Cancer Trial Data." *Science* 338 (6103):29. doi:10.1126/science.338.6103.29.

Bibliographic Services Task Force. 2005. "Rethinking How We Provide Bibliographic Services for the University of California." University of California Libraries. http://libraries.universityofcalifornia.edu/sopag/BSTF/Final.pdf.

Biemiller, Lawrence. 2013. "Universities Must Encourage Researchers to Share Data, Panel Says." *Chronicle of Higher Education.* http://chronicle.com/blogs/wiredcampus/universities-must-encourage-researchers-to-share-data-panel-says/45409.

Bietz, Matthew J., and Charlotte P. Lee. 2009. "Collaboration in Metagenomics: Sequence Databases and the Organization of Scientific Work." In *ECSCW 2009*, ed. Ina Wagner, Hilda Tellioğlu, Ellen Balka, Carla Simone, and Luigina Ciolfi, 243–262. London: Springer. http://link.springer.com/chapter/10.1007/978-1-84882-854-4_15.

Bietz, Matthew J., and Charlotte P. Lee. 2012. "Adapting Cyberinfrastructure to New Science: Tensions and Strategies." In *Proceedings of the 2012 iConference*, 183–190. New York: ACM. doi:10.1145/2132176.2132200.

Biglan, Anthony. 1973. "The Characteristics of Subject Matter in Different Academic Areas." *Journal of Applied Psychology* 57 (3):195–203. doi:10.1037/h0034701.

Bijker, Wiebe E. 1995. *Of Bicycles, Bakelites and Bulbs: Toward a Theory of Sociotechnical Change.* Cambridge, MA: MIT Press.

Bijker, Wiebe E., Thomas P. Hughes, and Trevor Pinch. 1987. *The Social Construction of Technological Systems: New Directions in the Sociology and History of Technology.* Cambridge, MA: MIT Press.

Binding, Ceri, Keith May, and Douglas Tudhope. 2008. "Semantic Interoperability in Archaeological Datasets: Data Mapping and Extraction via the CIDOC CRM." In *Research and Advanced Technology for Digital Libraries*, ed. Birte Christensen-Dalsgaard, Donatella Castelli, Bolette Ammitzbøll Jurik, and Joan Lippincott, 280–290. 5173. Berlin: Springer.

Birnholtz, Jeremy P., and Matthew J. Bietz. 2003. "Data at Work: Supporting Sharing in Science and Engineering." In *Proceedings of the 2003 International ACM SIGGROUP Conference*, 339–348. New York: ACM.

Bishop, Ann Peterson, and Susan Leigh Star. 1996. "Social Informatics of Digital Library Use and Infrastructure." *Annual Review of Information Science & Technology* 31:301–401.

Blair, Ann M. 2010. *Too Much to Know: Managing Scholarly Information before the Modern Age*. New Haven, CT: Yale University Press.

Blecksmith, E., S. Paltani, A. Rots, and Sherry L. Winkelman. 2003. "Chandra Data Archive Download and Usage Database." In *ASP Conference Series* 295:283. http://adsabs.harvard.edu/abs/2003ASPC.295.283B.

Blocker, Alexander W., and Xiao-Li Meng. 2013. "The Potential and Perils of Preprocessing: Building New Foundations." *Bernoulli* 19 (4):1176–1211. doi:10.3150/13-BEJSP16.

Blomberg, Jeanette, and Helena Karasti. 2013. "Reflections on 25 Years of Ethnography in CSCW." *Computer Supported Cooperative Work* 22 (4-6):373–423. doi:10.1007/s10606-012-9183-1.

Bloom, Harold. 1994. *The Western Canon: The Books and School of the Ages*. New York: Harcourt Brace.

Bohannon, John. 2013a. "Dance Your PhD: And the Winner Is...." *Science* (November 15). http://news.sciencemag.org/scientific-community/2013/11/dance-your-ph.d.-and -winner-%E2%80%A6.

Bohannon, John. 2013b. "Genealogy Databases Enable Naming of Anonymous DNA Donors." *Science* 339 (6117):262. doi:10.1126/science.339.6117.262.

Bollen, Johan, Huina Mao, and Xiao-Jun Zeng. 2010. "Twitter Mood Predicts the Stock Market." *Journal of Computational Science* 2 (1). doi:10.1016/j.jocs.2010.12.007.

Bollen, Johan, Herbert Van de Sompel, Aric Hagberg, and Ryan Chute. 2009. "A Principal Component Analysis of 39 Scientific Impact Measures." *PLoS ONE* 4 (6):e6022. doi:10.1371/journal.pone.0006022.

Bollier, David. 2007. "The Growth of the Commons Paradigm." In *Understanding Knowledge as a Commons: From Theory to Practice*, ed. Charlotte Hess and Elinor Ostrom, 27–40. Cambridge, MA: MIT Press.

Borges, Jorge Luis. 1999. "The Analytical Language of John Wilkins." Trans. Lilia Graciela Vazquez. *ALAMUT*. http://www.alamut.com/subj/artiface/language/johnWilkins.html.

Borgman, Christine L. 1990. *Scholarly Communication and Bibliometrics*. Newbury Park, CA: Sage.

Borgman, Christine L. 2000. *From Gutenberg to the Global Information Infrastructure: Access to Information in the Networked World*. Cambridge, MA: MIT Press.

Borgman, Christine L. 2003. "The Invisible Library: Paradox of the Global Information Infrastructure." *Library Trends* 51:652–674.

Borgman, Christine L. 2006. "What Can Studies of e-Learning Teach Us About e-Research? Some Findings from Digital Library Research." *Computer Supported Cooperative Work* 15 (4):359–383. doi:10.1007/s10606-006-9024-1.

Borgman, Christine L. 2007. *Scholarship in the Digital Age: Information, Infrastructure, and the Internet.* Cambridge, MA: MIT Press.

Borgman, Christine L. 2009. "The Digital Future Is Now: A Call to Action for the Humanities." *Digital Humanities Quarterly* 3. http://digitalhumanities.org/dhq/vol/3/4/000077/000077.html.

Borgman, Christine L. 2011. "Is Data to Knowledge as the Wasp Is to the Fig Tree? Reconsidering Licklider's Intergalactic Network in the Days of Data Deluge." In *Accelerating Discovery: Human-computer Symbiosis 50 Years On.* Park City, UT: Argonne National Labs, ICIS. https://sites.google.com/site/licklider50.

Borgman, Christine L. 2012a. "The Conundrum of Sharing Research Data." *Journal of the American Society for Information Science and Technology* 63 (6):1059–1078. doi:10.1002/asi.22634.

Borgman, Christine L. 2012b. "Why Are the Attribution and Citation of Scientific Data Important?" In *For Attribution—Developing Data Attribution and Citation Practices and Standards: Summary of an International Workshop*, 1–10. Washington, DC: National Academies Press. http://www.nap.edu/catalog.php?record_id=13564.

Borgman, Christine L. 2013. "Keynote Presentation: 'ADS, Astronomy and Scholarly Infrastructure'" presented at the Astrophysics Data System 20th Anniversary Symposium (May 8). Harvard-Smithsonian Center for Astrophysics, Cambridge, MA. http://conf.adsabs.harvard.edu/ADSXX.

Borgman, Christine L., and Jonathan Furner. 2002. "Scholarly Communication and Bibliometrics." *Annual Review of Information Science & Technology* 36:3–72.

Borgman, Christine L., Andrea L. Gallagher, Sandra G. Hirsh, and Virginia A. Walter. 1995. "Children's Searching Behavior on Browsing and Keyword Online Catalogs: The Science Library Catalog Project." *Journal of the American Society for Information Science American Society for Information Science* 46:663–684. doi:10.1002/(SICI)1097-4571(199510)46:9<663:AID-ASI4>3.0.CO;2-2.

Borgman, Christine L., Anne J. Gilliland-Swetland, Gregory H. Leazer, Richard Mayer, David Gwynn, Rich Gazan, and Patricia Mautone. 2000. "Evaluating Digital Libraries for Teaching and Learning in Undergraduate Education: A Case Study of the Alexandria Digital Earth ProtoType (ADEPT)." *Library Trends* 49 (2):228–250.

Borgman, Christine L., Dineh Moghdam, and Patti K. Corbett. 1984. *Effective Online Searching: A Basic Text.* New York: Marcel Dekker.

Borgman, Christine L., and Susan L. Siegfried. 1992. "Getty's Synoname™ and Its Cousins: A Survey of Applications of Personal Name Matching Algorithms." *Journal*

of the American Society for Information Science American Society for Information Science 43 (7):459–476. doi:10.1002/(SICI)1097-4571(199208)43:7<459:AID-ASI1>3.0.CO;2-D.

Borgman, Christine L., Sharon Traweek, Peter Darch, Milena Golshan, Elaine Levia, Camille Mathieu, Ashley E. Sands, and Jillian C. Wallis. 2014. "Knowledge Infrastructures Lab." *Los Angeles: University of California at Los Angeles, Department of Information Studies.* http://knowledgeinfrastructures.gseis.ucla.edu/index.html.

Borgman, Christine L., Jillian C. Wallis, and Noel Enyedy. 2006. "Building Digital Libraries for Scientific Data: An Exploratory Study of Data Practices in Habitat Ecology." In *10th European Conference on Digital Libraries*, Lecture Notes in Computer Science 4172:170–183. Berlin: Springer.

Borgman, Christine L., Jillian C. Wallis, and Noel Enyedy. 2007. "Little Science Confronts the Data Deluge: Habitat Ecology, Embedded Sensor Networks, and Digital Libraries." *International Journal on Digital Libraries* 7:17–30. doi:10.1007/s00799 -007-0022-9.

Borgman, Christine L., Jillian C. Wallis, and Matthew S. Mayernik. 2012. "Who's Got the Data? Interdependencies in Science and Technology Collaborations." *Computer Supported Cooperative Work* 21 (6):485–523. doi:10.1007/s10606-012-9169-z.

Borgman, Christine L., Jillian C. Wallis, Matthew S. Mayernik, and Alberto Pepe. 2007. "Drowning in Data: Digital Library Architecture to Support Scientific Use of Embedded Sensor Networks." In *Joint Conference on Digital Libraries*, 269–277. New York: ACM. http://doi.acm.org/10.1145/1255175.1255228.

Boruch, Robert F. 1985. "Definitions, Products, Distinctions in Data Sharing." In *Sharing Research Data*, ed. Stephen E. Fienberg, Margaret E. Martin, and Miron L. Straf, 89–122. Committee on National Statistics, Commission on Behavioral and Social Sciences and Education, National Research Council. Washington, DC: National Academies Press. http://books.nap.edu/catalog.php?record_id=2033.

Bos, Nathan, Ann Zimmerman, Judith Olson, Jude Yew, Jason Yerkie, Erik Dahl, and Gary M. Olson. 2007. "From Shared Databases to Communities of Practice: A Taxonomy of Collaboratories." *Journal of Computer-Mediated Communication* 12 (2). http://jcmc.indiana.edu/vol12/issue2/bos.html.

Boulton, Geoffrey. 2012. "Open Your Minds and Share Your Results." *Nature* 486 (7404):441. doi:10.1038/486441a.

Boulton, Geoffrey, Philip Campbell, Brian Collins, Peter Elias, Wendy Hall, Graeme Laurie, Onora O'Neill, et al. 2012. "Science as an Open Enterprise." The Royal Society. http://royalsociety.org/policy/projects/science-public-enterprise/report.

Boulton, Geoffrey, Michael Rawlins, Patrick Vallance, and Mark Walport. 2011. "Science as a Public Enterprise: The Case for Open Data." *Lancet* 377 (9778):1633–1635. doi:10.1016/S0140-6736(11)60647-8.

Bourne, Philip E. 2005. "Will a Biological Database Be Different from a Biological Journal?" *PLoS Computational Biology* 1:e34. doi:10.1371/journal.pcbi.0010034.

Bourne, Philip E., Timothy Clark, Robert Dale, and Anita de Waard, Eduard H. Hovy, and David Shotton, eds. 2011. "Force 11 Manifesto: Improving Future Research Communication and e-Scholarship." http://www.force11.org/white_paper.

Bowen, G. Michael, and Wolff Michael Roth. 2007. "The Practice of Field Ecology: Insights for Science Education." *Research in Science Education* 37:171–187.

Bowker, Geoffrey C. 2013. "Data Flakes: An Afterword to 'Raw Data' Is an Oxymoron." In *"Raw Data" Is an Oxymoron*, ed. Lisa Gitelman, 167–171. Cambridge, MA: MIT Press.

Bowker, Geoffrey C. 2005. *Memory Practices in the Sciences*. Cambridge, MA: MIT Press.

Bowker, Geoffrey C., Karen S. Baker, Florence Millerand, David Ribes, Jeremy Hunsinger, Lisbeth Klastrup, and Matthew Allen. 2010. "Toward Information Infrastructure Studies: Ways of Knowing in a Networked Environment." In *International Handbook of Internet Research*, ed. Jeremy Hunsinger, Lisbeth Klastrup, and Matthew Allen, 97–117. Dordrecht: Springer. http://www.springerlink.com/index/10.1007/978-1-4020-9789-8_5.

Bowker, Geoffrey C., and Susan Leigh Star. 1999. *Sorting Things Out: Classification and Its Consequences*. Cambridge, MA: MIT Press.

boyd, danah, and Kate Crawford. 2012. "Critical Questions for Big Data." *Information, Communication & Society* 15 (5): 662–679. doi:10.1080/1369118X.2012.678878.

Boyle, James, and Jennifer Jenkins. 2003. "The Genius of Intellectual Property and the Need for the Public Domain." In *The Role of Scientific and Technical Data and Information in the Public Domain*, ed. Julie M. Esanu and Paul F. Uhlir, 10–14. Office of Scientific and Technical Information Programs, Board on International Scientific Organizations, Policy and Global Affairs Division, National Research Council, National Academies. Washington, DC: National Academies Press.

Boyle, John. 2013. "Biology Must Develop Its Own Big-data Systems." *Nature* 499 (7456):7. doi:10.1038/499007a.

Boyle, Paul. 2013. "A U.K. View on the U.S. Attack on Social Sciences." *Science* 341 (6147):719. doi:10.1126/science.1242563.

Brady, Henry. 2004. "Testimony to the Commission on Cyberinfrastructure for the Humanities and Social Sciences." http://www.acls.org/cyberinfrastructure/cyber_meeting_notes_august.htm#brady_summary.

Brase, Jan, Yvonne Socha, Sarah Callaghan, Christine L. Borgman, Paul F. Uhlir, and Bonnie Carroll. 2014. "Data Citation." In *Managing Research Data: Practical Strategies*

for Information Professionals, ed. Joyce M. Ray, 167–186. Lafayette, IN: Purdue University Press.

The British Library Board. 2013. "Sacred Texts: Diamond Sutra." http://www.bl.uk/onlinegallery/sacredtexts/diamondsutra.html.

British Museum. 2013. "Parthenon Sculptures." http://www.britishmuseum.org/about_us/news_and_press/statements/parthenon_sculptures.aspx.

Brooks, Frederick. 1975. *The Mythical Man-Month: Essays on Software Engineering.* Reading, MA: Addison-Wesley.

Brown, Ian, and Christopher T. Marsden. 2013. *Regulating Code: Good Governance and Better Regulation in the Information Age.* Cambridge, MA: MIT Press.

Brown, John Seely, and Paul Duguid. 1996. "The Social Life of Documents." *First Monday* 1. http://firstmonday.org/ojs/index.php/fm/article/view/466/387.

Brown, John Seely, and Paul Duguid. 2000. *The Social Life of Information.* Boston: Harvard Business School Press.

Bruckman, Amy, Kurt Luther, and Casey Fiesler. Forthcoming. "When Should We Use Real Names in Published Accounts of Internet Research?" In *Digital Research Confidential*, ed. Eszter Hargittai and Christian Sandvig. Cambridge, MA: MIT Press.

Brumfiel, G. 2002. "Misconduct Finding at Bell Labs Shakes Physics Community." *Nature* 419:419–421.

Bruns, Axel, and Yuxian Eugene Liang. 2012. "Tools and Methods for Capturing Twitter Data during Natural Disasters." *First Monday* 17 (4). doi:10.5210/fm.v17i4.3937.

Bryson, Bill. 2008. *Bryson's Dictionary for Writers and Editors.* New York: Broadway Books.

Buckland, Michael K. 1991. "Information as Thing." *Journal of the American Society for Information Science American Society for Information Science* 42:351–360.

Budapest Open Access Initiative. 2002. "Budapest Declaration on Open Access." http://www.soros.org/openaccess/read.shtml.

Buneman, Peter, Sanjeev Khanna, and Wang-Chiew Tan. 2000. "Data Provenance: Some Basic Issues." In *Foundations of Software Technology and Theoretical Computer Science.* Vol. 1974, ed. S. Kapoor and S. Prasad, 87–93. Lecture Notes in Computer Science. Berlin: Springer.

Buneman, Peter, Sanjeev Khanna, and Wang-Chiew Tan. 2001. "Why and Where: A Characterization of Data Provenance." In *Database Theory—ICDT 2001.* Vol. 1973, ed. Jan Van den Bussche and Victor Vianu, 316–330. Berlin: Springer.

Burdick, Anne, Johanna Drucker, Peter Lunenfeld, Todd Presner, and Jeffrey Schnapp. 2012. *Digital_Humanities*. Cambridge, MA: MIT Press.

Burke, Peter. 2000. *A Social History of Knowledge: From Gutenberg to Diderot*. Cambridge, UK: Polity Press.

Burke, Peter. 2012. *A Social History of Knowledge II: From the Encyclopaedia to Wikipedia*. Cambridge, UK: Polity Press.

Burnard, Lou D. 1987. "Knowledge Base or Database? Computer Applications in Ethnology." In *Toward a Computer Ethnology*, ed. J. Raben, S. Sugita, and M. Kubo, 63–95. Osaka: National Museum of Ethnology. http://cat.inist.fr/?aModele=afficheN&cpsidt=11990052.

Burwell, Sylvia M., Steven VanRoekel, Todd Park, and Dominic J. Mancini. 2013. "Open Data Policy-Managing Information as an Asset." Executive Office of the President, Office of Management and Budget. www.whitehouse.gov/.../omb/memoranda/2013/m-13-13.p.

Busch, Lawrence. 2013. *Standards: Recipes for Reality*. Cambridge, MA: MIT Press.

California Digital Library. 2013. "DataUp." Home page. http://dataup.cdlib.org.

Callan, Jamie, and Alistair Moffat. 2012. "Panel on Use of Proprietary Data." *SIGIR Forum* 46 (2): 10–18. doi:10.1145/2422256.2422258.

Caltech. 2013a. "Caltech Announces Open-Access Policy." http://www.caltech.edu/content/caltech-announces-open-access-policy.

Caltech. 2013b. "Caltech Center for Advanced Computing Research." http://www.cacr.caltech.edu/main/?tag=astronomy&paged=2.

Campbell, Eric G., Brian R. Clarridge, Manjusha Gokhale, Lauren Birenbaum, Stephen Hilgartner, Neil A. Holtzman, and David Blumenthal. 2002. "Data Withholding in Academic Genetics: Evidence from a National Survey." *Journal of the American Medical Association* 287:473–480. http://jama.ama-assn.org/cgi/content/full/287/4/473.

Carata, Lucian, Sherif Akoush, Nikilesh Balakrishnan, Thomas Bytheway, Ripduman Sohan, Margo Selter, and Andy Hopper. 2014. "A Primer on Provenance." *Communications of the ACM* 57 (5):52–60. doi:10.1145/2596628.

Carpenter, Siri. 2012. "Psychology's Bold Initiative." *Science* 335 (6076):1558–1561. doi:10.1126/science.335.6076.1558.

Case, Donald O. 2002. *Looking for Information: A Survey of Research on Information Seeking, Needs, and Behavior*. San Diego: Academic Press.

Case, Donald O. 2006. *Looking for Information: A Survey of Research on Information Seeking, Needs, and Behavior*. 2nd ed. San Diego: Academic Press.

Case, Donald O. 2012. *Looking for Information: A Survey of Research on Information Seeking, Needs and Behavior*. 3rd ed. Bingley, UK: Emerald Group Publishing.

Cavendish, Henry. 1798. "Experiments to Determine the Density of the Earth." *Philosophical Transactions of the Royal Society of London* 88 (1):469–526. doi:10.1098/rstl.1798.0022.

CBETA Chinese Electronic Tripitaka Collection. 2013. Home page. http://www.cbeta.org.

Center for Embedded Networked Sensing. 2012. Home page. http://research.cens.ucla.edu.

Center for Embedded Networked Sensing. 2013. "CENS eScholarship Repository." http://repositories.cdlib.org/cens.

Centre National de la Recherche Scientifique. 2012. "Aladin Sky Atlas." http://aladin.u-strasbg.fr.

Centre National de la Recherche Scientifique. 2013. "CDS VizieR Service." http://vizier.u-strasbg.fr/viz-bin/VizieR.

Cha, Meeyoung, Hamed Haddadi, Fabrício Benevenuto, and Krishna P. Gummadi. 2010. "Measuring User Influence in Twitter: The Million Follower Fallacy." In *ICWSM '10: Proceedings of Fourth International AAAI Conference on Weblogs and Social Media*, 10–17. Palo Alto, CA: AAAI.

Chalmers, Iain. 2011. "Systematic Reviews and Uncertainties about the Effects of Treatments." *Cochrane Database of Systematic Reviews*. http://www.thecochrane library.com/details/editorial/691951/Systematic-reviews-and-uncertainties-about -the-effects-of-treatments.html.

Chamberlain, Scott. 2013. "Consuming Article-Level Metrics: Observations and Lessons." *Information Standards Quarterly* 25 (2):4. doi:10.3789/isqv25no2.2013.02.

Chang, Kevin, Nathan Yau, Mark Hansen, and Deborah Estrin. 2006. "SensorBase.org—A Centralized Repository to Slog Sensor Network Data." In *Proceedings of the International Conference on Distributed Networks (DCOSS)/EAWMS*. http://escholarship.org/uc/item/4dt82690.

Check Hayden, Erika. 2013. "Geneticists Push for Global Data-Sharing." *Nature* 498 (7452):16–17. doi:10.1038/498017a.

Chicago Manual of Style. 2010. 16th ed. Chicago: University of Chicago Press.

Cho, Adrian. 2012. "Who Invented the Higgs Boson?" *Science* 337 (6100):1286–1289. doi:10.1126/science.337.6100.1286.

Claerbout, Jon. 2010. "Reproducible Computational Research: A History of Hurdles, Mostly Overcome." http://sepwww.stanford.edu/sep/jon/reproducible.html.

CLARIN European Research Infrastructure Consortium. 2013. Home page. http://www.clarin.eu/external.

Cochrane Collaboration. 2013. Home page. http://www.cochrane.org.

CODATA-ICSTI Task Group on Data Citation Standards and Practices. 2013. "Out of Cite, Out of Mind: The Current State of Practice, Policy, and Technology for the Citation of Data." *Data Science Journal* 12:1–75. https://www.jstage.jst.go.jp/article/dsj/12/0/12_OSOM13-043/_article.

Cohen, Jon. 2012. "WHO Group: H5N1 Papers Should Be Published in Full." *Science* 335 (6071):899–900. doi:10.1126/science.335.6071.899.

Cohen, Julie E. 2012. *Configuring the Networked Self: Law, Code, and the Play of Everyday Practice*. New Haven, CT: Yale University Press.

Collins, Christopher E. 2011. "Twitter and Rheumatology Based Medical Education—Analysis of the First 100 Followers." *Arthritis and Rheumatism* 63 (S10):85. doi:10.1002/art.33310.

Collins, Harry M. 1975. "The Seven Sexes: A Study in the Sociology of a Phenomenon, or the Replication of Experiments in Physics." *Sociology* 9:205–224.

Collins, Harry M. 1998. "The Meaning of Data: Open and Closed Evidential Cultures in the Search for Gravitational Waves." *American Journal of Sociology* 104:293–338.

Collins, Harry M., and Robert Evans. 2007. *Rethinking Expertise*. Chicago: University of Chicago Press.

Committee on Networked Systems of Embedded Computers. 2001. *Embedded, Everywhere: A Research Agenda for Networked Systems of Embedded Computers*. Washington, DC: National Academies Press. http://www.nap.edu/catalog.php?record_id=10193.

Committee on Publication Ethics. 2013. Home page. http://publicationethics.org.

ConservationSpace. 2013. Home page. http://www.conservationspace.org/Home.html.

Consultative Committee for Space Data Systems. 2012. "Reference Model for an Open Archival Information System." Issue 2. Consultative Committee for Space Data Systems. http://public.ccsds.org/publications/RefModel.aspx.

Contadini, Anna. 1993. "Il Grifone Di Pisa." In *Eredità dell'Islam—Arte Islamica in Italia*, ed. Giovanni Curatola. Milan: Silvana Editoriale.

Contadini, Anna. 2010. "Translocation and Transformation: Some Middle Eastern Objects in Europe." In *The Power of Things and the Flow of Cultural Transformations: Art and Culture between Europe and Asia*, ed. Lieselotte E. Saurma-Jeltsch and Anja Eisenbeiss, 42–64. Berlin: Deutscher Kunstverlag.

Contadini, Anna, Richard Camber, and Peter Northover. 2002. "Beasts That Roared: The Pisa Griffin and the New York Lion." In *Cairo to Kabul: Afghan and Islamic Studies Presented to Ralph Pinder-Wilson*, ed. Warwick Ball and Leonard Harrow, 65–83. London: Melisende.

COordinated Molecular Probe Line Extinction Thermal Emission Survey of Star Forming Regions [COMPLETE]. 2011. Home page. http://www.cfa.harvard.edu/COMPLETE.

Corbyn, Zoë. 2011. "Researchers Failing to Make Raw Data Public." *NATNews* (9–14). doi:10.1038/news.2011.536.

Corporation for National Research Initiatives. 2013. "Handle System." http://www.handle.net.

Costello, Anthony, Mark Maslin, Hugh Montgomery, Anne M. Johnson, and Paul Ekins. 2011. "Global Health and Climate Change: Moving from Denial and Catastrophic Fatalism to Positive Action." *Philosophical Transactions of the Royal Society A* 369:1866–1882. doi:10.1098/rsta.2011.0007.

Council of Science Editors, and the Style Manual Committee. 2006. *Scientific Style and Format: The CBE Manual for Authors, Editors, and Publishers*. Reston, VA: CSE and Rockefeller University Press.

Courant, Paul N. 2009. "The Stakes in the Google Book Search Settlement." *The Economists' Voice* 6 (9):1–6. doi:10.2202/1553-3832.1665.

Couzin, Jennifer, and Catherine Unger. 2006. "Cleaning up the Paper Trail." *Science* 312:38–43. doi:10.1126/science.312.5770.38.

Couzin-Frankel, Jennifer. 2010. "As Questions Grow, Duke Halts Trials, Launches Investigation." *Science* 329 (5992):614–615. doi:10.1126/science.329.5992.614.

Couzin-Frankel, Jennifer. 2013a. "Return of Unexpected DNA Results Urged." *Science* 339 (6127):1507–1508. doi:10.1126/science.339.6127.1507.

Couzin-Frankel, Jennifer. 2013b. "Unmasking 'Invisible' Drug Trials." http://news.sciencemag.org/scienceinsider/2013/06/unmasking-invisible-drug-trials.html.

Crabtree, Pam J. 1990. "Zooarchaeology and Complex Societies: Some Uses of Faunal Analysis for the Study of Trade, Social Status, and Ethnicity." *Archaeological Method and Theory* 2:155–205. doi:10.2307/20170207.

Cragin, Melissa H., Carole L. Palmer, Jacob R. Carlson, and Michael Witt. 2010. "Data Sharing, Small Science and Institutional Repositories." *Philosophical Transactions of the Royal Society A: Mathematical, Physical and Engineering Sciences* 368:4023–4038. doi:10.1098/rsta.2010.0165.

Cragin, Melissa H., and Kalpana Shankar. 2006. "Scientific Data Collections and Distributed Collective Practice." *Computer Supported Cooperative Work* 15:185–204.

Crane, Diana. 1970. "Nature of Scientific Communication and Influence." *International Social Science Journal* 22:28–41.

Crane, Diana. 1972. *Invisible Colleges: Diffusion of Knowledge in Scientific Communities.* Chicago: University of Chicago Press.

Crane, Gregory R. 2006. "What Do You Do with a Million Books?" *D-Lib Magazine* 12 (3). http://www.dlib.org/dlib/march06/crane/03crane.html.

Crane, Gregory R., Alison Babeu, and David Bamman. 2007. "eScience and the Humanities." *International Journal on Digital Libraries* 7:117–122. doi:10.1007/s00799-007-0031-8.

Crane, Gregory R., and Amy Friedlander. 2008. "Many More Than a Million: Building the Digital Environment for the Age of Abundance. Report of a One-day Seminar on Promoting Digital Scholarship." Washington, DC: Council on Library and Information Resources. www.clir.org/activities/digitalscholar/Nov28final.pdf.

Creative Commons. 2013. "Creative Commons License Choices." http://creativecommons.org/choose.

Crombie, Alistair C. 1994. *Styles of Scientific Thinking in the European Tradition: The History of Argument and Explanation Especially in the Mathematical and Biomedical Sciences and Arts.* London: Duckworth.

Cronin, Blaise. 1981. "The Need for a Theory of Citing." *Journal of Documentation* 37 (1):16–24. doi:10.1108/eb026703.

Cronin, Blaise. 1984. *The Citation Process: The Role and Significance of Citations in Scientific Communication.* London: Taylor Graham. http://garfield.library.upenn.edu/cronin/citationprocess.pdf.

Cronin, Blaise. 1994. "Tiered Citation and Measures of Document Similarity." *Journal of the American Society for Information Science American Society for Information Science* 45 (7):537–538. doi:10.1002/(SICI)1097-4571(199408)45:7<537:AID-ASI8>3.0.CO;2-Q.

Cronin, Blaise. 1995. *The Scholar's Courtesy: The Role of Acknowledgement in the Primary Communication Process. London: Taylor Graham.* London: Taylor Graham.

Cronin, Blaise. 2005. *The Hand of Science: Academic Writing and Its Rewards.* Lanham, MD: Scarecrow Press.

Cronin, Blaise, and Sara Franks. 2006. "Trading Cultures: Resource Mobilization and Service Rendering in the Life Sciences as Revealed in the Journal Article's Paratext." *Journal of the American Society for Information Science and Technology* 57 (14):1909–1918. doi:10.1002/asi.20407.

Crosas, Mercè. 2011. "The Dataverse Network®: An Open-Source Application for Sharing, Discovering and Preserving Data." *D-Lib Magazine* 17 (1/2). doi:10.1045/january2011-crosas.

Crosas, Mercè, Todd Carpenter, David Shotton, and Christine L. Borgman. 2013. "Amsterdam Manifesto on Data Citation Principles." https://www.force11.org/AmsterdamManifesto.

CrossRef. 2009. "The Formation of CrossRef: A Short History." http://www.crossref.org/01company/02history.html.

CrossRef. 2013. "FundRef." http://www.crossref.org/fundref.

CrossRef. 2014. "Home Page." http://www.crossref.org.

Cuff, Dana, Mark Hansen, and Jerry Kang. 2008. "Urban Sensing: Out of the Woods." *Communications of the ACM* 51:24–33. http://doi.acm.org/10.1145/1325555.1325562.

Cummings, Jonathon, Thomas A. Finholt, Ian Foster, Carl Kesselman, and Katherine A. Lawrence. 2008. "Beyond Being There: A Blueprint for Advancing the Design, Development, and Evaluation of Virtual Organizations." Washington, DC: National Science Foundation. http://www.educause.edu/Resources/BeyondBeingThereABlueprintforA/163051.

Cuneiform Digital Library Initiative. 2013. Home page. http://cdli.ucla.edu.

Curwen, Thomas. 2013. "Capturing the Mysteries of the Sun One Drawing at a Time." *Los Angeles Times* (October 28). http://www.latimes.com/local/columnone/la-me-c1-mt-wilson-sun-spots-20131028-dto,0,4430093.htmlstory#axzz2jJfYqvCU.

Dalrymple, Dana. 2003. "Scientific Knowledge as a Global Public Good: Contributions to Innovation and the Economy." In *The Role of Scientific and Technical Data and Information in the Public Domain*, ed. Julie M. Esanu and Paul F. Uhlir, 35–51. Office of Scientific and Technical Information Programs, Board on International Scientific Organizations, Policy and Global Affairs Division, National Research Council, National Academies. Washington, DC: National Academies Press.

Darch, Peter, Annemarie Carusi, Sharon Lloyd, Marina Jirotka, Grace De La Flor, Ralph Schroeder, and Eric Meyer. 2010. "Shared Understandings in e-Science Projects." Technical Report. Oxford e-Research Centre, Oxford University. http://www.oerc.ox.ac.uk/sites/default/files/uploads/ProjectFiles/FLESSR/HiPerDNO/embedding/Shared_Understanding%2030%20June.pdf.

Das, Sudeshna, Lisa Girard, Tom Green, Louis Weitzman, Alister Lewis-Bowen, and Tim Clark. 2009. "Building Biomedical Web Communities Using a Semantically Aware Content Management System." *Briefings in Bioinformatics* 10 (2):129–138. doi:10.1093/bib/bbn052.

Daston, Lorraine J. 1988. "The Factual Sensibility." *Isis* 79 (3):452–467. doi:10.2307/234675.

Datacitation Synthesis Group. 2014. "Joint Declarion on Data Citation Principles—Final." *Force11: The Future of Research Communications and Scholarship*. http://www .force11.org/datacitation.

DataCite. 2013. Home page. http://www.datacite.org.

Conservancy, Data. 2010. Home page. http://www.dataconservancy.org/about.

Data Documentation Initiative. 2012. FAQ. http://www.ddialliance.org/resources/ faq.html.

Data Publishing. 2013. Home page. http://datapublishing.com/about.

Data Seal of Approval. 2014. Home page. http://www.datasealofapproval.org/en.

Davenport, Elisabeth, and Blaise Cronin. 2001. "Who Dunnit? Metatags and Hyper-authorship." *Journal of the American Society for Information Science and Technology* 52 (9):770–773. doi:10.1002/asi.1123.

David, Paul A. 1985. "Clio and the Economics of QWERTY." *American Economic Review* 75:332–337.

David, Paul A. 2003. "The Economic Logic of 'Open Science' and the Balance between Private Property Rights and the Public Domain in Scientific Data and Information: A Primer." In *The Role of the Public Domain in Scientific Data and Information*, ed. Julie M. Esanu and Paul F. Uhlir, 19–34. National Research Council. Washington, DC: National Academies Press. http://www.stanford.edu/group/siepr/cgi-bin/ siepr/?q=system/files/shared/pubs/papers/pdf/02-30.pdf.

David, Paul A. 2004a. "Can 'Open Science' Be Protected from the Evolving Regime of Intellectual Property Protections." *Journal of Institutional and Theoretical Economics* 160. http://www-siepr.stanford.edu/papers/pdf/02-42.pdf.

David, Paul A. 2004b. *Towards a Cyberinfrastructure for Enhanced Scientific Collaboration: Providing Its 'Soft' Foundations May Be the Hardest Part*. Oxford: University of Oxford.

David, Paul A., Matthijs den Besten, and Ralph Schroeder. 2010. "Will e-Science Be Open Science?" In *World Wide Research: Reshaping the Sciences and Humanities*, ed. William H. Dutton and Paul W. Jeffreys, 299–316. Cambridge, MA: MIT Press.

David, Paul A., and Michael Spence. 2003. "Towards Institutional Infrastructures for e-Science: The Scope of the Challenge." Oxford Internet Institute Research Reports. Oxford: University of Oxford. http://papers.ssrn.com/sol3/papers.cfm?abstract _id=1325240.

Day, Ronald E. 2001. *The Modern Invention of Information: Discourse, History, and Power*. Carbondale: Southern Illinois University Press.

De Angelis, Catherine D., Jeffrey M. Drazen, Frank A. Frizelle, Charlotte Haug, John Hoey, Richard Horton, Sheldon Kotzin, et al. 2005. "Is This Clinical Trial Fully Registered?—A Statement from the International Committee of Medical Journal Editors." *New England Journal of Medicine* 352 (23):2436–2438. doi:10.1056/NEJMe058127.

De La Flor, Grace, Marina Jirotka, Paul Luff, John Pybus, and Ruth Kirkham. 2010. "Transforming Scholarly Practice: Embedding Technological Interventions to Support the Collaborative Analysis of Ancient Texts." *Computer Supported Cooperative Work* 19 (3-4):309–334. doi:10.1007/s10606-010-9111-1.

De Roure, David, Carole Goble, and Robert Stevens. 2009. "The Design and Realisation of the Virtual Research Environment for Social Sharing of Workflows." *Future Generation Computer Systems* 25 (5):561–567. doi:10.1016/j.future.2008.06.010.

Declaration on Research Assessment. 2013. Home page. http://am.ascb.org/dora.

DeNardis, Laura. 2011. *Opening Standards the Global Politics of Interoperability*. Cambridge, MA: MIT Press. http://search.ebscohost.com/login.aspx?direct=true&scope=site&db=nlebk&db=nlabk&AN=386853.

Den Besten, Matthijs, Arthur J. Thomas, and Ralph Schroeder. 2009. "Life Science Research and Drug Discovery at the Turn of the 21st Century: The Experience of SwissBioGrid." *Journal of Biomedical Discovery and Collaboration* 4:5. doi:10.5210/disco.v4i0.2452.

Deshpande, Amol, Carlos Guestrin, Samuel R. Madden, Joseph M. Hellerstein, and Wei Hong. 2004. "Model-driven Data Acquisition in Sensor Networks." In *Proceedings of the Thirtieth International Conference on Very Large Data Bases*, ed. Mario A. Nascimento, M. T. Ozsu, Donald Kossmann, Renee J. Miller, Jose A. Blakeley, and K. B. Schiefer, 588–599. Toronto: Morgan Kaufmann. http://dl.acm.org/citation.cfm?id=1316689.1316741.

DeVorkin, David H., and Paul Routly. 1999. "The Modern Society: Changes in Demographics." In *The American Astronomical Society's First Century*, ed. David H. DeVorkin, 122–136. Washington, DC: American Astronomical Society.

Di Gennaro, Corinna, and William H. Dutton. 2007. "Reconfiguring Friendships: Social Relationships and the Internet." *Information Communication and Society* 10 (5):591–618. doi:10.1080/13691180701657949.

The Digital Archaeological Record. 2013. Home page. http://www.tdar.org/about.

Digital Curation Centre. 2013. "Disciplinary Metadata." http://www.dcc.ac.uk/resources/metadata-standards.

Digital Curation Centre. 2014. "Trustworthy Repositories." http://www.dcc.ac.uk/resources/repository-audit-and-assessment/trustworthy-repositories.

Digital Public Library of America. 2013. Home page. http://dp.la.

Digital Social Research. 2013. Home page. http://www.digitalsocialresearch.net/wordpress.

Directory of Open Access Journals. 2013. Home page. http://www.doaj.org.

Disco, Cornelis, and Eda Kranakis, eds. 2013. *Cosmopolitan Commons: Sharing Resources and Risks across Borders*. Cambridge, MA: MIT Press.

Doorn, Peter, Ingrid Dillo, and René van Horik. 2013. "Lies, Damned Lies and Research Data: Can Data Sharing Prevent Data Fraud?" *International Journal of Digital Curation* 8 (1):229–243. doi:10.2218/ijdc.v8i1.256.

Drago, Idilio, Marco Mellia, Maurizio M. Munafo, Anna Sperotto, Ramin Sadre, Aiko Pras, John Byers, and Jim Kurose. 2012. "Inside Dropbox: Understanding Personal Cloud Storage Services." In *Proceedings of the 2012 ACM Conference on Internet Measurement Conference*, 481–494. New York: ACM. doi:10.1145/2398776.2398827.

Dryad. 2013. Home page. http://datadryad.org.

Duderstadt, James J., Daniel E. Atkins, John Seely Brown, Marye Anne Fox, Ralph E. Gomory, Nils Hasselmo, Paul M. Horn, et al. 2002. *Preparing for the Revolution: Information Technology and the Future of the Research*. Washington, DC: National Academies Press.

Duguid, Paul. 2005. "'The Art of Knowing': Social and Tacit Dimensions of Knowledge and the Limits of the Community of Practice." *Information Society* 21:109–118. doi:10.1080/01972240590925311.

Duguid, Paul. 2007. "Inheritance and Loss? A Brief Survey of Google Books." *First Monday* 12. http://firstmonday.org/htbin/cgiwrap/bin/ojs/index.php/fm/article/view/1972/1847.

Dutton, William H., and Grant Blank. 2011. *Next Generation Internet Users: The Internet in Britain 2011*. Oxford: Oxford Internet Institute, University of Oxford.

Dutton, William H., Grant Blank, and Darja Groselj. 2013. *OxIS 2013 Report: Cultures of the Internet*. Oxford: Oxford Internet Institute, University of Oxford.

Dutton, William H., Corinna di Gennaro, and A. Millwood Hargrave. 2005. *Oxford Internet Survey 2005 Report: The Internet in Britain*. Oxford: Oxford Internet Institute, University of Oxford.

Dutton, William H., and Paul W. Jeffreys, eds. 2010. *World Wide Research: Reshaping the Sciences and Humanities*. Cambridge, MA: MIT Press.

Dutton, William H., and Adrian Shepherd. 2006. "Trust in the Internet as an Experience Technology." *Information Communication and Society* 9 (4):433–451. doi:10.1080/13691180600858606.

Dutton, William H., Ellen J. Helsper, and M. M. Gerber. 2009. *Oxford Internet Survey 2009 Report: The Internet in Britain*. Oxford: Oxford Internet Institute, University of Oxford.

Easterbrook, Steve M., and Timothy C. Johns. 2009. "Engineering the Software for Understanding Climate Change." *Computing in Science & Engineering* 11 (6):65–74. doi:10.1109/MCSE.2009.193.

eBird. 2013. Home page. http://ebird.org/content/ebird.

Edge, David O. 1979. "Quantitative Measures of Communication in Science: A Critical Review." *History of Science* 17:102–134.

Editors. 2013. "Authors, Plagiarists, or Tradents?" Chinese Buddhist Encyclopedia. http://chinabuddhismencyclopedia.com/en/index.php?title=Authors%2C_plagiarists%2C_or_tradents%3F.

Edwards, Aled M. 2008a. "Bermuda Principles Meet Structural Biology." *Nature Structural & Molecular Biology* 15 (2):116. doi:10.1038/nsmb0208-116.

Edwards, Aled M. 2008b. "Open-Source Science to Enable Drug Discovery." *Drug Discovery Today* 13 (17-18):731–733. doi:10.1016/j.drudis.2008.04.011.

Edwards, Aled M., Chas Bountra, David J. Kerr, and Timothy M. Willson. 2009. "Open Access Chemical and Clinical Probes to Support Drug Discovery." *Nature Chemical Biology* 5 (7):436–440. doi:10.1038/nchembio0709-436.

Edwards, Paul N. 2010. *A Vast Machine: Computer Models, Climate Data, and the Politics of Global Warming*. Cambridge, MA: MIT Press.

Edwards, Paul N. 2013. "Predicting the Weather: An Information Commons for Europe and the World." In *Cosmopolitan Commons: Sharing Resources and Risks Across Borders*, ed. Cornelis Disco and Eda Kranakis, 155–184. Cambridge, MA: MIT Press.

Edwards, Paul N., Steven J. Jackson, Geoffrey C. Bowker, and Cory P. Knobel. 2007. "Understanding Infrastructure: Dynamics, Tensions, and Design." National Science Foundation. Ann Arbor: University of Michigan.

Edwards, Paul N., Steven J. Jackson, Melissa K. Chalmers, Geoffrey C. Bowker, Christine L. Borgman, David Ribes, Matt Burton, and Scout Calvert. 2013. *Knowledge Infrastructures: Intellectual Frameworks and Research Challenges*. Ann Arbor: University of Michigan.

Edwards, Paul N., Matthew S. Mayernik, Archer L. Batcheller, Geoffrey C. Bowker, and Christine L. Borgman. 2011. "Science Friction: Data, Metadata, and Collaboration." *Social Studies of Science* 41:667–690. doi:10.1177/0306312711413314.

Ehrlich, Kate, and Debra Cash. 1999. "The Invisible World of Intermediaries: A Cautionary Tale." *Computer Supported Cooperative Work* 8 (1–2):147–167. doi:10.102 3/A:1008696415354.

Eichhorn, Guenther. 1994. "An Overview of the Astrophysics Data System." *Experimental Astronomy* 5:205–220. doi:10.1007/BF01583697.

Eisen, Michael. 2012. "Blinded by Big Science: The Lesson I Learned from ENCODE Is That Projects like ENCODE Are Not a Good Idea." http://www.michaeleisen.org/ blog/?p=1179.

Eisenstein, Elizabeth. 1979. *The Printing Press as an Agent of Change: Communications and Cultural Transformations in Early-Modern Europe*. Cambridge, UK: Cambridge University Press.

Embedded Metadata Initiative. 2013. "Embedded Metadata Manifesto." http://www .embeddedmetadata.org/embedded-metatdata-manifesto.php.

EndNote. 2013. Home page. http://endnote.com.

Enserink, Martin. 2006. "Avian Influenza: As H5N1 Keeps Spreading, a Call to Release More Data." *Science* 311:1224. doi:10.1126/science.311.5765.1224.

Enserink, Martin. 2012a. "Fraud-Detection Tool Could Shake Up Psychology." *Science Insider*. http://news.sciencemag.org/2012/07/fraud-detection-tool-could-shake -psychology?rss=1.

Enserink, Martin. 2012b. "Public at Last, H5N1 Study Offers Insight into Virus's Possible Path to Pandemic." *Science* 336 (6088):1494–1497. doi:10.1126/science.336 .6088.1494.

Enserink, Martin, and Jon Cohen. 2012. "One H5N1 Paper Finally Goes to Press; Second Greenlighted." *Science* 336 (6081):529–530. doi:10.1126/science.336.6081 .529.

Erdos, David. 2013a. "Freedom of Expression Turned on Its Head? Academic Social Research and Journalism in the European Privacy Framework." *Public Law*. http:// papers.ssrn.com/abstract=1928177.

Erdos, David. 2013b. "Mustn't Ask, Mustn't Tell: Could New EU Data Laws Ban Historical and Legal Research?" UK Constitutional Law Group (February 14). http:// ukconstitutionallaw.org/2013/02/14/david-erdos-mustnt-ask-mustnt-tell-could -new-eu-data-laws-ban-historical-and-legal-research.

Esanu, Julie M., and Paul F. Uhlir eds. 2004. *Open Access and the Public Domain in Digital Data and Information for Science: Proceedings of an International Symposium, March 10–11, Paris*. Washington, DC: National Academies Press.

Estrin, Deborah, K. Mani Chandy, R. Michael Young, Larry Smarr, Andrew Odlyzko, David Clark, Viviane Reding, et al. 2010. "Internet Predictions." *IEEE Internet Computing* 14 (1):12–42. doi:10.1109/MIC.2010.12.

Estrin, Judy. 2008. *Closing the Innovation Gap: Reigniting the Spark of Creativity in a Global Economy*. New York: McGraw-Hill.

Ettema, J. S., and F. G. Kline. 1977. "Deficits, Differences, and Ceilings: Contingent Conditions for Understanding the Knowledge Gap." *Communication Research* 4 (2):179–202. doi:10.1177/009365027700400204.

Europeana. 2013. Home page. http://www.europeana.eu.

European Southern Observatory. 2013. "Common Pipeline Library." http://www .eso.org/sci/software/cpl.

Eysenbach, Gunther. 2011. "Can Tweets Predict Citations? Metrics of Social Impact Based on Twitter and Correlation with Traditional Metrics of Scientific Impact." *Journal of Medical Internet Research* 13 (4). doi:10.2196/jmir.2012.

Falk, Harry. 2011. "The 'Split' Collection of Kharosthi Texts." In *Annual Report of the International Research Institute for Advanced Buddhology at Soka University for the Academic Year 2010*, 13–23. Tokyo: The International Research Institute for Advanced Buddhology, Soka University. iriab.soka.ac.jp/orc/Publications/ARIRIAB/pdf/ ARIRIAB-14.pdf.

Faniel, Ixchel M., and Trond E. Jacobsen. 2010. "Reusing Scientific Data: How Earthquake Engineering Researchers Assess the Reusability of Colleagues' Data." *Computer Supported Cooperative Work* 19:355–375. doi:10.1007/s10606-010-9117-8.

Faoláin, Simon Ó., and J. Peter Northover. 1998. "The Technology of Late Bronze Age Sword Production in Ireland." *Journal of Irish Archaeology* 9:69–88. doi:10.2307/30001693.

Fenner, Martin. 2013. "Letter from the Guest Content Editor: Altmetrics Have Come of Age." *Information Standards Quarterly* 25 (2): 3. doi:10.3789/isqv25no2.2013.01.

Field, Dawn, Susanna-Assunta Sansone, Amanda Collis, Tim Booth, Peter Dukes, Susan K. Gregurick, Karen Kennedy, et al. 2009. "'Omics Data Sharing." *Science* 326 (5950):234–236. doi:10.1126/science.1180598.

Fienberg, Stephen E., Margaret E. Martin, and Miron L. Straf. 1985. *Sharing Research Data*. Washington, DC: National Academies Press. http://books.nap.edu/catalog .php?record_id=2033.

Finch, Janet. 2012. "Accessibility, Sustainability, Excellence: How to Expand Access to Research Publications." Report of the Working Group on Expanding Access to Published Research Findings. London: Research Information Network. http://www .researchinfonet.org/publish/finch.

Finkbeiner, Ann K. 2010. *A Grand and Bold Thing: The Extraordinary New Map of the Universe Ushering in a New Era of Discovery*. New York: Free Press.

Fischman, Josh. 2012. "Fake Peer Reviews, the Latest Form of Scientific Fraud, Fool Journals." *Chronicle of Higher Education* (September 30). http://chronicle.com/article/ Fake-Peer-Reviews-the-Latest/134784.

Fisher, Celia B. 2006. "Clinical Trials Databases: Unanswered Questions." *Science* 311 (5758):180–181. doi:10.1126/science.1119685.

Fitzpatrick, Kathleen. 2011. *Planned Obsolescence: Publishing, Technology, and the Future of the Academy*. New York: New York University Press.

Forbes, Duncan. 2008. "So You Want to Be a Professional Astronomer." *Mercury Magazine*. http://www.astronomynotes.com/careers/Mercury-career.pdf.

Foster, Ian, Christine L. Borgman, P. Bryan Heidorn, William Howe, and Carl Kesselman. 2013. "Empowering Long Tail Research." https://sites.google.com/site/ieltrconcept.

Foster, Ian, and Luc Moreau. 2006. *Provenance and Annotation of Data*. Heidelberg: Springer. http://www.w3.org/2011/prov/wiki/Connection_Task_Force_Informal_Report.

Foster, Jonathan B., and Alyssa A. Goodman. 2006. "Cloudshine: New Light on Dark Clouds." *Astrophysical Journal Letters* 636 (2):L105. doi:10.1086/500131.

Foucault, Michel. 1994. *The Order of Things: An Archaeology of the Human Sciences*. New York: Vintage Books.

Fouchier, Ron A. M., Sander Herfst, and Albert D. M. E. Osterhaus. 2012. "Restricted Data on Influenza H5N1 Virus Transmission." *Science* 335 (6069):662–663. doi:10.1126/science.1218376.

Fox, Peter, and Ray Harris. 2013. "ICSU and the Challenges of Data and Information Management for International Science." *Data Science Journal* 12:WDS1–WDS12. https://www.jstage.jst.go.jp/article/dsj/12/0/12_WDS-001/_article.

Frankel, Henry. 1976. "Alfred Wegener and the Specialists." *Centaurus* 20 (4):305–324. doi:10.1111/j.1600-0498.1976.tb00937.x.

Freeman, Linton C. 2004. *The Development of Social Network Analysis: A Study in the Sociology of Science*. Vancouver, BC: Empirical Press.

Friedlander, Amy. 2009. "Asking Questions and Building a Research Agenda for Digital Scholarship." In *Working Together or Apart: Promoting the Next Generation of Digital Scholarship*, ed. Kathlin Smith and Brian Leney, 1–15. Washington, DC: Council on Library and Information Resources. http://www.clir.org/pubs/resources/pubs/reports/pub145/pub145.pdf.

Frischer, Bernard, Philip Stinson, Neil A. Silberman, and Dirk Callebaut. 2002. "Scientific Verification and Model-making Methodology: Case Studies of the Virtual Reality Models of the House of Augustus (Rome) and Villa of the Mysteries (Pompeii)." In *Interpreting the Past: Heritage, New Technologies & Local Development*. Belgium: Flemish Heritage Institute.

Furnas, Alexander, and Devin Gaffney. 2012. "Statistical Probability That Mitt Romney's New Twitter Followers Are Just Normal Users: 0%." *The Atlantic*. http://www.

theatlantic.com/technology/archive/2012/07/statistical-probability-that-mitt -romneys-new-twitter-followers-are-just-normal-users-0/260539.

Furner, Jonathan. 2003a. "Little Book, Big Book: Before and after Little Science, Big Science: A Review Article, Part I." *Journal of Librarianship and Information Science* 35:115–125. doi:10.1177/0961000603352006.

Furner, Jonathan. 2003b. "Little Book, Big Book: Before and after Little Science, Big Science: A Review Article, Part II." *Journal of Librarianship and Information Science* 35:189–201. doi:10.1177/0961000603353006.

Furner, Jonathan. 2004a. "Conceptual Analysis: A Method for Understanding Information as Evidence, and Evidence as Information." *Archival Science* 4:233–265. doi:10.1007/s10502-005-2594-8.

Furner, Jonathan. 2004b. "Information Studies Without Information." *Library Trends* 52:427–446.

Furner, Jonathan. 2010. "Philosophy and Information Studies." *Annual Review of Information Science & Technology* 44 (1):159–200. doi:10.1002/aris.2010.1440440111.

Gale Cengage Learning. 2013. "Eighteenth Century Collections Online." http://gale .cengage.co.uk/product-highlights/history/eighteenth-century-collections-online .aspx.

Galilei, Galileo. 1610. *Sidereus Nuncius*. Ed. Tommaso Baglioni and Herbert M. Evans. Venetiis: Apud Thomam Baglionum. http://archive.org/details/Sidereusnuncius00Gali.

Gallagher, Ryan. 2013. "NSA Phone Spying: EPIC, Privacy International File Lawsuits to Halt Government Surveillance." *Slate* (June 8). http://www.slate.com/blogs/future_ tense/2013/07/08/nsa_phone_spying_epic_privacy_international_file_lawsuits _to_halt_government.html.

Gamazon, Eric R. 2012. "Small Science: High Stakes." *Science* 338 (6109):883. doi:10.1126/science.338.6109.883-a.

Gamble, Matthew, and Carole Goble. 2011. "Quality, Trust, and Utility of Scientific Data on the Web: Towards a Joint Model." In *ACM WebSci'11*, 1–8. Koblenz, Germany. http://www.websci11.org/fileadmin/websci/Papers/177_paper.pdf.

Garfield, Eugene. 1955. "Citation Indexes for Science: A New Dimension in Documentation through Association of Ideas." *Science* 122 (3159):108–111. doi:10.1126/ science.122.3159.108.

Garfinkel, H. 1967. *Studies in Ethnomethodology*. Englewood Cliffs, NJ: Prentice Hall.

Geertz, Clifford. 1973. *The Interpretation of Cultures*. New York: Basic Books.

General Social Survey. 2013. Home page. http://www3.norc.org/gss+website.

Genova, Françoise. 2013. "Strasbourg Astronomical Data Center (CDS)." *Data Science Journal* 12:WDS56–WDS60. doi:10.2481/dsj.WDS-007.

Getty Research Institute. 2013. "Getty Vocabularies." http://www.getty.edu/research/tools/vocabularies.

Getty Trust. 2013. "Open Content Program." http://www.getty.edu/about/opencontent.html.

Gibbons, Ann. 2012. "A Crystal-Clear View of an Extinct Girl's Genome." *Science* 337 (6098):1028–1029. doi:10.1126/science.337.6098.1028.

Gil, Yolanda, James Cheney, Paul Groth, Olaf Hartig, Simon Miles, Luc Moreau, and Paulo Pinheiro da Silva. 2010. "Provenance XG Final Report." W3C Incubator Group. http://www.w3.org/2005/Incubator/prov/XGR-prov-20101214.

Gilliland, Anne J. 2008. "Setting the Stage." In *Introduction to Metadata*, ed. Murtha Baca, 3rd ed. Los Angeles: Getty Research Institute. http://www.getty.edu/research/publications/electronic_publications/intrometadata.

Gilliland-Swetland, Anne J. 1998. "Defining Metadata." In *Introduction to Metadata: Pathways to Digital Information*, ed. Murtha Baca, 1–8. Los Angeles: Getty Research Institute.

Ginsparg, Paul. 1994. "First Steps towards Electronic Research Communication." *Computers in Physics* 8 (4):390–396. http://dl.acm.org/citation.cfm?id=187178.187185.

Ginsparg, Paul. 2001. "Creating a Global Knowledge Network." In *Second Joint ICSU Press-UNESCO Expert Conference on Electronic Publishing in Science*. Paris: UNESCO. http://people.ccmr.cornell.edu/~ginsparg/blurb/pg01unesco.html.

Gitelman, Lisa, ed. 2013. *"Raw Data" Is an Oxymoron*. Cambridge, MA: MIT Press.

Gladwell, Malcolm. 2002. *The Tipping Point: How Little Things Can Make a Big Difference*. New York: Back Bay Books.

Glaser, Barney G., and Anselm L. Strauss. 1967. *The Discovery of Grounded Theory; Strategies for Qualitative Research*. Chicago: Aldine Publishing.

Gleick, P. H. 2011. "Climate Change and the Integrity of Science (Letter to Editor; 255 Signatories)." *Science* 328:689–690. doi:10.1126/science.328.5979.689.

Gnip. 2013a. "Gnip Twitter Activity Streams Format." http://support.gnip.com/customer/portal/articles/477765-twitter-activity-streams-format.

Gnip. 2013b. Home page. http://gnip.com.

Goble, Carole, and David De Roure. 2009. "The Impact of Workflow Tools on Data-intensive Research." In *The Fourth Paradigm: Data-Intensive Scientific Discovery*, ed. Tony Hey, Stewart Tansley, and Kristin Tolle, 137–146. Redmond, WA: Microsoft.

Goble, Carole, David De Roure, and Sean Bechhofer. 2013. "Accelerating Scientists' Knowledge Turns." In *Knowledge Discovery, Knowledge Engineering and Knowledge Management*, ed. Ana Fred, Jan L. G. Dietz, Kecheng Liu, and Joaquim Filipe, 3–25. Berlin: Springer.

Goenka, S. N., Myungsoo Kim, Lewis Lancaster, John R. McRae, Charles Muller, Min Bahadur Shakya, Morten Schlutter, and Christian Wittern. 2008. "CBETA 10 Years." Chinese Buddhist Electronic Text Association. http://www.cbeta.org/data/cbeta10y/friends.htm.

Goldacre, Ben. 2008. *Bad Science*. London: Fourth Estate.

Goldacre, Ben. 2012. *Bad Pharma: How Drug Companies Mislead Doctors and Harm Patients*. London: Fourth Estate.

Goldsmith, Jack L., and Tim Wu. 2006. *Who Controls the Internet? Illusions of a Borderless World*. Oxford: Oxford University Press.

Goodman, Alyssa A. 2012. "Principles of High-dimensional Data Visualization in Astronomy." *Astronomische Nachrichten* 333:505. doi:10.1002/asna.201211705.

Goodman, Alyssa A., Joao Alves, Chris Beaumont, Tom Dame, James Jackson, Jens Kauffmann, Thomas Robitaille, et al. 2013. "The Bones of the Milky Way." *Astrophysical Journal*. https://www.authorea.com/users/23/articles/249/_show_article.

Goodman, Alyssa A., Jonathan Fay, August Muench, Alberto Pepe, Patricia Udomprasert, and Curtis Wong. 2012. "WorldWide Telescope in Research and Education." *arXiv:1201.1285*. http://arxiv.org/abs/1201.1285.

Goodman, Alyssa A., August Muench, and Alicia Soderberg. 2012. "Introducing the Astronomy Dataverse (theastrodata.org)." Presentation and Panel Discussion (April 2). Cambridge, MA: Harvard-Smithsonian Center for Astrophysics. http://thedata.org/presentations/introducing-astronomy-dataverse-theastrodataorg.

Goodman, Alyssa A., Alberto Pepe, Alexander W. Blocker, Christine L. Borgman, Kyle Cranmer, Merce Crosas, Rosanne Di Stefano, et al. 2014. "10 Simple Rules for the Care and Feeding of Scientific Data." *PLoS Computational Biology* 10 (4):e1003542. doi:10.1371/journal.pcbi.1003542.

Goodman, Alyssa A., Jaime E. Pineda, and Scott L. Schnee. 2009. "The 'True' Column Density Distribution in Star-Forming Molecular Clouds." *Astrophysical Journal* 692:91–103. doi:10.1088/0004-637X/692/1/91.

Goodman, Alyssa A., Erik W. Rosolowsky, Michelle A. Borkin, Jonathan B. Foster, Michael Halle, Jens Kauffmann, and Jaime E. Pineda. 2009. "A Role for Self-gravity at Multiple Length Scales in the Process of Star Formation." *Nature* 457 (7225):63–66. doi:10.1038/nature07609.

Goodman, Alyssa A., and Curtis G. Wong. 2009. "Bringing the Night Sky Closer: Discoveries in the Data Deluge." In *The Fourth Paradigm: Data-Intensive Scientific Discovery*, ed. Tony Hey, Stewart Tansley, and Kristin Tolle, 39–44. Redmond, WA: Microsoft.

Grafton, Anthony. 2007. "Future Reading." *The New Yorker* (November 5). http://www.newyorker.com/reporting/2007/11/05/071105fa_fact_grafton?currentPage=all.

Gray, Jim, David T. Liu, Maria Nieto-Santisteban, Alexander Szalay, David DeWitt, and Gerd Heber. 2005. "Scientific Data Management in the Coming Decade." *CT Watch Quarterly* 1. http://www.ctwatch.org/quarterly/articles/2005/02/scientific-data-management.

Gray, Jim, and Alexander Szalay. 2002. "The World-wide Telescope." *Communications of the ACM* 45:51–55.

Groth, Paul, Yolanda Gil, James Cheney, and Simon Miles. 2012. "Requirements for Provenance on the Web." *International Journal of Digital Curation* 7 (1):39–56. doi:10.2218/ijdc.v7i1.213.

Groth, Paul, and Luc Moreau eds. 2013. "PROV-Overview." W3C. http://www.w3.org/TR/prov-overview.

Guibault, Lucie. 2013. "Licensing Research Data under Open Access Conditions." In *Information and Knowledge: 21st Century Challenges in Intellectual Property and Knowledge Governance*, ed. Dana Beldiman. Cheltenham: Edward Elgar.

Gutmann, Myron, Mark Abrahamson, Margaret Adams, Micah Altman, Caroline R. Arms, and Gary King. 2009. "From Preserving the Past to Preserving the Future: The Data-PASS Project and the Challenges of Preserving Digital Social Science Data." *Library Trends* 57:315–337. doi:10.1353/lib.0.0039.

Gymrek, Melissa, Amy L. McGuire, David Golan, Eran Halperin, and Yaniv Erlich. 2013. "Identifying Personal Genomes by Surname Inference." *Science* 339 (6117):321–324. doi:10.1126/science.1229566.

Haak, Laurel L., David Baker, Donna K. Ginther, Gregg J. Gordon, Matthew A. Probus, Nirmala Kannankutty, and Bruce A. Weinberg. 2012. "Standards and Infrastructure for Innovation Data Exchange." *Science* 338 (6104):196–197. doi:10.1126/science.1221840.

Hackett, Edward J., Olga Amsterdamska, Michael Lynch, and Judy Wajcman. 2007. *The Handbook of Science and Technology Studies*. 3rd ed. Cambridge, MA: MIT Press.

Hamilton, David P. 1990. "Information Decontrol Urged." *Science* 248 (4958):957–958. doi:10.1126/science.248.4958.957.

Hamilton, Michael P., Eric A. Graham, Philip W. Rundel, Michael F. Allen, William Kaiser, Mark H. Hansen, and Deborah L. Estrin. 2007. "New Approaches in

Embedded Networked Sensing for Terrestrial Ecological Observatories." *Environmental Engineering Science* 24 (2):149–150.

Hanisch, Robert J. 2013. "The Future of the Virtual Observatory—US Virtual Astronomical Observatory." (August 12). http://www.usvao.org/2013/08/12/the-future -of-the-virtual-observatory.

Hanisch, Robert J., A. Farris, E. W. Greisen, W. D. Pence, B. M. Schlesinger, P. J. Teuben, R. W. Thompson, and A. Warnock. 2001. "Definition of the Flexible Image Transport System (FITS)." *Astronomy and Astrophysics* 376 (1): 359–380. http://adsabs .harvard.edu/abs/2001A%26A...376.359H.

Hanisch, Robert J., and Peter J. Quinn. 2002. "The International Virtual Observatory." http://www.ivoa.net/about/TheIVOA.pdf.

Hanson, Karen, Alisa Surkis, and Karen Yacobucci. 2012. *Data Sharing and Management Snafu in 3 Short Acts*. Film and Animation. http://www.youtube.com/ watch?v=N2zK3sAtr-4&sns=em.

Hardin, Garrett. 1968. "The Tragedy of the Commons." *Science* 162 (3859):1243–1248. doi:10.1126/science.162.3859.1243.

Harnad, Stevan. 1998. "The Invisible Hand of Peer Review." *Nature* 5. http://www .nature.com/nature/webmatters/invisible/invisible.html.

Harpring, Patricia. 2010. *Introduction to Controlled Vocabularies: Terminology for Art, Architecture, and Other Cultural Works*. Los Angeles: Getty Publications.

Hart, Michael S. 1992. "History and Philosophy of Project Gutenberg." http://www .gutenberg.org/about/history.

Hart, Michael S. 2013. "Project Gutenberg." http://www.gutenberg.org.

Harvard Law Review Association. 2005. *The Bluebook: A Uniform System of Citation*. Cambridge, MA: Author.

Harvard-Smithsonian Astrophysical Observatory. 2013a. "Chandra X-ray Observatory." Home page. http://chandra.harvard.edu.

Harvard-Smithsonian Astrophysical Observatory. 2013b. "Digitizing the Harvard College Observatory Astronomical Plate Stacks." http://tdc-www.harvard.edu/plates.

Harvard-Smithsonian Astrophysical Observatory. 2013c. "The SAO/NASA Astrophysics Data System." http://adswww.harvard.edu.

Harvard University. 2010. "Open Access Policies." Harvard University Library, Office for Scholarly Communication. https://osc.hul.harvard.edu/policies.

Harvard University and Wellcome Trust. 2012. International Workshop on Contributorship and Scholarly Attribution. http://projects.iq.harvard.edu/files/attribution _workshop/files/iwcsa_report_final_18sept12.pdf.

Hedstrom, Margaret, Lee Dirks, Nicholas Economides, Peter Fox, Michael F. Good-child, Heather Joseph, Ronald L. Larsen, et al. 2014. "Future Career Opportunities and Educational Requirements for Digital Curation." http://sites.nationalacademies.org/PGA/brdi/PGA_069853.

Heidorn, Bryan. 2008. "Shedding Light on the Dark Data in the Long Tail of Science." *Library Trends* 57 (2):280–299. doi:10.1353/lib.0.0036.

Hess, Charlotte, and Elinor Ostrom. 2007a. "Introduction: An Overview of the Knowledge Commons." In *Understanding Knowledge as a Commons: From Theory to Practice*, ed. Charlotte Hess and Elinor Ostrom, 3–26. Cambridge, MA: MIT Press.

Hess, Charlotte, and Elinor Ostrom. 2007b. *Understanding Knowledge as a Commons: From Theory to Practice*. Cambridge, MA: MIT Press.

Hettne, Kristina, Katy Wolstencroft, Khalid Belhajjame, Carole Goble, Eleni Mina, and Harish Dharuri. 2012. "Best Practices for Workflow Design: How to Prevent Workflow Decay." In *Proceedings of the ESWC 2012 Workshop on the Future of Scholarly Communication in the Semantic Web*, ed. Frank Van Harmelen, Alexander G. Castro, Christoph Lange, and Benjamin Good. Greece: Sepublica. http://ceur-ws.org/Vol-952/paper_23.pdf.

Hey, Tony, Stewart Tansley, and Kristin Tolle. 2009. "Jim Gray on eScience: A Transformed Scientific Method." In *The Fourth Paradigm: Data-Intensive Scientific Discovery*, ed. Tony Hey, Stewart Tansley, and Kristin Tolle, xix–xxxiii. Redmond, WA: Microsoft.

Hey, Tony, and Anne Trefethen. 2005. "Cyberinfrastructure and e-Science." *Science* 308:818–821. doi:10.1126/science.1110410.

Higgins, D., C. Berkley, and M. B. Jones. 2002. "Managing Heterogeneous Ecological Data Using Morpho." In *Proceedings 14th International Conference on Scientific and Statistical Database Management*, 69–76. Edinburgh, UK: IEEE Computer Society.

Hilgartner, Stephen. 1997. "Access to Data and Intellectual Property: Scientific Exchange in Genome Research." In *Intellectual Property Rights and the Dissemination of Research Tools in Molecular Biology. Summary of a Workshop Held at the National Academy of Science, February 15–16, 1996*, 28–39. Washington, DC: National Academies Press.

Hilgartner, Stephen, and Sherry I. Brandt-Rauf. 1994. "Data Access, Ownership and Control: Toward Empirical Studies of Access Practices." *Knowledge* 15:355–372.

Hine, Christine. 2000. *Virtual Ethnography*. London: Sage.

Hine, Christine. 2008. *Systematics as Cyberscience: Computers, Change, and Continuity in Science*. Cambridge, MA: MIT Press.

Hirsh, Sandra G. 1996. *The Effect of Domain Knowledge on Elementary School Children's Information Retrieval Behavior on an Automated Library Catalog.* Los Angeles: UCLA.

Hirtle, Peter B. 2011. "Introduction to Intellectual Property Rights in Data Management." https://confluence.cornell.edu/display/rdmsgweb/introduction-intellectual-property-rights-data-management.

Hirtle, Peter B. 2012. "When Is 1923 Going to Arrive and Other Complications of the U.S. Public Domain." *Searcher* 20 (6). http://www.infotoday.com/searcher/sep12/Hirtle--When-Is-1923-Going-to-Arrive-and-Other-Complications-of-the-U.S.-Public-Domain.shtml.

Hirtle, Peter B., Emily Hudson, and Andrew T. Kenyon. 2009. *Copyright and Cultural Institutions: Guidelines for U.S. Libraries, Archives, and Museums.* http://hdl.handle.net/1813/14142.

H-Net. 2013a. "H-Buddhism Discussion Network." https://www.h-net.org/~buddhism.

H-Net. 2013b. "What Is H-Net?" http://www.h-net.org/about.

Hockey, Susan. 1999. "Making Technology Work for Scholarship: Investing in the Data." In *Technology and Scholarly Communication,* ed. Richard Ekman and Richard E. Quandt. Berkeley: University of California Press; published in association with the Andrew K. Mellon Foundation. http://ark.cdlib.org/ark:/13030/ft5w10074r.

Hogg, David W., and Dustin Lang. 2008. "Astronomical Imaging: The Theory of Everything." *arXiv:0810.3851.* doi:10.1063/1.3059072.

Holdren, John P. 2013a. "Increasing Access to the Results of Federally Funded Scientific Research." Executive Office of the President, Office of Science and Technology Policy. http://www.whitehouse.gov/sites/default/files/microsites/ostp/ostp_public_access_memo_2013.pdf.

Holdren, John P. 2013b. "Memorandum for the Heads of Executive Departments and Agencies." Executive Office of the President, Office of Science and Technology Policy. http://www.whitehouse.gov/sites/default/files/microsites/ostp/ostp_public_access_memo_2013.pdf.

Hollan, Jim, and Scott Stornetta. 1992. "Beyond Being There." In *CHI '92,* ed. Penny Bauersfeld, John Bennett, and Gene Lynch, 119–125. New York: ACM.

Hollinger, David A. 2013. "The Wedge Driving Academe's Two Families Apart." *Chronicle of Higher Education* (October 14). http://chronicle.com/article/Why-Cant-the-Sciencesthe/142239/?cid=cr&utm_source=cr&utm_medium=en.

Howard, Jennifer. 2013a. "Posting Your Latest Article? You Might Have to Take It Down." *Chronicle of Higher Education [Blog]* (December 6). http://chronicle.com/blogs/wiredcampus/posting-your-latest-article-you-might-have-to-take-it-down/48865.

Howard, Jennifer. 2013b. "White House Delivers New Open-Access Policy That Has Activists Cheering." *Chronicle of Higher Education* (February 22). http://chronicle.com/article/White-House-Delivers-New/137549/?cid=at&utm_source=at&utm_medium=en.

Howard, Jennifer. 2014. "Born Digital, Projects Need Attention to Survive." *Chronicle of Higher Education* (January 6). http://chronicle.com/article/Born-Digital-Projects-Need/143799.

Howe, Doug, Maria Costanzo, Petra Fey, Takashi Gojobori, Linda Hannick, Winston Hide, David P. Hill, et al. 2008. "Big Data: The Future of Biocuration." *Nature* 455 (7209):47–50. doi:10.1038/455047a.

Hrynaszkiewicz, Iain, and Douglas G. Altman. 2009. "Towards Agreement on Best Practice for Publishing Raw Clinical Trial Data." *Trials* 10:17. doi:10.1186/1745-6215-10-17.

HubbleSite. 2013a. Home page. http://hubblesite.org.

HubbleSite. 2013b. "The Telescope: Hubble Essentials." http://hubblesite.org/the_telescope/hubble_essentials.

Hughes, Thomas P. 1989. "The Evolution of Large Technological Systems." In *The Social Construction of Technological Systems: New Directions in the Sociology and History of Technology*, ed. Wiebe E. Bijker, Thomas P. Hughes, and Trevor J. Pinch, 51–82. Cambridge, MA: MIT Press.

Hughes, Thomas P. 2004. *Human-Built World: How to Think About Technology and Culture*. Chicago: University of Chicago Press.

Hugo, W. 2013. "A Maturity Model for Digital Data Centers." *Data Science Journal* 12:WDS189–WDS192.

Hunter, Jane. 2009. "Collaborative Semantic Tagging and Annotation Systems." *Annual Review of Information Science & Technology* 43:187–239.

Hvistendahl, Mara. 2013. "China's Publication Bazaar." *Science* 342 (6162):1035–1039. doi:10.1126/science.342.6162.1035.

IAU Working Group Libraries. 2013. "Best Practices for Creating a Telescope Bibliography." *IAU-Commission5—WG Libraries*. http://iau-commission5.wikispaces.com/WG+Libraries.

Incorporated Research Institutions for Seismology. 2013. Home page. http://www.iris.edu/hq.

Ingwersen, Peter. 1998. "The Calculation of Web Impact Factors." *Journal of Documentation* 54:236–243.

Ingwersen, Peter, and Kalervo Jarvelin. 2005. *The Turn: Integration of Information Seeking and Retrieval in Context*. Dordrecht: Springer.

Institute for Quantitative Social Sciences. 2011. "Data Citation Principles Workshop." Harvard University, May 16–17. http://projects.iq.harvard.edu/datacitation_workshop.

Institute for Quantitative Social Sciences. 2013. Home page. Harvard University. http://www.iq.harvard.edu.

Institute of Electrical and Electronics Engineers. 2013. "IEEE Code of Ethics." http://www.ieee.org/about/corporate/governance/p7-8.html.

International Astronomical Union. 2013. "About the International Astronomical Union." http://www.iau.org/about.

International Committee of Medical Journal Editors. 2013. "Recommendations for the Conduct, Reporting, Editing, and Publication of Scholarly Work in Medical Journals." http://www.icmje.org/recommendations.

International Council of Museums. 2013. "CIDOC Conceptual Reference Model." http://www.cidoc-crm.org/who_we_are.html.

International Dunhuang Project. 2013. Home page. http://idp.bl.uk.

International Social Survey Programme. 2013. Home page. http://www.issp.org.

International Standard Book Number Agency. 2013. Home page. http://www.isbn.org.

International Standard Name Identifier International Agency. 2013. Home page. http://www.isni.org.

International Standard Serial Number International Centre. 2013. "Understanding the ISSN: What Is an ISSN?" http://www.issn.org/2-22636-All-about-ISSN.php.

International Virtual Observatory Alliance. 2013a. Home page. http://www.ivoa.net.

International Virtual Observatory Alliance. 2013b. "Virtual Observatory Applications for Astronomers." http://www.ivoa.net/astronomers/applications.html.

Inter-University Consortium for Political and Social Research. 2012. "Guide to Social Science Data Preparation and Archiving: Best Practice Throughout the Data Life Cycle." 5th edition. Ann Arbor, MI: ICPSR. https://www.icpsr.umich.edu/icpsrweb/content/deposit/guide/index.html.

Inter-University Consortium for Political and Social Research. 2013. Home page. http://www.icpsr.umich.edu/icpsrweb/landing.jsp.

Ioannidis, John P. A., and Muin J. Khoury. 2011. "Improving Validation Practices in 'Omics' Research." *Science* 334 (6060):1230–1232. doi:10.1126/science.1211811.

IRIS Data Management Center. 2013. Home page. http://www.iris.edu/data.

ISO 10646. 2013. "Ideograph Characters." http://glyph.iso10646hk.net/english/icharacters_1.jsp.

Jackson, Brian A., Tora K. Bikson, and Patrick P. Gunn. 2013. "Human Subjects Protection and Research on Terrorism and Conflict." *Science* 340 (6131):434–435. doi:10.1126/science.1231747.

Jackson, Steven J. 2006. "Water Models and Water Politics: Deliberative Design and Virtual Accountability." In *Proceedings of the 7th Annual International Conference on Digital Government Research*, ed. Jose A.B. Fortes and Ann MacIntosh, 95–104. San Diego: Digital Government Research Center.

Jackson, Steven J., and Ayse Buyuktur. 2014. "Who Killed WATERS? Mess, Method, and Forensic Explanation in the Making and Unmaking of Large-Scale Science Networks." *Science, Technology & Human Values* 39 (2):285–308. doi:10.1177/0162243913516013.

Jackson, Steven J., David Ribes, Ayse Buyuktur, and Geoffrey C. Bowker. 2011. "Collaborative Rhythm: Temporal Dissonance and Alignment in Collaborative Scientific Work." In *Proceedings of the ACM 2011 Conference on Computer Supported Cooperative Work*, 245–254. New York: ACM. doi:10.1145/1958824.1958861.

Jacobs, Neil. 2006. *Open Access: Key Strategic, Technical and Economic Aspects*. Oxford: Chandos.

James San Jacinto Mountains Reserve. 2013. "Data Resources." http://www.jamesreserve.edu/data_arch.html.

Janee, Greg, and James Frew. 2002. "The ADEPT Digital Library Architecture." In *Second ACM/IEEE-CS Joint Conference on Digital Libraries*, 342–350. New York: ACM.

Jantz, Ronald, and Michael J. Giarlo. 2005. "Digital Preservation: Architecture and Technology for Trusted Digital Repositories." *D-Lib Magazine* 11. http://www.dlib.org/dlib/june05/jantz/06jantz.html.

Jasny, B. R., G. Chin, L. Chong, and S. Vignieri. 2011. "Again, and Again, and Again...." *Science* 334 (6060):1225. doi:10.1126/science.334.6060.1225.

JavaScript Object Notation. 2013. Home page. http://www.json.org.

Jenkins, Henry, Ravi Purushotma, Margaret Weigel, and Katie Clinton. 2009. *Confronting the Challenges of Participatory Culture: Media Education for the 21st Century*. Cambridge, MA: MIT Press.

Jirotka, Marina, Rob Procter, Tom Rodden, and Geoffrey C. Bowker. 2006. "Special Issue: Collaboration in e-Research." *Computer Supported Cooperative Work* 15:251–255.

Johnson, George. 2007. "A Trip Back in Time and Space." *New York Times* (July 10). http://www.nytimes.com/2007/07/10/science/10astro.html.

Johnston, E. H. 1938. "The Gopālpur Bricks." *Journal of the Royal Asiatic Society* 70 (04):547–553. doi:10.1017/S0035869X00078242.

Jones, James Howard. 1981. *Bad Blood: The Tuskegee Syphilis Experiment*. New York: Free Press.

Journal of Open Archaeology Data. 2013. Home page. http://openarchaeologydata .metajnl.com.

JoVE: Peer Reviewed Scientific Video Journal. 2013. Home page. http://www.jove.com.

Kahin, Brian, and Dominique Foray. 2006. *Advancing Knowledge and the Knowledge Economy*. Cambridge, MA: MIT Press.

Kaiser, Jocelyn. 2008. "Making Clinical Data Widely Available." *Science* 322 (5899):217–218. doi:10.1126/science.322.5899.217.

Kaiser, Jocelyn. 2013. "Rare Cancer Successes Spawn 'Exceptional' Research Efforts." *Science* 340 (6130):263. doi:10.1126/science.340.6130.263.

Kanfer, Alana G., Caroline Haythornthwaite, B. C. Bruce, Geoffrey C. Bowker, N. C. Burbules, J. F. Porac, and J. Wade. 2000. "Modeling Distributed Knowledge Processes in Next Generation Multidisciplinary Alliances." *Information Systems Frontiers* 2 (3–4):317–331. doi:10.1109/AIWORC.2000.843277.

Kansa, Eric C. 2012. "Openness and Archaeology's Information Ecosystem." *World Archaeology* 44 (4):498–520. doi:10.1080/00438243.2012.737575.

Kansa, Sarah W., Eric C. Kansa, and J. M. Schultz. 2007. "An Open Context for Near Eastern Archaeology." *Near Eastern Archaeology* 70 (4): 188–194.

Karabag, Solmaz Filiz, and Christian Berggren. 2012. "Retraction, Dishonesty and Plagiarism: Analysis of a Crucial Issue for Academic Publishing, and the Inadequate Responses from Leading Journals in Economics and Management Disciplines." *Journal of Applied Economics and Business Research* 4 (2). http://www.aebrjournal.org/ volume-2-issue-4.html.

Karasti, Helena, Karen S. Baker, and Eija Halkola. 2006. "Enriching the Notion of Data Curation in E-Science: Data Managing and Information Infrastructuring in the Long Term Ecological Research (LTER) Network." *Computer Supported Cooperative Work* 15 (4):321–358. doi:10.1007/s10606-006-9023-2.

Kelty, Christopher M. 2008. *Two Bits: The Cultural Significance of Free Software*. Durham, NC: Duke University Press.

Kelty, Christopher M. 2012. "This Is Not an Article: Model Organism Newsletters and the Question of 'Open Science.'" *Biosocieties* 7 (2):140–168. doi:10.1057/biosoc.2012.8.

Kessler, Elizabeth A. 2012. *Picturing the Cosmos: Hubble Space Telescope Images and the Astronomical Sublime*. Minneapolis: University of Minnesota Press.

King, C. Judson, Diane Harley, Sarah Earl-Novell, Jennifer Arter, Shannon Lawrence, and Irene Perciali. 2006. "Scholarly Communication: Academic Values and Sustainable Models." Berkeley: Center for Studies in Higher Education. http://cshe.berkeley.edu/publications/scholarly-communication-academic-values-and-sustainable-models.

King, Christopher. 2013. "Single-Author Papers: A Waning Share of Output, but Still Providing the Tools for Progress." *ScienceWatch*. http://sciencewatch.com/articles/single-author-papers-waning-share-output-still-providing-tools-progress.

King, Gary, Jennifer Pan, and Margaret E. Roberts. 2013. "How Censorship in China Allows Government Criticism but Silences Collective Expression." *American Political Science Review* 107 (02):326–343. doi:10.1017/S0003055413000014.

Kintisch, Eli. 2010. "Embattled U.K. Scientist Defends Track Record of Climate Center." *Science* 327 (5968):934. doi:10.1126/science.327.5968.934.

Klump, J., R. Bertelmann, J. Brase, Michael Diepenbroek, Hannes Grobe, H. Höck, M. Lautenschlager, Uwe Schindler, I. Sens, and J. Wächter. 2006. "Data Publication in the Open Access Initiative." *Data Science Journal* 5:79–83. doi:10.2481/dsj.5.79.

Knorr-Cetina, Karin. 1999. *Epistemic Cultures: How the Sciences Make Knowledge*. Cambridge, MA: Harvard University Press.

Knowledge Network for Biocomplexity. 2010. "Ecological Metadata Language." http://knb.ecoinformatics.org/software/eml.

Knowledge Network for Biocomplexity. 2013. "Ecological Metadata Language (EML) Specification." http://knb.ecoinformatics.org/software/eml/eml-2.1.1/index.html.

Knox, Keith T. 2008. "Enhancement of Overwritten Text in the Archimedes Palimpsest." In *Computer Image Analysis in the Study of Art*, ed. David G. Stork and Jim Coddington, 6810:681004. SPIE. doi:10.1117/12.766679.

Kolb, David A. 1981. "Learning Styles and Disciplinary Differences." In *The Modern American College*, ed. Arthur W. Chickering. San Francisco: Jossey-Bass.

Kolowich, Steve. 2014. "Hazards of the Cloud: Data-Storage Service's Crash Sets Back Researchers." *The Chronicle of Higher Education [Blog]* (May 12). http://chronicle.com/blogs/wiredcampus/hazards-of-the-cloud-data-storage-services-crash-sets-back-researchers/52571.

Korn, Naomi, and Charles Oppenheim. 2011. "Licensing Open Data: A Practical Guide." JISC. http://discovery.ac.uk/files/pdf/Licensing_Open_Data_A_Practical_Guide .pdf.

Korsmo, Fae L. 2010. "The Origins and Principles of the World Data Center System." *Data Science Journal* 8:55–65. doi:10.2481/dsj.SS_IGY-011.

Koshland, Daniel. 1987. "Sequencing the Human Genome." *Science* 236 (4801):505. doi:10.1126/science.3576182.

Kouw, Matthijs, Charles Van den Heuvel, and Andrea Scharnhorst. 2013. "Exploring Uncertainty in Knowledge Representations: Classifications, Simulations, and Models of the World." In *Virtual Knowledge: Experimenting in the Humanities and the Social Sciences*, ed. Paul Wouters, Anne Beaulieu, Andrea Scharnhorst, and Sally Wyatt, 127–149. Cambridge, MA: MIT Press.

Kranich, Nancy. 2004. "The Information Commons: A Public Policy Report." New York: The Free Expression Policy Project, Brennan Center for Justice, NYU School of Law. http://www.fepproject.org/policyreports/InformationCommons.pdf.

Kranich, Nancy. 2007. "Countering Enclosure: Reclaiming the Knowledge Commons." In *Understanding Knowledge as a Commons: From Theory to Practice*, ed. Charlotte Hess and Elinor Ostrom, 85–122. Cambridge, MA: MIT Press.

Kraut, Robert, Sara Kiesler, Bonka Boneva, Jonathon Cummings, Vicki Helgeson, and Anne Crawford. 2002. "Internet Paradox Revisited." *Journal of Social Issues* 58 (1):49–74. doi:10.1111/1540-4560.00248.

Kuhn, Thomas S. 1962. *The Structure of Scientific Revolutions*. Chicago: University of Chicago Press.

Kuhn, Thomas S. 1970. *The Structure of Scientific Revolutions*. 2nd ed. Chicago: University of Chicago Press.

Kurtz, Donna, and T. S. Lipinski. 1995. "Telecommunications for the Arts in Archive, Museum and Gallery: The Beazley Archive and Cast Gallery, Ashmolean Museum, Oxford." In *Networking in the Humanities: Proceedings of the Second Conference on Scholarship and Technology in the Humanities*, ed. Stephanie Kenna and Seamus Ross, 97–109. London: Bowker-Saur.

Kurtz, Donna, Greg Parker, David Shotton, Graham Klyne, Florian Schroff, Andrew Zisserman, and Yorick Wilks. 2009. "CLAROS—Bringing Classical Art to a Global Public." In *Proceedings of the 2009 Fifth IEEE International Conference on e-Science*, 20–27. Oxford: IEEE. doi:10.1109/e-Science.2009.11.

Kurtz, Michael J., and Johan Bollen. 2010. "Usage Bibliometrics." In *Annual Review of Information Science and Technology*. vol. 44. ed. Blaise Cronin. Medford, NJ: Information Today.

Kurtz, Michael J., G. Eichhorn, A. Accomazzi, C. Grant, M. Demleitner, and S. S. Murray. 2005. "Worldwide Use and Impact of the NASA Astrophysics Data System Digital Library." *Journal of the American Society for Information Science and Technology* 56 (1):36–45. doi:10.1002/asi.20095.

Kurtz, Michael J., Güenther Eichhorn, Alberto Accomazzi, Carolyn S. Grant, Stephen S. Murray, and Joyce M. Watson. 2000. "The NASA Astrophysics Data System: Overview." *Astronomy & Astrophysics. Supplement Series* 143 (1):41–59. doi:10.1051/aas:2000170.

Kwa, Chunglin. 2005. "Local Ecologies and Global Science: Discourses and Strategies of the International Geosphere-Biosphere Programme." *Social Studies of Science* 35:923–950.

Kwa, Chunglin. 2011. *Styles of Knowing*. Pittsburgh: University of Pittsburgh Press.

Kwa, Chunglin, and Rene Rector. 2010. "A Data Bias in Interdisciplinary Cooperation in the Sciences: Ecology in Climate Change Research." In *Collaboration in the New Life Sciences*, ed. John N. Parker, Niki Vermeulen, and Bart Penders, 161–176. Farnheim, UK: Ashgate.

Kwak, Haewoon, Changhyun Lee, Hosung Park, and Sue Moon. 2010. "What Is Twitter, a Social Network or a News Media?" In *Proceedings of the 19th International Conference on World Wide Web*, 591–600. New York: ACM. doi:10.1145/1772690.1772751.

Laakso, Mikael, and Bo-Christer Björk. 2013. "Delayed Open Access: An Overlooked High-impact Category of Openly Available Scientific Literature." *Journal of the American Society for Information Science and Technology* 64 (7):1323–1329. doi:10.1002/asi.22856.

Laakso, Mikael, Patrik Welling, Helena Bukvova, Linus Nyman, Bo-Christer Björk, and Turid Hedlund. 2011. "The Development of Open Access Journal Publishing from 1993 to 2009." *PLoS ONE* 6 (6):e20961. doi:10.1371/journal.pone.0020961.

Lagerstrom, Jill, Sherry L. Winkelman, Uta Grothkopf, and Marsha Bishop. 2012. "Observatory Bibliographies: Current Practices." In *Observatory Operations: Strategies, Processes, and Systems IV*. vol. 8448. ed. Alison B. Peck, Robert L. Seaman, and Fernando Comeron. Amsterdam: SPIE.

Lagoze, Carl, and Theresa Velden. 2009a. "Communicating Chemistry." *Nature Chemistry* 1:673–678. doi:10.1038/nchem.448.

Lagoze, Carl, and Theresa Velden. 2009b. "The Value of New Scientific Communication Models for Chemistry." http://ecommons.cornell.edu/handle/1813/14150.

Laine, Christine, Richard Horton, Catherine D. DeAngelis, Jeffrey M. Drazen, Frank A. Frizelle, Fiona Godlee, Charlotte Haug, et al. 2007. "Clinical Trial

Registration—Looking Back and Moving Ahead." *New England Journal of Medicine* 356 (26):2734–2736. doi:10.1056/NEJMe078110.

Lakoff, George. 1987. *Women, Fire, and Dangerous Things: What Categories Reveal about the Mind*. Chicago: University of Chicago Press.

Lampland, Martha, and Susan Leigh Star, eds. 2009. *Standards and Their Stories: How Quantifying, Classifying, and Formalizing Practices Shape Everyday Life*. Ithaca, NY: Cornell University Press.

Landsberger, Henry A. 1958. *Hawthorne Revisited: Management and the Worker: Its Critics, and Developments in Human Relations in Industry*. Ithaca, NY: Cornell University Press.

Laney, Doug. 2001. "3D Data Management: Controlling Data Volume, Velocity, and Variety." http://blogs.gartner.com/doug-laney/files/2012/01/ad949-3D-Data-Manage ment-Controlling-Data-Volume-Velocity-and-Variety.pdf.

Lang, Dustin, David W. Hogg, Keir Mierle, Michael Blanton, and Sam Roweis. 2009. "Astrometry.net: Blind Astrometric Calibration of Arbitrary Astronomical Images." *arXiv:0910.2233*. doi:10.1088/0004-6256/139/5/1782.

Large Synoptic Survey Telescope Corporation. 2010. Home page. http://www.lsst .org/lsst.

Latour, Bruno. 1987. *Science in Action: How to Follow Scientists and Engineers through Society*. Cambridge, MA: Harvard University Press.

Latour, Bruno. 1988. "Drawing Things Together." In *Representation in Scientific Practice*, ed. Michael E. Lynch and Steve Woolgar, 19–68. Cambridge, MA: MIT Press.

Latour, Bruno. 1993. *We Have Never Been Modern*. Cambridge, MA: Harvard University Press.

Latour, Bruno. 2004. *Politics of Nature: How to Bring Sciences into Democracy*. Cambridge, MA: Harvard University Press.

Latour, Bruno, and Steve Woolgar. 1979. *Laboratory Life: The Construction of Scientific Facts*. Beverly Hills, CA: Sage.

Latour, Bruno, and Steve Woolgar. 1986. *Laboratory Life: The Construction of Scientific Facts*. Princeton, NJ: Princeton University Press.

Lave, Jean, and Etienne Wenger. 1991. *Situated Learning: Legitimate Peripheral Participation*. Cambridge, UK: Cambridge University Press.

Lawrence, Bryan, Catherine Jones, Brian Matthews, Sam Pepler, and Sarah Callaghan. 2011. "Citation and Peer Peview of Data: Moving towards Formal Data Publication." *International Journal of Digital Curation* 6 (2):4–37. doi:10.2218/ijdc. v6i2.205.

Lee, Charlotte P., Paul Dourish, and Gloria Mark. 2006. "The Human Infrastructure of Cyberinfrastructure." In *Proceedings of the 2006 20th Anniversary Conference on Computer Supported Cooperative Work*, 483–492. New York: ACM.

Lehman, Richard, and Elizabeth Loder. 2012. "Missing Clinical Trial Data: A Threat to the Integrity of Evidence Based Medicine." *British Medical Journal* 344:d8158. doi:10.1136/bmj.d8158.

Leland, John. 2013. "Online Battle over Ancient Scrolls Spawns Real-World Consequences." *New York Times* (February 16) http://www.nytimes.com/2013/02/17/nyregion/online-battle-over-ancient-scrolls-spawns-real-world-consequences.html.

Leptin, Maria. 2012. "Open Access—Pass the Buck." *Science* 335 (6074):1279. doi:10.1126/science.1220395.

Lessig, Lawrence. 1999. *Code and Other Laws of Cyberspace*. New York: Basic Books.

Lessig, Lawrence. 2001. *The Future of Ideas: The Fate of the Commons in a Connected World*. New York: Random House.

Lessig, Lawrence. 2004. *Free Culture: How Big Media Uses Technology and the Law to Lock Down Culture and Control Creativity*. New York: Penguin.

Levi-Strauss, Claude. 1966. *The Savage Mind*. Chicago: University of Chicago Press.

Levien, Roger. S. Robert Austein, Christine L. Borgman, Timothy Casey, Hugh Dubberly, Patrik Faltstrom, Per-Kristian Halvorsen, et al. 2005. *Signposts in Cyberspace: The Domain Name System and Internet Navigation*. Washington, DC: National Academies Press.

Lewis, Anthony, Paul N. Courant, Laine Farley, Paula Kaufman, and John Leslie King. 2010. "Google & the Future of Books: An Exchange." *New York Review of Books* (January 14). http://www.nybooks.com/articles/archives/2010/jan/14/google-the-future-of-books-an-exchange.

Libicki, M. C. 1995. "Standards: The Rough Road to the Common Byte." In *Standards Policy for Information Infrastructure*, ed. Brian Kahin and Janet Abbate, 35–78. Cambridge, MA: MIT Press.

Licklider, J. C. R. 1960. "Man-Computer Symbiosis." *IRE Transactions on Human Factors in Electronics* 1: 4–11. http://groups.csail.mit.edu/medg/people/psz/Licklider.html.

Lide, David R., and Gordon H. Wood. 2012. *CODATA @ 45 Years: 1966 to 2010*. The Story of the ICSU Committee on Data for Science and Technology (CODATA) from 1966 to 2010. Paris: CODATA. http://www.codata.org/about/CODATA@45years.pdf.

Lievrouw, Leah A. 2010. "Social Media and the Production of Knowledge: A Return to Little Science?" *Social Epistemology* 24 (3):219–237. doi:10.1080/02691728.2010.499177.

Lievrouw, Leah A., and Sonia Livingstone. 2002. *The Handbook of New Media*. London: Sage Publications.

Lin, Rong Gong, Rosanna Xia, and Doug Smith. 2014a. "In Reversal, Quake Researchers to Turn over List of Concrete Buildings." *Los Angeles Times* (January 17). http://www.latimes.com/local/la-me-01-18-concrete-building-quake-20140118,0,3 71340.story#axzz2tcxSukHC.

Lin, Rong Gong, Rosanna Xia, and Doug Smith. 2014b. "UC Releases List of 1,500 Buildings; Big Step for L.A. Quake Safety." *Los Angeles Times* (January 25). http:// www.latimes.com/local/lanow/la-me-ln-concrete-buildings-list-20140125,0,425 6501.story#axzz2tcxSukHC.

Lipetz, Ben-Ami. 1965. "Improvement of the Selectivity of Citation Indexes to Science Literature through Inclusion of Citation Relationship Indicators." *American Documentation* 16 (2):81–90.

Liu, Alan. 2004. *The Laws of Cool: Knowledge Work and the Culture of Information*. Chicago: University of Chicago Press.

Lofland, John, David Snow, Leon Anderson, and Lyn H. Lofland. 2006. *Analyzing Social Settings: A Guide to Qualitative Observation and Analysis*. Belmont, CA: Wadsworth/Thomson Learning.

Lozano, George A., Vincent Lariviere, and Yves Gingras. 2012. "The Weakening Relationship between the Impact Factor and Papers' Citations in the Digital Age." *Journal of the American Society for Information Science and Technology* 63 (11):2140–2145. doi:10.1002/asi.22731.

Lyman, Peter. 1996. "What Is a Digital Library? Technology, Intellectual Property, and the Public Interest." *Daedalus: Proceedings of the American Academy of Arts and Sciences* 125: 1–33.

Lynch, Clifford A. 2009. "Jim Gray's Fourth Paradigm and the Construction of the Scientific Record." In *The Fourth Paradigm: Data-Intensive Scientific Discovery*, ed. Tony Hey, Stewart Tansley, and Kristin Tolle, 177–184. Redmond, WA: Microsoft.

Lynch, Clifford A. 2013. "The Next Generation of Challenges in the Curation of Scholarly Data." In *Research Data Management: Practical Strategies for Information Professionals*, ed. Joyce M. Ray. West Lafayette, IL: Purdue University Press.

Lynch, Michael E., and Steve Woolgar. 1988a. "Introduction: Sociological Orientations to Representational Practice in Science." In *Representation in Scientific Practice*, ed. Michael E. Lynch and Steve Woolgar, 1–19. Cambridge, MA: MIT Press.

Lynch, Michael E., and Steve Woolgar, ed. 1988b. *Representation in Scientific Practice*. Cambridge, MA: MIT Press.

Machlup, Fritz, and Una Mansfield. 1983. *The Study of Information: Interdisciplinary Messages*. New York: Wiley.

MacLean, Don. 2004. *Internet Governance: A Grand Collaboration*. New York: United Nations ICT Task Force.

MacRoberts, Michael H., and Barbara R. MacRoberts. 1989. "Problems of Citation Analysis: A Critical Review." *Journal of the American Society for Information Science American Society for Information Science* 40 (5):342–349.

MacRoberts, Michael H., and Barbara R. MacRoberts. 2010. "Problems of Citation Analysis: A Study of Uncited and Seldom-cited Influences." *Journal of the American Society for Information Science and Technology* 61 (1):1–12. doi:10.1002/asi.21228.

Makice, Kevin. 2009. *Twitter API: Up and Running*. Sebastopol, CA: O'Reilly Media.

Mandell, Rachel Alyson. 2012. "Researchers' Attitudes towards Data Discovery: Implications for a UCLA Data Registry." http://escholarship.org/uc/item/5bv8j7g3.

Manyika, James, Michael Chui, Diana Farrell, Steve Van Kuiken, Peter Groves, and Elizabeth Almasi Doshi. 2013. "Open Data: Unlocking Innovation and Performance with Liquid Information." McKinsey & Company. http://www.mckinsey.com/ insights/business_technology/open_data_unlocking_innovation_and_performance _with_liquid_information.

Marchionini, Gary, and Gregory R. Crane. 1994. "Evaluating Hypermedia and Learning: Methods and Results from the Perseus Project." *ACM Transactions on Information Systems* 12:5–34.

Marcus, Adam. 2013. "Influential Reinhart-Rogoff Economics Paper Suffers Spreadsheet Error." *Retraction Watch* (April 18). http://retractionwatch.wordpress.com/ 2013/04/18/influential-reinhart-rogoff-economics-paper-suffers-database-error.

Marcus, George E. 1995. "Ethnography In/of the World System: The Emergence of Multi-Sited Ethnography." *Annual Review of Anthropology* 24 (1):95–117. doi:10.1146/ annurev.an.24.100195.000523.

Markus, M. Lynne, and Mark Keil. 1994. "If We Build It, They Will Come: Designing Information Systems That People Want to Use." *MIT Sloan Management Review* 35 (4):11–25.

Marshall, Catherine C. 2008a. "Rethinking Personal Digital Archiving, Part 1." *D-Lib Magazine* 14 (3/4). doi:10.1045/march2008-marshall-pt1.

Marshall, Catherine C. 2008b. "Rethinking Personal Digital Archiving, Part 2." *D-Lib Magazine* 14 (3/4). doi:10.1045/march2008-marshall-pt2.

Marshall, Catherine C. 2009. "No Bull, No Spin: a Comparison of Tags with Other Forms of User Metadata." In *Proceedings of the 9th ACM/IEEE-CS Joint Conference on Digital Libraries*, 241–250. New York: ACM. doi:10.1145/1555400.1555438.

Marshall, Eliot. 2011. "Unseen World of Clinical Trials Emerges From U.S. Database." *Science* 333 (6039):145. doi:10.1126/science.333.6039.145.

Mathae, Kathie Bailey, and Paul F. Uhlir eds. 2012. *The Case for International Sharing of Scientific Data: A Focus on Developing Countries; Proceedings of a Symposium.* Washington, DC: National Academies Press.

Maunsell, John. 2010. "Announcement Regarding Supplemental Material." *Journal of Neuroscience* 30 (32):10599–10600. http://www.jneurosci.org/content/30/32/10599.

Mayer, Rob. 2010. "Authors, Plagiarists, or Tradents?" *Kīli Kīlaya.* http://blogs.orient.ox.ac.uk/kila/2010/10/09/authors-plagiarists-or-tradents.

Mayer-Schonberger, Viktor, and Kenneth Cukier. 2013. *Big Data: A Revolution That Will Transform How We Live, Work, and Think.* Boston: Houghton Mifflin Harcourt.

Mayernik, Matthew S. In press. "Research Data and Metadata Curation as Institutional Issues." *Journal of the Association for Information Science and Technology.*

Mayernik, Matthew S. 2011. "Metadata Realities for Cyberinfrastructure: Data Authors as Metadata Creators." PhD diss., Los Angeles: University of California at Los Angeles. http://papers.ssrn.com/sol3/papers.cfm?abstract_id=2042653.

Mayernik, Matthew S., Archer L. Batcheller, and Christine L. Borgman. 2011. "How Institutional Factors Influence the Creation of Scientific Metadata." In *Proceedings of the 2011 iConference,* 417–425. New York: ACM. doi:10.1145/1940761.1940818.

Mayernik, Matthew S., Jillian C. Wallis, and Christine L. Borgman. 2007. "Adding Context to Content: The CENS Deployment Center." In *Proceedings of the American Society for Information Science & Technology.* Vol. 44. Milwaukee, WI: Information Today.

Mayernik, Matthew S., Jillian C. Wallis, and Christine L. Borgman. 2012. "Unearthing the Infrastructure: Humans and Sensors in Field-based Research." *Computer Supported Cooperative Work* 22 (1):65–101. doi:10.1007/s10606-012-9178-y.

McCain, Katherine W. 2012. "Assessing Obliteration by Incorporation: Issues and Caveats." *Journal of the American Society for Information Science and Technology* 63 (11):2129–2139. doi:10.1002/asi.22719.

McCray, W. Patrick. 2000. "Large Telescopes and the Moral Economy of Recent Astronomy." *Social Studies of Science* 30 (5):685–711. doi:10.1177/030631200030005002.

McCray, W. Patrick. 2001. "What Makes a Failure? Designing a New National Telescope, 1975–1984." *Technology and Culture* 42 (2):265–291. doi:10.1353/tech.2001.0076.

McCray, W. Patrick. 2003. "The Contentious Role of a National Observatory." *Physics Today* 56 (10):55–61. doi:10.1063/1.1629005.

McCray, W. Patrick. 2004. *Giant Telescopes: Astronomical Ambition and the Promise of Technology*. Cambridge, MA: Harvard University Press.

McCray, W. Patrick. In press. "How Astronomers Digitized the Sky." *Technology & Culture*.

McGuire, Amy L., Steven Joffe, Barbara A. Koenig, Barbara B. Biesecker, Laurence B. McCullough, Jennifer S. Blumenthal-Barby, Timothy Caulfield, Sharon F. Terry, and Robert C. Green. 2013. "Ethics and Genomic Incidental Findings." *Science* 340 (6136):1047–1048. doi:10.1126/science.1240156.

McLaughlin, Jamie, Michael Meredith, Michael Pidd, and Katherine Rogers. 2010. "A Review of the AHRC Technical Appendix and Recommendations for a Technical Plan." Sheffield, UK: Humanities Research Institute, University of Sheffield. http://digital.humanities.ox.ac.uk/Support/technicalappendix_final3.pdf.

Meadows, A. J. 1974. *Communication in Science*. London: Butterworths.

Meadows, A. J. 1998. *Communicating Research*. San Diego: Academic Press.

Meadows, Jack. 2001. *Understanding Information*. Munchen: K. G. Saur.

Mele, Salvatore. 2013. "Higgs Boson Discovery at CERN: Physics and Publishing." *The Oxford Internet Institute, Innovation and Digital Scholarship Lecture Series Events*. http://www.oii.ox.ac.uk/events/?id=598.

Mendeley. 2013. Home page. http://www.mendeley.com/features.

Meng, Xiao-Li. 2011. "Multi-party Inference and Uncongeniality." In *International Encyclopedia of Statistical Science*, ed. Miodrag Lovric, 884–888. Berlin: Springer.

Merton, Robert K. 1963a. "The Ambivalence of Scientists." *Bulletin of the Johns Hopkins Hospital* 112:77–97.

Merton, Robert K. 1963b. "The Mosaic of the Behavioral Sciences." In *The Behavioral Sciences Today*, by Bernard Berelson, 247–272. New York: Basic Books.

Merton, Robert K. 1968. "The Matthew Effect in Science." *Science* 159:56–63. doi:10.1126/science.159.3810.56.

Merton, Robert K. 1970. "Behavior Patterns of Scientists." *Leonardo* 3:213–220.

Merton, Robert K. 1973. *The Sociology of Science: Theoretical and Empirical Investigations*. Ed. Norman W. Storer. Chicago: University of Chicago Press.

Merton, Robert K. 1988. "The Matthew Effect in Science II: Cumulative Advantage and the Symbolism of Intellectual Property." *Isis* 79:606–623.

Merton, Robert K. 1995. "The Thomas Theorem and the Matthew Effect." *Social Forces* 74:379–422. doi:10.1093/sf/74.2.379.

Meyer, Eric T. 2009. "Moving from Small Science to Big Science: Social and Organizational Impediments to Large Scale Data Sharing." In *e-Research: Transformations in Scholarly Practice*, ed. Nicholas W Jankowski, 147–159. New York: Routledge.

Meyer, Eric T., and Ralph Schroeder. 2014. *Digital Transformations of Research*. Cambridge, MA: MIT Press.

Meyer, Eric T., Ralph Schroeder, and Linnet Taylor. 2013. "Big Data in the Study of Twitter, Facebook and Wikipedia: On the Uses and Disadvantages of Scientificity for Social Research." Presented at the Annual Meeting of the American Sociological Association Annual Meeting, Hilton New York and Sheraton New York.

Miles, Alistair, Jun Zhao, Graham Klyne, Helen White-Cooper, and David Shotton. 2010. "OpenFlyData: An Exemplar Data Web Integrating Gene Expression Data on the Fruit Fly Drosophila Melanogaster." *Journal of Biomedical Informatics* 43 (5):752–761. doi:10.1016/j.jbi.2010.04.004.

Milgram, Stanley. 1974. *Obedience to Authority: An Experimental View*. New York: Harper & Row.

Miller, Mary K. 2007. "Reading between the Lines." *Smithsonian Magazine*. http://www.smithsonianmag.com/science-nature/archimedes.html.

Millerand, Florence, and Geoffrey C. Bowker. 2009. "Metadata Standards: Trajectories and Enactment in the Life of an Ontology." In *Standards and Their Stories*, ed. Martha Lampland and Susan Leigh Star, 149–165. Ithaca, NY: Cornell University Press.

Mimno, David, Gregory Crane, and Alison Jones. 2005. "Hierarchical Catalog Records: Implementing a FRBR Catalog." *D-Lib Magazine* 11 (10). http://www.dlib.org/dlib/october05/crane/10crane.html.

Ministry of Education, Republic of China. 2000. "Dictionary of Chinese Character Variants." http://dict.variants.moe.edu.tw.

MIT Libraries. 2009. "MIT Faculty Open Access Policy." Scholarly Publishing @ MIT Libraries. http://libraries.mit.edu/scholarly/mit-open-access/open-access-at-mit/mit-open-access-policy.

Modern Language Association of America. 2009. *MLA Handbook for Writers of Research Papers*. New York: The Modern Language Association of America.

Moffett, Jonathan. 1992. "The Beazley Archive: Making a Humanities Database Accessible to the World." *Bulletin of the John Rylands University of Manchester* 74 (3):39–52.

Monaghan, Peter. 2013. "'They Said at First That They Hadn't Made a Spreadsheet Error, When They Had.'" *Chronicle of Higher Education* (April 24). http://chronicle.com/article/UMass-Graduate-Student-Talks/138763.

Moreau, Luc. 2010. "The Foundations for Provenance on the Web." *Foundations and Trends® in Web Science* 2 (2-3): 99–241. doi:10.1561/1800000010.

Moreau, Luc, Paul Groth, Simon Miles, Javier Vazquez-Salceda, John Ibbotson, Sheng Jiang, Steve Munroe, et al. 2008. "The Provenance of Electronic Data." *Communications of the ACM* 51 (4):52–58. doi:10.1145/1330311.1330323.

Mullaney, Thomas S. 2012. "The Moveable Typewriter: How Chinese Typists Developed Predictive Text During the Height of Maoism." *Technology and Culture* 53 (4):777–814. doi:10.1353/tech.2012.0132.

Munns, David P. D. 2012. *A Single Sky: How an International Community Forged the Science of Radio Astronomy*. Cambridge, MA: MIT Press.

Murphy, Fiona. 2013. "The Now and the Future of Data Publishing." *Wiley Exchanges*. http://exchanges.wiley.com/blog/2013/07/05/the-now-and-the-future-of-data publishing.

Murray-Rust, Peter, and Henry S. Rzepa. 2004. "The Next Big Thing: From Hypermedia to Datuments." *Journal of Digital Information* 5 (1). http://journals.tdl.org/jodi/article/view/130.

Murray-Rust, Peter, Cameron Neylon, Rufus Pollock, and John Wilbanks. 2010. "Panton Principles." http://pantonprinciples.org.

Murray-Rust, Peter, Henry S. Rzepa, S. Tyrrell, and Y. Zhang. 2004. "Representation and Use of Chemistry in the Global Electronic Age." *Organic & Biomolecular Chemistry* 2:3192–3203.

Murthy, Dhiraj. 2011. "Twitter: Microphone for the Masses?" *Media Culture & Society* 33 (5):779–789. doi:10.1177/0163443711404744.

Naik, Gautam. 2011. "Scientists' Elusive Goal: Reproducing Study Results." *Wall Street Journal*. http://online.wsj.com/news/articles/SB10001424052970203764804577059841672541590.

NASA's Earth Observing System Data and Information System. 2013. "Processing Levels." *EOS DIS*. http://earthdata.nasa.gov/data/standards-and-references/processing-levels.

NASA Spitzer Space Telescope. 2013. Home page. http://www.spitzer.caltech.edu.

The National Academies. 2010. *Astro2010: The Astronomy and Astrophysics Decadal Survey*. Washington, DC: National Academies Press. http://sites.nationalacademies.org/bpa/BPA_049810.

National Aeronautics and Space Administration, Goddard Space Flight Center. 2014. "BSC5P—Bright Star Catalog." http://heasarc.gsfc.nasa.gov/W3Browse/star-catalog/bsc5p.html.

National Aeronautics and Space Administration, Goddard Space Flight Center. 2013a. "FITS Documentation." http://fits.gsfc.nasa.gov/fits_documentation.html.

National Aeronautics and Space Administration, Goddard Space Flight Center. 2013b. "FITS World Coordinate System." http://fits.gsfc.nasa.gov/fits_wcs.html.

National Aeronautics and Space Administration, Infrared Processing and Analysis Center. 2014a. "NASA Extragalactic Database (NED)." http://ned.ipac.caltech.edu.

National Aeronautics and Space Administration, Infrared Processing and Analysis Center. 2014b. "NASA Exoplanet Archive." http://www.ipac.caltech.edu/project/25.

National Aeronautics and Space Administration, Infrared Processing and Analysis Center. 2014c. "Two Micron All Sky Survey." http://www.ipac.caltech.edu/2mass.

National Aeronautics and Space Administration, Jet Propulsion Laboratory. 2014. "NASA Planetary Data System." http://pds.jpl.nasa.gov.

National Aeronautics and Space Administration, Mikulski Archive for Space Telescopes. 2013. "About MAST." http://archive.stsci.edu/aboutmast.html.

The National Archives. 2013. "Domesday Book." http://www.nationalarchives.gov.uk/domesday.

National Center for Biotechnology Information. 2013. "Taxonomy Database." http://www.ncbi.nlm.nih.gov/taxonomy.

National Health and Medical Research Council. 2007. "Australian Code for the Responsible Conduct of Research." http://www.nhmrc.gov.au/guidelines/publications/r39.

National Information Standards Organization. 2004. *Understanding Metadata*. Bethesda, MD: NISO Press.

National Information Standards Organization. 2013. "Recommended Practice for Online Supplemental Journal Article Materials." http://www.niso.org/publications/rp/rp-15-2013.

National Institutes of Health. 2003. "NIH Data Sharing Policy." http://grants2.nih.gov/grants/policy/data_sharing.

National Institutes of Health. 2013. "NIH Public Access Policy." http://publicaccess.nih.gov/submit_process.htm.

National Optical Astronomy Observatory. 2003. "NOAO Policies for the Allocation of Observing Time." http://www.noao.edu/noaoprop/help/policies.html#dr.

National Optical Astronomy Observatory. 2013a. "AURA/NOAO Data Rights Policy." http://www.noao.edu/noaoprop/help/datarights.html.

National Optical Astronomy Observatory. 2013b. "Data." http://ast.noao.edu/data.

National Research Council. 1997. *Bits of Power: Issues in Global Access to Scientific Data*. Washington, DC: National Academies Press.

National Research Council. 1999. *A Question of Balance: Private Rights and the Public Interest in Scientific and Technical Databases*. Washington, DC: National Academies Press.

National Research Council. 2001. *The Internet's Coming of Age*. Washington, DC: National Academies Press.

National Research Council. 2013. *Proposed Revisions to the Common Rule: Perspectives of Social and Behavioral Scientists: Workshop Summary*. Washington, DC: National Academies Press.

National Science Board. 2005. "Long-Lived Digital Data Collections." http://www.nsf.gov/pubs/2005/nsb0540.

National Science Foundation. 2010a. "NSF Data Management Plans." Washington, DC: NSF. http://www.nsf.gov/pubs/policydocs/pappguide/nsf11001/gpg_2.jsp#dmp.

National Science Foundation. 2010b. "NSF Data Sharing Policy." Washington, DC: NSF. http://www.nsf.gov/pubs/policydocs/pappguide/nsf11001/aag_6.jsp#VID4.

Natural Reserve System, University of California. 2013. Home page. http://nrs.ucop.edu.

Nature Staff. 2012. "Data Standards Urged." *Nature* 492 (7427): 145. doi:10.1038/nj7427-145a. http://www.nature.com/naturejobs/science/articles/10.1038/nj7427-145a.

Naylor, Bernard, and Marilyn Geller. 1995. "A Prehistory of Electronic Journals: The EIES and BLEND Projects." In *Advances in Serials Management*, ed. Marcia Tuttle and Karen D. Darling, 27–47. Greenwich, CT: JAI Press.

Nelson, Bryn. 2009. "Data Sharing: Empty Archives." *NATNews* 461 (7261):160–163. doi:10.1038/461160a.

Nexleaf. 2013. Home page. http://nexleaf.org/about-us-0.

Nguyên, Tánh Trầntiễn Khanh, and Hiển Trần Tiễn Huyến Nguyên. 2006. "Computer Translation of the Chinese Taisho Tripitaka." http://www.daitangvietnam.com/Computer%20Translation%20of%20the%20Chinese%20Tripitaka.pdf.

Nielsen, Michael. 2011. *Reinventing Discovery: The New Era of Networked Science*. Princeton, NJ: Princeton University Press.

Nisbet, Miriam M. 2005. "Library Copyright Alliance, Orphan Works Notice of Inquiry." http://www.copyright.gov/orphan/comments/OW0658-LCA.pdf.

Normile, Dennis, Gretchen Vogel, and Jennifer Couzin. 2006. "Cloning—South Korean Team's Remaining Human Stem Cell Claim Demolished." *Science* 311:156–157. doi:10.1126/science.311.5758.156.

Norris, Ray, Heinz Andernach, Guenther Eichhorn, Françoise Genova, Elizabeth Griffin, Robert J. Hanisch, Ajit Kembhavi, Robert Kennicutt, and Anita Richards. 2006. "Astronomical Data Management." In *Highlights of Astronomy, XXVIth IAU General Assembly*, ed. K. A. van der Hucht. Cambridge, UK: Cambridge University Press.

Northover, J. Peter, and Shirley M. Northover. 2012. "Applications of Electron Backscatter Diffraction (EBSD) in Archaeology." In *Historical Technology, Materials and Conversation: SEM and Microanalysis*, ed. Nigel Meeks. London: Archetype.

The NSA files. 2013. Home page. *The Guardian* (June 8). http://www.guardian.co.uk/world/the-nsa-files.

Nunberg, Geoffrey. 2009. "Google's Book Search: A Disaster for Scholars." *Chronicle of Higher Education*. http://chronicle.com/article/Googles-Book-Search-A/48245.

Nunberg, Geoffrey. 2010. "Counting on Google Books." *Chronicle Review* (December 16). https://chronicle.com/article/Counting-on-Google-Books/125735.

NVivo 10. 2013. "NVivo 10 Research Software for Analysis and Insight." http://www.qsrinternational.com/products_nvivo.aspx.

O'Brien, Danny. 2004. "How to Mend a Broken Internet." *New Scientist*. http://www.newscientist.com/article/mg18424736.100-how-to-mend-a-broken-internet.html.

Odlyzko, Andrew M. 2000. "The Internet and Other Networks: Utilization Rates and Their Implications." *Information Economics and Policy* 12 (4):341–365.

Office of Scholarly Communication. 2013. "UC Open Access Policy." University of California. http://osc.universityofcalifornia.edu/openaccesspolicy.

Office of Science and Technology Policy. 2013. "Expanding Public Access to the Results of Federally Funded Research." *The White House*. http://www.whitehouse.gov/blog/2013/02/22/expanding-public-access-results-federally-funded-research.

Ohm, Paul. 2010. "Broken Promises of Privacy: Responding to the Surprising Failure of Anonymization." *UCLA Law Review* 57:1701. http://ssrn.com/abstract=1450006.

Olsen, Mark, Russell Horton, and Glenn Roe. 2011. "Something Borrowed: Sequence Alignment and the Identification of Similar Passages in Large Text Collections." *Digital Studies / Le Champ Numérique* 2 (1). http://www.digitalstudies.org/ojs/index.php/digital_studies/article/view/190.

Olson, Gary M., and Judith S. Olson. 2000. "Distance Matters." *Human-Computer Interaction* 15 (2):139–178.

Olson, Gary M., Ann Zimmerman, and Nathan Bos. 2008. *Scientific Collaboration on the Internet*. Cambridge, MA: MIT Press.

Open Access Infrastructure for Research in Europe (OpenAIRE). 2014. Frequently Asked Questions. http://www.openaire.eu/en/support/faq.

Open Bibliography and Open Bibliographic Data. 2013. Home page. http://openbiblio.net.

Open Biological, Open, and Biomedical Ontology Foundry. 2013. Home page. http://www.obofoundry.org.

Open Context. 2013. http://opencontext.org.Open Geospatial Consortium. 2014. "Home Page." http://www.opengeospatial.org.

Open Data Commons. 2013. Home page. http://opendatacommons.org.

Open Geospatial Consortium. 2014. "Home Page." http://www.opengeospatial.org.

Open Researcher and Contributor ID. 2011. Home page. http://www.orcid.org.

Oransky, Ivan. 2012. "Why Aren't There More Retractions in Business and Economics Journals?" *Retraction Watch*. http://retractionwatch.wordpress.com/2012/12/12/why-arent-there-more-retractions-in-business-and-economics-journals.

Organisation for Economic Co-operation and Development. 2007. "OECD Principles and Guidelines for Access to Research Data from Public Funding." www.oecd.org/dataoecd/9/61/38500813.pdf.

Osterlund, Carsten, and Paul Carlile. 2005. "Relations in Practice: Sorting through Practice Theories on Knowledge Sharing in Complex Organizations." *Information Society* 21:91–107.

Ostrom, Elinor, and Charlotte Hess. 2007. "A Framework for Analyzing the Knowledge Commons." In *Understanding Knowledge as a Commons: From Theory to Practice*, ed. Charlotte Hess and Elinor Ostrom, 41–81. Cambridge, MA: MIT Press.

Ostrom, Vincent, and Elinor Ostrom. 1977. "Public Goods and Public Choices." In *Alternatives for Delivering Public Services: Toward Improved Performance*, ed. E. S. Savas, 7–49. Boulder, CO: Westview Press.

Overpeck, Jonathan T., Gerald A. Meehl, Sandrine Bony, and David R. Easterling. 2011. "Climate Data Challenges in the 21st Century." *Science* 331:700–702. doi:10.1126/science.1197869.

Owen, Whitney J. 2004. "In Defense of the Least Publishable Unit." *Chronicle of Higher Education* (February 9). http://chronicle.com/article/In-Defense-of-the-Least/44761.

Oxford English Dictionary. 2014. Home page. www.oed.com.

Ozsoy, Selami. 2011. "Use of New Media by Turkish Fans in Sport Communication: Facebook and Twitter." *Journal of Human Kinetics* 28:165–176. doi:10.2478/v10078-011-0033-x.

Paisley, William J. 1980. "Information and Work." In *Progress in the Communication Sciences*. vol. 2. ed. Brenda Dervin and Melvin J. Voigt, 114–165. Norwood, NJ: Ablex.

Paisley, William J. 1990. "The Future of Bibliometrics." In *Scholarly Communication and Bibliometrics*, ed. Christine L. Borgman, 281–299. Newbury Park, CA: Sage.

Palfrey, John G, and Urs Gasser. 2012. *Interop: The Promise and Perils of Highly Interconnected Systems*. New York: Basic Books.

PANGAEA. Data Publisher for Earth & Environmental Science. 2013. Home page. http://www.pangaea.de.

Pan-STARRS. 2012. "Pan-STARRS Data Release of PS1 Surveys." http://ps1sc.org/Data_Release.shtml.

Pan-STARRS. 2013a. "Camera Design—Pan-Starrs—Panoramic Survey Telescope & Rapid Response System." http://pan-starrs.ifa.hawaii.edu/public/design-features/cameras.html.

Pan-STARRS. 2013b. Home page. http://pan-starrs.ifa.hawaii.edu/public.

Parry, Marc. 2014. "How the Humanities Compute in the Classroom." *Chronicle of Higher Education* (January 6). http://chronicle.com/article/How-the-Humanities-Compute-in/143809.

Parsons, M. A., and P. A. Fox. 2013. "Is Data Publication the Right Metaphor?" *Data Science Journal* 12:WDS32–WDS46. doi:10.2481/dsj.WDS-042.

Paskin, Norman. 1997. "Information Identifiers." *Learned Publishing* 10:135–156.

Paskin, Norman. 1999. "Toward Unique Identifiers." *Proceedings of the IEEE* 87:1208–1227.

Pearson, Sarah Hinchcliff. 2012. "Three Legal Mechanisms for Sharing Data." In *For Attribution—Developing Data Attribution and Citation Practices and Standards: Summary of an International Workshop*, ed. Paul F. Uhlir, 71–76. Washington, DC: National Academies Press. http://www.nap.edu/openbook.php?record_id=13564&page=71.

Peng, Roger D. 2011. "Reproducible Research in Computational Science." *Science* 334 (6060):1226–1227. doi:10.1126/science.1213847.

Pepe, Alberto. 2010. "Structure and Evolution of Scientific Collaboration Networks in a Modern Research Collaboratory." Los Angeles: University of California at Los Angeles. http://papers.ssrn.com/sol3/papers.cfm?abstract_id=1616935.

Pepe, Alberto. 2011. "The Relationship between Acquaintanceship and Coauthorship in Scientific Collaboration Networks." *Journal of the American Society for Information Science and Technology* 62 (11):2121–2132. doi:10.1002/asi.21629.

Pepe, Alberto, Christine L. Borgman, Jillian C. Wallis, and Matthew S. Mayernik. 2007. "Knitting a Fabric of Sensor Data and Literature." In *Information Processing in Sensor Networks*. New York: ACM/IEEE.

Pepe, Alberto, Alyssa A. Goodman, and August Muench. 2011. "The ADS All-Sky Survey." *arXiv:1111.3983*. http://arxiv.org/abs/1111.3983.

Pepe, Alberto, Alyssa A. Goodman, August Muench, Mercè Crosas, and Christopher Erdmann. In press. "Sharing, Archiving, and Citing Data in Astronomy." *PLoS ONE*. https://www.authorea.com/users/3/articles/288/_show_article.

Pepe, Alberto, Matthew S. Mayernik, Christine L. Borgman, and Herbert Van de Sompel. 2010. "From Artifacts to Aggregations: Modeling Scientific Life Cycles on the Semantic Web." *Journal of the American Society for Information Science and Technology* 61:567–582. doi:10.1002/asi.21263.

Perseus Digital Library. 2009. Home page. http://www.perseus.tufts.edu/hopper.

Petersen, Arthur C. 2012. *Simulating Nature: a Philosophical Study of Computer-simulation Uncertainties and Their Role in Climate Science and Policy Advice*. Boca Raton, FL: CRC Press.

Phelps, Thomas A., and Robert Wilensky. 1997. "Multivalent Annotations." In *Proceedings of the First European Conference on Research and Advanced Technology for Digital Libraries*, ed. Rachel Heery and Liz Lyon, 287–303. London: Springer-Verlag.

Phelps, Thomas A., and Robert Wilensky. 2000. "Multivalent Documents." *Communications of the ACM* 43:83–90.

Pienta, Amy M., George C. Alter, and Jared A. Lyle. 2010. "The Enduring Value of Social Science Research: The Use and Reuse of Primary Research Data." http://deepblue.lib.umich.edu/bitstream/handle/2027.42/78307/pienta_alter_lyle_100331.pdf?sequence=1.

Pine, Kathleen, Christine T. Wolf, and Melissa Mazmanian. 2014. "The Work of Reuse: Quality Measurement in Healthcare Organizations." Paper presented at Workshop on Sharing, Re-Use, and Circulation of Resources in Cooperative Scientific Work, Baltimore, February.

Pineda, Jaime E., Erik W. Rosolowsky, and Alyssa A. Goodman. 2009. "The Perils of Clumpfind: The Mass Spectrum of Sub-structures in Molecular Clouds." *Astrophysical Journal* 699 (2):L134–L138. doi:10.1088/0004-637X/699/2/L134.

Pinter, Frances. 2012. "Open Access for Scholarly Books?" *Publishing Research Quarterly* 28 (3):183–191. doi:10.1007/s12109-012-9285-0.

The Pisa Griffin Project. 2013. Home page. http://vcg.isti.cnr.it/griffin.

Planck Collaboration. P.A.R. Ade, N. Aghanim, C. Armitage-Caplan, M. Arnaud, M. Ashdown, F. Atrio-Barandela, et al. 2013. "Planck 2013 Results: Overview of Products and Scientific Results." *arXiv:1303.5062.* http://arxiv.org/abs/1303.5062.

PLoS Medicine Editors. 2006. "The Impact Factor Game." *PLoS Medicine* 3 (6):e291. doi:10.1371/journal.pmed.0030291.

Polanyi, Michael. 1966. *The Tacit Dimension.* Garden City, NY: Doubleday.

Poovey, Mary. 1998. *A History of the Modern Fact: Problems of Knowledge in the Sciences of Wealth and Society.* Chicago: University of Chicago Press.

Porter, Theodore M. 1995. *Trust in Numbers: The Pursuit of Objectivity in Science and Public Life.* Princeton, NJ: Princeton University Press.

Prayle, Andrew, Matthew N. Hurley, and Alan R. Smyth. 2012. "Compliance with Mandatory Reporting of Clinical Trial Results on ClinicalTrials.gov: Cross Sectional Study." *British Medical Journal* 344:d7373. doi:10.1136/bmj.d7373.

Presner, Todd Samuel. 2010. "HyperCities: Building a Web 2.0 Learning Platform." In *Teaching Literature at a Distance,* ed. Anastasia Natsina and Takis Tagialis. London: Continuum Books.

Prewitt, Kenneth. 2013. "Is Any Science Safe?" *Science* 340 (6132):525. doi:10.1126/science.1239180.

Price, Derek John de Solla. 1963. *Little Science, Big Science.* New York: Columbia University Press.

Price, Derek John de Solla. 1975. *Science since Babylon.* New Haven, CT: Yale University Press.

Priem, Jason, Dario Taraborelli, Paul Groth, and Cameron Neylon. 2010. "Altmetrics: A Manifesto—Altmetrics.org." http://altmetrics.org/manifesto.

Pritchard, Sarah M., Larry Carver, and Smiti Anand. 2004. "Collaboration for Knowledge Management and Campus Informatics." Santa Barbara: University of California, Santa Barbara. http://www.immagic.com/eLibrary/ARCHIVES/GENERAL/UCSB_US/S040823P.pdf.

Project Bamboo. 2013. Home page. http://projectbamboo.org.

Protein Data Bank. 2011. Home page. http://www.rcsb.org/pdb.

PubMed Central. 2009. Home page. http://www.ncbi.nlm.nih.gov/pmc.

Rabesandratana, Tania. 2013. "Drug Watchdog Ponders How to Open Clinical Trial Data Vault." *Science* 339 (6126):1369–1370. doi:10.1126/science.339.6126.1369.

Rahtz, Sebastian, Alexander Dutton, Donna Kurtz, Graham Klyne, Andrew Zisserman, and Relja Arandjelovic. 2011. "CLAROS—Collaborating on Delivering the

Future of the Past." http://dh2011abstracts.stanford.edu/xtf/view?docId=tei/ab-224 .xml;query=;brand=default.

Raymond, Eric S. 2001. *The Cathedral & the Bazaar: Musings on Linux and Open Source by an Accidental Revolutionary*. Cambridge, MA: O'Reilly.

reCAPTCHA. 2013. "What Is reCAPTCHA?" http://www.google.com/recaptcha/ intro/index.html.

Reichman, Jerome H., Tom Dedeurwaerdere, and Paul F. Uhlir. 2009. *Designing the Microbial Research Commons: Strategies for Accessing, Managing, and Using Essential Public Knowledge Assets*. Washington, DC: National Academies Press.

Reichman, O. J., Matthew B. Jones, and Mark P. Schildhauer. 2011. "Challenges and Opportunities of Open Data in Ecology." *Science* 331:703–705. doi:10.1126/science .1197962.

Reimer, Thorsten, Lorna Hughes, and David Robey. 2007. "After the AHDS: The End of National Support?" *Arts-Humanities.net: Digital Humanities and Arts*. http://www .arts-humanities.net/forumtopic/after_ahds_end_national_support.

Renear, Allen H., and Carole L. Palmer. 2009. "Strategic Reading, Ontologies, and the Future of Scientific Publishing." *Science* 325:828–832. doi:10.1126/science.1157784.

Renear, Allen H., Simone Sacchi, and Karen M. Wickett. 2010. "Definitions of Dataset in the Scientific and Technical Literature." *Proceedings of the 73rd ASIS&T Annual Meeting : Navigating Streams in an Information Ecosystem* 47 (1): 1–4. doi:10.1002/meet .14504701240.

Research Acumen. 2013. Home page. http://research-acumen.eu.

Research Councils UK. 2011. "RCUK Common Principles on Data Policy." http:// www.rcuk.ac.uk/research/datapolicy.

Research Councils UK. 2012a. "Guidance for the RCUK Policy on Access to Research Output."

Research Councils UK. 2012b. "RCUK Policy on Open Access and Supporting Guidance." http://www.rcuk.ac.uk/documents/documents/RCUKOpenAccessPolicy.pdf .http://roarmap.eprints.org/671/1/RCUK%20_Policy_on_Access_to_Research _Outputs.pdf.

Research Councils UK. 2012c. "Research Councils UK Announces New Open Access Policy." http://www.rcuk.ac.uk/media/news/120716.

Research Councils UK. 2013. "RCUK Policy on Open Access: Frequently Asked Questions." http://www.rcuk.ac.uk/RCUK-prod/assets/documents/documents/Openaccess FAQs.pdf.

Research Data Alliance. 2013. Home page. https://rd-alliance.org/node.

Ribes, David, Karen S. Baker, Florence Millerand, and Geoffrey C. Bowker. 2005. "Comparative Interoperability Project: Configurations of Community, Technology, Organization." *Proceedings of the 5th ACM/IEEE-CS Joint Conference on Digital Libraries*: 65–66. doi:10.1145/1065385.1065399.

Ribes, David, and Thomas Finholt. 2009. "The Long Now of Technology Infrastructure: Articulating Tensions in Development." *Journal of the Association for Information Systems* 10 (5). http://aisel.aisnet.org/jais/vol10/iss5/5.

Ribes, David, and Steven J. Jackson. 2013. "Data Bite Man: The Work of Sustaining a Long-term Study." In *"Raw Data" Is an Oxymoron*, ed. Lisa Gitelman, 147–166. Cambridge, MA: MIT Press.

Ridge, Naomi A., James Di Francesco, Helen Kirk, Di Li, Alyssa A. Goodman, João F. Alves, Héctor G. Arce, et al. 2006. "The COMPLETE Survey of Star-Forming Regions: Phase I Data." *Astronomical Journal* 131 (6):2921. doi:10.1086/503704.

Roberts, L. 1987. "Who Owns the Human Genome?" *Science* 237 (4813):358–361. doi:10.1126/science.2885920.

Roberts, L. 1990. "Genome Project: An Experiment in Sharing." *Science* 248 (4958):953. doi:10.1126/science.2343307.

Robertson, C. Martin. 1976. "The Beazley Archive." *American Journal of Archaeology* 80 (4):445. doi:10.2307/503600.

Robey, David. 2007. "Consequences of the Withdrawal of AHDS Funding." Swindon, UK: Arts & Humanities Research Council. http://www.ahrcict.reading.ac.uk/activities/review/consequences%20of%20the%20withdrawl%20of%20ahds%20funding.pdf.

Robey, David. 2011. "Sustainability and Related Issues for Publicly Funded Data Resources." In *Evaluating & Measuring the Value, Use and Impact of Digital Collections*, ed. Lorna Hughes. London: Facet Publishing.

Robey, David. 2013. "Infrastructure Needs for the Digital Humanities." *e-Research South*. http://www.eresearchsouth.ac.uk/news/infrastructure-needs-for-the-digital-humanities.

Robinson, W. S. 1950. "Ecological Correlations and the Behavior of Individuals." *American Sociological Review* 15 (3):351–357. doi:10.2307/2087176.

Rodriguez, Laura L., Lisa D. Brooks, Judith H. Greenberg, and Eric D. Green. 2013. "The Complexities of Genomic Identifiability." *Science* 339 (6117):275–276. doi:10.1126/science.1234593.

Rodriguez, Marko A., Johan Bollen, and Herbert Van de Sompel. 2007. "A Practical Ontology for the Large-scale Modeling of Scholarly Artifacts and Their Usage." In

Proceedings of the 7th ACM/IEEE-CS Joint Conference on Digital Libraries, 278–287. New York: ACM. http://portal.acm.org/citation.cfm?id=1255229.

Rogers, Everett M. 1962. *Diffusion of Innovations*. New York: Free Press of Glencoe.

Rosenberg, Daniel. 2013. "Data before the Fact." In *"Raw Data" Is an Oxymoron*, ed. Lisa Gitelman, 15–40. Cambridge, MA: MIT Press.

Rosenthal, David S. H. 2010. "Stepping Twice into the Same River." JCDL 2010 Keynote Address, Queensland, Australia. http://blog.dshr.org/2010/06/jcdl-2010-keynot .html.

Rosenthal, David S. H. 2014. "Storage Will Be Much Less Free Than It Used to Be." Presented at the Seagate Corporation. http://blog.dshr.org/2014/05/talk-at-seagate .html.

Rosolowsky, E. W., J. E. Pineda, J. B. Foster, M. A. Borkin, J. Kauffmann, P. Caselli, P. C. Myers, and Alyssa Goodman. 2008. "An Ammonia Spectral Atlas of Dense Cores in Perseus." *Astrophysical Journal. Supplement Series* 175 (2):509–521. doi:10.1086/ 524299.

Ross, Joseph S., Tony Tse, Deborah A. Zarin, Hui Xu, Lei Zhou, and Harlan M. Krumholz. 2012. "Publication of NIH-funded Trials Registered in ClinicalTrials.gov: Cross Sectional Analysis." *British Medical Journal* 344:d7292. doi:10.1136/bmj.d7292.

Roth, Wendy D., and Jal D. Mehta. 2002. "The Rashomon Effect: Combining Positivist and Interpretivist Approaches in the Analysis of Contested Events." *Sociological Methods & Research* 31 (2):131–173. doi:10.1177/0049124102031002002.

Rots, Arnold H., and Sherry L. Winkelman. 2013. "Observatory Bibliographies as Research Tools." Paper presented at American Astronomical Society, AAS Meeting #221. http://adsabs.harvard.edu/abs/2013AAS...22115603R.

Rots, Arnold H., Sherry L. Winkelman, and Glenn E. Becker. 2012. "Meaningful Metrics for Observatory Publication Statistics." In *Society of Photo-Optical Instrumentation Engineers (SPIE) Conference Series*. Vol. 8448. doi:10.1117/12.927134.

Ruhleder, Karen. 1994. "Rich and Lean Representations of Information for Knowledge Work: The Role of Computing Packages in the Work of Classical Scholars." *ACM Transactions on Information Systems* 12 (2):208–230. doi:10.1145/196734.196746.

Ruixin, Yang. 2002. "Managing Scientific Metadata Using XML." *IEEE Internet Computing* 6:52–59.

Ryan, Michael J. 2011. "Replication in Field Biology: The Case of the Frog-Eating Bat." *Science* 334:1229–1230. doi:10.1126/science.1214532.

Sage Bionetworks. 2013. Home page. http://sagebase.org.

Salaheldeen, Hany M., and Michael L. Nelson. 2013. "Resurrecting My Revolution." In *Research and Advanced Technology for Digital Libraries*, ed. Trond Aalberg, Christos Papatheodorou, Milena Dobreva, Giannis Tsakonas, and Charles J. Farrugia, 333–345. Berlin: Springer.

Salerno, Emanuele, Anna Tonazzini, and Luigi Bedini. 2007. "Digital Image Analysis to Enhance Underwritten Text in the Archimedes Palimpsest." *International Journal of Document Analysis and Recognition* 9:79–87. doi:10.1007/s10032-006-0028-7.

Salk, Jonas. 1986. "Foreword." In *Laboratory Life: The Construction of Scientific Facts*, by Bruno Latour and Steve Woolgar, 2nd ed. Princeton, NJ: Princeton University Press.

Samuelson, Pamela. 2009a. "Legally Speaking: The Dead Souls of the Google Book-search Settlement." (April 17). http://toc.oreilly.com/2009/04/legally-speaking-the -dead-soul.html.

Samuelson, Pamela. 2009b. "The Dead Souls of the Google Book Search Settlement." *Communications of the ACM* 52:28–30. doi:10.1145/1538788.1538800.

Samuelson, Pamela. 2010. "Should the Google Book Settlement Be Approved?" *Communications of the ACM* 53:32–34.

Sands, Ashley, Christine L. Borgman, Laura Wynholds, and Sharon Traweek. 2014. "'We're Working on It:' Transferring the Sloan Digital Sky Survey from Laboratory to Library." Paper presented at International Conference on Digital Curation, San Francisco. http://www.dcc.ac.uk/events/idcc14/programme.

Santer, B. D., T. M. L. Wigley, and K. E. Taylor. 2011. "The Reproducibility of Observational Estimates of Surface and Atmospheric Temperature Change." *Science* 334:1232–1233. doi:10.1126/science.1216273.

Savage, Mike, and Roger Burrows. 2007. "The Coming Crisis of Empirical Sociology." *Sociology* 41:885–899.

Savage, Mike, and Roger Burrows. 2009. "Some Further Reflections on the Coming Crisis of Empirical Sociology." *Sociology* 43 (4):762–772. doi:10.1177/00380385 09105420.

Sawyer, Steve. 2008. "Data Wealth, Data Poverty, Science and Cyberinfrastructure." *Prometheus* 26 (4):355–371. doi:10.1080/08109020802459348.

Schiffman, Lawrence H. 2002. "The Many Battles of the Scrolls." *Journal of Religious History* 26:157–178.

Schiller, Dan. 2007. *How to Think About Information*. Urbana: University of Illinois Press.

Schirrwagen, Jochen, Paolo Manghi, Natalia Manola, Lukasz Bolikowski, Najla Rettberg, and Birgit Schmidt. 2013. "Data Curation in the OpenAIRE Scholarly

Communication Infrastructure." *Information Standards Quarterly* 25 (3):13. doi:10.3789/isqv25no3.2013.03.

Schmidt, Kjeld. 2012. "The Trouble with 'Tacit Knowledge.'" *Computer Supported Cooperative Work* 21 (2-3):163–225. doi:10.1007/s10606-012-9160-8.

Schnee, Scott, Thomas Bethell, and Alyssa A. Goodman. 2006. "Estimating the Column Density in Molecular Clouds with Far-Infrared and Submillimeter Emission Maps." *Astrophysical Journal Letters* 640 (1):L47. doi:10.1086/503292.

Schrier, Bill. 2011. "Bright Shiny Objects." *Chief Seattle Geek Blog*. http://schrier .wordpress.com/tag/bright-shiny-objects.

Schroeder, Ralph. 2007. *Rethinking Science, Technology, and Social Change*. Stanford, CA: Stanford University Press.

Schroeder, Ralph. 2014. "Big Data: Towards a More Scientific Social Science and Humanities?" In *Society and the Internet: How Information and Social Networks Are Changing Our Lives*, ed. Mark Graham and William H. Dutton. Oxford: Oxford University Press.

SciDrive. 2014. Home page. http://www.scidrive.org.

Science Exchange Network. 2012. "The Reproducibility Initiative." http://validation .scienceexchange.com/#/reproducibility-initiative.

Science Staff. 1987. "Ownership of the Human Genome." *Science* 237 (4822):1555. doi:10.1126/science.3629252.

Science Staff. 2011. "Challenges and Opportunities." *Science* 331 (6018):692–693. doi:10.1126/science.331.6018.692.

Science Staff. 2012. "The Runners-Up." *Science* 338 (6114):1525–1532. doi:10.1126/ science.338.6114.1525.

Science Staff. 2013. "Random Sample: Was the Downfall of Louis XVI in His DNA?" *Science* 340 (6135):906–907. doi:10.1126/science.340.6135.906-c.

Scotchmer, Suzanne. 2003. "Intellectual property—When Is It the Best Incentive Mechanism for S&T Data and Information?" In *The Role of Scientific and Technical Data and Information in the Public Domain*, ed. Julie M. Esanu and Paul F. Uhlir, 15–18. Washington, DC: National Academies Press.

Segal, Judith. 2005. "When Software Engineers Met Research Scientists: A Case Study." *Empirical Software Engineering* 10:517–536. doi:10.1007/s10664-005-3865-y.

Segal, Judith. 2009. "Software Development Cultures and Cooperation Problems: A Field Study of the Early Stages of Development of Software for a Scientific Community." *Computer Supported Cooperative Work* 18 (5-6):1–26. doi:10.1007/ s10606-009-9096-9.

Sensor Modeling Language. 2010. http://vast.uah.edu/SensorML.

Servick, Kelly. 2013. "House Subpoena Revives Battle over Air Pollution Studies." *Science* 341 (6146):604. doi:10.1126/science.341.6146.604.

Shadish, William R, Thomas D. Cook, and Donald T. Campbell. 2002. *Experimental and Quasi-experimental Designs for Generalized Causal Inference.* Boston: Houghton Mifflin.

Shankar, Kalpana. 2003. "Scientific Data Archiving: The State of the Art in Information, Data, and Metadata Management." http://works.bepress.com/borgman/234.

Shankland, Stephen. 2013. "Big Blue, Big Bang, Big Data: Telescope Funds Computing R&D." *CNET.* http://news.cnet.com/8301-11386_3-57572519-76/big-blue-big-bang-big-data-telescope-funds-computing-r-d.

Shapley, Alan H., and Pembroke J. Hart. 1982. "World Data Centers." *Eos, Transactions, American Geophysical Union* 63 (30):585. doi:10.1029/EO063i030p00585-01.

Shatz, David. 2004. *Peer Review: A Critical Inquiry.* Lanham, MD: Rowman & Littlefield.

Shea, Christopher. 2011. "Fraud Scandal Fuels Debate over Practices of Social Psychology." *Chronicle of Higher Education* (November 13). http://chronicle.com/article/As-Dutch-Research-Scandal/129746/?sid=wb&utm_source=wb&utm_medium=en.

SHERPA/RoMEO. 2014. "Publisher Copyright Policies & Self-archiving." http://www.sherpa.ac.uk/romeo.

Shilton, Katie. 2011. "Building Values into the Design of Pervasive Mobile Technologies." Los Angeles: University of California, Los Angeles. http://ssrn.com/paper=1866783.

Shotton, David. 2011. "Why Researchers Don't Publish Data." *Semantic Publishing.* http://semanticpublishing.wordpress.com/2011/08/04/why-researchers-dont-publish-data.

Shotton, David. 2013. "SCoRO, the Scholarly Contributions and Roles Ontology." http://www.essepuntato.it/lode/http://purl.org/spar/scoro.

Shotton, David, Katie Portwin, Graham Klyne, and Alistair Miles. 2009. "Adventures in Semantic Publishing: Exemplar Semantic Enhancements of a Research Article." *PLoS Computational Biology* 5 (4):e1000361. doi:10.1371/journal.pcbi.1000361.

Shuai, Xin, Alberto Pepe, and Johan Bollen. 2012. "How the Scientific Community Reacts to Newly Submitted Preprints: Article Downloads, Twitter Mentions, and Citations." *PLoS ONE* 7 (11):e47523. doi:10.1371/journal.pone.0047523.

SIMBAD Astronomical Database. 2013. Home page. http://simbad.u-strasbg.fr/simbad.

Siminovitch, Lou. 2012. "Small Science: Big Science Will Prevail." *Science* 338 (6109):882–883. doi:10.1126/science.338.6109.882-c.

Simonite, Tom. 2013. "Chinese Censorship of Twitter-Style Social Networks Weibo, Tencent, and Sina Offers Clues to Government Plans | MIT Technology Review." *MIT Technology Review.* http://www.technologyreview.com/news/511011/social-media-censorship-offers-clues-to-chinas-plans.

Sloan Digital Sky Survey. 2013a. Home page. http://www.sdss.org.

Sloan Digital Sky Survey. 2013b. "The Ninth Sloan Digital Sky Survey Data Release (DR9)." http://www.sdss3.org/dr9.

Smith, David A., Anne Mahoney, and Gregory R. Crane. 2002. "Integrating Harvesting into Digital Library Content." In *2nd ACM IEEE-CS Joint Conference on Digital Libraries*, 183–184. New York: ACM. http://www.perseus.tufts.edu/Articles/oaishort.pdf.

Smith, Doug, Rosanna Xia, and Rong Gong Lin. 2013. "Earthquake Risk: L.A. Formally Requests List of Concrete Buildings." *Los Angeles Times* (October 24). http://articles.latimes.com/2013/oct/24/local/la-me-ln-earthquake-concrete-list-20131024.

Smith, Michael E., Gary M. Feinman, Robert D. Drennan, Timothy Earle, and Ian Morris. 2012. "Archaeology as a Social Science." *Proceedings of the National Academy of Sciences of the United States of America* 109 (20):7617–7621. doi:10.1073/pnas.1201714109.

Smith, T. R., and M. Zheng. 2002. "ADEPT Knowledge Organization Team. Structured Models of Scientific Concepts as a Basis for Organizing, Accessing and Using Learning Materials." In *Joint Conference on Digital Libraries*, 202. New York: ACM.

Snow, Charles P. 1956. "The Two Cultures." *New Statesman.* http://www.newstatesman.com/cultural-capital/2013/01/c-p-snow-two-cultures.

Sobel, Dava. 2007. *Longitude: The True Story of a Lone Genius Who Solved the Greatest Scientific Problem of His Time.* New York: Walker.

Social Media Research Foundation. 2013. Home page. http://smrfoundation.com.

Social Science Data Archive. 2014. Home page. http://www.sscnet.ucla.edu/issr/da.

Social Science Research Network. 2014. Home page. http://www.ssrn.com/en.

Society of American Archivists. 2009. "Orphan Works: Statement of Best Practices." http://www.archivists.org/standards/OWBP-V4.pdf.

Spitzer Science Center. 2013. "Spitzer Observing Rules." http://ssc.spitzer.caltech.edu/warmmission/propkit/sor/15.

Square Kilometre Array. 2013. Home page. http://www.skatelescope.org.

Srinivasan, Ramesh. 2013. "Re-thinking the Cultural Codes of New Media: The Question Concerning Ontology." *New Media & Society* 15 (2):203–223. doi:10.1177/1461444812450686.

Srinivasan, Ramesh, Robin Boast, Katherine M. Becvar, and Jonathan Furner. 2009. "Blobgects: Digital Museum Catalogs and Diverse User Communities." *Journal of the American Society for Information Science and Technology* 60:666–678. doi:10.1002/asi.21027.

Srinivasan, Ramesh, Robin Boast, Jonathan Furner, and Katherine M. Becvar. 2009. "Digital Museums and Diverse Cultural Knowledges: Moving Past the Traditional Catalog." *Information Society* 25 (4):265–278. doi:10.1080/01972240903028714.

Stallman, Richard M. 2002. *Free Software, Free Society: Selected Essays of Richard M. Stallman.* Ed. Joshua Gay. Boston: The Free Software Foundation.

Stanley, Barbara, and Michael Stanley. 1988. "Data Sharing: The Primary Researcher's Perspective." *Law and Human Behavior* 12 (1):173–180.

Star, Susan Leigh. 1983. "Simplification in Scientific Work: An Example from Neuroscience Research." *Social Studies of Science* 13:205–228.

Star, Susan Leigh. 1989. "The Structure of Ill-structured Solutions: Boundary Objects and Heterogenous Distributed Problem Solving." In *Distributed Artificial Intelligence,* ed. Les Gasser and M. Huhns. Vol. 2, 37–54. San Mateo, CA: Morgan Kaufmann.

Star, Susan Leigh. 1991. "Power, Technologies, and the Phenomenology of Standards: On Being Allergic to Onions." In *A Sociology of Monsters? Power, Technology and the Modern World*, ed. John Law, 27–57. Oxford: Basic Blackwell.

Star, Susan Leigh. 1995. "The Politics of Formal Representations: Wizards, Gurus and Organizational Complexity." In *Ecologies of Knowledge: Work and Politics in Science and Technology*, ed. Susan Leigh Star, 88–118. Albany: State University of New York Press.

Star, Susan Leigh. 1999. "The Ethnography of Infrastructure." *American Behavioral Scientist* 43 (3):377–391. doi:10.1177/00027649921955326.

Star, Susan Leigh, and Geoffrey C. Bowker. 2002. "How to Infrastructure." In *Handbook of New Media*, ed. Leah A. Lievrouw and Sonia Livingstone, 151–162. London: Sage.

Star, Susan Leigh, Geoffrey C. Bowker, and Laura J. Neumann. 2003. "Transparency beyond the Individual Level of Scale: Convergence between Information Artifacts and Communities of Practice." In *Digital Library Use: Social Practice in Design and Evaluation*, ed. Ann Peterson Bishop, Nancy Van House, and Barbara P. Buttenfield, 241–270. Cambridge, MA: MIT Press.

Star, Susan Leigh, and J. Griesemer. 1989. "Institutional Ecology, 'Translations,' and Boundary Objects: Amateurs and Professionals in Berkeley's Museum of Vertebrate Zoology, 1907–1939." *Social Studies of Science* 19:387–420. doi:10.1177/03063128901 9003001.

Star, Susan Leigh, and Karen Ruhleder. 1996. "Steps toward an Ecology of Infrastructure: Design and Access for Large Information Spaces." *Information Systems Research* 7:111–134.

Star, Susan Leigh, and Anselm Strauss. 1999. "Layers of Silence, Arenas of Voice: The Ecology of Visible and Invisible Work." *Computer Supported Cooperative Work* 8 (1–2):9–30. doi:10.1023/A:1008651105359.

Starke, Marcus. 2013. "The Bright Shiny Object Syndrome of Marketing: Avoid It or Assess It?" *Business Innovation from SAP.* http://blogs.sap.com/innovation/sales -marketing/the-bright-shiny-object-syndrome-of-marketing-avoid-it-or-assess -it-024063.

Stata Data Analysis and Statistical Software (STATA). 2013. Home page. http://www .stata.com.

Steve: The Museum Social Tagging Project. 2013. "Welcome to the Steve Project." http://www.steve.museum.

Structural Genomics Consortium. 2013. "SGC Mission and Philosophy." http:// www.thesgc.org/about/what_is_the_sgc.

Stodden, Victoria C. 2009a. "Enabling Reproducible Research: Open Licensing for Scientific Innovation." *International Journal of Communications Law and Policy* 13:1– 55. http://papers.ssrn.com/sol3/papers.cfm?abstract_id=1362040.

Stodden, Victoria C. 2009b. "The Legal Framework for Reproducible Scientific Research: Licensing and Copyright." *Computing in Science & Engineering* 11:35–40. doi:10.1109/MCSE.2009.19.

Stodden, Victoria C. 2010. "Reproducible Research: Addressing the Need for Data and Code Sharing in Computational Science." *Computing in Science & Engineering* 12 (5):8–12. doi:10.1109/MCSE.2010.113.

Stokes, Donald. 1997. *Pasteur's Quadrant: Basic Science and Technological Innovation.* Washington, DC: Brookings Institution Press.

Storer, Norman W. 1973. "The Normative Structure of Science." In *The Sociology of Science: Theoretical and Empirical Investigations*, by Robert K. Merton, 267–278. Chicago: University of Chicago Press.

Suber, Peter. 2012a. *Open Access.* Cambridge, MA: MIT Press.

Suber, Peter. 2012b. "SPARC Open Access Newsletter" (September 2). http://www .earlham.edu/~peters/fos/newsletter/09-02-12.htm#uk-ec.

Sullivan, Woodruff T., Dan Werthimer, Stuart Bowyer, Jeff Cobb, David Gedye, and David Anderson. 1997. "A New Major SETI Project Based on Project SERENDIP Data and 100,000 Personal Computers." In *IAU Colloq. 161: Astronomical and Biochemical Origins and the Search for Life in the Universe*, 1:729. http://adsabs.harvard.edu/abs/1997abos.conf.729S.

Summers, Lawrence. 2013. "The Buck Does Not Stop with Reinhart and Rogoff." *Financial Times* (May 3). http://www.ft.com/cms/s/2/41d14954-b317-11e2-b5a5-00144feabdc0.html#axzz2chzkbMZX.

Svenonius, Elaine. 2000. *The Intellectual Foundation of Information Organization*. Cambridge, MA: MIT Press.

Sweeney, Latanya. 2002. "K-anonymity: a Model for Protecting Privacy." *International Journal on Uncertainty, Fuzziness and Knowledge-based Systems* 10 (5):557–570. doi:10.1142/S0218488502001648.

Szalay, Alexander. 2008. "Jim Gray, Astronomer." *Communications of the ACM* 51:59–65.

Szalay, Alexander. 2011. "Cosmology: Science in an Exponential World." *TEDxCaltech*. http://www.youtube.com/watch?v=hB92o4H46hc&NR=1.

Takakusu, Junjirō, and Kaikyoku Watanabe. 1932. *Taishō Shinshū Daizōkyō (The Buddhist Canon, New Compilation of the Taishō [1912–1925] Era)*. Vol. 1–85. Tokyo: Taishō Issaikyō Kankōkai.

Taper, Mark L., and Subhash R. Lele, eds. 2004. "Models of Scientific Inquiry and Statistical Practice: Implications for the Structure of Scientific Knowledge." In *The Nature of Scientific Evidence: Statistical, Philosophical, and Empirical Considerations*, 17–50. Chicago: University of Chicago Press.

Tenopir, Carol, Suzie Allard, Kimberly Douglass, Arsev Umur Aydinoglu, Lei Wu, Eleanor Read, Maribeth Manoff, and Mike Frame. 2011. "Data Sharing by Scientists: Practices and Perceptions." *PLoS ONE* 6 (6):e21101. doi:10.1371/journal.pone.0021101.

Text Encoding Initiative. 2013. Home page. http://www.tei-c.org.

Thelwall, Mike, Stefanie Haustein, Vincent Larivière, and Cassidy R. Sugimoto. 2013. "Do Altmetrics Work? Twitter and Ten Other Social Web Services." *PLoS ONE* 8 (5):e64841. doi:10.1371/journal.pone.0064841.

Thelwall, Mike, Liwen Vaughan, and Lennart Bjorneborn. 2005. "Webometrics." *Annual Review of Information Science & Technology* 39:81–135.

Thomas, Katie. 2013. "Breaking the Seal on Drug Research." *New York Times* (June 29). http://www.nytimes.com/2013/06/30/business/breaking-the-seal-on-drug-research.html.

Thomson Reuters. 2013. "Unlocking the Value of Research Data: A Report from the Thomson Reuters Industry Forum." Thomson Reuters. http://researchanalytics .thomsonreuters.com/m/pdfs/1003903-1.pdf.

Tichenor, Philip J., George A. Donohue, and Clarice N. Olien. 1970. "Mass Media and Differential Growth in Knowledge." *Public Opinion Quarterly* 34:158–170.

Tomasello, Michael, and Josep Call. 2011. "Methodological Challenges in the Study of Primate Cognition." *Science* 334:1227–1228. doi:10.1126/science.1213443.

Udomprasert, Patricia, and Alyssa A. Goodman. 2012. "WWT Ambassadors: World-Wide Telescope for Interactive Learning." In *Annual Meeting of the American Astronomical Society*. Austin, TX: AAS.

Uhlir, Paul F. 2006. "The Emerging Role of Open Repositories as a Fundamental Component of the Public Research Infrastructure." In *Open Access: Open Problems*, ed. Giandomenico Sica. Monza, Italy: Polimetrica.

Uhlir, Paul F. 2007. "Open Data for Global Science: A Review of Recent Developments in National and International Scientific Data Policies and Related Proposals." *Data Science Journal* 6:1–3. http://www.codata.org/dsj/special-open-data.html.

Uhlir, Paul F., ed. 2012. *For Attribution—Developing Data Attribution and Citation Practices and Standards: Summary of an International Workshop*. Board on Research Data and Information. Washington, DC: National Academies Press.

Uhlir, Paul F., and Daniel Cohen. 2011. "Internal Document." Board on Research Data and Information, Policy and Global Affairs Division, National Academy of Sciences.

Uhlir, Paul F., and Peter Schröder. 2007. "Open Data for Global Science." *Data Science Journal* 6:36–53. http://www.codata.org/dsj/special-open-data.html.

UK Data Archive. 2014. Home page. http://www.data-archive.ac.uk.

Unicode, Inc. 2013. "Chronology of Unicode Version 1.0." http://www.unicode.org/ history/versionone.html.

United Nations Educational, Scientific and Cultural Organization. 1970. "Convention on the Means of Prohibiting and Preventing the Illicit Import, Export and Transfer of Ownership of Cultural Property." http://portal.unesco.org/en/ev.php -URL_ID=13039&URL_DO=DO_TOPIC&URL_SECTION=201.html.

United Nations Educational, Scientific and Cultural Organization. 2013. "UNESCO Database of National Cultural Heritage Laws." http://www.unesco.org/culture/ natlaws.

United States Copyright Office. 2006. "Report on Orphan Works." Washington, DC: Register of Copyrights. http://www.copyright.gov/orphan/orphan-report.pdf.

University of Arizona Science Mirror Lab. 2013. "Casting for GMT3 to Start!" University of Arizona. *Steward Observatory Mirror Lab* (August 24). http://mirrorlab.as.arizona.edu/castings/projects/gmt/gmt3_casting.

University of Maryland University Libraries. 2013. "Primary, Secondary and Tertiary Sources." http://www.lib.umd.edu/ues/guides/primary-sources.

University of Oxford. 2013a. "Bodleian Libraries Launch Shakespeare's First Folio Online." *Oxford Thinking* (April 23). http://www.campaign.ox.ac.uk/news/first_folio.html.

University of Oxford. 2013b. "CLAROS: The World of Art on the Semantic Web." http://www.clarosnet.org/XDB/ASP/clarosHome/index.html.

University of Oxford Podcasting Service. 2011. *CLAROS—A Virtual Art Collection.* http://podcasts.ox.ac.uk/claros-virtual-art-collection-video.

Unsworth, John, Paul Courant, Sarah Fraser, Mike Goodchild, Margaret Hedstrom, Charles Henry, Peter B. Kaufman, Jerome McGann, Roy Rosenzweig, and Bruce Zuckerman. 2006. "Our Cultural Commonwealth: The Report of the American Council of Learned Societies Commission on Cyberinfrastructure for Humanities and Social Sciences." New York: American Council of Learned Societies. http://www.acls.org/cyberinfrastructure/cyber.htm.

Urbina, Ian. 2013. "I Flirt and Tweet. Follow Me at #Socialbot." *New York Times* (August 10). http://www.nytimes.com/2013/08/11/sunday-review/i-flirt-and-tweet-follow-me-at-socialbot.html.

US Department of Health and Human Services. 1979. *The Belmont Report.* Washington, DC: U.S. Government Printing Office. http://www.hhs.gov/ohrp/humansubjects/guidance/belmont.html.

Van de Sompel, Herbert. 2013. "From the Version of Record to a Version of the Record" presented at the Coalition for Networked Information (April 15). http://www.youtube.com/watch?v=fhrGS-QbNVA&feature=youtube_gdata_player.

Van de Sompel, Herbert, and Carl Lagoze. 2009. "All Aboard: Toward a Machine-Friendly Scholarly Communication System." In *The Fourth Paradigm: Data-Intensive Scientific Discovery,* ed. Tony Hey, Stewart Tansley, and Kristin Tolle, 1–8. Redmond, WA: Microsoft.

Van de Sompel, Herbert, Robert Sanderson, Martin Klein, Michael L. Nelson, Berhard Haslhofer, Simeon Warner, and Carl Lagoze. 2012. "A Perspective on Resource Synchronization." *D-Lib Magazine* 18 (9/10). doi:10.1045/september2012-vandesompel.

Van House, Nancy A. 2004. "Science and Technology Studies and Information Studies." *Annual Review of Information Science & Technology* 38:3–86. doi:10.1002/aris.1440380102.

Van Houweling, Molly Shaffer. 2009. "Author Autonomy and Atomism in Copyright Law." *Virginia Law Review* 96 (549):549–642.

Van Noorden, Richard. 2013a. "Half of 2011 Papers Now Free to Read." *Nature* 500 (7463):386–387. doi:10.1038/500386a.

Van Noorden, Richard. 2013b. "Open Access: The True Cost of Science Publishing." *Nature* 495 (7442):426–429. doi:10.1038/495426a.

Van Raan, Anthony F. J. 1988. *Handbook of Quantitative Studies of Science and Technology*. Amsterdam: Elsevier.

Vandewalle, Patrick, Jelena Kovacevic, and Martin Vetterli. 2009. "Reproducible Research in Signal Processing." *IEEE Signal Processing Magazine* 26:37–47. doi:10.1109/msp.2009.932122.

Vardigan, Mary, Pascal Heus, and Wendy Thomas. 2008. "Data Documentation Initiative: Toward a Standard for the Social Sciences." *International Journal of Digital Curation* 3 (1). doi:10.2218/ijdc.v3i1.45.

Vargas, Rodrigo, Alisha Glass, Mike Taggart, Kuni Kitajima, Michael Hamilton, and Michael Allen. 2006. "Linking Minirhizotron Images to Soil Physical Properties and Microbial Diversity (TER 2)." *Center for Embedded Network Sensing*. http://escholarship.org/uc/item/4312j473.

Vertesi, Janet, and Paul Dourish. 2011. "The Value of Data: Considering the Context of Production in Data Economies." In *Computer Supported Cooperative Work*, 533–542. New York: ACM. doi:10.1145/1958824.1958906.

Virtual International Authority File. 2013. Home page. http://viaf.org.

Visual Resources Association. 2012. "Statement on the Fair Use of Images for Teaching, Research, and Study." http://www.vraweb.org/organization/pdf/VRAFairUse GuidelinesFinal.pdf.

Vita, Silvio. 2003. "Printings of the Buddhist 'Canon' in Modern Japan." In *Buddhism Asia 1: Papers from the First Conference of Buddhist Studies Held in Naples*, ed. Giovanni Verard and Silvio Vita, 217–245. Kyoto: ISEAS.

Vogel, Gretchen, and Jennifer Couzin-Frankel. 2013. "Europe Debates Ethics Reviews, Data Release." *Science* 339 (6123):1024. doi:10.1126/science.339.6123.1024.

Voltaire. 1759. *Candide: Or, All for the Best*. London: Printed for J. Nourse.

Von Ahn, Luis, Benjamin Maurer, Colin McMillen, David Abraham, and Manuel Blum. 2008. "reCAPTCHA: Human-Based Character Recognition via Web Security Measures." *Science* 321 (5895):1465–1468. doi:10.1126/science.1160379.

Waldrop, M. Mitchell. 2001. *The Dream Machine: J.C.R. Licklider and the Revolution That Made Computing Personal*. New York: Viking Penguin.

Wallis, Jillian C. 2012. "The Distribution of Data Management Responsibility within Scientific Research Groups." University of California, Los Angeles. http://gradworks .umi.com/35/13/3513859.html.

Wallis, Jillian C., and Christine L. Borgman. 2011. "Who Is Responsible for Data? An Exploratory Study of Data Authorship, Ownership, and Responsibility." *Proceedings of the American Society for Information Science and Technology* 48 (1):1–10. doi:10.1002/ meet.2011.14504801188.

Wallis, Jillian C., Christine L. Borgman, and Matthew S. Mayernik. 2010. "Who Is Responsible for Data? A Case Study Exploring Data Authorship, Ownership, and Responsibility and Their Implications for Data Curation." In *6th International Digital Curation Conference*. Chicago: Digital Curation Center. http://www.dcc.ac.uk/events/ conferences/6th-international-digital-curation-conference.

Wallis, Jillian C., Christine L. Borgman, Matthew S. Mayernik, and Alberto Pepe. 2008. "Moving Archival Practices Upstream: An Exploration of the Life Cycle of Ecological Sensing Data in Collaborative Field Research." *International Journal of Digital Curation* 3. doi:10.2218/ijdc.v3i1.46.

Wallis, Jillian C., Christine L. Borgman, Matthew S. Mayernik, Alberto Pepe, Nithya Ramanathan, and Mark Hansen. 2007. "Know Thy Sensor: Trust, Data Quality, and Data Integrity in Scientific Digital Libraries." In *Research and Advanced Technology for Digital Libraries*, ed. Laszlo Kovacs, Norbert Fuhr, and Carlo Meghini. Vol. 4675, 380–391. Berlin: Springer.

Wallis, Jillian C., Matthew S. Mayernik, Christine L. Borgman, and Alberto Pepe. 2010. "Digital Libraries for Scientific Data Discovery and Reuse: From Vision to Practical Reality." In *Proceedings of the 10th Annual Joint Conference on Digital Libraries*, 333–340. New York: ACM. doi:10.1145/1816123.1816173.

Wallis, Jillian C., Stasa Milojevic, Christine L. Borgman, and William A. Sandoval. 2006. "The Special Case of Scientific Data Sharing with Education." In *Proceedings 69th Annual Meeting of the American Society for Information Science and Technology*. Medford, NJ: Information Today.

Wallis, Jillian C., Elizabeth Rolando, and Christine L. Borgman. 2013. "If We Share Data, Will Anyone Use Them? Data Sharing and Reuse in the Long Tail of Science and Technology." *PLoS ONE* 8 (7):e67332. doi:10.1371/journal.pone.0067332.

Wallis, Jillian C., Laura A. Wynholds, Christine L. Borgman, Ashley E. Sands, and Sharon Traweek. 2012. "Data, Data Use, and Inquiry: A New Point of View on Data Curation." Full paper (long version) submitted to the 12th ACM/IEEE-CS Joint Conference on Digital Libraries. http://works.bepress.com/borgman/280.

Watson, J. 1990. "The Human Genome Project: Past, Present, and Future." *Science* 248 (4951):44–49. doi:10.1126/science.2181665.

Weigelt, Johan. 2009. "The Case for Open-Access Chemical Biology. A Strategy for Pre-competitive Medicinal Chemistry to Promote Drug Discovery." *EMBO Reports* 10 (9):941–945. doi:10.1038/embor.2009.193.

Weinberg, Alvin M. 1961. "Impact of Large-Scale Science on the United States." *Science* 134:161–164. doi:10.1126/science.134.3473.161.

Weinberger, David. 2012. *Too Big to Know: Rethinking Knowledge Now That the Facts Aren't the Facts, Experts Are Everywhere, and the Smartest Person in the Room Is the Room.* New York: Basic Books.

Weller, Ann C. 2001. *Editorial Peer Review: Its Strengths and Weaknesses.* Medford, NJ: Information Today.

Wellman, Barry, and Caroline Haythornthwaite. 2002. *The Internet in Everyday Life.* Oxford: Blackwell.

Wells, Don C., Eric W. Greisen, and R. H. Harten. 1981. "FITS—A Flexible Image Transport System." *Astronomy & Astrophysics. Supplement Series* 44:363. http://adsabs .harvard.edu/abs/1981A%26AS...44.363W.

Wenger, Etienne. 1998. *Communities of Practice: Learning, Meaning, and Identity.* New York: Cambridge University Press.

Whalen, Maureen. 2009. "What's Wrong with This Picture? An Examination of Art Historians' Attitudes about Electronic Publishing Opportunities and the Consequences of Their Continuing Love Affair with Print." *Art Documentation* 28:13–22.

What's Invasive! 2010. Home page. http://whatsinvasive.com.

White, Howard D. 1990. "Author Co-citation Analysis: Overview and Defense." In *Scholarly Communication and Bibliometrics*, ed. Christine L. Borgman, 84–106. Newbury Park, CA: Sage.

White, Richard L., Alberto Accomazzi, G. Bruce Berriman, Giuseppina Fabbiano, Barry F. Madore, Joseph M. Mazzarella, Arnold Rots, Alan P. Smale, Lombardi Storrie, and Sherry L. Winkelman. 2009. "The High Impact of Astronomical Data Archives." *Astro2010: The Astronomy and Astrophysics Decadal Survey, Position Papers, No. 64.* http://adsabs.harvard.edu/abs/2009astro2010P.64W.

Whitley, Richard. 2000. *The Intellectual and Social Organization of the Sciences.* Oxford: Oxford University Press.

Whitlock, Michael C. 2011. "Data Archiving in Ecology and Evolution: Best Practices." *Trends in Ecology & Evolution* 26:61–65. doi:10.1016/j.tree.2010.11.006.

Whitlock, Michael C., Mark A. McPeek, Mark D. Rausher, Loren Rieseberg, and Allen J. Moore. 2010. "Data Archiving." *American Naturalist* 175:E45–E146. doi:10.1086/650340.

Wickham, Chris, and Nigel Vincent. 2013. "Debating Open Access: Introduction." *Debating Open Access*: 4–12. http://issuu.com/thebritishacademy/docs/debating_open _access-introduction__.

Wiener, Jon. 2002. "How the Critics Shot up Michael Bellesiles's Book Arming America." *Nation* 275 (15):28–32.

Wieseler, Biete, Michaela F. Kerekes, Volker Vervoelgyi, Natalie McGauran, and Thomas Kaiser. 2012. "Impact of Document Type on Reporting Quality of Clinical Drug Trials: a Comparison of Registry Reports, Clinical Study Reports, and Journal Publications." *British Medical Journal* 344:d8141. doi:10.1136/bmj.d8141.

Wiesenthal, Joe. 2013. "REINHART AND ROGOFF: 'Full Stop,' We Made a Microsoft Excel Blunder in Our Debt Study, and It Makes a Difference." *Business Insider* (April 17). http://www.businessinsider.com/reinhart-and-rogoff-admit-excel-blunder-2013-4.

Wilbanks, John. 2006. "Another Reason for Opening Access to Research." *British Medical Journal* 333 (7582):1306–1308. doi:10.1136/sbmj.39063.730660.F7.

Wilbanks, John. 2009. "I Have Seen the Paradigm Shift and It Is Us." In *The Fourth Paradigm: Data-Intensive Scientific Discovery*, ed. Tony Hey, Stewart Tansley, and Kristin Tolle, 209–214. Redmond, WA: Microsoft.

Wilbanks, John. 2011. "Openness as Infrastructure." *Journal of Cheminformatics* 3 (36). doi:10.1186/1758-2946-3-36.

Wilbanks, John. 2013. "Licence Restrictions: A Fool's Errand." *Nature* 495 (7442):440–441. doi:10.1038/495440a.

Williams, Antony J., John Wilbanks, and Sean Ekins. 2012. "Why Open Drug Discovery Needs Four Simple Rules for Licensing Data and Models." *PLoS Computational Biology* 8 (9). doi:10.1371/journal.pcbi.1002706.

Willinsky, John. 2006. *The Access Principle: The Case for Open Access to Research and Scholarship*. Cambridge, MA: MIT Press.

Willis, Craig, Jane Greenberg, and Hollie White. 2012. "Analysis and Synthesis of Metadata Goals for Scientific Data." *Journal of the American Society for Information Science and Technology* 63 (8):1505–1520. doi:10.1002/asi.22683.

Winkelman, Sherry L., and Arnold Rots. 2012a. "Observatory Bibliographies: Not Just for Statistics Anymore." In *Observatory Operations: Strategies, Processes, and Systems IV. Proceedings of the SPIE*, ed. Alison B. Peck, Robert L. Seaman, and Fernando Comeron. Vol. 8448. Amsterdam: SPIE. doi:10.1117/12.925207.

Winkelman, Sherry L., and Arnold Rots. 2012b. "The Chandra Observational Ontology: Tying the Threads Together." In *Astronomical Data Analysis Software and Systems XXI*, ed. P. Ballester, D. Egret, and N.P.F. Lorente, 461:241. San Francisco: Astronomical Society of the Pacific. http://adsabs.harvard.edu/abs/2012ASPC.461.241W.

Winkelman, Sherry L., Arnold Rots, Michael McCollough, Glenn Becker, Aaron Watry, and Joan Hagler. 2009. "The Chandra Bibliography Cataloging System: A Scientific Research Aid." In *Chandra's First Decade of Discovery, Proceedings of the Conference Held 22–25 September, 2009 in Boston, MA*, 207. http://adsabs.harvard.edu/abs/2009cfdd.confE.207W.

Wiseman, James. 1964. "Archaeology and the Humanities." *Arion* 3 (2):131–142. doi:10.2307/20162908.

Wohn, D. Yvette, and Dennis Normile. 2006. "Korean Cloning Scandal: Prosecutors Allege Elaborate Deception and Missing Funds." *Science* 312:980–981.

Wolf, Susan M., George J. Annas, and Sherman Elias. 2013. "Patient Autonomy and Incidental Findings in Clinical Genomics." *Science* 340 (6136):1049–1050. doi:10.1126/science.1239119.

Wood, John, Thomas Andersson, Achim Bachem, Christopher Best, Françoise Genova, Diego R. Lopez, Wouter Los, et al. 2010. *Riding the Wave: How Europe Can Gain from the Rising Tide of Scientific Data*. Final report of the High Level Expert Group on Scientific Data. http://cordis.europa.eu/fp7/ict/e-infrastructure/docs/hlg-sdi-report.pdf.

Woolgar, Steve. 1988. *Knowledge and Reflexivity: New Frontiers in the Sociology of Knowledge*. London: Sage.

World Internet Project. 2013. Home page. http://www.worldinternetproject.net.

WorldWide Telescope. 2012. Home page. http://www.worldwidetelescope.org/Home.aspx.

Wouters, Paul, Anne Beaulieu, Andrea Scharnhorst, and Sally Wyatt, eds. 2012. *Virtual Knowledge: Experimenting in the Humanities and Social Sciences*. Cambridge, MA: MIT Press.

Wuchty, Stefan, Benjamin F. Jones, and Brian Uzzi. 2007. "The Increasing Dominance of Teams in the Production of Knowledge." *Science* 316 (5827):1036–1039.

Wynholds, Laura A., David S. Fearon, Christine L. Borgman, and Sharon Traweek. 2011. "Awash in Stardust: Data Practices in Astronomy." In *iConference: Proceedings of the 2011 iConference*, 802–804. New York: ACM. doi:10.1145/1940761.1940912.

Wynholds, Laura A., Jillian C. Wallis, Christine L. Borgman, Ashley Sands, and Sharon Traweek. 2012. "Data, Data Use, and Scientific Inquiry: Two Case Studies of Data Practices." In *Proceedings of the 12th ACM/IEEE-CS Joint Conference on Digital Libraries*, 19–22. New York: ACM. doi:10.1145/2232817.2232822.

Xia, Rosanna, Doug Smith, and Michael Finnegan. 2013. "UC Quake Researchers Refuse to Share Building Data with L.A." *Los Angeles Times* (October 18). http://

www.latimes.com/local/la-me-concrete-quake-20131019,0,1097898.story#axzz 2lPPa1ctb.

Yan, Koon-Kiu, and Mark Gerstein. 2011. "The Spread of Scientific Information: Insights from the Web Usage Statistics in PLoS Article-Level Metrics." *PLoS ONE* 6 (5):e19917. doi:10.1371/journal.pone.0019917.

Yoffee, Norman, and Severin Fowles. 2011. "Archaeology in the Humanities." *Diogenes* 58 (1-2):35–52. doi:10.1177/0392192112441906.

Younis, Mohamed, and Kemal Akkaya. 2008. "Strategies and Techniques for Node Placement in Wireless Sensor Networks: A Survey." *Ad Hoc Networks* 6 (4):621–655. doi:10.1016/j.adhoc.2007.05.003.

Zacchetti, Stefano. 2002. "An Early Chinese Translation Corresponding to Chapter 6 of the Petakopadesa: An Shigao's Yin Chi Ru Jing T 603 and Its Indian Original: a Preliminary Survey." *Bulletin of the School of Oriental and African Studies, University of London* 65 (01):74–98. doi:10.1017/S0041977X02000046.

Zacchetti, Stefano. 2005. *In Praise of the Light: A Critical Synoptic Edition with an Annotated Translation of Chapters 1–3 of Dharmaraksa's Guang Zan Jing, Being the Earliest Chinese Translation of the Larger Prajnaparamita*. Open Research Centre Project. Tokyo, Japan: The International Research Institute for Advanced Buddhology, Soka University. http://iriab.soka.ac.jp/orc/Publications/BPPB/index_BPPB.html.

Zappavigna, Michele. 2011. "Ambient Affiliation: A Linguistic Perspective on Twitter." *New Media & Society* 13 (5):788–806. doi:10.1177/1461444810385097.

ZENODO. 2013. Frequently Asked Questions. http://zenodo.org/faq.

Zerhouni, Elias A. 2006. "Report on the NIH Public Access Policy." Department of Health and Human Services, National Institutes of Health. http://publicaccess.nih.gov/Final_Report_20060201.pdf.

Zhang, Guo, Ying Ding, and Staša Milojević. 2013. "Citation Content Analysis (CCA): A Framework for Syntactic and Semantic Analysis of Citation Content." *Journal of the American Society for Information Science and Technology* 64 (7):1490–1503. doi:10.1002/asi.22850.

Zimmer, Michael. 2010. "'But the Data Is Already Public': On the Ethics of Research in Facebook." *Ethics and Information Technology* 12 (4):313–325. doi:10.1007/s10676-010-9227-5.

Zimmerman, Ann S. 2003. "Data Sharing and Secondary Use of Scientific Data: Experiences of Ecologists." PhD diss., Ann Arbor, MI: University of Michigan.

Zimmerman, Ann S. 2007. "Not by Metadata Alone: The Use of Diverse Forms of Knowledge to Locate Data for Reuse." *International Journal on Digital Libraries* 7:5–16. doi:10.1007/s00799-007-0015-8.

Zittrain, Jonathan. 2005. *The Future of the Internet—and How to Stop It.* Cambridge, MA: MIT Press.

Zooniverse. 2014. Home page. https://www.zooniverse.org/projects.

Zorich, Diane. 2008. "A Survey of Digital Humanities Centers in the United States." Washington, DC: Council on Library and Information Resources. http://www.clir .org/pubs/reports/pub143/contents.html.

Zotero. 2013. Home page. http://www.zotero.org.

Zotero. 2014. "Zotero Style Repository." https://www.zotero.org/styles.

Index